1991
Children's Writer's & Illustrator's Market

Edited by
Lisa Carpenter
Assisted by Veronica Gliatti

Writer's
Digest
Books

Cincinnati, Ohio

Distributed in Canada by McGraw-Hill,
330 Progress Ave.,
Scarborough, Ontario M1P 2Z5.
Also distributed in Australia by
Kirby Books, Private Bag No. 19, P.O. Alex-
andria NSW/2015.

Managing Editor, Market Books Department:
Constance J. Achabal; Assistant Managing
Editor: Glenda Tennant Neff.

Children's Writer's & Illustrator's Market.
Copyright © 1990
by Writer's Digest Books. Published by
F&W Publications, 1507 Dana Ave.,
Cincinnati, Ohio 45207. Printed and bound
in the United States of America. All rights
reserved. No part of this book may be repro-
duced in any manner whatsoever without
written permission from the publisher, except
by reviewers who may quote brief passages to
be printed in a magazine or newspaper.

International Standard Serial Number
0897-9790
International Standard Book Number
0-89879-429-3

Contents

1 From the Editor

3 How to Use Children's Writer's & Illustrator's Market

6 Children's Books: Trends and Guidelines for the Current Market, *by Leslie Prosak-Beres, Ph.D.*

9 How to Make a Dummy: A Guide for Picture Book Writers and Illustrators, *by Frieda Gates.*

20 The Business of Children's Writing & Illustrating

20	*Marketing Your Work*	27	*Rights*
20	*Format for Submitting Work*	29	*Taxes*
23	*Packing and Mailing*	30	*Insurance*
24	*Pricing*	30	*Building Skills*
25	*Business Records*	31	*Books of Interest*
26	*Recording Submissions*	31	*Publications of Interest*

Special Business Feature

32 Simultaneous Submissions, *by Lisa Carpenter*

The Markets

35 Book Publishers

54 Close-up:
Russell Freedman, Children's Writer
The 1988 Newbery medalist discusses how he got started, his research methods and the state of children's nonfiction today.

87 Close-up:
Maria Modugno, Little, Brown & Co.
Editor-in-chief of the children's division, Modugno reveals what she looks for in a book and offers advice to aspiring writers and illustrators.

109 Close-up:
Johanna Hurwitz, Children's Writer
This popular author discusses her late start as a published writer, how she gets ideas for books and her approach toward writing a novel.

124 **Magazine Publishers**

143 Close-up:
Donald Evans, Hopscotch
Where are the magazines for little girls? That's what Evans wanted to know. Read about why he started one just for them and what he needs most from freelancers.

167 Close-up:
Al Nagy, 3-2-1 Contact
Fresh, lively illustration is what this art director wants in order to make science fun for kids. Read his tips for artists.

177 **Audiovisual Markets**

182 **Audiotapes**

190 **Scriptwriter's Markets**

192 Close-up:
Deedra Bébout, Children's Story Scripts
Prose stories for children have a different format than regular scripts, says Bébout. Find out the difference.

198 **Special Markets**

203 **Young Writer's/Illustrator's Markets**

210 Close-up:
Mike Joyer and Zach Robert, Authors
Two kids wrote a book on a summer day and got it published. They both share how they managed to "strike gold" the first time out.

219 **Contests and Awards**

Resources

239 **Agents**

251 **Clubs/Organizations**

257 Close-up:
Sue Alexander, The Society of Children's Book Writers
Chairperson of the Board of Directors, Alexander explains the benefits of being a SCBW member. Also, she offers her observations on the most common mistakes made by beginning writers and illustrators.

259 **Workshops**

264 **Glossary**

267 **Key to Symbols**

268 **Age-Level Index**

275 **General Index**

From the Editor

Writing and illustrating for children are truly labors of love. The people who appreciate this the most are those who are successful in the field.

"I don't think you write because something is in demand," says author (and "Close-up" — see page 54) Russell Freedman. "I don't think anybody ever writes a book because they think it's going to sell. You write because you find something that fits in with your interests and your abilities. You do what comes naturally." To do this, Freedman says it is imperative for writers and illustrators to find the child inside of themselves. He himself does this by visiting children in schools. At times, he says, the kids are the ones who actually spark his book ideas.

Johanna Hurwitz (also a "Close-up" personality — see page 109) maintains her ability to see through a child's eyes by working with children a few hours a week in her local library. "I love working with the young readers," she says.

A common misconception is that children's books are easier to write than adult books. Not true. Good children's literature requires special insight and understanding of the audience. Remember, children are tough critics. Whereas most adults might give a book with a slow beginning a chance to improve, children will just get up and walk away. With children's stories, the audience must be "hooked" as soon as possible.

The markets

The growth in the area of writing and illustrating for children is reflected by the 152 new listings in this year's book. This third edition is 288 pages, up from 266 pages in 1990 and 186 in 1989. A proper assumption from the two-year, 100-page growth is that industry is cashing in on the lucrativeness of the field. This book is produced in order to give you a competitive edge. Hopefully, the purchase of *Children's Writer's & Illustrator's Market* will prove to be a worthwhile investment as it aids your burgeoning career.

What's new in '91

Exciting additions in this year's book include an article detailing trends in children's literature and the necessary ingredients required for a good book. For picture book writers and illustrators, there is a step-by-step guide to making a dummy, complete with diagrams and illustrations. Finally, as a supplement to the business section, an article arguing the pros and cons of simultaneous submissions.

Besides Freedman and Hurwitz, you'll find "Close-up" interviews with Maria Modugno, editor-in-chief of the children's division at Little, Brown & Co.; Donald Evans, editor of *Hopscotch*, a new periodical which is just starting to take off; Al Nagy, art director at *3-2-1 Contact*; and Deedra Bébout, founder of Children's Story Scripts. Also, junior authors Zach Robert, 12, and Mike Joyer, 11, share their experience of writing and publishing their first book and the beginner's luck that provided the extra "push." In the Clubs/Organizations section, Sue Alexander of the Society of Children's Book Writers offers information about her organization and practical advice about breaking into the field.

Enthusiasm is the key

One thing writers, illustrators and editors alike will agree on is this is not a field for money-motivated people. Monetarily, few get rich by writing and illustrating for children, especially with the traditionally low advances and trickling royalty payments. The intangible rewards, however, are treasures money can't buy. So for those of you who thrive on a glint in a child's eye, feel excitement at the mere prospect of enlightening a young mind, and want nothing more than to enhance a child's creative, developmental and educational worlds, welcome to *Children's Writer's and Illustrator's Market* — this book is for you.

How to Use Children's Writer's & Illustrator's Market

Take a few minutes to familiarize yourself with this sample listing before browsing through the book. Each component of the listing is numbered for your convenience and corresponds to an explanation following this sample. "Ms" or "mss" refers to "manuscript" or "manuscripts" respectively.

Be sure to *always* include a self-addressed, stamped envelope (SASE) with submissions. If you are a foreigner marketing to a listing within the United States, or a United States citizen marketing work abroad, send a self-addressed envelope (SAE) and the appropriate number of International Reply Coupons (IRCs).

Throughout many listings you will find four categories of children's writing/illustrating; they are defined as: "picture books," written/illustrated for preschool-8 year olds; "young readers" for 5-8 year olds; "middle readers" for 9-11 year olds; and "young adults" for those 12 and older.

(1) HARBINGER HOUSE INC., (2) 2802 North Alvenon Way, Tucson AZ 85712. (602)326-9595. **(3)** (Some listings specify whether the business is a book publisher or book packager.) **(4)** Publisher: Laurel Gregory. Editor, Children's Books: Jeffrey H. Lockridge. Publishes 4 picture books/year; 2 young reader titles/year; 2-3 middle reader titles/year. **(5)** 40% of books by first-time authors; 10% of books from agented writers. **(6)** (Some listings will provide information on the percent of books subsidy published.)

Fiction: (7) Picture books: "all kinds." Young readers: adventure, fantasy, history. Middle readers: animal, fantasy, problem novels, science fiction, sports, spy/mystery/adventure. **(8)** (Some listings specify a word or page length here.) **(9)** Published *The Marsh King's Daughter*, by Andersen/Gentry (all ages/classic fantasy); *One Green Mesquite Tree*, by Jernigan (ages 3-5, counting rhyme); *Mystery on Mackinac Island*, (ages 8-11).

Nonfiction: (10) Picture books: "all kinds." Young readers: animal, history, nature/environment, geography. Middle readers: animal, biography, history, music/dance, nature/environment, space science, geography. **(11)** (Some listings specify a word or page length here.) **(12)** Published *The Reef & the Wrasse*, by Steere & Ring (ages 8-11, natural history); *Out in the Night*, by Liptak (ages 8-11, natural history); *Zoot Zoot Zaggle Splot or, What to Do With A Scary Dream*, (ages 4-8).

How to Contact/Writers: (13) Fiction/nonfiction: Submit outline/synopsis and sample chapters. **(14)** (Some listings request a Social Security number with a submission.) **(15)** Reports on queries in 3-4 weeks; on mss in 6-8 weeks. **(16)** Publishes a book 12-18 months after acceptance. **(17)** Will consider simultaneous submissions.

Illustration: (18) Average number of illustrations used for fiction: picture books—14; young readers—12; middle readers—12. Number of illustrations used for nonfiction: picture books—14; young readers—20; middle readers—18. **(19)** Editorial will review all varieties of ms/illustration packages. **(20)** (Some listings will include information about the medium/style/size of artwork the editor or art director prefers to review.)

How to Contact/Illustrators: (21) "For picture books and young readers only: Minimum of 3 pieces of finished art." Illustrations only: Tearsheets and slides. **(22)** Reports on art samples in 4 weeks. **(23)** Original artwork returned at job's completion.

Terms/Writers & Illustrators: (24) Pays authors in royalties based on net receipts. **(25)** Average advance payment $800-1,000. **(26)** Factors used to determine final payment for ms/illustration package include "color art vs. black and white and number of illustrations for outright purchase." Pay for separate authors and illustrators: "royalties split between author and artist." Pay for illustrators: "royalties based on net receipts." **(27)** Sends galleys to authors; sometimes sends dummies to illustrators. **(28)** Book catalog free on request. **(29)** (Some listings specify availability of manuscript and/or artist's guidelines.)

Tips: (30) (Some listings give general advice about breaking into the field.) **(31)** Looks for "manuscripts with a particular, well-articulated message or purpose." Illustrators: Looks for "art of imagination and skill that has something special." **(32)** In children's book publishing there has been "a gradual improvement in the standards of quality in both the ideas and their presentation."

(1)(2) The full name, mailing address, and phone number of the book or magazine publishing company, agency, organization, workshop, or contest. A phone number in a listing does not mean the market accepts phone queries. Make a phone query only when your story's timeliness would be lost by following the usual procedures. As a rule, don't call unless you have been invited to do so.

(3) The type of business.

(4) Title and name of contact person. Address your query or submission to a specific name when possible. If no contact name is given consult a sample copy of the publication or catalog. As a last resort, you can address your query to "Editor" or "Art Director" or whatever is appropriate. The next of information is a breakdown of the type and number of books published annually: picture books, young readers, middle readers, young adults. Use this breakdown to help you choose a company most receptive to your type of book.

(5) The percentage of books by first-time authors will give you an indication of how open a market is to new authors. Also given is the percentage of submissions accepted through agents.

(6) Information to let you know which companies subsidy publish.

(7) The specific fictional material desired is listed. Follow the guidelines.

(8) Editors know the length of most material they buy; follow their word or page range. If your manuscript is longer or shorter by a large margin, submit to a more appropriate market.

(9) A list of the publisher's recent fiction is provided.

(10) Specific nonfiction material desired.

(11) The appropriate page or word length for nonfiction material is given.

(12) A list of recently published nonfiction.

(13) Submission specifications.

(14) If requested, include your Social Security number.

(15) Reporting times indicate how soon a market will respond to your query or manuscript, but times listed are approximate. Wait four weeks beyond the stated reporting time before you send a polite inquiry.

(16) If your material is accepted this information gives you the approximate time it will take for your manuscript to be published.

(17) This information tells you if if is possible to submit a manuscript via disk or modem. Also indicated is the publisher's policy on simultaneous submissions. Send manuscripts or queries to one market at a time unless it indicates simultaneous submissions are OK. If you do send your manuscript to more than one market at a time, always mention in your cover letter that it is a simultaneous submission.

(18) The average number of illustrations required per type of book gives the illustrator an idea of how much work a project might entail.

(19) This information tells the illustrator if the company will see manuscripts with illustrations by the same person and/or manuscripts by an author with illustrations done by a separate artist. It also tells if the market is open to the use of freelance illustrators for the company's own book projects and provides a contact name if different from the contact at the beginning of the listing. If all of the above applies, the listing merely states all varieties of manuscript/illustration packages are accepted.

(20) Specific information regarding preferences in the medium/style/size of art submissions is provided here.

(21) Submit illustrations only in the manner an art director/editor asks.

(22) The approximate amount of time taken to report back on illustrations is provided. If an art director/editor doesn't respond within the stated time, wait four weeks before sending a polite inquiry.

(23) Information that states whether original artwork is returned.

(24) Terms for payment of authors.

(25) If an advance is given, the average amount will be provided here.

(26) Payment information for ms/illustration packages and freelance illustration projects is provided here.

(27) If galleys are sent to authors and/or dummies to illustrators for review prior to publication, you will read the notification here.

(28)(29) If catalogs or guidelines are available, it's important to send for them.

(30)(31)(32) Helpful suggestions for writers and illustrators are listed under the subhead, "Tips."

Important Market Listing Information

• *Listings are based on questionnaires, phone calls and updated copy. They are not advertisements nor are markets reported here necessarily endorsed by the editor of this book.*

• *Information in the listings comes directly from the company and is as accurate as possible, but situations change and needs fluctuate between the publication of this directory and the time you use it.*

• **Children's Writer's & Illustrator's Market** *reserves the right to exclude any listing that does not meet its requirements.*

Children's Books: Trends and Guidelines for the Current Market

by Leslie Prosak-Beres, Ph. D.

Children read for many reasons. They read to dream, to learn, to laugh, to enjoy the familiar and to explore the unknown. For the most part, children read for sheer pleasure. Through their travels in the uncharted waters of a good book, they build a concept of the society in which they live and their place in that society.

Reading is an active experience. Each time a good piece of literature is encountered, the reader is changed by the experience; the world is seen in a new and different way. Literature transforms human experience and reflects it back to us, and in that reflection we can see our own lives and experiences as part of the larger human experience. The catalytic quality of literature enables children to better understand themselves and contributes to making tomorrow's world more humane and considerate.

There is an amazing variety of material in printed format intended for children. There are picture books, some without text, some with text and some designed to teach concepts or clarify information; easy-to-read books for the beginning reader; pop-up books and adventure books; books with "easy to read" vocabulary, but with an engaging plot. There is poetry for children; folk literature that includes epics and legends, folk tales, myths and fables; modern fantasy which includes embellishments of folk tales and science fiction; historical fiction and biography; animal stories, sports stories, mysteries; family stories and problem novels; realistic fiction; multicultural literature and informational books. Underlying all of these many and varied possibilities remains the fact that quality and integrity in development are significant to the lasting and universal nature of books for children.

Where is children's literature and where is it going tomorrow?

It was not until the twentieth century that children's literature was taken seriously enough to warrant a special place in the academic or publishing world. Today we no longer need to justify the existence of a body of literature specifically for children. The number of books published each year has nearly doubled since 1980, reflecting the economic health of producing and selling children's books. In the same way, the number of children's bookstores has grown from a minority representation to a community landmark. In spite of the increasing

Leslie Prosak-Beres *is a professor of Education at Xavier University in Cincinnati, Ohio. She directs the graduate program in Reading and teaches Children's Literature and Reading Theory and Methodology.*

prices of quality books for children, the market shows owners of content-specific children's bookstores are riding a financial wave of success. Schools, becoming more aware of the "whole language" philosophy of teaching reading, are integrating literature-based programs and materials into their curriculums. Parental awareness of early and continuous exposure to the written word for scholastic success has certainly enhanced the prospects of opportunities for newcomers to the world of children's literature. Valuing the gift of a book has returned to the scene of the 90s.

Between 1900 and 1990, vast changes have taken place in our society, and in turn, those changes have influenced children's books. Society is recognizing the variety of children in general and their needs for books aimed toward them in particular.

Books written for children reflect their intellectual ability, their demographic data, their racial heritage and the conflict and controversy in our society regarding moral standards and lifestyles. It is clear that change has become a predominant fact of life—so fast, in fact that there has been confusion about traditional values. Many of the enduring values of the past are reflected in books for children, yet so too are the values of a contemporary society that is less secure and more mobile than earlier generations.

It appears that change reflecting society's standards is visible in children's books for the 1990s. Although topics addressed focus on everything from crime and violence to contemporary sex patterns, children's books are substantially better today than they were even a few decades ago. They cover more children-inspired topics and are more accurate and candid. The writing styles are better crafted, being influenced from previous generations of writers. The art in books today includes every medium and every style. While some illustrations may be mediocre, for the most part they are of superlative quality.

Trends

One thing that emerges is that trends develop for practical reasons; they derive from market and or need.

Market indicators show the focus for fiction in children's books may take a decided twist back to areas that have appeared to be almost silenced in the 1980s: minority voices, women's legacy in all areas of society, and racial/ethnic response to stereotyping. A resurgence of interest in the art of storytelling will also necessitate the need for quality retelling of folk tales or collections of unique generational stories. Other areas of topical interest may include: increased awareness of and concern for the rights of children, peace topics, environmental concerns, death and dying, handicaps and family.

There are two significant trends in nonfiction: one is the coverage of topics that formerly were considered to interest only adults; and two is the care given to produce quality books that are both accurate and authoritative. Topics in this area for writers to be concerned with are: pollution, war, peace, international relations, nuclear power and multi-ethnic heritage. Included in these trends is the need for contemporary biographies, more representation of minorities, varied depictions of women in a broad spectrum of careers and more candid portraits of prominent people as human beings.

Editorial concerns

Children's book editors are eager to produce the best books they can, but they are also aware that the books they produce must sell. Most adult books are sold directly to the consumer. The primary market for children's books is still schools and libraries. For this reason, editors can't afford to take chances with children's books that have no hope at attaining a reasonable profit margin. However, editors will take a look at a manuscript that has unusual qualities, even if it doesn't promise immediate material rewards. Because the market is highly competitive, editors are turning more frequently to subject-matter experts to check and screen manuscripts.

Children's books are affected perhaps above all by our society's concept of the roles of children, what they should learn and how they should learn. The books children read are formative in their lives. Parents note that sharing books creates a special closeness with their children; teachers realize the value of a well-written book in the teaching of reading.

What constitutes a good book for children?

Children's books, just as adult novels, need to have some direct guidelines to determine the appropriateness as well as the level of "enjoyable" readability. You cannot judge a book simply by its well-illustrated cover; it must be read all of the way through. If it appeals to you the writer, it may also appeal to a younger audience. Here are some general questions to ask yourself when writing your manuscript:

• Will the book call into play the child's imagination?
• Will it invite the exercise of compassion or humor?
• Will it exploit the capacity for being curious?
• Will its language challenge the child's awareness of rhythms and structures.
• Will its characters and events call for—and even strengthen—an understanding of human motives and circumstances?
• Will it provide the joy that comes with achievement, understanding and new encounters?

Answering yes to most of the above questions indicates the possibility of a good book, perhaps even a great book.

The aim the writer sets himself is the same as that of a magician—to penetrate to the secret, beating heart of life, according to noted children's writer Mollie Hunter. Instinctually the writer senses that words are inherently magical, and that by setting one with another he may formulate the language which is his spell.

How to Make A Dummy: A Guide for Picture Book Writers And Illustrators

by Frieda Gates

Because pictures play such an important role in children's books, publishers need to see page-by-page layouts in order to make an accurate judgment of a book design. Sometimes these lay-outs are presented as individual sheets of two-page spreads, but more often they are presented in actual book form. Such a handmade mock-up of a book is called a dummy.

Publishers usually employ a designer to lay out the book and prepare the dummy. Working with the editor and illustrator, the designer chooses the typeface and determines the size and location of the type and illustrations on every page plus the cover. However, if you plan to design and illustrate you own book, you must prepare the dummy yourself.

Even if you plan to do only the illustrations, or only the writing, a dummy can be very helpful. For illustrators, a dummy aids in determining the number, size and composition of illustrations. For writers, a dummy, however crudely executed, aids in determining if more or less text is needed and if the text provides sufficient potential for successful graphic depiction by the illustrator.

Book formats

Format refers to the shape, size and general make-up of a book, and this is determined by the publisher. However, if you are preparing a dummy for a proposed book to be submitted to various publishers for consideration, you must determine the format yourself. Although every publisher has specific format preferences, general publishing guidelines can be acquired by examining a broad variety of children's books at your public library.

Size: Since there are many technical considerations that influence page size, it is wise to conform to the size of an already-published book. You will notice that the average picture book, counting each side of the paper as an individual page, contains 32, 40 or 48 pages, the maximum length being 64 pages. Books are bound in signatures of 32, 16, 12 and occasionally 8 pages. A signature is one sheet of paper printed on both sides and folded and trimmed in such a way that it results in a series of consecutive pages.

Front matter: The first six to eight pages of most books contain "front matter," which includes the half title, copyright, dedication and possibly a table of

Frieda Gates *is author and artist of numerous successful children's books. She lives in Monsey, New York. See page 19 for more information about her book,* How to Write, Illustrate, and Design Children's Books, *from which this article is reprinted.*

contents, preface, foreword, introduction and/or information about the book. Books will vary in the way this information is laid out, but the Library of Congress dictates that the copyright notice appear on the "title verso" page, which is the reverse side of the title page. (In publishing, recto means the right-hand page and verso means the reverse or left-hand page.) The title page generally states the title, author, illustrator and the name and address of the publishing company. The front-matter section may also include illustrations and/or blank pages.

Back matter: The last pages of some children's books contain "back matter," which includes biographical information about the author and illustrator and possibly an index, bibliography and/or picture credits.

Most hardcover books have endpapers, which are sheets that are glued to the inside of the front and back covers and the binding edge of the first and last pages. They are frequently of heavier stock than the pages and may be either white or colored. Although it is not common to do so, they may be used for illustrations.

Thumbnail sketches

The first step in designing a book is to lay out the pages in thumbnail sketches, or thumbnails. These are rough sketches done in miniature on a pad of layout, or visualizer, paper with a soft pencil. While the thumbnails can be any size that is convenient, it is important that they be in proportion to the actual page size. For example, if your actual page size is $6 \times 9''$, then your thumbnail page size should be $2 \times 3''$, $3 \times 4\frac{1}{2}''$, $4 \times 6''$, etc.

After you have decided on a thumbnail size, a fast and accurate method of drawing page outlines on the layout pad is with a cardboard template cut to the size of a two-page spread. (Thumbnail sketches are always executed as two-page spreads in order to judge the graphic relationship of facing pages.) Use heavy cardboard, such as illustration or matboard, so that a pencil can easily follow its edges, and cut notches in the top and bottom of the template to indicate the centerfold. (**See Figure 1**)

Figure 1: Cardboard Template

Lay out as many two-page outlines as possible on the layout pad, but leave enough room between them for page numbers as well as to avoid visual confusion. Work directly on the pad; it provides a resilient drawing surface and, because layout paper is somewhat transparent, previous sketches and other reference material can easily be slipped under the top sheet for use as a drawing guide. The usual procedure is to first try a number of layout variations on scrap paper. The best one, then, can be slipped under the top sheet and copied. Further layout adjustments can be made by shifting the underlying sketch.

If you or the publisher have decided on the number of pages, then make that many page outlines with the template and number them before proceeding further. If the number of pages has not been decided on, make the page outlines (and number them) as you go along, keeping in mind that the average book length ranges from 32 to 64 pages in multiples of 8.

After you have laid out the page outlines, the next step is to determine how much space the text will occupy. For lengthy stories, the typewritten manuscript has to be character-counted and then converted to typographic measurements. This is called copyfitting. For short stories, the text will occupy such a small space on any one page that an accurate preliminary character count is not necessary. As you layout the pages you can easily adjust the illustrations to accommodate the type.

To determine how much space is available for illustrations, first indicate the pages that will be used for front and back matter by writing "half title," "title," "blank," etc. in the middle of the appropriate pages on the thumbnail layout. Then count the remaining pages and deduct from them the approximate number of pages the text would occupy if it were set in full pages. In a 48-page book, for example, there might be 9 pages of front and back matter and 13 full pages of story text, leaving 26 pages for illustrations. Thus, the average page would be two-thirds illustrative and one-third textual. This ratio, of course, can and should vary from page to page, so long as the total book averages out to it.

The final step before starting the page layouts is to read through the manuscript to identify those images and situations that convey the essence of the story and have the best potential for graphic depiction. Small spot, or single-image, illustrations can be interspersed among the larger situational illustrations. Make a numbered list of the potential illustrations using words and/or small sketches, and mark the illustration number at the appropriate place on the manuscript. **(See Figure 2)**

At this point you are ready to begin the layout design. As mentioned previously, use a soft graphite pencil, and try out a few layout ideas on scrap paper first. The purpose of thumbnail layouts is to achieve, in a given number of pages, pleasing overall page compositions with well-synchronized words and pictures. Therefore, while the size, shape, position, and subject matter of illustrations are important, the drawing technique and accuracy of details are not. In fact, many illustrators who are fine draftsmen employ a crude, stick-figure technique for thumbnails. The text, too, can be crudely indicated, using a horizontal line to represent each line of type. As with the illustrations, of course, the overall block of type should be reasonably accurate in regard to size, shape, and position. Type larger than 14 points should be block-lettered. Colored pencils or pointed color markers are good mediums for indicating color illustrations. **(See Figure 3)**

It is almost always necessary to do a second series of thumbnail sketches.

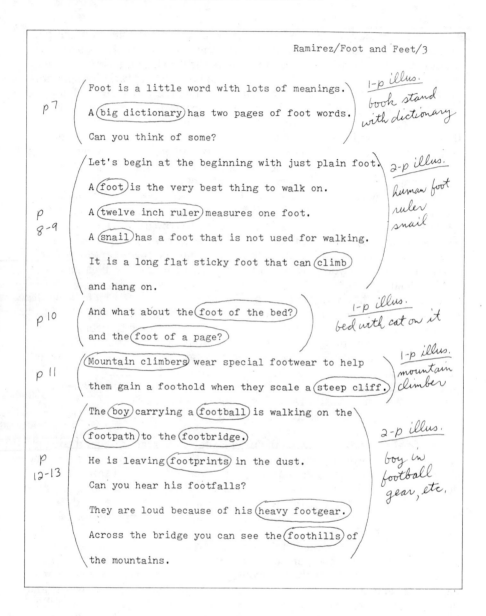

Ramirez/Foot and Feet/3

p 7

Foot is a little word with lots of meanings.
A big dictionary has two pages of foot words.
Can you think of some?

1-p illus.
book stand with dictionary

p 8-9

Let's begin at the beginning with just plain foot.
A foot is the very best thing to walk on.
A twelve inch ruler measures one foot.
A snail has a foot that is not used for walking.
It is a long flat sticky foot that can climb
and hang on.

2-p illus.
human foot
ruler
snail

p 10

And what about the foot of the bed?
and the foot of a page?

1-p illus.
bed with cat on it

p 11

Mountain climbers wear special footwear to help
them gain a foothold when they scale a steep cliff.

1-p illus.
mountain climber

p 12-13

The boy carrying a football is walking on the
footpath to the footbridge.
He is leaving footprints in the dust.
Can you hear his footfalls?
They are loud because of his heavy footgear.
Across the bridge you can see the foothills of
the mountains.

2-p illus.
boy in football gear, etc.

Figure 2: A typical method of indicating page distribution and potential illustrations on the manuscript. Another method is to make a separate list of potential illustrations, using words and/or small sketches.

Even if you were lucky enough in the first series to end up on the right page, you will find, upon later overall evaluation, that some spreads are less satisfying than others. A common problem is that two or more consecutive spreads are either so similar in layout as to be boring, or so different as to be discordant. When revising them, try to achieve a pleasing variety of compositions from spread to spread, while at the same time employing certain common factors to provide unity.

Don't rush through the thumbnail sketches, and don't hesitate to revise them one or more times. The most important aspect of a book is its overall graphic structure or "look," which involves the sizes, shape, and color relationships of elements on individual spreads (the abstract composition), as well as the relationship between the spreads. Beginners tend to believe that beautifully executed illustrations will hide any deficiencies in the layout composition, but just the opposite is true. The better the illustrations are, the more obvious the layout deficiencies become.

Figure 3: Thumbnail sketches for the first 23 pages of a 48-page book, **Foot and Feet** *(1973), written by Carolyn Ramirez and illustrated by Frieda Gates.*

Rough layouts

When you are satisfied with the thumbnail sketches, you must enlarge them to reproduction size for further refinement before starting the dummy. Working on a layout pad, accurately measure and draw the outlines of two-page spreads, using a ruler, T-square, triangle, and sharp pencil, roughly lay out the page elements, paying particular attention to their size, shape and position. Such a conversion from thumbnail to rough layout size is usually done by visual estimation.

After you have roughly laid out the pages, you can then begin to refine the illustrations in regard to the larger issues of proportions, perspective, and overall composition. Don't be concerned with details and the technique to be used in the finished art; these are issues to be resolved in the finished art itself. As on the thumbnails, the lines of small type are indicated with horizontal pencil lines, while large type (over 14 points) must be block-lettered.

It is usually necessary to do two or three roughs to fully resolve the layout and illustration problems. **(See Figure 4)** For color illustrations, therefore, do the earlier sketches in black graphite pencil to resolve the formal composition, reserving color for the later sketches. The best color mediums for roughs are colored pencils, color markers, and pastels. To avoid smudging, spray pastel sketches with workable matte fixative, either as each shape is rendered or when the sketch is finished.

Figure 4: On top is a reproduction-size rough layout. The bottom illustration is a more refined layout for use in the dummy.

Executing the dummy

Since the dummy is time-consuming to construct and render, you don't want to have to execute if more than once. Therefore, make sure you are fully satisfied with your rough layouts before proceeding further.

There are various methods of constructing a dummy, and each has certain advantages and disadvantages. Read through the following descriptions of some of the most common methods, and select one that best suits your purposes. If your book has already been accepted by a publisher, you will need only an original dummy for presentation. However, if your book will be sent to one or more publishers for consideration, you will need to make a photocopy of the dummy, since it would be too risky to send the original.

For pages with color illustrations, do the original art in black, using thin outlines to delineate color areas, and apply the color to the photocopy with markers. Of course, you can also make full-color photocopies of color pages, but these are substantially more expensive than black & white copies, and are not as easily available. When making a photocopy dummy, keep in mind that you may be able to make copies of your rough layouts, which will eliminate the need to re-execute them for the dummy.

Saddle-stiched blank dummy: This dummy is constructed in the following steps:

(1) Carefully measure and draw the outlines of the two-page spreads on white bond paper, adding ¼" to all four sides for later trimming.

(2) Mark the hole positions for two staples on the centerfold of each spread, using a strip of paper as a measuring guide to insure that the holes will later align perfectly.

(3) Trim the spreads with a sharb blade and a straightedge, puncture the staple holes with a pushpin, and score the centerfolds with the end of a paper clip.

(4) Fold and then unfold the individual spreads, insert the two staples through one spread at a time (from the outside), and bend them over at the center spread.

(5) Fold the assembled dummy and trim ¼" off the top, bottom, and unbound side with a sharp blade and a straightedge. **(See Figure 5)**

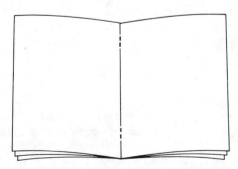

Figure 5: Saddle-stitched blank dummy showing staples clinched at the center spread.

The layouts are not executed directly on this type of dummy. Rather, they are executed separately on thin layout paper (either page by page or spread by spread), rubber cemented onto the dummy, and trimmed to page size. The reason for this is that later changes can easily be made by replacing individual pages or spreads. A rubber cemented sheet can be removed with a squirt can of rubber cement thinner. Squirt the thinner between the sheets as they are being pulled part. Xerographic copies can also be used in this type of dummy. For books over 48 pages, it may be necessary to divide the dummy into two sets of stapled sheets. They can later be bound together with a strip of tape.

Cemented-spread dummy: This type of dummy, which eliminates the need to make a separate blank dummy, is constructed in the following steps:

(1) Carefully measure and draw the outlines of a two-page spread on opaque white bond paper, adding ¼" to all four sides for later trimming, and execute the layout on it. Because bond paper is quite opaque, you may need to use a tracing box to see your underlying rough layout.

(2) Trim the spread with a sharp knife and a straightedge, and score the center-fold with the end of a paper clip.

(3) After all the spreads are executed, fold them inwardly, and rubber cement them together, attaching the back of the right-hand page of one spread to the back of the left-hand page of the next spread.

(4) Trim ¼" off the top, bottom, and right side of the assembled dummy with a sharp blade and a straightedge. **(See Figure 6)**

Figure 6: Binding procedure for cemented-spread dummy.

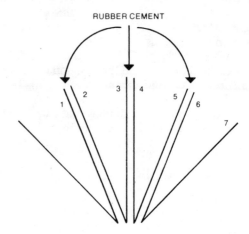

RUBBER CEMENT

Cemented-page dummy. This method is used primarily for xerographic dummies where the page size is too large for the cemented-spread method. However, because a ½" binding tab plus ¼" trim margins are required, the largest page that can be made from 8½ × 14" copier paper is 7¾ × 13½" for an upright book (bound on its long dimension) and 13¼ × 8" for an oblong book (bound on its short dimension). For page sizes larger than this (up to 8½ × 14" in either dimension, you will have to use the saddle-stitched blank dummy described earlier.

Following are the steps required to make a cemented-page dummy (**See Figure 7**):

(**1**) Make a xerographic copy of each page layout, allowing for trim and binding edges as described in the following steps.

(**3**) Measure and draw the page outlines on the copies, adding ¼″ at the top, bottom, and right side of right-hand pages, and ¼″ at the top, bottom and left side of left-hand pages, also add a ½″ binding tab.

(**3**) Trim the pages with a sharp blade and a straightedge, score the binding tabs with the end of a paper clip, and fold them toward you.

(**4**) With rubber cement, attach the back of page 1 (RH) to the back of page 2 (LH); unfold the tab on page 2 and attach the back of page 3 to it; attach the back of page 4 to the back of page 3; and so forth.

(**5**) Trim the assembled dummy at top, bottom, and right side with a sharp blade and a straightedge, and remove any excess cement at the binding edges of pages.

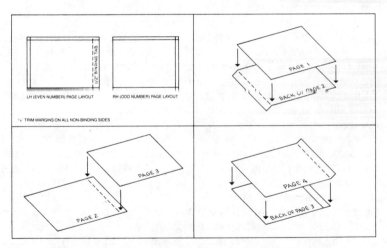

Figure 7: Layout and binding procedure for cemented-page dummy.

Spiral-wire dummy. An easy way to make a dummy is with a spiral-wire notebook. The drawback to this method, however, is that the spiral is always visible, and also disrupts two-page illustrations. Use a notebook that has a small spiral and unruled pages. Remove the covers and unneeded pages, trim the notebook to dummy size, and clip off the excess spiral. Execute the layouts on layout paper (or make xerographic copies of the layouts), trim to page size, and rubber-cement them on the notebook pages.

The cover or jacket

The printed cover or jacket is very important because it serves to attract attention to the book. Even though your book may be limited to one or two colors, most publishers will agree to the use of an extra color or two on the cover or jacket.

The cover of a dummy is of much simpler construction than that of a manufactured book. Usually it is nothing more than a folder made of heavyweight paper that may or may not be attached to the enclosed page dummy. It is possible, however, to simulate a hardcover book by wrapping and gluing the rendered layout around two pieces of cardboard, and reinforcing the interior of the spine with tape.

If your book has not yet been commissioned, the only copy required is that for the front cover, which includes the title and the names of the author and illustrator.

When designing the cover, it is first necessary to construct a trial cover to see that it properly fits the enclosed dummy. Note that the front cover is on the right and the back cover is on the left. Make a number of layouts, from rough to tight, before executing the final dummy cover. For the rough layouts, use a soft graphite pencil to resolve the larger issues of proportions, perspective, and composition. Details and color can be resolved in the tighter layouts. Keep in mind that the back cover can be blank or illustrated. Frequently the front-cover illustration extends onto the back cover.

Don't treat type as an afterthought. It is a very important design element that must be included on all the layouts. It can be roughly executed on the rough layouts, but it should be fairly accurate in regard to size, weight, and position. For the tight layouts, find an appropriate type style and size in a type reference book and, using a piece of tracing paper that has been ruled with horizontal guidelines, trace the outlines of the desired letters, shifting the paper to compose them into words. If the type sample is not the right size, enlarge or reduce it on an art projector or a photocopier.

Transfer the type to the cover design. When executing the type to the cover, use pointed color markers or colored pencils if the background is white or light in value. For white or colored type on a dark background, it is necessary to use gouache (opaque watercolor). To obtain maximum brightness, colored type on a dark background must first be painted white. If you fail to follow this procedure, you'll not only be disappointed with the color, but you'll find that any number of additional coats will not improve it.

The final dummy cover can be executed on layout paper and then cemented onto the cover paper, or it can be executed directly on the cover paper itself. A xerographic copy can also be cemented onto the cover paper, but if the cover is largely in color, only a full-color copy would be worthwhile in regard to rendering time saved. With all methods, don't trim, score, and fold the cover until after the graphics are applied.

The cover can be attached to the enclosed page dummy with strips of tape along the inside binding edges. It can also be attached with endpapers, which are like two-page spreads that are cemented to the insides of the cover and the first and last pages of the dummy.

Putting type on the dummy

If your book has been commissioned by a publisher, then by the time you do the dummy the editor will have copyedited the manuscript, the type will have been set to your specifications, and you will have received the rough, or galley, proofs. In that case, simply cut up the galley proofs and paste them on the dummy.

If your book has not been commissioned, the easiest way to indicate type on the dummy is to paste in typewritten copy. This is not a very accurate method, but since copy and layout changes are bound to occur after the book is accepted, it is adequate for dummy purposes. Use a typewriter that produces 10 characters per inch (pica size), and set it at single spacing for normally-spaced paragraphs. This approximates 12-point type, which is a common size used in children's books.

A slower but more accurate method of indicating type is to hand-letter it, using a single-stroke technique. This method is preferable for books that don't contain much copy and thus usually require larger type.

Frieda Gates' book, How to Write, Illustrate, and Design Children's Books *describes every aspect involved in putting together a children's book and serves as a step-by-step guide for novices and professionals alike. Available from Library Research Associates, Inc., Dunderberg Road RD 5, Box 41, Monroe NY 10950, $23.50. (LRA pays shipping. New York State residents add sales tax.)*

The Business of Children's Writing & Illustrating

In many children's fantasy stories, a magic potion is all that is needed to cure all and assure happiness ever after. Unfortunately, unlike the characters in the story, aspiring children's writers and illustrators must face reality—there is no magic potion for success.

You may like to believe superb writing or illustrating is all that is needed to be discovered in this industry. Actually, knowledge of the business is essential. The Business of Children's Writing & Illustrating is devoted to writers and artists who are adept at the craft of writing or illustrating, but may be a little unsure of the business techniques needed to successfully compete in the growing industry of children's publishing.

So though your energies have been drained from working on your children's book, remember that if you ever want your "labor of love" to be seen by more than the walls of your desk drawer, you are going to have to market it. Hopefully, this section will answer some of your questions when you wonder, "Okay, I've finished the book. What do I do now?"

Marketing your work

There are two basic elements to submitting your work successfully: good research and persistence. Read through the listings in this book and familiarize yourself with the publications that interest you. Then study the specific needs and the required submission procedures of each publisher or publication. Editors hate to receive inappropriate submissions because handling them wastes precious time. By randomly sending out manuscripts without knowledge of whom you're sending them to, you risk irritating the editors. This practice can actually hurt you more than it can help you.

If you're interested in submitting to a particular magazine, acquire a sample copy. For a book publisher, buy a couple of books produced by that publisher or obtain a book catalog. By doing this, you can better acquaint yourself with that market's writing and illustration styles and formats.

Most of the book publishers and magazines listed offer some sort of writer's/artist's guidelines. It is recommended you read these guidelines before submitting. This way, you can tailor your work more closely to the needs of the publisher or publication.

Format review for submitting work

Throughout these listings you will read editors' requests for a query letter, cover letter, book proposal, complete manuscript or resume as all or part of the initial contact procedure.

Query letters. A query letter should be no more than a one-page, well written, concise piece to arouse an editor's interest in your manuscript. Queries are usually required from writers submitting nonfiction material to a publisher. Such a letter should be single-spaced and include the editor's name, if available, though you will want to avoid using a first name during an initial contact until more familiarity is established. In the query letter you want to convince the editor that your idea is perfect for his readership and that you're the writer qualified to do the job. Include any previous writing experience in your letter plus published samples to prove your credentials, especially any samples that relate to the subject matter about which you're querying.

Many query letters start with a lead similar to the lead that would be used in the actual manuscript. Next, you want to briefly outline the work and include facts, anecdotes, interviews or any other pertinent information that give the editor a feel for the manuscript's premise. Your goal is to entice him to want to know more. End your letter with a straight-forward request to write the work, and include information on its approximate length, date it could be completed and the availability of accompanying photos or artwork.

Queries are rarely used for fiction manuscripts, but occasionally there are exceptions. For a fiction query you want to explain the story's plot, main characters, conflict and resolution. Just as in nonfiction queries, you want to make the editor eager to see more. For more information on writing good queries, consult *How to Write Irresistible Query Letters*, by Lisa Collier Cool (Writer's Digest Books).

Cover letters. Many editors prefer to review a complete manuscript, especially for fiction. In such a case, the cover letter will serve to introduce you and establish your credentials as a writer plus give the editor an overview of the manuscript. Unlike the query letter, a cover letter sent with a manuscript doesn't need to take a hard-sell orientation; the manuscript, at this point, will be the selling mechanism. Be sure to let the editor know whether the unsolicited manuscript is a simultaneous submission. However, if you're just sending a photocopy of your manuscript, and not a simultaneous submission, you might want to reassure him that he is the only one considering your work at this time. Some editors might assume a photocopied manuscript is being considered elsewhere. If you're sending the manuscript after a "go-ahead" from the editor, the cover letter should serve as a reminder of this commitment.

For an illustrator, the cover letter will also serve as your introduction to the art director and establish your credentials as a professional artist. Type the cover letter on your letterhead and, in addition to introducing yourself and your abilities, be sure to explain what services you can provide as well as what type of follow-up contact you plan to make, if any. If you are sending samples of your work, indicate whether they should be returned or filed. If you wish them returned include a self-addressed, stamped envelope (SASE) with your submission packet. Cover letters, like the query, should be no longer than one page.

Resumes. Often illustrators are asked to submit a resume with their cover letter and samples. A resume provides you with a vehicle to showcase your experience, education and awards. Resumes can be created in a variety of formats ranging from a single page listing information to color brochures featuring your art. Keep the resume brief, and focus on your artistic achievements, not your whole life. On your resume you want to include your name and address, your clients and the work you did for them. Also include your educational background and any awards you've won.

Book proposals. Throughout the listings in the Book Publishers section you will find references to submission of a synopsis, outline and sample chapters. Depending on an editor's preference, some or all of these components, as well as inclusion of a cover letter, comprise a book proposal.

A synopsis summarizes the book. Such a summary includes the basic plot of the book (including the ending), is easy to read and flows well.

An outline can also be used to set up fiction, but is more effective as a tool for nonfiction. The outline covers your book chapter by chapter and provides highlights of each. If you are developing an outline for fiction you will want to include major characters, plots and subplots, and length of the book. An outline can run 3 to 30 pages depending on the complexity of your manuscript.

Sample chapters give a more comprehensive idea of your writing skill. Some editors may request the first two or three chapters to see how your material is set up; others may request a beginning, middle and ending chapter to get a better feel for the entire plot. Be sure to determine what the editor needs to see before investing time in writing sample chapters.

Many picture book editors require an outline or synopsis, sample chapters and a variation of roughs or finished illustrations from the author/illustrator. Listings specifying an interest in picture books will detail what type of artwork should accompany manuscripts. You will also want to query the editor or art director prior to submitting material for more detailed information that will tailor your illustrations to their needs. If you want to know more about putting together a book proposal, read *How to Write a Book Proposal*, by Michael Larsen (Writer's Digest Books).

Manuscript formats. If an editor specifies that you should submit a complete manuscript for review, here is some format information to guide you. In the upper left corner type your legal name (not pseudonym), address, phone number and Social Security number (publishers must have this to file payment records with the government). In the upper right corner you should type the approximate word length, what rights are being offered for sale (this is not necessary for book manuscripts; rights will be covered in your contract) and your copyright notice, which should appear as © Joe Writer 1991 (a copyright notice is no longer necessary, though advisable; see "Rights for the Writer and Illustrator" for details). All material in the upper corners should be typed single-spaced, not double.

There is no need for a cover page or title page on a manuscript: The first page should include the title (centered) one-third of the way down. Two spaces under that type "by" and your name or pseudonym. To begin the body of your manuscript, drop down two double spaces and indent five spaces for each new paragraph. There should be 1¼ inch margins around all sides of a full typewritten page. (Manuscripts with wider margins are easier to edit. Also, a page that isn't cramped with a lot of words is more readable and appealing to an editor.) Be sure to set your typewriter on "double-space" for the manuscript body. From page 2 to the end of your manuscript just include your last name followed by a dash and the page number in the upper left corner. You can include the title of your piece under your name if you wish. Drop down two double spaces to begin the body of the page and follow this format throughout the manuscript.

If you're submitting a novel, type the chapter title one-third of the way down the page. On subsequent pages you again will want to include your name, dash symbol, page number and title of the manuscript.

On the last page of your manuscript skip down three double spaces after your last sentence and type "The End." Some nonfiction writers use the journalistic symbols "###" or "-30-." For more information on manuscript formats read *Manuscript Submission*, by Scott Edelstein (Writer's Digest Books).

To get an approximate word count for your manuscript, first count the number of characters and spaces in an average line, next count the number of lines on a representative page and multiply these two factors to get your average number of characters per page. Finally, count the number of pages in your manuscript, multiply by the characters per page, then divide by 6 (the average number of characters in a word). You will have your approximate word count.

Packing and mailing submissions

Your primary concern in packaging material is to ensure that it arrives undamaged.

If your manuscript is fewer than six pages it is safe to simply fold it in thirds and send it out in a #10 (business-size) envelope. For a self-addressed, stamped envelope (SASE) you can then fold another #10 envelope in thirds or insert a #9 (reply) envelope which fits in a #10 neatly without any folding at all. Some editors appreciate receiving a manuscript folded in half into a 6x9 envelope. For larger manuscripts you will want to use a 9x12 envelope both for mailing the submission out and as a SASE for its return. The SASE envelope can be folded in half. Book manuscripts will require a sturdy box such as a typing paper or envelope box for mailing. Include a self-addressed mailing label and return postage so it can also double as your SASE.

Artwork requires a bit more packaging care to guarantee that it arrives in presentable form. Sandwich illustrations between heavy cardboard that is slightly larger than the work and tape it closed. You will want to write your name and address on each piece in case the inside material becomes separated from the outer envelope upon receipt. For the outer wrapping you can use either a manila envelope, foam-padded envelope, a mailer with plastic air bubbles as a liner or brown wrapping paper. Bind non-joined edges with reinforced mailing tape and clearly write your address.

You will want to mail material first-class to ensure quick delivery. Also, first-class mail is forwarded for one year if the addressee has moved (which does happen with some magazine and book publishers), and can be returned if undeliverable. If you are mailing a package that weighs between one and 70 pounds it can go fourth class unless you specifically request first-class mail treatment. Fourth-class mail tends to be handled with less care, so pack your material with this in mind. If you have enclosed a letter, write "first-class letter enclosed" on the package and add the correct amount of postage. Also write "return postage guaranteed" on your package so it can be returned to you if undeliverable.

If you are concerned about your material safely reaching its destination, consider certified mail as an option. Material sent this way must be signed when it reaches its destination, and if you wish, a return receipt will be sent to you. Material sent certified mail is also automatically insured for $100.

Your packages can also be sent UPS. Since UPS isn't legally allowed to carry first-class mail, your letter will have to be mailed separately.

If material needs to reach your editor or art director quickly, you can elect to use overnight deliveries such as U.S. Priority Mail and Express Mail Next Day Services, UPS's Two-Day Blue Label Air Service, and dozens of privately owned overnight services such as Federal Express, Emery Worldwide or Purolater Courier. Fees and delivery destinations vary.

Occasionally throughout this book you will see the term International Reply Coupon (IRC). Keep in mind foreign markets cannot use U.S. postage when returning a manuscript to you, which therefore renders moot any SASE you may have sent. When mailing a submission to another country (Canada too), include IRCs in lieu of U.S. postage. The U.S. Post Office can help you determine, based on your package's weight, the correct number of IRCs to include to ensure its return. Two IRCs are recommended for packages being shipped via air.

It is not necessary for an editor to return your work, such as with photocopies of manuscripts or art, don't include return postage. It will be cheaper on your postage bill. Instead, track the status of your submissions by enclosing a postage-paid reply postcard (which requires less postage) with options for the editor to check, such as "yes, I am interested" or "no, the material is not appropriate for my needs at this time."

Some writers or illustrators simply set a deadline date. The manuscript or artwork is automatically withdrawn from consideration. If nothing is heard from the editor or art director by this date. Because many publishing houses are overstocked with manuscripts, a minimum deadline should be no less than 3 months.

Pricing, negotiating and contracts

Negotiation is a two-way street on which, hopefully, both the author/artist and editor/art director will feel mutual satisfaction prior to signing a contract.

Book publishers pay authors and artists in royalties, or rather, a percentage of the cover price of each book sold. Usually, before the book is published, the author or artist receives an advance issued against future royalties. Half of the advance amount is issued upon signing the book contract. The other half is issued when the book is finished. After your book has sold enough copies to earn back your advance, you will start to get royalty checks. Though royalty percentages vary with each publisher, the following are general guidelines to consider when negotiating the sale of your first book (figures taken from the May 1990 issue of *Children's Book Insider*):
• Picture Books: For 24-40 pages of text, full-color artwork on each page, the writer and illustrator (if two people) should each be able to command $2,000-5,000 advances. The 8-10% hardcover royalty and 6-8% paperback royalty is split equally between the two. If one person is writing and illustrating the book, the advance for the one person is higher ($4,000-7,000) and that person receives the full royalty.
• Chapter Books and Middle Grade Novels: For 40-80 pages, 10-15 black and white illustrations and a color cover, the writer should receive a $3,000-6,000

advance, 7-10% hardcover royalty and 5-8% paperback royalty. The illustrator should get a $3,000-5,000 advance, 3-5% hardcover royalty and 1.5-3% paperback royalty.

• Young Adult Novels: For 100 or more pages, no illustrations and a color cover, writers should be offered a $3,500-6,000 advance, 8-10% hardcover royalty and a 6-8% paperback royalty. The illustrators get a flat fee (up to $1,000) for the cover.

One way to determine a fair advance is to multiply the print run by the cover price and then multiply that figure with the royalty percentage. If you feel the advance is too low, ask for higher royalties.

Price structures for magazines are based on a per-word rate or range for a specific length of article.

Artists have a few more variables to contend with prior to contracting their services. Payment for illustrations can be set by such factors as whether the piece will be rendered in black and white or four-color, how many illustrations are to be purchased and the artist's prior experience. Determine an hourly rate by using the annual salary of a staff artist doing similar work in an economically similar geographic area (try to find an artist willing to share this information), then dividing that salary by 52 (the number of weeks in a year) and again by 40 (the number of hours in a work week). You will want to add your overhead expenses such as rent, utilities, art supplies, etc. to this answer by multiplying your hourly rate by 2.5. Research, again, may have to come into play to be sure your rate is competitive within the marketplace.

Once you make a sale you will probably sign a contract. A contract is an agreement between two or more parties that specifies the fee to be paid, services to be rendered, deadlines, rights purchased and, for artists, return (or not) of original artwork. Be sure to get a contract in writing rather than agreeing to oral stipulations; written contracts protect both parties from misunderstandings and faulty memories. Also, look out for clauses that may not be in your best interest, such as "work-for-hire." Be sure you know whether or not your contract contains an option clause. This clause requires the author to give the publisher a first look at his next work before marketing it to other publishers. Though it is editorial etiquette to give the publisher the first chance at publishing your next work, be wary of statements in the contract which could trap you. Don't allow the publisher to consider the next project for more than 30 days and be specific about what type of work should actually be considered "next work" (i.e., if the book under contract is a young adult novel, specify that the publisher will only receive an exclusive look at the next young adult novel). If there are clauses that appear vague or confusing, get some legal advice. The time and money invested in counseling up front could protect you from more serious problems down the road. If you have an agent, he will review any contract.

Business records

It is imperative to keep accurate business records in order to determine if you are making a profit as a writer or illustrator. You will definitely want to keep a separate bank account and ledger apart from your personal finances. Also, if writing or illustrating is secondary to another freelance career, maintain separate business records from that career.

If you're just starting your career, you will most likely be accumulating some business expenses prior to showing any profit. To substantiate your income and expenses to the IRS be sure to keep all invoices, cash receipts, sales slips, bank statements, cancelled checks plus receipts related to entertaining clients such as for dinner and parking. For entertainment expenditures you also will want to record the date, place and purpose of the business meeting as well as gas mileage. Be sure to file all receipts in chronological order; if you maintain a separate file for each month of the year it will provide for easier retrieval of records at year's end. Keeping receipts is important for all purchases, big and small. Don't take the small purchases for granted. Enough of them can result in a rather substantial monetary figure.

When setting up a single-entry bookkeeping system you will want to record income and expenses separately. It may prove easier to use some of the sub-heads that appear on Schedule C of the 1040 tax form. This way you can transfer information more easily onto the tax form when filing your return. In your ledger you will want to include a description of each transaction—date, source of income (or debts from business purchases), description of what was purchased or sold; whether pay was by cash, check or credit card, and the amount of the transaction.

You don't have to wait until January 1 to start keeping records, either. The moment you first make a business-related purchase or sell an article, book manuscript or illustrations you will need to begin tracking your profits and losses. If you keep records from January 1 to December 31 you are using a calendar-year accounting method. Any other accounting period is known as a fiscal year. You also can choose between two types of accounting methods— the cash method and the accrual method. The cash method is used more often: You record income when it is received and expenses when they are disbursed. Under the accrual method you report income at the time you earn it rather than when it is actually received. Similarly, expenses are recorded at the time they are incurred rather than when you actually pay them. If you choose this method you will need to keep separate records for "accounts receivable" and "accounts payable."

Recording submissions

An offshoot of recording income and expenses is keeping track of submissions under consideration in the marketplace. Many times writers and illustrators devote their attention to submitting material to editors or art directors, then fail to follow up on overdue responses because they feel the situation is out of their hands. By tracking those submissions still under consideration and then following up, you may be able to refresh a buyer's memory who temporarily forgot about your submission, or revise a troublesome point to make your work more enticing to him. At the very least you will receive a definite "no," thereby freeing you to send your material to another market.

It is especially important to keep track of submissions when you are submitting simultaneously. This way if you get an offer on that manuscript, you will be able to notify the other publishers to withdraw your work from consideration.

When recording your submissions be sure to include the date they were sent, the business and contact name; and any enclosures that were inserted such as samples of writing, artwork or photography. Keep copies of the article or manuscript as well as related correspondence for easier follow up. When you sell rights to a manuscript or artwork you can "close" your file by noting the date the material was accepted, what rights were purchased, the publication date and payment.

Rights for the writer and illustrator

The Copyright Law of 1976, which became effective January 1, 1978, was modified in 1989. So that the United States may have copyright relations with 80 other countries, Congress voted to amend our copyright law and ratify the Berne Convention. This means that it is no longer necessary to attach a copyright notice to works; material published after March 1, 1989 automatically carries copyright protection via this amendment.

The international recognition of copyright protection provided in the Berne Convention prevents foreign piracy of works copyrighted in the U.S. and allows prosecution of foreign copyright infringers in foreign courts. (Principal countries that haven't yet adopted the convention are China and the Soviet Union.)

From the second words hit the paper, they are protected by the copyright law. However, in order to proceed with an infringement lawsuit, the work must be registered. A copyright notice—© (your name, year of work)—should be included on all your work, registered or not, and should be enough to keep most people from stealing it. But if you are really concerned about truly making the work yours, it is a good idea to register it.

Keep in mind that ideas and concepts are not copyrightable, but rather the expression of those ideas and concepts. Though it is a fact of life that ideas do get taken, a character type or basic plot outline is not subject to a copyright infringement lawsuit.

In general, copyright protection ensures that you, the writer or illustrator, have the power to decide how the work is used and that you receive payment for each use. Not only does a copyright protect you, it essentially encourages you to create new works by guaranteeing you the power to sell rights to their use in the marketplace. As the copyright holder you can print, reprint or copy your work; sell or distribute copies of your work; or prepare derivative works such as plays, collages or recordings. The Copyright Law is designed to protect a writer's or illustrator's work for his lifetime plus 50 years. If you collaborate with someone else on a written or artistic project, the copyright will last for the lifetime of the last survivor plus 50 years. In addition, works created anonymously or under a pseudonym are protected for 100 years, or 75 years after publication, whichever is shorter. Incidentally, this latter rule is also true of work-for-hire agreements. Under work-for-hire you relinquish your copyright to your "employer." Try to avoid agreeing to such terms.

For more information about the proper procedure to register works, contact the Register of Copyrights, Library of Congress, Washington D.C. 20559. The forms available are **TX** for writing (books, articles, etc.); **VA** for pictures (photographs, illustrations); and **PA** for plays and music. To learn more about how to go about using the copyright forms, request a copy of Circular I on Copyright Basics. All of these forms are free. Send the completed form along with the stated fee and a copy of the work to the Copyright Office. You can register a group of articles or illustrations if:

- the group is assembled in order, such as in a notebook;
- the works bear a single title, such as "Works by (your name)";
- they are the work of one writer or artist;
- the material is the subject of a single claim to copyright.

It is the publisher's responsibility to register your book for copyright. If you have previously registered the same material, you must inform your editor and supply the previous copyright information. Otherwise, the publisher cannot register the book in its published form.

The copyright law specifies that writers generally sell one-time rights to their work unless they and the buyer agree otherwise in writing. Be forewarned that many editors aren't aware of this. Many publications will want more exclusive rights from you than just one-time usage of your work; some will even require you to sell all rights to your work. Be sure that you are monetarily compensated for the additional rights you give up to your material. It is always to your benefit to retain as much control as possible over your work. Writers who give up limited rights to their work can then sell reprint rights to other publications, foreign rights to international publications, or even movie rights, should the opportunity arise. Likewise, artists can sell their illustrations to other book and magazine markets as well as to paper-product companies who may use an image on a calendar or greeting card. You can see that exercising more control over ownership of your work gives you a greater marketing edge for resale. If you do have to give up all rights to a work, think about the price you are being offered to determine whether it will compensate you for the loss of other sales.

Rights acquired through sale of a book manuscript are explained in each publisher's contract. Take the time to read through relevant clauses to be sure you understand what each contract is specifying prior to signing. The rights you will most often be selling to periodicals in the marketplace are:

- One-time rights—The buyer has no guarantee that he is the first to use a piece. One-time permission to run a written or illustrated work is acquired, then the rights revert back to the creator.
- First serial rights—The creator offers rights to use the work for the first time in any periodical. All other rights remain with the creator. When material is excerpted from a soon-to-be-published book for use in a newspaper or periodical, first serial rights are also purchased.
- First North American serial rights—This is similar to first serial rights, except that publishers who distribute both in the U.S. and Canada will stipulate these rights to ensure that a publication in the other country won't come out with simultaneous usage of the same work.
- Second serial (reprint) rights—In this case newspapers and magazines are granted the right to reproduce a work that already has appeared in another publication. These rights also are purchased by a newspaper or magazine editor who wants to publish part of a book after the book has been published. The proceeds from reprint rights are often split 50/50 between the author and his publishing company.
- Simultaneous rights—Use of such rights occurs among magazines with circulations that don't overlap, such as many religious publications. Many "moral guidance" stories or illustrations are appropriate for a variety of denominational publications. Be sure you submit to a publication that allows simultaneous submissions, and be sure to state in your cover letter to the editor that the

submission is being considered elsewhere.

● All rights—Rights such as this are purchased by publishers who pay premium usage fees, have an exclusive format, or have other book or magazine interests from which the purchased work can generate more "mileage" for their interests. When the writer or illustrator sells all rights to a market he no longer has any say in who acquires rights to use his piece. Synonymous with purchase of all rights is the term "work-for-hire." Under such an agreement the creator of a work gives away all rights—and his copyright—to the company buying his work. Try to avoid such agreements; they're not in your best interest. If a market is insistent upon acquiring all rights to your work, see if you can negotiate for the rights to revert back to you after a reasonable period of time. It can't hurt to ask. If they're agreeable to such a proposal, be sure you get it in writing.

● Foreign serial rights—Be sure before you market to foreign publications that you have only sold North American—not worldwide—serial rights to previous markets. If not, you are free to market to publications you think may be interested in using material that has appeared in a U.S. or North American-based periodical.

● Syndication rights—This is a division of serial rights. For example, if a syndicate prints portions of a book in installments in its newspapers, it would be syndicating second serial rights. The syndicate would receive a commission and leave the remainder to be split between the author and publisher.

● Subsidiary rights—These are rights, other than book rights, and should be specified in a book contract. Subsidiary rights include serial rights, dramatic rights, book club rights or translation rights. The contract should specify what percentage of profits from sales of these rights go to the author and publisher.

● Dramatic, television and motion picture rights—During the specified time the interested party tries to sell the story to a producer or director. Many times options are renewed because the selling process can be lengthy.

Taxes

To successfully (and legally) compete in the business of writing or illustrating you must have knowledge of what income you should report and deductions you can claim. Before you can do this however, you must prove to the IRS that you are in business to make a profit, that your writing or illustrations are not merely a hobby. Under the Tax Reform Act of 1986 it was determined that you should show a profit for three years out of a five-year period to attain professional status. What does the IRS look for as proof of your professionalism? Keeping accurate financial records (see Business records), maintaining a business bank account separate from your personal account, the time you devote to your profession and whether it is your main or secondary source of income, and your history of profits and losses. The amount of training you have invested in your field also is a contributing factor to your professional status, as well as your expertise in the field.

If your business is unincorporated, you will fill out tax information on Schedule C of Form 1040. If you're unsure of what deductions you can take, request Publication 553 from the IRS. Under the Tax Reform Act only 80 percent (formerly it was 100 percent) of business meals, entertainment and related tips and parking charges are deductible. Other deductibles allowed on Schedule C include: capital expenditures (such as a computer), car expenses for business-related trips, professional courses and seminars, depreciation of office equipment, dues and publications and miscellaneous expenses, such as postage used for business needs, etc.

If you're working out of a home office, a portion of your mortgage (or rent), related utilities, property taxes, repair costs and depreciation can be deducted as business expenses. To qualify though, your office must be used only for business activities. It can't double as a family room during nonbusiness hours. To determine what portion of business deductions can be taken, simply divide the square footage of your business area into the total square footage of your house. You will want to keep a log of what business activities, and sales and business transactions occur each day; the IRS may want to see records to substantiate your home office deductions.

The method of paying taxes on income not subject to withholding is your "estimated tax." If you expect to owe more than $500 at year's end and if the total amount of income tax that will be withheld during the year will be less than 90% of the tax shown on the previous year's return, you will generally make estimated tax payments. Estimated tax payments are made in four equal installments due on April 15, June 15, September 15 and January 15. For more information, request Publication 505, Tax Withholding and Estimated Tax.

Depending on your net income you may be liable for a self-employment tax. This is a Social Security tax designed for those who don't have Social Security withheld from their paychecks. You're liable if your net income is $400 or more per year. Net income is the difference between your income and allowable business deductions. Request Schedule SE, Computation of Social Security Self-Employment Tax if you qualify.

If completing your income tax return proves to be a complex affair, call the IRS for assistance. In addition to walk-in centers, the IRS has 90 publications to instruct you in various facets of preparing a tax return.

Insurance

As a self-employed professional you need to be aware of what health and business insurance coverage is available to you. Personal insurance needs to research include life, health and disability coverage.

Disability insurance is offered through many private insurance companies and state governments, and pays a monthly fee that covers living and business expenses during periods of long-term recuperation from a health problem. The amount of money paid monthly is based on the writer's or artist's annual earnings.

Before contacting any insurance representative, talk to other writers or illustrators to find out about insurance companies they could recommend. If you belong to a writer's or artist's organization, be sure to contact them to determine if any insurance coverage for professionals is offered to members. Such group coverage may prove less expensive and yield more comprehensive coverage than an individual policy.

Building business—and creative—skills

Now that you have an idea of what it takes to set up your freelance writing or illustrating practice, you may want to consult further publications to read in depth about business, writing or illustrating specialties you don't feel quite as comfortable with. Many of the publications recommended here incorporate business-oriented material with information about how to write or illustrate more creatively and skillfully.

Books of interest
The Artist's Friendly Legal Guide. Conner, Floyd; Karlen, Peter; Perwin, Jean; Spatt, David M. North Light Books, 1988.
Children's Media Marketplace. Jones, Delores B., ed. Neal-Schuman, 1988.
The Children's Picture Book: How to Write It, How to Sell It. Roberts, Ellen E.M. Writer's Digest Books, 1984.
How to Write, Illustrate, and Design Children's Books. Gates, Frieda. Lloyd-Simone Publishing Company, 1986.
How to Write a Children's Book & Get It Published. Seuling, Barbara. Charles Scribner's Sons, 1984.
How to Write and Illustrate Children's Books. Bicknell, Treld Pelkey; Trotman, Felicity, eds. North Light Books, 1988.
Illustrating Children's Books. Hands, Nancy S. Prentice Hall Press, 1986.
Market Guide for Young Writers. Henderson, Kathy. Shoe Tree Press, 1989.
Nonfiction for Children: How to Write It, How to Sell It. Roberts, Ellen E.M. Writer's Digest Books, 1986.
A Writer's Guide to a Children's Book Contract. Flower, Mary. Fern Hill Books, 1988.
Writing Books for Children. Yolen, Jane. The Writer, Inc., 1983.
Writing for Children & Teenagers. Wyndham, Lee & Madison, Arnold. Writer's Digest Books, 1988.
Writing Short Stories for Young People. Stanley, George Edward. Writer's Digest Books, 1987.
Writing Young Adult Novels. Irwin, Ann; Hadley, Lee and Eyerly, Jeannette. Writer's Digest Books, 1988.

Publications of interest
Children's Book Insider. Backes, Laura, Ed. Suite 303, 80 Eighth Ave., New York NY 10011.
Children's Magazine Guide. Sinclair, Patti, ed. 7 North Pinckney St., Madison WI 53703.
The Horn Book. Silvey, Anita, ed. The Horn Book, Inc., Park Square Building, 31 St. James Ave., Boston MA 02116.
Society of Children's Book Writers Bulletin. Mooser, Stephen; Oliver, Lin, eds. Society of Children's Book Writers, Box 296, Mar Vista Station, Los Angeles CA 90066.

Simultaneous Submissions

by Lisa Carpenter

One issue that puzzles beginning writers is whether it is okay to submit the same work to more than one publisher at a time. Is it ethical to send a manuscript to several publishers simultaneously?

In the past, the practice was considered taboo. Today, though most editors don't like getting simultaneous submissions, they will accept them. Part of the reason for the relaxed, though reluctant, attitude is editors realize writers usually have to wait many months for a reply because there are just too many manuscripts and not enough staff to review these manuscripts. What also hampers the process is that reading unsolicited manuscripts is usually low on an editor's priority list.

The author's side

"Multiple submitting, which seems to be increasingly in use, was forced upon writers by editors who keep manuscripts for sometimes interminable lengths of time. For whatever reason, work overload or whatever, it does seem unconscionable to expect a writer, whose income accrues from his writing, to wait around for six months to a year and longer for an editorial response," says Barbara True in a letter to the editor of the *Society of Children's Book Writers Bulletin* (January/February 1990).

Who can blame the logic of a simultaneous submittor? After all, by sending work out to several publishers at the same time, it is being seen and considered by more people; therefore, you're more likely to sell it. Also, multiple submitting could actually expedite the review process. Some publishers say if they know other houses have the same manuscript, they are more inclined to look at it sooner. Considering the length of time it takes some publishers to report, it could take a writer years to place a piece by submitting singly. "We feel strongly that an author has a right to make multiple submissions," says Bob Schildgen, Senior Editor at China Books. "It is the author's product, and as such he or she should be free to market it as anyone else would market a product. The idea of single submission is mere paternalistic nonsense, which puts a given publisher in a priveleged position. Since publishing houses treat books as products, why shouldn't the authors have the same prerogative?"

In his book *Manuscript Submission*, (Writer's Digest Books), Scott Edelstein says some nonfiction editors discourage this practice, but simultaneous submission is the rule for fiction. He goes on to say it is not necessary for a writer to indicate to the editor that more than one market has his work. "If a market notice or listing says, 'no simultaneous submissions,' multiple submit the piece anyway."

The editors speak

However, many publishers disagree with Edelstein. Publishers hate simultaneous submissions for several reasons. Amy Shields of Walker and Company says, "I have had some manuscripts for up to four months before I had a chance to respond. I have also spent the weekend reading a manuscript only to find out the author had received an offer days before. One solution might be for authors to consider more critically if they are making appropriate submissions. Forty percent of my slush pile is material we would never publish."

Some editors feel an author who submits simultaneously is not interested in tailoring work toward the publisher's needs and lacks the desire to work specifically with their company. Nina Kooij, editor at Pelican Publishing Company, says she wishes to work with authors who expressly want to work with the company. Dianne Hess, senior editor at Scholastic, Inc. says, "We prefer not to get simultaneous submissions. It shows lack of commitment to a company on the part of the writer."

Editors of periodicals are especially insistent that submissions be written exclusively with their publication in mind. "Quite simply, I expect an article submitted to *SuperScience* be tailored to our magazine. If an author is shopping it around to other magazines, then it's unlikely to be written in our style, tone, and reading level," says Lorraine Hopping Egan, editor. More than a few magazine editors expressed the same sentiments to *Children's Writer's & Illustrator's Market*.

Mary Lee Donovan, editor at Houghton Mifflin Co., says she will accept simultaneous submissions, but the author shouldn't expect a free consultation. "We will accept and respond to simultaneous submissions, but we will judge them on the writing submitted and not on its potential. We believe in the editor/author relationship. The best books evolve through this give and take process. Editors here are already overworked and do not have time to give extensive notes or constructive criticism on manuscripts that are being considered by another house."

The SCBW compromise

Realizing this was an important issue with writers, the Society of Children's Book Writers (SCBW) acknowledged the writers' and illustrators' grievances and took a stand in 1990. Though some members felt the single submission policy was old-fashioned and impractical, the SCBW recommended against multiple submission as a general practice. The logic was if they encouraged the practice, publishers would quit accepting unsolicited manuscripts altogether. Instead, the organization advised its members to send a photocopy of their submission (let the editor know it's a photocopy) and wait three months for a response (noting you will do so in the cover letter). If no response is received, the writer should then send a note withdrawing the work from consideration and submit the work elsewhere. That way, writers' works aren't tied up for many months and publishers have sufficient time to consider the work.

The SCBW did specify two instances in which they would consider multiple submissions acceptable: (1) If the subject matter depends on timing (i.e., if it is a seasonal story, or if the subject has to do with an upcoming event occurring within the next three years); and (2) If you are so much in demand that editors are vigorously competing for specifically you and your manuscripts.

Show some courtesy

If you decide to submit simultaneously, editors request you at least have a heart when doing so. Most consider it a sneaky practice not to inform them about the submission and request writers indicate whether it is a simultaneous submission.

Send your manuscript to appropriate markets. When you send material out randomly, you not only waste postage, you also irritate the overworked editors. It really burns them when they waste time on worthless manuscripts. So research those markets!

Keep a record of whom you send your manuscripts to. If the work is accepted, you can notify the other editors your work has been sold. By doing this, you are more likely to stay on the editor's good side (unless, of course, he has already spent time reading your manuscript). Remember, you may want to send him another piece in the future, so it is important to maintain good graces.

Give the editor some time. In other words, don't expect a response within a matter of days. Standard time to wait for a response is three months. If after then you haven't heard anything, it is okay to write or call regarding the status of the work.

Once you accept an offer, don't later try to "weasel out" of the deal if you get a better offer. Though not illegal, it is not an ethical practice to withdraw a manuscript once it has been accepted. You may get more money with the second offer, but if you bite the original hand that feeds you, it will probably never feed you again. On the same note, you may experience severe consequences if you try to create a bidding war with two publishers interested in your work. The bluff may work, but unless you're highly renowned, it is more likely to backfire. You may make both editors so mad that neither one of them will have anything to do with you, much less publish your work.

Important listing information

When using listings in the book and magazine sections, be aware that age categories can be found under the "Fiction" and "Nonfiction" headings for solicited material. They are given to aid you in targeting material for those age groups for which you write/illustrate. "Picture books" are geared toward the preschool-8-year-old group; "Young readers" to 5-8-year-olds; "Middle readers" to 9-11 year-olds; and "Young adults" to those 12 and up. These age breakdowns may vary slightly from publisher to publisher.

The Markets

Book Publishers

Books for children are hot—the growth within the industry in the last few years has been spectacular. Producing children's books was once just a small sideline for most publishers, but now business is booming. Consider these figures from the Book Industry Study Group (taken from the August 31, 1990 issue of *Publishers Weekly*): In 1991, sales are expected to top $1 billion for the first time ever. Projections are this figure will be $1.6 billion by 1994. The significance of these figures is better illustrated by taking into account past sales figures.

In 1955, sales of children's books totaled $42.7 million. From 1955 to 1980 the industry enjoyed steady, but unextraordinary, growth. It was in the '80s that things started happening. From 1980 to 1985, sales of children's books more than doubled (from $210.8 million to $475.6 million). Sales in 1990 exceeded $991 million, more than double the 1985 figure. Of course, inflation is part of the reason the sales figures have increased so dramatically from 1955.

Hardbound children's books rarely cost less than $10. However, this isn't dissuading consumers. Children's books are continuing to sell in record numbers, children's bookstores are popping up all over the country and more book clubs for children are appearing (mainly as offspring of adult book clubs), especially in the schools.

Though forecasters admit this rate of growth can't continue forever and will eventually level off, the future is nevertheless bright. Because of the promising outlook for children's books, many publishers are grabbing for a piece of the action. In fact, several of the 31 new markets listed in this section are "testing the waters" and are just entering the children's book market.

Why the boom?

The increased demand for children's books can be attributed to a variety of reasons.

First and foremost, more babies are being born. The original baby boomers are now starting to have babies themselves. What is significant about this is that so many of these parents delayed starting families in order to become established in their professional careers. Therefore, new parents today tend to possess more disposable income.

Fortunately, they are choosing to spend some of this extra money on books for their kids. John Keller, publisher of children's books at Little, Brown & Co. was quoted in the *Wall Street Journal* saying, "Parents with disposable income are now willing as they never were before to build home libraries for their children." Why? Because young parents today (as well as the general population) have more formal education. They are aware of the benefits of education and want their children to reap those benefits.

"If the parents of today can be largely credited for the current growth in children's books, buying more books per child than ever before in our history, hopefully the rest of the nation is not far behind in recognizing that to survive and compete in the world of today we must educate our children," says Janet Schulamn, publisher and division vice president of Random House Books for Young Readers in the January 5, 1990 edition of *Publishers Weekly*.

More and more, schools are utilizing trade books in lieu of textbooks, the attitude being trade books (or "real" books, as kids call them) are more fun to read than the dull, boring contents found in many textbooks. In fact, some critics actually encourage teachers to discard textbooks altogether and teach with trade books.

What's hot?

Picture books are hot property right now, perhaps because the bulk of the baby boomer babies are of the target picture book age. One thing about most picture books today is they're not cheap. Some of them are as high as $16.95. But the quality of the books is now superb—so much so, that it almost seems a shame to risk letting children handle them!

As the toddlers get older, expect young reader books to gain in popularity. Increasing sales in young reader books support the idea that a new generation of avid readers can be reared if children start reading early.

On the downside, young adult novels are lagging behind in sales. One reason is economics. Preteens buy their own books and are unable to afford the more expensive hardbacks. Therefore, they buy paperbacks. Another explanation is that kids 12 and up are more exposed to and better understand adult situations than in the past and opt for adult books. "There is less emphasis on the YA market, especially novels. The ones we do are very carefully selected," says Virginia Buckley, Editorial Director of Lodestar Books.

Books for pre-schoolers and younger readers, though, won't be the top sellers forever. Many publishers are aware that there is already a group of children ready for middle readers and this age group will shift into the young adult reading group as well. These publishers intend to service the kids' reading needs as they get older.

Publishers are beginning to accept the challenge of producing more books with multicultural themes. "The trend that will most affect us is the movement for more bilingual/bicultural education and a mulicultural emphasis in curricula at all levels of education," says Bob Schildgen, Senior Editor at China Books. In June 1990, children's author Candy Dawson Boyd gave a stirring speech at the American Booksellers Association convention about why books reflecting cultural diversity were important for today's children. She said children must receive realistic messages about the world through reading, and that can only be achieved by including racial and cultural diversity within today's books. She implied these books will help promote positive multicultural and racial attitudes among young people in the future. "I'm looking forward to seeing the results of the census. We all know we should be publishing more for the Hispanic community, for example, but perhaps the figures will help get us to that point a little faster," says Amy Shields of Walker & Co.

Multicultural diversity isn't the only social issue being explored as a topic for children. In 1990, books about the environment were published. Children are being informed in simple words about what's happening to the environment and what they can do to help the situation.

Indications are retellings of folk tales are being sought by publishers. "Any trend toward increasing interest in the modern fairy tale or fantasy for today's children will insure our interest and attention, as we help our children to value and appreciate their natural gifts of learning, spontaneity, and the light of imagination beyond the graphic realities put before them," says Patrique Quintahlen of Jordan Enterprises Publishing Company.

Poetry is being seen more today than in the last few years. Publishers are now recognizing the profitability of poetry. Margaret McElderry was once quoted in *Publishers Weekly* saying "The rhythm, the imagery, the beauty, in addition to the fun, are all immensely important. Small children respond to nursery rhymes, and if we don't keep introducing children to poetry as they grow older, their sense of language may never develop as much as it otherwise might." This year Highlights launched an imprint devoted exclusively to printing poetry. The imprint will publish out-of-print classics as well as new work by established poets.

Finally, children's nonfiction is more recognized now than it has been in decades. As Russell Freedman says in a close-up in this section, nonfiction today is freer, more honest, and definitely given more recognition. Nonfiction trade books are being used more in schools to teach history and science. Also, publishers have made works of nonfiction more attractive visually. Read too the close-up with Sue Alexander in the Organizations section for her insight on the status of nonfiction today.

Book packagers

Occasionally at the beginning of each listing you will notice markets that describe themselves as "book packagers" rather than "publishers." While the majority of packaged books for children have been nonfiction, there is currently an increase in the production of picture books. Book packagers, or "book producers" or "developers," work for publishers and offer services that range from hiring writers, photographers and/or illustrators to editing and producing the final book. What they don't do is market the book; you won't see a catalog of books a packager has produced since such publications will appear in the client/ publisher's catalog instead. Book packagers can offer experienced manpower to a small publisher in which, for instance, the inhouse staff may not be skilled in a certain subject area or where experience in dealing with illustrations may be lacking.

What is the difference, besides marketing, between a book publisher and book packager? The book publisher reviews (and hopefully accepts) queries and/or manuscripts (mss) sent to them by writers. The book packager already has the book idea. They then go out to hire a writer and/or illustrator whose skills match their needs. It is often felt that this is a good outlet for the fledgling writer who wants to get started in book publishing. This isn't necessarily true — book packagers will ask to see a writer's credentials to ensure they are getting the best person for the job. Also, writing and/or illustrating for a book packager doesn't always get you credit for the work you have done. Many times you will labor under a work-for-hire arrangement, or will be offered a large advance with low royalty percentage.

Subsidy publishing

Let's say you've sent out that manuscript too many times to count. Every time, it has come back rejected, but you're convinced that it's the greatest thing since non-stick bubble gum. If you're really determined to get that work into print (and all of your other chances at getting published haven't worked out), you may want to consider subsidy publishing, also known as "vanity" publishing. You will notice that some of the listings in this section give percentages of subsidy-published material. Listings that offer subsidy publishing are marked with a solid block (■) before the company name.

Subsidy publishers ask writers to pay all or part of the costs of producing a book. There are different reasons people use subsidy publishers: they have had their material rejected by other publishers and believe they can't improve the work with further rewrites, or writing is more a hobby and they want a book they can share with family and friends.

Aspiring writers will want to strongly consider working only with publishers who pay. Paying publishers will more actively market your work because this is where they make their profit; subsidy publishers make their money from each writer who pays them to publish a book. In other words, if you go the subsidy route, the marketing and promotion is entirely up to you.

If you are comfortable with the idea of working with a subsidy publisher, be sure you understand all points of a contract. If you're willing to underwrite the cost of producing a book, you should be willing to have an attorney look over your contract to spot any "small print" and clarify any unclear terms. All in all, just be careful. Some businesses are out only to get your money and don't care how they do it. "Buyer beware" is the attitude that should be taken by consumers considering subsidy services.

Listing information

This year's listings contain a few format changes.

As you will see, the listings no longer contain information about whether to send a self-addressed, stamped envelope (SASE) with your submission. Any writer serious about submitting material should automatically assume a SASE is required. *Always* send a SASE with your manuscript! Otherwise, you'll probably never see your manuscript again. Publishers should not be expected to return manuscripts at their cost.

Always present your manuscript neatly typed, double-spaced and free of any messy typos. Since a high percentage of writers today own word processors or computers, the listings no longer indicate whether computer printout submissions are acceptable. But do make sure the type is letter quality. Dot matrix printouts, for the most part, are not good to send. Also, the listings no longer indicate whether photocopied submissions are acceptable. If you have a computer, it is best to send fresh printouts. For writers who are still using typewriters, good quality photocopies are acceptable. If you must send copies, make sure they are done with a high quality copier. Also, when sending copies, you may want to indicate to the publisher your manuscript is *not* being simultaneously submitted (unless, of course, it is). Publishers tend to suspect writers who submit copies because photocopying technology has made it easier for writers to submit simultaneously.

Now a word to illustrators: In the "Illustration" section of each listing, you will often find the statement that the editorial staff will review all varieties of manuscript/illustration packages. "All varieties" in the context of this book is defined by these three types of manuscript/illustration packages: (1) ms/illustration packages submitted by authors/artists (one person being both the author and artist); (2) ms/illustration packages submitted by authors with illustrations done by separate artists; and (3) artists' illustration packages for possible use in separate authors' texts (the publisher matches an author with an illustrator). Usually, when publishers claim they will review all varieties of manuscript/illustration packages, they will also review artist portfolios for future work.

One thing that cannot be stressed enough is the importance of actually reading the listings. Too many times people buy this book only for the company names and addresses and don't bother to read about the editorial and art needs of these companies. Publishers get too much inappropriate material as it is. You have this book, so you have no excuse for sending inappropriate material.

Know your stuff

Editors are often amazed at how novice writers and artists perceive children's books as easy and quick projects. The most successful writers and illustrators have had material rejected time after time before being published. Nobody knows better than professional writers and illustrators how truly difficult it can be to seek out the child in themselves and recall reactions to childhood events. Also, it helps to know your subject. Make sure it is something you can get excited about. After all, if you can't get excited about the subject as a writer, how do you expect to relay any enthusiasm in your writing? Not every writer or artist has the instinct to "tune in" to today's children, and it is for this reason that editors and art directors are excited every time they find an outstanding manuscript or unique style of artwork.

ACCENT BOOKS, a div. of Accent Publications, Inc., Box 15337, Denver CO 80215. (303)988-5300. Book publisher. Executive Editor: Mary B. Nelson. "Books for young readers is a new category for us. Publishes 1 young reader title/year.
Fiction: "We are an evangelical Christian publishing house. All books must reflect that." Easy-to-read contemporary Christian books for beginning readers. Average word length: 700-1,000. "Now looking for first book to publish for beginning readers."
Nonfiction: Young readers. "All books must be Christian in orientation and message—family, church, friends, etc." Average word length: 700-1,000. "Now looking for first book to publish for beginning readers."
How to Contact/Writers: Fiction/Nonfiction: Submit complete ms; include Social Security number with submission. Reports on queries/mss 10-12 weeks. Publishes a book 12 months after acceptance. Will consider simultaneous submissions.
Illustration: Editorial will review ms/illustration packages submitted by authors/artists and ms/illustration packages submitted by author with illustrations done by separate artists.

How to Contact/Illustrators: Ms/illustration packages: Submit "samples of final art with rest in roughs." Illustrations only: "No separate freelance artists yet. Artists can send samples of their work for us to hold as file reference." Reports on ms/art samples only if interested.

Terms/Writers & Illustrators: Pays authors in royalties. Additional payment for ms/illustration packages is "uncertain yet; may put both names on contract and split royalties." Book catalog for $1.05 and 9×12 SAE; manuscript guidelines for SASE.

Tips: "Be sure you understand children's interests, interest level, reading level and vocabulary as well as the doctrinal position of the company. Ms/illustration packages "need to be interesting to children as well as their parents, cute and easily illustrated. There are many more children's books coming into the bookstores, creating a broader, more competitive marketplace. In competing with the visual impact of television and other products, children's books must be top quality."

ADDISON-WESLEY PUBLISHING CO., Trade Dept., Subsidiary of Pearson PLC, Route 128, Reading MA 01867. (617)944-3700. Book publisher. Estab. 1942. Assistant Editor: John Bell. Publishes 6 middle reader titles/year. 33% of books by first-time authors.

Nonfiction: Middle readers: history, hobbies, nature/environment. "All of our children's books are science activity books." Recently published *The Fossil Factory*, by Niles Eldredge et al. (science activity); *Weatherwatch*, by Valerie Wyatt (ages 7-12, science activity).

How to Contact/Writers: Nonfiction: Query. Reports on queries/mss in 6 weeks. Publishes a book 24 months after acceptance. Will consider simultaneous submissions.

Illustration: Number of illustrations used for fiction and nonfiction: middle readers—90 full page. Editorial will review all varieties of ms/illustration packages. Prefers "4-color representational art for covers and b&w for interior."

How to Contact/Illustrators: Ms/illustration packages: "Query first." Illustrations only: Send "résumé and tearsheets." Original artwork returned at job's completion.

Terms/Writers & Illustrators: Pays authors in royalties based on retail price. Factors used to determine payment for ms/illustration package include: "number of illustrations, technical nature of same." Pays for illustrators: by the project. Sends galleys to authors; dummies to illustrators. Book catalog for 7×10 SAE and 85¢ postage.

Tips: The writer and/or illustrator have the best chance of selling "science activity books *only*. Increasing competition in our field (science projects) means finding more focused and more imaginative books."

ADVOCACY PRESS, div. of The Girls Club of Santa Barbara, Box 236, Santa Barbara CA 93102. (805)962-2728. FAX: (805)963-3580. Book publisher. Editorial Contact: Kathy Araujo. Publishes 3-5 picture books/year; 2-4 young reader titles/year. 25% of books by first-time authors.

Fiction: "We are only allowed to publish books that are relevant to Equity (equal opportunity) issues. Two series: self-esteem concept stories and little known women in history "role models." Award winners: *My Way Sally*, by P. Paine and M. Bingham (ages 3-9, picture book); *Tonia the Tree*, by Sandy Stryker (ages 3-9, picture book); and newest release *Berta Benz and the Motorwagen*, by Mindy Bingham (ages 3-9, picture book).

 The asterisk before a listing indicates the listing is new in this edition.

How to Contact/Writers: Fiction/nonfiction: Submit outline/synopsis and sample chapters. Reports on queries/mss in 2 weeks. Publishes a book 6 months after acceptance. Will consider simultaneous submissions. Send for editorial policy.

Illustration: Number of illustrations used for fiction/nonfiction: picture books—30; middle readers—200; young adults—200. Editorial will review all varieties of ms/illustration packages. Marketing Director, Penny Paine, will review an illustrator's work for possible use in author's texts.

How to Contact/Illustrators: Ms/illustration packages: Query first. Reports on art samples in 4 weeks.

Terms/Writers & Illustrators: Illustrators paid by the project. Sends galleys to authors; dummies to illustrators. Book catalog/manuscript guidelines available for legal-size SASE

■**AEGINA PRESS/UNIVERSITY EDITIONS, INC.**, 59 Oak Lane, Spring Valley, Huntington WV 25704. (304)429-7204. Book publisher. Estab. 1983. Managing Editor: Ira Herman. Publishes 1 picture book/year; 1-2 young reader titles/year; 2 middle reader titles/year; 2-3 young adult titles/year. 20% of books by first-time authors; 5% of books from agented writers; "over 50% of books are subsidy published."

Fiction: Picture books: animal. Young readers: animal, easy-to-read, fantasy. Middle readers: history, sports. Young adults: problem novels, romance, science fiction. "Will consider most categories." Average word length: picture books—1,000; young readers—2,000; middle readers—10,000; young adults—20,000. Recently published *Captain and Joey and the Tumbled Down Cabin*, by Mary Joachim (grades 1-3, children's adventure); *Chester the Ant*, by Andrea Ross (K-3, picture book).

Nonfiction: "We have not previously published any juvenile nonfiction. We may consider doing so in the future, however."

How to Contact/Writers: Fiction/nonfiction: Submit complete ms. Reports on queries in 1 week; on mss in 1 month. Publishes a book 5-6 months after acceptance. Will consider simultaneous submissions.

Illustration: Number of illustrations used for fiction: picture books—15-20; young readers—10; middle readers—5-6. Editorial will review ms/illustration packages submitted by authors/artists and ms/illustration packages submitted by authors with illustrations done by separate artists.

How to Contact/Illustrators: Ms/illustration packages: Query first. "We generally use our own artists. We will consider outside art. Artists should send photocopies or non-returnable samples." Reports on art samples in 1 month. Original artwork returned at job's completion.

Terms/Writers & Illustrators: Pays authors in royalties of 10-15% based on retail price. Pays freelance artists per project. Payment "negotiated individually for each book." Sends galleys to authors. Book catalog available for $2 and SAE and 4 first-class stamps; manuscript guidelines for #10 envelope and 1 first-class stamp.

Tips: "Focus your subject and plot-line. For younger readers, stress visual imagery and fantasy characterizations. A cover letter should accompany the manuscript, which states the approximate length (not necessary for poetry). A brief synopsis of the manuscript and a listing of the author's publishing credits (if any) should also be included. Queries, sample chapters, synopses and completed manuscripts are welcome."

 The solid block before a listing indicates the market subsidy publishes manuscripts.

ALADDIN BOOKS/COLLIER BOOKS FOR YOUNG READERS, Paperback imprints of Macmillan Children's Book Group, 24th floor, 866 Third Avenue, New York NY 10022. (212)702-9043. Book publisher. Estab. 1986. Associate Editor: Sarah Lehman Schwartz. Publishes 30 picture books/year; 5 young reader titles/year; 15 middle reader titles/year; 8 young adult titles/year; 10 novelty titles/year. 5% of books by first-time authors; 40% of books from agented writers.
Fiction: Young readers: easy-to-read. Middle readers: contemporary, fantasy, romance, science fiction, sports, spy/mystery/adventure. Young adults: contemporary, fantasy, romance, science fiction, sports, spy/mystery/adventure. Recently published *Megan's Island*, by Willo Davis Roberts (8-12, mystery, suspense); *The Dragon Circle*, by Stephen Krensky (8-12, fantasy); and *When the Tripods Came*, by John Christopher (12 and up, science fiction).
Nonfiction: Middle readers, young adults: sports, self-help. Recently published *The Baseball Book and Trophy*, by William Humber (8-12, sports).
How to Contact/Writers: Fiction/nonfiction: Query; submit outline/synopsis and sample chapters. Reports on queries in 2-6 weeks; on mss in 12-16 weeks. Publishes a book 1-2 years after acceptance. Will consider simultaneous submissions. Book catalog and ms guidelines available for SASE.
Illustration: Editorial will review illustration package submitted by artists. Seeks cover artists for paperback fiction for middle grades and young adults. No original picture books.
How to Contact/Illustrators: Illustrations only: submit résumé/tearsheets. Reports on art samples only if interested. Original artwork returned at job's completion. Pay for illustrators: by the project.
Tips: "We are currently concentrating on reprinting successful titles originally published by the hardcover imprints of the Macmillan Children's Book Group. However, we do occasionally publish original material. We will be publishing fewer young adult titles (Collier imprint) and will be concentrating on several genres for this age group: science fiction, fantasy, and mysteries. The bulk of our purchases will be novelty projects: lift-the-flaps, musical books, books with an interactive component etc. Other purchases of original material are the exception, rather than the rule. We prefer that longer manuscripts be preceded by a query letter and two or three sample chapters. We do not generally consider picture book manuscripts. Please do not submit more than two short (under 15 typed pages) or one longer manuscript at one time. If you wish to confirm that your manuscript has arrived safely, please include a self-addressed stamped postcard, or send the manuscript via registered mail. Read children's books — and talk to children, get a sense of their world. Learn something about the business of publishing — that way you can have an idea as to what editors are looking for and why they make the decisions that they do. Be clear-eyed and professional." Regarding illustrations: "Remember that what appeals to adults may not necessarily appeal to children." (See also Atheneum Publishers, Bradbury Press, Four Winds Press, Margaret K. McElderry Books.)

*ALYSON PUBLICATIONS, INC., 40 Plympton Street, Boston MA 02118. (617)542-5679. Book publisher. Editorial Contact: Sasha Alyson. Publishes 5 (projected) picture books/year; 3 (projected) young adult titles/year. "Alyson Wonderland is a new line of kids' books. We are looking for diverse depictions of family life for children of gay and lesbian parents."
Fiction: All levels: Books aimed at the children of lesbian and gay parents. Our YA books should deal with issues faced by kids growing up gay or lesbian." Recently published *Heather Has Two Mommies*, by Lesléa Newman/Diana Souza (ages 3-5); *Daddy's Roommate*, by Michael Willhoite (ages 2-7).
How to Contact/Writers: Submit outline/synopsis and sample chapters (young adults); submit complete manuscript (picture books/young readers). Reports on queries in 2 weeks; reports on mss in 3-4 weeks.

Illustration: Send "representative art that can be *kept on file*. Good quality photocopies are OK."

Terms/Writers & Illustrators: Prefer to discuss terms with the authors and artists. "We *do* offer advances." Book catalog and/or manuscript guidelines free on request.

Tips: "We only publish kids' books aimed at the children of gay or lesbian parents."

AMERICAN BIBLE SOCIETY, 1865 Broadway, New York NY 10023. (212)408-1235. FAX: (212)408-1512. Book publisher. Estab. 1816. Manager of Scripture Resource Development: Charles Houser. Publishes 2 picture books/year; 4 young reader titles /year; 4 young adult titles/year.

Nonfiction: Picture books, young readers, middle readers, young adults: religion. Recently published *A Book About Jesus*, (young readers, collection of scripture passages); *A Few Who Dared to Trust God*, (young reader, scripture passages about Bible heroes and heroines).

How to Contact/Writers: "All manuscripts developed in-house; unsolicited mss rejected."

Illustration: Number of illustrations used for nonfiction: picture book—5-10; young reader—5-60; middle reader—1-5 (cover); young adult—1-5 (cover). Editorial will review an illustrator's work for possible use in separate authors' texts. "Would be more interested in artwork for teens which is influenced by the visual 'vocabulary' of videos."

How to Contact/Illustrators: Ms/illustration packages: "Query first." Illustrations only: send "résumés, tearsheets to keep; slides will be returned promptly." Reports back in 6 weeks. Factors used to determine payment for ms/illustration package include "Nature and scope of project; complexity of illustration and continuity of work; number of illustrations." Pay for illustrators: Pays $200-$30,000; based on fair market value. Sends two complimentary copies of published work to illustrators. Book catalog free on request.

Tips: Illustrators must have the "ability to communicate traditional values about faith and worship in a fresh and modern way. Sensitivity to needs of children today and a realistic representation of their world (intergenerational, interracial, intercultural pictures are desirable)."

■ARCADE PUBLISHING, Imprint of Little Brown & Co., 141 Fifth Ave., New York NY 10010. (212)475-2633. Book publisher. President and Publisher: Richard Seaver. Publishes 8-12 picture books/year; 3-5 young reader titles/year; 5-8 middle reader titles/ year; 3 young adult titles/year. 50% of books from agented writers. 25% of books by first-time authors. 50% of books subsidy published.

Fiction: Young readers, middle readers. Recently published *Good Morning, River*, by Lisa Westberg Peters (4-7 picture book); *Moon Glows*, by Bethea verDorn (4-7 picture book); *Winter-Broken*, by Marya Smith (10-14 novel).

Nonfiction: Will consider general nonfiction—"all ages." Recently published *Global Warming: Assessing the Greenhouse Threat*, by Laurence Pringle (7-11 middle reader).

How to Contact/Writers: Fiction: Submit complete ms. Nonfiction: Query. Reports on queries in 2 weeks. Publishes ms 12 months after acceptance. Will consider simultaneous submissions.

Illustration: Number of illustrations used for fiction: picture books—30; young readers—12; middle readers 8-12. Number of illustrations used for nonfiction: picture books—30; young readers—25; middle readers—25. Will review all varieties of ms/illustration packages.

How to Contact/Illustrators: "*No* original art—send slides or color photocopies." Illustrations only: Send tear sheets and slides. Reports on ms/art samples in 3 weeks. Original artwork returned at job's completion.

"We were looking for an artist who could capture the action and drama of the events being depicted, portray historical settings and dress accurately, and make the art engaging for children 9 years old and younger," says Charles Houser of the American Bible Society. This picture of the Nativity of Christ was one of 120 full-color illustrations that appeared in A Few Who Dared to Trust God, *published in 1989. "It was important that children could quickly identify the main characters in each picture as they read through the book," says Houser. The artist, Carolyn Ewing, was paid $65,000 for her illustrations.*

Reprinted with permission. Copyright© 1990 by the American Bible Society.

Terms/Writers & Illustrators: Pays authors in variable royalties; or buys ms outright for $400-$3,000; "also flat fees per b&w books and jackets." Offers average advance of $2,500. Additional payment for ms/illustration package is percentage of book. Sends galleys to authors; book catalog for 8×10 SASE; manuscript guidelines for legal-size SASE.

ARCHWAY/MINSTREL BOOKS, Pocket Books, 1230 Avenue of the Americas, New York NY 10020. (212)698-7000. Book publisher. Editorial contact: Patricia McDonald. Publishes originals and reprints. Minstrel Books (ages 7-11) and Archway Paperbacks (ages 12-16).
Fiction: Middle readers: animal, funny school stories. Young adults: contemporary, fantasy, romance, sports, suspense/mystery/adventure, humor, funny school stories.
Nonfiction: Middle readers: animal, sports. Young adults: sports.
How to Contact/Writers: Fiction/nonfiction: Query, submit outline/synopsis and sample chapters.
Terms/Writers & Illustrators: Pays authors in royalties.

ATHENEUM PUBLISHERS, Macmillan Children's Book Group, 866 Third Ave., New York NY 10022. (212)702-2000. Book Publisher. Editorial Director: Jonathan Lanman. Editorial Contacts: Gail Paris, Marcia Marshall. Publishes 15-20 picture books/year; 4-5 young reader titles/year; 20-25 middle reader titles/year; 10-15 young adult titles/year. 20% of books by first-time authors; 50% of books from agented writers.
Fiction: Picture books: animal, contemporary, fantasy. Young readers: contemporary, fantasy. Middle readers: animal, contemporary, fantasy. Young adults: contemporary, fantasy. Recently published *Tehanu*, by Ursula Le Guin (YA, fantasy); *Turtle People*, by Brenda L. Guikerson (ages 8-12, contemporary); *Nessa's Fish*, by Nancy Luenn (ages 4-8, picture book).
Nonfiction: Picture books: animal, biography, education, history. Young readers: animal, biography, education, history. Middle readers: animal, biography, education, history. Young adults: animal, biography, education, history. Recently published *The Big*

Rock, by Bruce Hiscock (ages 6-8, science); *Inca and Spaniard*, by Albert Mami (ages 10-14, history)

How to Contact/Writers: Fiction/nonfiction: Query; will consider complete picture book manuscript; submit outline/synopsis and sample chapters for longer works. Reports on queries 6-8 weeks; on mss 12 weeks. Publishes a book 18-24 months after acceptance. Will consider simultaneous submissions from previously unpublished authors; "we request that the author let us know it is a simultaneous submission."

Illustration: Editorial will review ms/illustration packages submitted by authors/artists and ms/illustration packages submitted by authors with illustrations done by separate artists.

How to Contact/Illustrators: Ms/illustration packages: query first, 3 chapters of ms with 1 piece of final art. Illustrations only: résumé, tear sheets. Reports on art samples only if interested. Original artwork returned at job's completion.

Terms/Writers & Illustrators: Pays authors in royalties of 8-12½% based on retail price. Illustrators paid royalty or flat fee depending on the project. Sends galleys to authors; proofs to illustrators. Book catalog available for 9×12 SAE and 5 first-class stamps; manuscript guidelines for #10 SAE and 1 first-class stamp. (See also Aladdin Books/Collier Books for Young Adults, Bradbury Press, Four Winds Press, Margaret K. McElderry Books.)

AVON BOOKS/BOOKS FOR YOUNG READERS (AVON FLARE AND AVON CAMELOT), div. of The Hearst Corporation, 105 Madison Ave., New York NY 10016. (212)481-5609. Book publisher. Editorial Director: Ellen Krieger. Editorial Contact: Gwen Montgomery. Editorial Assistant: Lisa Norment. Publishes 25-30 middle reader titles/year; 20-25 young adult titles/year. 10% of books by first-time authors; 20% of books from agented writers.

Fiction: Middle readers: contemporary, problem novels, sports, spy/mystery/adventure, comedy. Young adults: contemporary, problem novels, romance. Average length: middle readers—100-150 pages; young adults—150-250 pages. Recently published *The Plant That Ate Dirty Socks*, by Nancy McArthur (middle readers, comedy); *Cross Your Heart*, by Bruce and Carole Hart (young adults, contemporary); *At the Edge*, by Michael Behrens (young adults, coming of age).

Nonfiction: Middle readers: hobbies, music/dance, sports. Young adults: music/dance, "growing up." Average length: middle readers—100-150 pages; young adults—150-250 pages. Recently published *Why Am I So Miserable If These Are the Best Years of My Life?*, by A. B. Eagan (young adults, growing up); *Dead Serious*, by Jane Mersky Leder (young adults, suicide).

How to Contact/Writers: Fiction: Submit complete ms. Nonfiction: Submit outline/synopsis and sample chapters. Reports on queries in 2 weeks; on mss in 4-8 weeks. Publishes book 18-24 months after acceptance. Will consider simultaneous submissions.

Illustration: Number of illustrations used for fiction: middle readers 6-8. Number of illustrations used for nonfiction: middle readers 8-10; young adults 6-8. Very rarely will review ms/illustration packages submitted by authors/artists and ms/illustration packages submitted by authors with illustrations done by separate artists.

"Picture books" are geared toward the preschool — 8 year old group; "Young readers" to 5-8 year olds; "Middle readers" to 9-11 year olds; and "Young adults" to those 12 and up.

How to Contact/Illustrators: "Send samples we can keep. Need line art and cover art."

Terms/Writers & Illustrators: Pays authors in royalties of 6% based on retail price. Average advance payment is "very open." Sends galleys to authors; sometimes sends dummies to illustrators. Book catalog available for 9 × 12 SAE and 4 first-class stamps; manuscript guidelines for letter-size SAE and 1 first-class stamp.

Tips: "We have two Young Readers imprints, Avon Camelot books for the middle grades, and Avon Flare for young adults. Our list is weighted more to individual titles than to series, with the emphasis in our paperback originals on high quality recreational reading—a fresh and original writing style; identifiable, three dimensional characters; a strong, well-paced story that pulls readers in and keeps them interested." Writers: "Make sure that you really know what a company's list looks like before you submit work. Is your work in line with what they usually do? Is your work appropriate for the age group that this company publishes for? Keep aware of what's in your bookstore (but not what's in there for too long!)" Illustrators: "Submit work to art directors and people who are in charge of illustration at publishers. This is usually not handled entirely by the editorial department."

BARRONS EDUCATIONAL SERIES, 250 Wireless Blvd., Hauppauge NY 11788. (516)434-3311. FAX: (516)434-3723. Book publisher. Estab. 1945. Acquisitions Editor (picture books): Grace Freedson. Editorial contact (young/middle readers, young adult titles): Don Reis. Publishes 20 picture books/year; 20 young reader titles/year; 20 middle reader titles/year; 10 young adult titles/year. 25% of books by first-time authors; 25% of books from agented writers.

Fiction: Picture books: animal, easy-to-read, sports. Recently published *Elephant Plus Mouse Get Ready for Christmas*, by Lois Grambling (ages 3-6, holiday story book).

Nonfiction: Picture books: animal. Young readers: biography, sports. Recently published *Cooking Wizardry for Kids*, by Margaret Kwoa/Phyllis Williams (ages 8-12, kitchen science, crafts, recipes).

How to Contact/Writers: Fiction: Query. Nonfiction: Submit outline/synopsis and sample chapters. Reports on queries in 3-8 weeks; on mss in 3-12 weeks. Publishes a book 1 year after acceptance. Will consider simultaneous submissions.

Illustration: Number of illustrations used for fiction/nonfiction: picture books—16. Editorial will review all varieties of ms/illustration packages.

How to Contact/Illustrators: Ms/illustration packages: Query first; 3 chapters of ms with 1 piece of final art, remainder roughs. Illustrations only: Tearsheets or slides plus résumé. Reports in 3-8 weeks.

Terms/Writers & Illustrators: Pays authors in royalties based on retail price. Illustrators paid by the project based on retail price. Sends galleys to authors; dummies to illustrators. Book catalog, manuscript/artist's guidelines free on request.

Tips: Writers: "We are predominately on the lookout for preschool storybooks and concept books." Illustrators: "We are happy to receive a sample illustration to keep on file for future consideration. Periodic notes reminding us of their work is acceptable." Children's book themes "are becoming much more contemporary and relevant to a child's day-to-day activities."

BEACON PRESS, 25 Beacon St., Boston MA 02108. (617)742-2110. Book publisher. Publishes 2 picture books/year; Editorial Contact: Wendy Strothman. Publishes 2 young reader titles/year; 2 middle reader titles/year.

Always include a self-addressed stamped envelope (SASE) or International Reply Coupon (IRC) with submissions.

Fiction: Young reader: contemporary, easy-to-read. Middle reader: contemporary. Other: "folktales and multicultural stories." Average word length: picture books—2,500; middle readers—7,000. Recently published *Ntombi's Song*, by Jenny Seed (picture books and young reader, multicultural picture book); *Tales of an Ashanti Father*, by Peggy Appiah (middle reader, African folktales); *Aditi and the One-Eyed Monkey*, by Suniti Namjoshi (middle reader, feminist multicultural fantasy).

Nonfiction: Young reader: biography, nature/environment, "handicaps." No nonfiction titles yet.

How to Contact/Writers: Fiction/nonfiction: Query, submit outline/synopsis and sample chapters. Reports on queries/mss in 2 months. Publishes a book 1 year after acceptance. Will consider simultaneous submissions.

Illustration: Number of illustrations used for fiction: picture books—30; young reader—10; middle reader—10. Editorial will review ms/illustration packages submitted by authors/artists or ms/illustration packages submitted by authors with illustrations done by separate artists. Production and Design Manager, Pam Suwinsky, will review illustrator's work for possible use in author's texts.

How to Contact/Illustrators: Reports in 1 month. Original art work returned at job's completion.

Terms/Writers & Illustrators: Pays authors in royalties based on wholesale price. Offers average advance payment of $2,000. Factors used to determine payment of ms/illustration package include "color art vs. black-and-white, number of illustrations used, plus percentage of art to text." Pay for illustrators: by the project. Sends galleys to authors; dummies to illustrators. Book catalog, manuscript/artist's guidelines free on request.

Tips: "Do your homework. Find out what kind of books a publisher produces before you send in something that might be totally inappropriate." Looking for "feminist, multi-cultural, multi-racial (picture book, young reader, middle reader), folktales."

BEHRMAN HOUSE INC., 235 Watchung Ave., West Orange NJ 07052. (201)669-0447. Book publisher. Project Editor: Adam Siegel. Publishes 2 young reader titles/year; 2 middle reader titles/year; 2 young adult titles/year. 12% of books by first-time authors; 2% of books from agented writers.

Nonfiction: All levels: Jewish Educational textbooks. Average word length: young reader—1,200; middle reader—2,000; young adult—4,000.

How to Contact/Writers: Fiction/nonfiction: Submit outline/synopsis and sample chapters. Recently published *A Child's Bible*, by Seymour Rossel (ages 9-10, Bible stories and activity book); *My Jewish World*, by Robert Tinm (ages 8-9, a kid's view of Jewish life). Reports on mss/queries in 2 months. Publishes a book 2½ years after acceptance. Will consider simultaneous submissions.

Illustration: Number of illustrations used for nonfiction: young reader—40; middle reader—35; young adult—30. Editorial will review all varieties of ms/illustration packages. Project Editor Adam Siegel will review illustrator's work for possible use in separate texts.

How to Contact/Illustrators: Ms/illustration packages: "Query first." Illustrations only: Send "tearsheets or photocopies." Reports in 2 months.

Terms/Writers & Illustrators: Pays authors in royalties of 3-8% based on retail price or buys ms outright for $1,000-5,000. Offers average advance payment of $500. Factors used to determine payment for ms/illustration package include color art vs. black-and-white, number of illustrations. Pay for illustrators: by the project; $500-5,000. Sends galleys to authors; dummies to illustrators. Book catalog free on request.

Tips: Looking for "religious school texts."

*BEYOND WORDS PUBLISHING, Route 3, Box 492B, Hillsboro OR 97123. (503)647-5109. Book publisher. Editor: Cynthia Black. Publishes 2-3 picture books/year. 75% of books by first-time authors; 25% of books by agented authors.
Fiction: Picture books and young readers: animal, easy-to-read and fantasy. Middle readers: joke books. Average word length: 250. Recently published *Davy's Dream*, *The Starlight Bride* and *P. Bear's New Year's Party*, all by Paul O. Lewis (picture books).
Nonfiction: Picture books: animal, nature/environment. Young readers and middle readers: nature/environment. Average word length: 250-400.
How to Contact/Writers: Fiction/nonfiction: Query; submit outline/synopsis and sample chapters. Reports on queries in 3 weeks; reports on mss in 3 months. Publishes a book one year after acceptance. Accepts simultaneous submissions.
Illustration: Uses 15-20 illustrations per fiction title. Will review ms/illustration packages submitted by authors/artists and ms/illustration packages submitted by authors with illustrations done by separate artists.
How to Contact/Illustrators: Ms/illustration packages: submit three chapters of manuscript with one piece of final art. Illustrations only: submit color photocopies. Reports back to artists within 3 months. Originals returned to artist at job's completion.
Terms/Writers and Illustrators: Authors paid 10% maximum royalty based on wholesale price. "No advances paid." Illustrators paid by the project. Authors see galleys for review.
Tips: Seeing "more books by children and more nature-oriented books, as well as multicultural books in the future."

BRADBURY PRESS, imprint of Macmillan Publishing Company, 866 Third Ave., New York NY 10022. (212)702-9809. Book publisher. Editorial Director: Barbara Lalicki. Publishes 15-20 picture books/year; 5 young reader titles/year; 5 middle reader titles/year; 3 young adult titles/year. 25% of books by first-time authors; 75% of books from previously published or agented writers.
Fiction: Picture books: animal, contemporary, history. Young readers: animal, contemporary, easy-to-read, history. Middle readers: contemporary, fantasy, history, science fiction, spy/mystery/adventure. Young adults: science fiction, spy/mystery/adventure. Average length: picture books—32 pages; young readers—48 pages; middle readers—112 pages; young adults—140 pages. Recently published *Hatchet*, by Gary Paulsen (ages 11-13, adventure/survival); *Her Seven Brothers*, by Paul Goble (all ages, picture book); *Henry and Mudge in the Sparkle Days*, by Cynthia Rylant (ages 6-8, easy-to-read).
Nonfiction: Picture books: animal, history, music/dance, nature/environment. Young readers: animal, biography, education, history, hobbies, music/dance, nature/environment, sports. Middle readers: animal, biography, education, history, hobbies, music/dance, nature/environment, sports. Average length: picture books—32-48 pages; young and middle readers—48-64 pages; *African Journey*, by John Chiasson (8 and up, photoessay); *Dinosaurs Walked Here*, by Patricia Lauber (8 and up, photoessay/nature/history); *When I See My Doctor*, by Susan Kuklin (ages 3-5, photoessay).
How to Contact/Writers: Fiction: Query. Nonfiction: Submit outline/synopsis and sample chapters. Reports on queries in 2-3 weeks; on mss in 6-8 weeks. Publishes a book 18 months after acceptance.
Illustration: Number of illustrations used for fiction and nonfiction: picture books—30; young readers—1; middle readers—1; young adults—1. Art Director, Julie Quan will review illustrator's work for possible use in separate texts.
How to Contact/Illustrators: Submit ms with color photocopies of art. Illustrations only: Portfolio drop off last Thursday of every month. Reports on art samples only if interested. Original artwork returned at job's completion.
Terms/Writers & Illustrators: Pays author in royalties based on retail price. Average advance: "Percentage of estimated sales." Additional payment for ms/illustration packages. Pay for separate authors and illustrators: "advance, royalty." Sends galleys to

authors; dummies to illustrators. Book catalog available for 8 × 10 SAE and 4 first-class stamps; manuscript and/or artist's guidelines for business-size SAE and 1 first-class stamp.

Tips: Illustrators: "Know how to draw and paint children." Looks for "a strong story, nothing gimmicky, no pop-ups." Trends include "nonfiction for pre-schoolers."

*BRANDEN PUBLISHING CO., 17 Station St., Box 843, Brookline Village MA 02147. (617)734-2045. Book publisher. Estab. 1903. Editor: Adolph Caso. Publishes 2 picture books/year; 2 young adult titles/year. 100% of books by first-time authors.

Fiction: Middle readers: history. Young adults: sports.

Nonfiction: Recently published *Jack Johnson*, by Sal Fradella (young adults, biography); *Better Than Our Best: Women of Valor in American History*, by E. Ferman et al (young adults, biographies).

How to Contact/Writers: Fiction/nonfiction: Query. All unsolicited ms returned unopened. Reports on queries in 2 weeks; on mss in 8 weeks. Publishes a book 10 months after acceptance. Will consider electronic submissions via disk or modem.

Illustration: Editorial will review ms/illustration packages submitted by authors/artists and ms/illustration packages submitted by authors with illustrations done by separate artists.

How to Contact/Illustrators: Ms/illustration packages: Query only with SASE. Illustrations only: résumé. "Do not send originals." Reports in 2 weeks.

Terms/Writers & Illustrators: Pays authors in royalties of 10%. Pay for separate authors and illustrators: by agreement between author and illustrator. Sends galleys to authors; dummies to illustrators.

BRIGHT RING PUBLISHING, 1900 N. Shore Dr., Box 5768, Bellingham WA 98227-5768. (206)734-1601. Estab. 1985. Editor: MaryAnn Kohl. Publishes 1 young reader title/year. 50% of books by first-time authors.

Nonfiction: Picture books/young reader/middle reader: education and hobbies. Average word length: "about 125 ideas/book." Recently published *Mudworks* and *Scribble Cookies*, by Kohl (picture book, young reader, middle reader — art ideas). "We are moving into only recipe-style resource books in any variety of subject areas — useful with children 2-12. 'Whole language' is the buzz word in early education — so books to meet the new demands of that subject will be needed."

How to Contact/Writers: Nonfiction: submit complete ms. Include Social Security number with submission. Reports in 1-6 weeks. Publishes a book 12 months after acceptance. Will consider simultaneous submissions.

Illustration: Editorial will review all varieties of ms/illustration packages. Prefers to review "black line (drawings) for text."

How to Contact/Illustrators: Ms/illustration packages: "Query first." Illustrations only: Send tearsheets and "sample of ideas I request after query." Reports in 6-8 weeks. Original art work returned at job's completion.

Terms/Writers & Illustrators: Pays authors in royalties of 5-10% based on wholesale or retail price. Pays illustrators $500-1,000. Also offers "free books and discounts for future books." Book catalog, ms/artist's guidelines for business-size SAE and 25¢ postage.

Refer to the Business of Children's Writing & Illustrating
for up-to-date marketing, tax and legal information.

Tips: Illustrators: "Build your portfolio by taking a few jobs at lower pay—then grow." Looks for "creative ideas for children, recipe format, open-ended results" and for artists "black line drawings of children doing projects or project materials."

Bright Ring Publishing's recent craft book for kids, **Mudworks: Creative Clay, Dough, and Modeling Experiences,** *was written by editor MaryAnn Kohl. Kohl paid artist Kathleen Kerr $900 for 130 line drawings. "She reached me by submitting some unsolicited samples. I loved her simple, fresh drawings. She set herself apart from other illustrators who only illustrated and did not embellish or interpret," says Kohl.*

CAROLINA WREN PRESS/LOLLIPOP POWER BOOKS, Box 277, Carrboro NC 27510. (919) 560-2738 (office). (919)376-8152 (main editor). Book publisher. Carolina Wren estab. 1976; Lollipop Power estab. 1971. Editor-in-Chief: Judy Hogan. Regular Children's Editor: Elizabeth Core. Minority Children's Editor: Pauletta Bracy. Publishes 2 picture books/year; 1 young reader title in '89. 100% of books by first-time authors.
Fiction: Picture books: contemporary, easy-to-read, fantasy, history, problem novels, science fiction, black family, "especially interested in non-sexist, multi-racial." Average length: picture books— 30 pages. Recently published *The Boy Toy*, by Phyllis Johnson (grade 1, picture book); *I Like You to Make Jokes*, by Ellen Bass (grades 1-2, picture book); *In Christina's Toolbox*, by Dianne Homan (grades 1-2, picture book).
Nonfiction: Picture books: biography, education, history, hobbies, music/dance, "children of divorce and lesbian homes and black families." Average length: picture books— 30 pages.
How to Contact/Writers: Fiction/nonfiction: Query and request guidelines. Reports on queries/ms in 12 weeks. Publishes a book 24-36 months after acceptance "at present."
Illustration: Number of illustrations used for fiction and nonfiction: picture books— 12. Editorial will review ms/illustration packages submitted by authors/artists and ms/ illustration packages submitted by authors with illustrations done by separate artists. Designer, Martha Lange (215 Monmouth St., Durham NC 27701) will review illustrator's work for possible use in separate texts.
How to Contact/Illustrators: Query first to Martha Lange. Reports on art samples only if interested. Original artwork returned at job's completion.
Terms/Writers & Illustrators: Pays authors in royalties of 5% of print-run based on retail price, or cash, if available. Additional payment for ms/illustration packages: author gets 5%; illustrator gets 5%. Pays illustrators in royalties of 5% "of print-run based on retail price, or cash, if available." Sends galleys to authors; dummies to illustrators.

Book catalog, manuscript guidelines for business-size SASE.

Tips: "Our books aim to show children that girls and women are self-sufficient; boys and men can be emotional and nurturing; families may consist of one parent only, working parents, extended families; families may rely on daycare centers or alternative child care; all children, whatever their race, creed or color, are portrayed often and fairly in ways true to their own experience. We require that childhood be taken seriously. Children's lives can be no less complex than adults; we expect that their problems are presented honestly and completely. The validity of their feelings must be recognized, as children will benefit from reading of others coping with emotions or conflicts and finding solutions to their own problems. Current publishing priorities: strong female protagonists, especially Black, Hispanic or Native-American girls and women; friendship and solidarity among girls; children working to change values and behavior; nontraditional family situations; stories with evident concern for the world around us." Writers: "Be sure you can hold the attention of a child. Practice stories on real children and become a good writer." Beginning illustrators: "Try to get classes with someone who understands illustration professionally. We are seeking new illustrators for our files. Please send us your name and current address and we will notify you when we have a manuscript ready for illustration. Keep us notified of any address change, as it may be a while before we contact you."

CAROLRHODA BOOKS, INC., Lerner Publications, 241 First Ave. N., Minneapolis MN 55401. (612)332-3344. Book publisher. Estab. 1969. Submissions Editor: Rebecca Poole. Publishes 5 picture books/year; 2 young reader titles/year; 20 middle reader titles/year. 20% of books by first-time authors; 10% of books from agented writers.

Fiction: Picture books: general. Young readers: historical. Average word length: picture books—1,000-1,500; young readers—2,000. Recently published *Miss Hindy's Cats*, by Helena Clare Pittman (ages 4-8, story book); *How the Guinea Fowl Got Her Spots*, by Barbara Knutson (ages 4-8, story book); and *My Grandpa and the Sea*, by Katherine Orr (ages 5-9, story book).

Nonfiction: Young readers: history, hobbies, music/dance, nature/environment. Middle readers: animal, biography, history, music/dance, nature/environment. Average word length: young readers— 2,000; middle readers—6,000. Recently published *Arctic Explorer*, by Jeri Ferris (ages 8-11, biography); *Ostriches*, by Caroline Arnold (ages 7-10, nature/science); and *A Skyscraper Story*, by Charlotte Wilcox (ages 5-9, photo essay).

How to Contact/Writers: Fiction/nonfiction: Submit complete ms. Reports on queries in 3 weeks; on mss in 12 weeks. Publishes a book 18 months after acceptance. Will consider simultaneous submissions.

Illustration: Number of illustrations used for fiction: picture books—15-20; young readers—20. Number of illustrations used for nonfiction: young readers—15-20; middle readers—10-12. Editorial will review all varieties of ms/illustration packages.

How to Contact/Illustrators: Ms/illustration packages: At least one sample illustration (in form of photocopy, slide, duplicate photo) with full ms. Illustrations only: résumé/slides. Reports on art samples only if interested.

Terms/Writers & Illustrators: Buys ms outright for variable amount. Factors used to determine final payment: color vs. black-and-white, number of illustrations, quality of work. Sends galleys to authors; dummies to illustrators. Book catalog available for 9 × 12 SAE and 2 first-class stamps; manuscript guidelines for letter-size SAE and 1 first-class stamp.

Tips: Writers: "Research the publishing company to be sure it is in the market for the type of book you're interested in writing. Familiarize yourself with the company's list. We specialize in beginning readers, photo essays, and books published in series. We do very few single-title picture books, and no novels. For more detailed information about our publishing program, consult our catalog. We do not publish any of the following: textbooks, workbooks, songbooks, puzzles, plays and religious material. In general, we suggest that you steer clear of alphabet books; preachy stories with a moral to convey; stories featuring anthropomorphic protagonists ('Amanda the Amoeba,' 'Frankie the Fire Engine,' 'Tonie the Tornado'); and stories that revolve around trite, hackneyed plots: Johnny moves to a new neighborhood and is miserable because he can't make any new friends; Steve and Jane find a sick bird with a broken wing, and they nurse it back to health; lonely protagonist is rejected by his peers—usually because he's 'different' from them in some way—until he saves the day by rescuing them from some terrible calamity; and so on. You should also avoid racial and sexual stereotypes in your writing, as well as sexist language." (See also Lerner Publications.)

CHARLESBRIDGE, Subsidiary of Mastery Education, 85 Main St., Watertown MA 02172. (617)926-0329. Book publisher. Publishes 9 picture books/year. Managing Editor: Elena Wright. 50% of books by first-time authors; 50% of books from agented writers.
Nonfiction: Recently published *The Yucky Reptile Book*, by Jerry Pellotta (ages 6-9, nonfiction); *Going Lobstering*, by Jerry Pellotta (ages 3-8, environment).
How to Contact/Writers: Nonfiction: Submit complete ms. Reports on queries in 1 month. Publishes a book 1 year after acceptance.
How to Contact/Illustrators: Illustrations only: Send résumé, tearsheets. Reports only when interested—will keep work on file.

*CHILDREN'S WRITER'S & ILLUSTRATOR'S MARKET, Imprint of F&W Publications, 1507 Dana Ave., Cincinnati OH 45207. Contact: Lisa Carpenter. Publishes annual directory of freelance markets for children's writers and illustrators. Send b&w samples—photographs, photostats or good quality photocopies of artwork. "Since *Children's Writer's & Illustrator's Market* is published only once a year, submissions are kept on file for the next upcoming edition until selections are made. Material is then returned by SASE." Buys one-time rights. Buys 10-20 illustrations/year. "I need examples of art that have been sold to one of the listings in *CWIM*. Thumb through the book to see the type of art I'm seeking. The art must be freelance; it cannot have been done as staff work. Include the name of the listing that purchased the work, what the art was used for and the payment you received." Pays $25 to holder of reproduction rights and free copy of *CWIM* when published.

■CHINA BOOKS, 2929 24th St., San Francisco CA 94110. (415)282-2994. FAX: (415)282-0994. Book publisher. Independent book producer/packager. Estab. 1960. Senior Editor: Bob Schildgen. 10% of books by first-time authors; 10% of books from agented writers. Subsidy publishes 10%.
Nonfiction: Young readers, middle readers: hobbies, nature/environment. Average word length: young readers—2,000; middle readers—4,000. Recently published *Paper Pandas and Jumping Frogs*, by Florence Temko (young adults, hobby); *Long Is a Dragon*, by Peggy Goldstein (ages 8-12, writing Chinese).
How to Contact/Writers: Fiction/nonfiction: Query; submit outline/synopsis and sample chapters. Publishes a book 9 months after acceptance. Will consider simultaneous and electronic submissions via disk or modem.
Illustration: Editorial will review all varieties of ms/illustration packages.
Terms/Writers & Illustrators: Pays authors in royalties of 8-10% based on retail price; buys ms outright for $100-$500. Offers average advance payment of "1/3 of total royalty." Pay for illustrators: by the project $100-$500; royalties of 8% based on retail price. Sends galleys to authors; dummies to illustrators. Book catalog free on request; manuscript/artist's guidelines for SASE.
Tips: Looks for "something related to China or to Chinese-Americans."

CHRONICLE BOOKS, 275 Fifth St., San Francisco CA 94103. (415)777-7240. Book publisher. Editor: Victoria Rock. Publishes 12-16 picture books/year; 4-6 young reader titles/year; 0-1 middle reader titles/year; 0-1 young adult titles/year. 10-50% of books by first-time authors; 10-50% of books from agented writers.

Fiction: Picture books: animal, contemporary, easy-to-read, fantasy, history. Young readers: anthology, contemporary, easy-to-read, history, sports. Middle readers: Anthology, animal, contemporary, easy-to-read. Recently published *C is for Curious*, by Woodleigh Hubbard (2-6 yrs., picture books); *George & His Giant Shadow*, by Jeffrey Severn (2-6 yrs., picture book); *Aesop's Fables*, edited by Russel Ash/Bernard Higton (all ages, picture book).

Nonfiction: All levels: various categories. Recently published *The Long Ago Lake*, by Marne Wilken's (ages 8-12, nature/craft); *Wildlife California*, to be published in 1991, (ages 6-12, nature); *The Forest*, by Susan Deming (ages 3-8, nature/board book).

How to Contact/Writers: Fiction and nonfiction: Submit complete manuscript (picture books); submit outline/synopsis and sample chapters (for older readers). Reports on queries in 1 month; 2-3 months on mss. Publishes a book 1-3 years after acceptance. Will consider simultaneous submissions.

Illustration: Number of illustrations used for fiction/nonfiction: picture books—13-30. Editorial will review ms/illustration packages submitted by authors/artists. "Indicate if project *must* be considered jointly, or if editor may consider text and art separately." Editor, Victoria Rock, will review illustrator's work for possible use in separate author's text. Wants "unusual art. Something that will stand out on the shelves. Either bright and modern or very traditional. Fine art, not mass market."

How to Contact/Illustrators: Picture books: complete ms and samples and artist's work (not necessarily from book, but in the envisioned style.) Slides and color photocopies. Okay. Dummies helpful. Slides and tearsheets preferred. Photocopies okay. Resumé helpful. "If samples sent for files, generally no response—unless samples are not suited to list, in which case samples are returned. Queries and project proposals responded to in same time frame as author query/proposals."

Terms/Writers & Illustrators: Pays authors in royalties based on retail price. Advance "varies greatly." Retail price and number of copies printed used to determine final payment. Pay for separate authors and illustrators "Generally 50/50%, though this can vary from project to project." Illustrators paid royalty based on retail price or flat fee. Sends galleys to authors; proofs to illustrators. Book catalog for 8 × 11 SAE and 8 first class stamps; manuscript guidelines for #10 SAE and 1 first class stamp.

Tips: "The children's book world is becoming increasingly competitive which means that potential projects must not only be editorially and artistically solid, but they must also be *outstanding* in some way."

CLARION BOOKS, Houghton Mifflin Company, 215 Park Ave. South, New York NY 10003. (212)420-5800. Book publisher. Editor and Publisher: Dorothy Briley. Publishes 10 picture books/year; 7 young reader titles/year; 14 middle reader titles/year; 4 young adult titles/year. 10% of books by first-time authors; 15% of books from agented writers.

Fiction: Picture books: animal, contemporary, fantasy, history, problem novels. Young readers: animal, contemporary, fantasy, history, problem novels. Middle readers: animal, contemporary, fantasy, history, problem novels, sports, spy/mystery/adventure. Young adults: history, problem novels, spy/mystery/adventure. Average word length: picture books—50-1,000; young readers—1,000-2,500; middle readers—10,000-30,000; young adults—20,000—30,000. Recently published *Alice's Special Room*, by Dick Gackenbach (6-12, picture book); *A Perfect Father's Day*, by Eve Bunting (6-12, picture book); *A Wave in Her Pocket*, by Lynn Joseph (9 and up, middle readers); *A Place to Claim As Home*, by Patricia Willis (9-12, young adult novel).

Close-up

Russell Freedman
Writer
New York City

"All along I had wanted to write books," says nonfiction author Russell Freedman. "It was just I didn't know what kind of books I could write successfully." Thirty years ago Freedman, a former Associated Press journalist and television publicity writer, was working for an advertising agency writing television copy for such classics as "Kraft Television Theatre," "Father Knows Best" and "The Real McCoys." It was quite by accident he ended up writing children's books.

What sparked the idea for his first book was an article in *The New York Times* about a 16-year-old blind boy who invented a Braille typewriter. Upon reading further, he learned the Braille system itself was invented by a 16-year-old. This aroused Freedman's curiosity about other teenagers who had carved a place in history. Using some connections, he landed a lunch date with Vernon Ives, the head man at Holiday House in 1960. Ives liked the book idea and asked him to write a sample chapter. "It took me six months to write that chapter," says Freedman. "It was my first book and it was quite intimidating. I wrote it, rewrote it, revised it and rewrote it again."

Ives liked the sample chapter and gave Freedman his first book contract and an advance of $500. Freedman spent the next year writing *Famous Teenagers Who Made History* in his spare time.

"After the book was published, Vernon Ives told me, 'whatever you do, don't quit your job.' So of course, I quit my job." After his second book he realized it was possible to support himself as a fulltime children's writer. Since then, he says, "I've never had an honest job."

Today Freedman is a master at his craft. His current book, *The Wright Brothers: How They Invented the Airplane*, is his thirty-seventh. In 1988 he received the highest award given to a children's book writer, the Newbery Medal. *Lincoln: A Photobiography*, published by Clarion Books, is only the sixth work of nonfiction to win the award since it was established in 1926. "I had never imagined myself as winning the Newbery Award. I was flabbergasted! No nonfiction book has won the Newbery since I've been in the field and it didn't occur to me that nonfiction could win." He credits part of his accomplishment to the resurging interest in nonfiction. His book, he says, for the most part rode the crest of nonfiction's heightened popularity.

Nonfiction is more honest today, says Freedman. "It deals in more realistic terms with the real world." He cites the example of his researching life in the

"Wild West" and finding "the reality of the cowboy was such a dramatic contrast to the idealized notion of the cowboy I had grown up with." Though he claims there is less hero worship in today's books, "they're just as idealistic as they ever were." He explains where in the past children's biographies contained invented dialogue and fictionalized scenes (such as the story of George Washington cutting down the cherry tree), biographies today use actual quotes. Using facts can be just as effective in building a dramatic scene, says Freedman.

Writers today are more willing to tackle controversial subjects, he says. "If I decide to write a book about Franklin Roosevelt (which he did), I feel I cannot write a book about him without mentioning his affair with Lucy Mercer. If I thought it was objectionable, I wouldn't put it into the book. If I didn't feel as though I could mention it, I would have had to find another subject."

Freedman says there are certain fundamental tasks involved in writing children's nonfiction. His research starts with a trip to the library. "Find the most recent books on the subject; they will have pages and pages of bibliography. At a glance you can begin to see everything that's been published. I try to pick what are the most important and representative books," though he says it is impossible to read everything there is on a subject. "I read until I feel saturated, until it's coming out of my pores. At that point I think I'm ready to start writing."

On-site research adds essence to the text, says Freedman. "I like to do whatever field and actual eyewitness research I can do, but I don't like to do it until after I've written the first draft. I like to do the first draft based on my reading. This gets me really immersed in the subject, and then I know what all of my questions are." He says on-site research allows for the addition of flavor and texture to the text.

Early on Freedman decided using pictures (rather than drawings) was best for his books, saying photos are more effective in "driving the point home." This gives him complete control over his books. "Once I started doing natural history books with photographs, I actually did a dummy. I design the basic book myself, so I know exactly where to position text and photos. Doing this gives me the feeling I'm actually 'making' the book.

"A book determines its own length," he says. "It depends on the subject and the approach to the subject. Those things will tell you how long it will be and how long it will take to write it." Freedman says rookie writers often do not think in visual terms. "Every sentence, every paragraph has to conjure up a picture in the reader's mind."

His advice for hopeful authors: Avoid patronizing and condescending tones by remembering how smart kids really are. Then "read, read, read. Also, don't write about a subject you're not excited about." Writing books takes time, he says, and it is imperative authors be enthusiastic about their subjects. Otherwise, the motive is not there.

—Lisa Carpenter

Nonfiction: Picture books: animal. Young readers: animal, history, nature/environment. Middle readers: biography, history, nature/environment. Average word length: picture books—750-1,000; young readers—1,000-2,500; middle readers—10,000-30,000. Recently published *Franklin Delano Roosevelt*, by Russell Freedman (9 and up, biography); *Voyager to The Planets*, by Necia H. Apfel (8-12, science); *Hey, Hay! Funny Homonym Riddles*, by Marvin Terban (8-12, wordplay).
How to Contact/Writers: Fiction: Query on all ms over 50 pages. Nonfiction: Query. Reports on queries in 4 weeks; mss in 8-12 weeks. Publishes a book 18 months after acceptance. Will consider simultaneous submissions.
Illustration: Number of illustrations used for fiction: picture books—20; young readers—15. Number of illustrations used for nonfiction: picture books—20; young readers—40; middle readers—20-50. Editorial will review ms/illustration packages submitted by authors/artists and ms/illustration packages submitted by authors with illustrations done by separate artists. Art Director, Carol Goldenberg, will review illustrator's work for possible use in separate texts.
How to Contact/Illustrators: Ms/illustration packages: "Query first." Illustrations only: "tearsheets, photos or photocopies of samples." Reports on art samples only if interested. Original artwork returned at job's completion.
Terms/Writers & Illustrators: Pays authors in royalties of 10-12½% based on retail price. Offers average advance payment of $2,500-$5,000. Pay for separate authors and illustrators: "Separately, on an advance and royalty basis." Sends galleys to authors; dummies to illustrators. Book catalog, manuscript/artist's guidelines free on request.

*****CLOVERDALE PRESS**, 96 Morton St., New York NY 10014. (212)727-3370. Independent book producer/packager. Editorial Contact: Marian Vaarn. 25% of books by first-time authors; 50% of books from agented writers.
Fiction: Categories for consideration open on all levels. Average word length: picture books—500-1,000; young readers—10,000-15,000; middle readers—20,000-30,000; young adult/teens—30,000-40,000. Recently published *On The Edge*, by Jesse Maguire (young adult, problem novel); *Caroline Zucker* series, by Jan Bradford (young readers, contemporary); *Animal Inn* series, by Virginia Vail (middle readers, animal/contemporary).
Nonfiction: Picture books, young readers, middle readers and young adults/teens: animal, biography, education, history, hobbies, music/dance, nature/environment, religion, sports and science. Average word length: picture books—500-1,000; young readers—10,000-15,000; middle readers—20,000-30,000; young adult/teens—30,000-40,000. Recently published *Make the Team: Basketball* (middle readers, sports); *Smart Talk* series (young adult, grooming/manners).
How to Contact/Writers: Fiction/nonfiction: Query or submit outline/synopsis and sample chapters. Reports on queries in 4-6 weeks; mss in 2-3 months. Publishing of book "Varies according to publisher—usually about 1 year."
Terms/Writers & Illustrators: Pays authors in royalties or purchases outright. Advance varies. Additional payment for ms/illustration package varies. Pay for separate authors and illustrators: separately. Illustrators are paid by the illustration. Sometimes sends galleys to authors and dummies to illustrators. Manuscript guidelines for #10 SAE and 1 first class stamp.

COBBLEHILL BOOKS, affiliate of Dutton Children's Books, a division of Penguin Books USA Inc., 375 Hudson St., New York NY 10014. (212)366-2000. Book publisher. Editorial Director: Joe Ann Daly. Sr. Editor: Rosanne Lauer. Publishes 6 picture books/year; 14 young reader titles/year; 9 middle reader titles/year; 5 young adult titles/year.
Fiction: Picture books: animal, contemporary, easy-to-read, sports, spy/mystery/adventure. Young readers: animal, contemporary, easy-to-read, sports, spy/mystery/adventure. Middle readers: contemporary, problem novels, sports, spy/mystery/adventure.

Young adults: spy/mystery/adventure. Recently published *Snow Company*, by Marc Harshman, Illus. by Leslie W. Bowman (preschool-grade 3, picture book); *Maybe She Forgot*, by Ellen Kandoian (preschool-grade 2, picture book); *Gamebuster*, by Annabel and Edgar Johnson (grades 7 and up, novel).

Nonfiction: Picture books: animal, nature/environment, sports. Young readers: animal, nature/environment, sports. Middle readers: nature/environment. Recently published *Elephants on the Beach*, by Colleen Stanley Bare (preschool-grade 3, picture book); *Sea Otter Rescue*, by Roland Smith (grades 5 and up, nonfiction); *A Capital for the Nation*, by Stan Hoig (grades 6 and up, nonfiction).

How to Contact/Writers: Fiction/nonfiction: query. Reports on queries in 2 weeks; mss in 1 month. Will consider simultaneous submissions "if we are informed about them."

How to Contact/Illustrators: Illustrations only: Send samples to keep on file, no original art work. Original art work returned at job's completion.

Terms/Writers & Illustrators: Pays authors in royalties. Illustrators paid in a flat fee or by royalty. Book catalog for 8½ × 11 SAE and 2 first class stamps; manuscript guidelines for #10 SAE and 1 first class stamp.

COLORMORE, INC., Box 111249, Carrollton TX 75011-1249. (316)636-9326. Book publisher. Estab. 1987. President: Susan Koch. Publishes 4-6 young reader titles/year. 25% of books by first-time authors.

Nonfiction: Young readers: history, travel and world cultures. Average word length: 3,000. Recently published *Colormore Travels—Dallas, Texas—The Travel Guide for Kids*; and *Colormore Travels—San Diego, California—The Travel Guide for Kids*, by Mary Stack (young reader, travel guide/activity book).

How to Contact/Writers: Nonfiction: Submit outline/synopsis and sample chapters; submit complete ms. Reports on queries/mss in 2-4 weeks. Publishes a book 9 months after acceptance.

Illustration: Number of illustrations used for nonfiction: young readers—25. Editorial will review all varieties of ms/illustration packages. Preference for "8½ × 11 format books, mainly black and white, coloring-type pictures and activities."

How to Contact/Illustrators: Ms/illustration packages: Send "complete ms with 1 piece of final art." Illustrations only: Send "example(s) of black line drawing suitable for coloring." Reports in 2-4 weeks. Original art work returned at job's completion.

Terms/Writers & Illustrators: Authors paid a 5% royalty based on invoice price. Ms/illustration packages: 5% royalty. Pay for separate authors and illustrators: "separate royalty percentage." Pay for illustrators: 5% royalty based on invoice price. Sends galleys to authors; dummies to illustrators. Ms/artist's guidelines for legal SASE.

Tips: Looking for "a regional/local travel guide with lively, interesting illustrations and activities specifically for kids."

*CONCORDIA PUBLISHING HOUSE, 3558 S. Jefferson Ave., St. Louis MO 63118. (314)664-7000 ext. 498. Book publisher. Contact: Ruth Geisler, Family and Children's Resources Editor. "Concordia Publishing House publishes a number of quality children's books each year. Most are fiction, with some nonfiction, based on a religious subject. Reader interest ranges from picture books to young adults. All books must contain explicit Christian content." Recently published *Hear Me Read Bible Story Series*, by Mary Manz Simon (primer, limited vocabulary Bible stories); *Jennifer of the Jungle*, by Corbin Hillam (grade 2, picture book); *Some of My Best Friends Are Trees*, by Joanne Marxhausen (grade 3, picture book).

How to Contact/Writers: Fiction: Query. Submit complete manuscript (picture books); submit outline/synopsis and sample chapters (novel-length). Include Social Security number with submission. Reports on queries in 2 weeks; 2 months on mss. Publishes a book one year after acceptance. Will consider simultaneous submissions.

Illustration: Art director, Ed Luhmann, will review illustrator's work for possible use in separate author's text.

Terms/Writers & Illustrators: Pays authors in royalties based on retail price and outright purchase. Sends galleys to author. Manuscript guidelines for 1 first class stamp and a #10 envelope.

Tips: "Do not send finished artwork with the manuscript. If sketches will help in the presentation of the manuscript, they may be sent. If stories are taken from the Bible, they should follow the Biblical account closely. Liberties should not be taken in fantasizing Biblical stories."

CONSUMER REPORT BOOKS, Consumer Union, 51 East 42nd St., New York NY 10017. (212)983-8250. Book publisher. Editorial Contact: Sarah Uman. Publishes 2 young adult titles/year. 50% of books from agented writers.

Nonfiction: Young adults: education, nature/environment, health. Average word length: young adults—50,000. Published *How and Why?*, by Catherine O'Neill (young adults, health); *AIDS: Trading Fears for Facts*, by Karen Hein, M.D. and Theresa DiGeronimo (young adults, health).

How to Contact/Writers: Nonfiction: Submit outline/synopsis and sample chapters; submit complete ms; submit table of contents. Reports on queries/mss in 6 weeks. Publishes a book 24 months after acceptance. Will consider simultaneous submissions.

Illustrations: Number of illustrations used for nonfiction: young adults—50. Editorial will review ms/illustration packages submitted by authors/artists and ms/illustration packages submitted by authors with illustrations done by separate artists.

How to Contact/Illustrators: Ms/illustration packages: Query first.

Terms/Writers & Illustrators: Pays authors in royalties based on retail price. Factors used to determine payment for ms/illustration packages include "number of illustrations." Pay for separate authors and illustrators: Pay for "author—advance against royalty; illustrator—flat fee by the project." Sends galleys to authors. Book catalog/manuscript guidelines free on request.

COUNCIL FOR INDIAN EDUCATION, 517 Rimrock Rd., Billings MT 59102. (406)252-7451. Book publisher. Estab. 1968. Editor: Hap Gilliland. Publishes 1 picture book/year; 1 young reader title/year; 3 middle reader titles/year; 1 young adult title/year. 75% of books by first-time authors. "Have done only one shared expense book but may do one a year—larger books that we can't afford alone."

Fiction: Picture books: animal, easy-to-read. Young readers: animal, easy-to-read, history. Middle readers: animal, history. Young adults: animal, history. All must relate to Native American life, past and present. Recently published *The Vision of the Spokane Prophet*, by Egbert (grade 5-10, Indian legend); *Chief Stephen's Party*, by Chardonnet (grade 4-12, Alaskan Indian life); and *Sacajawea*, by Martha Bryant (grade 6, adult biography).

Nonfiction: Picture books: animal, nature/environment. Young readers: animal, biography, history, hobbies, nature/environment. Middle readers: animal, biography, history, hobbies, music/dance, nature/environment. Young adults: animal, biography, history, hobbies, music/dance, nature/environment, sports. All of above must be related to American Indian life and culture, past and present. Recently published *Havasupai Years*, by Knobloch (high school-adult, journal of reservation teacher); *Red Power on the Rio Grande*, by Folsom (grade 9-adult, history of Pueblo Indians).

How to Contact/Writers: Fiction: Submit complete ms. Nonfiction: Submit outline/synopsis and sample chapters, or submit complete ms. Reports on queries in 2 months; mss in 3 months. "We accept 10% of the manuscripts received. Those with potential must be evaluated by all the members of our Indian Editorial Board, who make the final selection. This board makes sure the material is true to the Indian way of life and is the kind of material they want their children to read." Publishes a book 4 months after acceptance. Will consider simultaneous submissions.

Illustration: Number of illustrations used for fiction: picture books—25; young readers—12; middle readers—10; young adults—10. Number of illustrations used for nonfiction: picture books—20; young readers—10; middle readers—10; young adults—10. Editor will review ms/illustration packages submitted by authors/artists and ms/illustration packages submitted by authors with illustrations done by separate artists. "Black and white artwork only."

How to Contact/Illustrators: Ms/illustration packages: "Samples sent with manuscript." Illustrations only: "samples." Reports on art samples in 3 months "when we report back to author on ms." Original artwork returned at job's completion "if requested."

Terms/Writers & Illustrators: Pays authors in royalties of 10% based on wholesale price or buys ms outright for "1½¢ per word." Additional payment for ms/illustration packages "sometimes." Factors used to determine payment for ms/illustration package include "number of illustrations used." Sends galleys to authors. Book catalog/manuscript guidelines available for SAE and 1 first-class stamp.

Tips: "For our publications, write about one specific tribe or group and be sure actions portrayed are culturally correct for the group and time period portrayed. What kind of material can we use? These are our preferences, in the order listed: Contemporary Indian Life—exciting stories that could happen to Indian children now. (Be sure the children act like present-day Indians, not like some other culture.) Indians of the old days—authentically portrayed. Be specific about who, where, and when. How-to—Indian arts, crafts, and activities. Biography—Indians past and present. History and culture—factual material of high interest only. If you are Indian express your ideas and ideals. Folk stories and legends—high interest expressing Indian ideas. Name the specific tribe. Poetry—possibly—if it expresses real Indian ideals. Instructional material and information for teachers of Indian children."

CROCODILE BOOKS, USA, Imprint of Interlink Publishing Group, Inc., 99 Seventh Ave., Brooklyn NY 11215. (718)797-4292. Book publisher. Vice President: Ruth Moushabeck. Publishes 16 picture books/year. 25% of books by first-time authors.
Fiction: Picture books: animal, contemporary, history, spy/mystery/adventure. Recently published *Ella & the Rabbit*, by Helen Cooper (ages 2-6, picture book); *The Woodcutter's Mitten*, by Loek Koopmans (ages 2-6, picture book).
Nonfiction: Picture book: history, nature/environment. Recently published Ecology Story Books Series by Chris Baines and Penny Ives (ages 4-8, picture books).
How to Contact/Writers: Fiction/nonfiction: Submit outline/synopsis and sample chapters. Reports on queries in 2-3 weeks; on ms in 8 weeks. Publishes a book 12 months after acceptance.
Illustrations: Editorial will review ms/illustration packages submitted by authors/artists, and ms/illustration packages submitted by authors with illustrations done by separate artists.
How to Contact/Illustrators: Ms/illustration packages: Send "2-3 sample chapters (whole ms if less than 48 pages) and sample art." Original art work returned at job's completion.
Terms/Writers & Illustrators: Pays authors in royalties. If ms/illustration package is the work of a writer and a separate illustrator, "royalties will be shared equally." Sends galleys to author; dummies to illustrator. Book catalog free on request.

*CROSSWAY BOOKS, Good News Publishers, 1300 Crescent, Wheaton IL 60187. Book Publisher. Editorial assistant: Jennifer Narstad. Publishes 2 young reader titles/year; 4 middle readers/year;1-2 young adult titles/year. 20% of books by first-time authors. 5% of books by agented authors.

Fiction: Young readers, middle readers and young adult/teens: contemporary, fantasy, science fiction, sports, history and spy/mystery/adventure. Recently published *Sadie Rose and the Mad Fortune Hunters*, by Hilda Stahl (9-12, novel); *Sendi Lee Mason and the Stray Striped Cat*, by Hilda Stahl (6-8, novel).

How to Contact/Writers: Fiction/nonfiction: Query. Reports on queries in 5 months. Publishes a book up to 12 months after acceptance. Accepts simultaneous submissions.

Illustration: Art director Mark Schramm will review an illustrator's work for possible use in authors' texts.

How to Contact/Illustrators: Query first. Submit resume, color photocopies or slides. Reports back only if interested. Originals returned to artist at job's completion.

Terms/Writers & Illustrators: Pays by royalty based on wholesale price. Illustrators paid by the project (negotiable). Authors see galleys for review; illustrators see dummies for review. Book catalog for $1.05 and 9 × 12 SASE. Manuscript/artist's guidelines for #10 SAE and 1 first class stamp.

*CROWN PUBLISHERS (CROWN BOOKS FOR CHILDREN), Imprint of Random House, Inc. 225 Park Ave. S., New York NY 10003. (212)254-1600. Book publisher. Editor-in-Chief: Andrea Cascardi. Publishes 20 pictures/year; 10 middle reader titles/year; 5 young adult titles/year. 2% of books by first-time authors; 70% of books from agented writers.

Fiction: Picture books, young readers and middle readers: sports, humorous, animal. All levels: contemporary. Average word length: picture books—750; young readers—20,000; middle readers—50,000; young adult/teens—50,000. Recently published: *Ace: The Very Important Pig*, by D. King-Smith (middle reader, novel); *Baby Beluga*, by Raffi (pre-school-8 yrs., picture book); *Hey! Get Off Our Train*, by John Burningham (4-9 yrs., picture book).

Nonfiction: Picture books: animal, biography, history, music/dance, nature/environment, sports, science. Young readers: animal, biography, history, nature/environment, sports, science. Middle readers: animal, history, nature/environment, sports, science. Average word length: picture books—750-1,000; young readers—20,000; middle readers—50,000; young adult/teens—50,000. Recently published: *Journey to the Planets*, by Patricia Lauber (9 yrs. and up, science); *Playing Hockey*, by Chuck Solomon (5-9 yrs., photo-essay); *Hidden Life of the Meadow*, by David Schwartz (6-10 yrs., photo-picture book).

How to Contact/Writers: Fiction/nonfiction: Submit complete manuscript. Reports on queries in 1 month; 2-4 months on mss. Publishes book 2 years after acceptance. Will consider simultaneous submissions.

Illustration: Number of illustrations used for fiction and nonfiction: picture books—33; young readers—10; middle readers—1; young adult/teens—1. Reviews all varieties of ms/illustration packages. "Double-spaced, continuous manuscripts; do not supply page-by-page breaks. One or two photocopies of art are fine. *Do Not Send Original Art.* Dummies are acceptable."

How to Contact Illustrators: Photocopies or slides with SASE. Reports in ms/art samples in 2 months. Original artwork returned at job's completion. Pays author royalty. Advance "varies greatly." Additional payment for ms/illustration package. Quality and experience determine final payment. Illustrators paid royalty. Sends galleys to authors; proofs to illustrators. Book catalog for 9 × 12 SAE and 4 first class stamps. Manuscript guidelines for 4¼ × 9½ SAE and 1 first class stamp. Artists' guidelines not available.

MAY DAVENPORT, PUBLISHERS, 26313 Purissima Rd., Los Altos Hills CA 94022. (415)948-6499. Book publisher. Estab. 1976. Independent book producer/packager. Editor: May Davenport. Publishes 1-2 picture books/year; 2-3 young adult titles/year. 99% of books by first-time authors.

Fiction: Young adults: fantasy. Average word length: 20,000-30,000 words. Recently published *Pompey Poems*, by Ellen Langill (grades 7-12, paper and hardcover); *Creeps*, by Shelly Fredman, (grades 7-12 hardcover); *The Chase of the Sorceress*, by Philip R. Johnson (grades 7-12, paperback).

Nonfiction: Picture books: animal. Recently published *Willie, Zilly and the Bantams*, by Grace Collins (preschool-1, hardcover); *All About Turtles*, by Andrea Ross (coloring book/read-along cassette).

How to Contact/Writers: Fiction: Query. Reports on queries in 2-3 weeks. Publishes a book 6-12 months after acceptance.

Terms/Writers: Pays authors in royalties based on retail price. Pays "by mutual agreement, no advances." Book listing, manuscript guidelines free on request with SASE.

Tips: "If you are a writer—write so the words will communicate your thoughts and feelings. If your characters come alive, they will live on in great literature, and classroom teachers will appreciate your talent as models of writers for the present generation, whose models are television writers. We receive many senior citizens' flashback of humor in their childhood which are nostalgic for senior citizens, but the characters and dialogue need to be dramatized in order for this young television-oriented youth to read such common material which comes over the tube. Usually the television version is traumatized. Fictional approach of dramatized youth narration is worth rereading, and that means such wonderful flashbacks need to be focused to an audience (TV-oriented youth who do not like to read) which will not appreciate their stories. Since many senior citizens are print-oriented, they are familiar with the tools of writing. If only they could use their tools. Haven't found many yet."

*DELACORTE PRESS, Dell Publishing, 666 5th Avenue, New York NY 10103. Book publisher. Publisher: George Nicholson. Associate Publisher: Craig Virden. Senior Editors: Mary Cash and David Gale. Publishes 10 picture books/year; 10 young reader titles/year; 20 middle reader titles/year; 10 young adult titles/year. 10% of books by first-time authors; 70% of books from agented writers.

Fiction: Picture books: animal, contemporary, fantasy, history. Young Readers: animal, contemporary, easy-to-read, fantasy, sports, spy/mystery/adventure. Middle Readers: animal, contemporary, fantasy, sports, spy/mystery/adventure; Young Adults/Teens: anthology, contemporary, fantasy, problem novels, sports, spy/mystery/adventure. Recently published *Matthew Jackson Meets the Wall*, by Patricia Reilly Giff (2nd grade, chapter book); *A Blossom Promise*, by Betsy Byars (grades 3-7, novel); *Canyons*, by Gary Paulsen (grades 7 and up, novel).

Nonfiction: "Delacorte publishes a very limited number of nonfiction titles."

How to Contact/Writers: Submit through agent only. All unsolicited manuscripts returned unopened. "Unsolicited picture book mss accepted. Unsolicited manuscripts accepted for the Delcorte Press Prize for a First Young Adult Novel contest (see contest section)." Reports on queries sent to individual editors in 6 weeks; reports on mss in 3 months.

Illustration: Number of illustrations used per fiction title varies considerably. Will review all varieties of manuscript illustration packages.

How to Contact/Illustrators: Query first. Do not send originals. All samples will be filed and not returned. Illustrations only: tearsheets, résumé, samples that do not need returned. Reports on ms/art samples only if interested. Original artwork returned at job's completion. "Unfortunately we cannot accept appointments."

Terms/Writers & Illustrators Pays authors royalty based on retail price or outright purchase on some art only. If the ms/illustration package is the work of a writer and a separate illustrator, royalty and advance split. Pay for illustrators: royalty based on retail price. Sends galleys to authors.

DIAL BOOKS FOR YOUNG READERS, Penguin Books USA Inc., 375 Hudson St., New York NY 10014. (212)725-1818. Editor-in-Chief: Phyllis J. Fogelman. Publishes 40-50 picture books/year; 10 young reader titles/year; 5 middle reader titles/year; 10 young adult titles/year.

Fiction: Picture books: animal, contemporary, fantasy, history, sports, spy/mystery/adventure. Young readers: animal, contemporary, easy-to-read, fantasy, history, sports, spy/mystery/adventure. Middle readers, young adults: contemporary, fantasy, history, problem novels, science fiction, sports, spy/mystery/adventure. Recently published *Nora and the Great Bear*, by Ute Krause (ages 4-8, picture book); *The Christmas Fox*, by John Bush (ages 4-8, poetry picture book); and *Bailey's Bones*, by Victor Kelleher (YA novel).

Nonfiction: Uses very little nonfiction but will consider submissions of outstanding artistic and literary merit. Recently published *A Flower Grows*, by Ken Robbins (ages 4-8, picture book); *How Animals See*, by Sandra Sinclair (middle readers).

How to Contact/Writers: Fiction: Query, submit outline/synopsis and sample chapters for longer work, submit complete ms for short material.

Illustration: Editorial will review ms/illustration packages submitted by author/artist (i.e. a single individual who does both art and text). Prefers to use own artists for mss submitted by authors. Will review an illustrator's work for possible use in author's texts.

How to Contact/Illustrators: Ms/illustration packages: Query first or 1 piece of final color art and sketches. Illustrations only: Résumé, tearsheets.

Terms/Writers & Illustrators: Pays authors and illustrators in royalties based on retail price. Average advance payment "varies." Manuscript guidelines for SASE.

DILLON PRESS, INC., 242 Portland Ave. S., Minneapolis MN 55415. (612)333-2691. Book publisher. Nonfiction: Tom Schneider, Senior Editor. Publishes 10 young reader titles/year; 20 middle reader titles/year. 30% of books by first-time authors; 10% of books from agented writers. Currently not accepting fiction mss.

Nonfiction: Young readers and middle readers: animal, biography, Native American tribes and leaders, foreign countries (especially children in other nations), nature/environment, contemporary issues. Average word length: young readers—3,000; middle readers—5,000-7,000. Recently published *Pakistan*, by Jabeen Yusufali (grades 5-9, educational geography); *Those Amazing Leeches*, by by Cheryl Halton (grades 4-7, educational natural science); and *Could You Ever Fly to the Stars?*, by Dr. David Darling (grades 5-9, educational physical science).

How to Contact/Writers: Nonfiction: Query, with writing sample. Reports on queries in 2-3 weeks; on mss in 6-8 weeks. Publishes a book 12-18 months after acceptance. Will consider simultaneous submissions.

Illustration: Number of illustrations used for nonfiction: young readers—20; middle readers—25. Editorial will review ms/illustration packages submitted by authors/artists and ms/illustration packages submitted by authors with illustrations done by separate artists. Editorial Director, Uva Dillon, will review an illustrator's work for possible use in separate texts.

How to Contact/Illustrators: Ms/illustration packages: Query with sample chapters and art sample. Illustrations only: Slides and/or samples. Reports on art samples only if interested.

Terms/Writers & Illustrators: Pays authors in royalties of 5-10%. Outright purchase "negotiated." Average advance "negotiated." Additional payment for ms/illustration packages "negotiated." Factors to determine final payment include number of illustrations or photos quality. Pay for separate authors and illustrators "negotiated." Illustrators paid by the project via negotiation. Sends galleys to authors. Book catalog for 9 × 12 SASE; manuscript guidelines for 4 × 9 SASE.

Tips: Writers: "Research competitive books and ideas and submit a complete well-organized proposal with sample chapters or complete manuscript." Illustrators: "Provide evidence of artistic ability and knowledge of book publishing." Looks for a book "that matches our current publishing plans for existing or new series of educational books (nonfiction) for young readers K-12, with an emphasis on 2nd grade through 7th grade."

DOUBLE M PRESS, 16455 Tuba St., Sepulveda CA 91343. (818)360-3166. Book publisher. Estab. 1975. Publisher: Charlotte Markman Stein. Publishes young reader titles, middle reader titles, and young adult titles. 50% of books by first-time authors.
Fiction: Middle readers: contemporary, fantasy, historical. Young readers: contemporary; fantasy. Young adults: contemporary, problem novels. Average word length: young adults—40,000-60,000. "We are trade publishers, who, started in 1989, concentrating on children's books, all ages." Recent titles include *The Stained Glass Window*, by Charlotte M. Stein (young adult, historical/love); *Journey to a Magic Castle*, by Gershen Kaufman, Ph.D. (picture story).
Nonfiction: Young readers: biography, education, history, mythology. Middle readers: biography, education, history, mythology. Young adults: biography, education, history, mythology. Distributes *Greek Mythology* (Series A, B, C and D), by Stephanides Brothers (middle reader, mythology).
How to Contact/Writers: Fiction/nonfiction: Query. Reports on queries in 4 weeks; on mss in 6-8 weeks. Publishes a book 1-2 years after acceptance.
Illustration: Number of illustrations used for fiction/nonfiction: middle readers—3-4; young adults—3-4. Editorial will review all varieties of ms/illustration packages. Query first. Michele P. Bodenheimer will review an illustrator's work for possible use in separate texts.
How to Contact/Illustrators: Ms/illustration packages: Query first. Illustrations only: Tearsheets, slides. Reports on art samples in 4 weeks.
Terms/Writers & Illustrators: Pays authors in royalties based on retail price. Buys ms outright "based on work." Additional payment for ms/illustration packages. Factors used to determine final payment include color art and number of illustrations. Pay for separate authors and illustrators: "royalties to each." Pay for illustrators: by the project; "we also pay royalties, depends on work." Sends galleys to authors; dummies to illustrators.
Tips: Looks for: "Imaginative handling of contemporary problems and a constructive outlook. Illustrations that appeal to the imaginative or fantasy in children."

DOUBLEDAY, div. of Bantam Doubleday Dell, 666 Fifth Ave., New York NY 10103. (212)492-9772. Book publisher. Publisher: Michael Palgon. Publishes 15-20 picture books/year; 20 young reader titles/year; 20 middle reader titles/year. 10% of books by first-time authors; 40% of books from agented writers.
How to Contact/Writers: Fiction/nonfiction: Query. Reports on queries in 5 weeks; on mss in 12 weeks. Publishes a book 24 months after acceptance. Will consider simultaneous submissions.
Illustration: Editorial will review all varieties of ms/illustration packages.
How to Contact/Illustrators: Ms/illustration packages: Query. Illustrations only: "Previous books, slides, tearsheets." Reports on art samples only if interested. Original art work returned at job's completion.
Terms/Writers & Illustrators: Pays authors in royalties based on retail price. Buys ms outright. Additional payment for ms/illustration packages. Separate writers and illustrators paid separately. Illustrators paid by the project. Sends galleys to authors; dummies to illustrators. Book catalog, manuscript guidelines free on request.
Tips: Writers: "Learn the marketplace and fill a need." Illustrators: "Do a sample dummy and sample art for an available, well-known text to show ability."

DUTTON CHILDREN'S BOOKS, Penguin USA, 375 Hudson St., New York NY 10014. (212)366-2600. Book publisher. Editor-in-Chief: Lucia Monfried. Publishes approximately 60 picture books/year; 4 young reader titles/year; 10 middle reader titles/year; 8 young adult titles/year. 15% of books by first-time authors.
Fiction: Picture books: animal, fantasy, spy/mystery/adventure. Young readers: easy-to-read, fantasy, science fiction. Middle readers: animal, contemporary, fantasy, history, science fiction, spy/mystery/adventure. Young adults: animal, contemporary, fantasy, history, romance, science fiction, spy/mystery/adventure. Recently published *Archie, Follow Me,*, by Lynne Cherry (picture book, ages 4-6); *The Fireplug is First Base*, by P.J. Petersen and Betsy James (Speedsters series for reluctant readers, ages 7-10); *Fudge-A-Mania*, by Judy Blume (novel, ages 8-12).
Nonfiction: Picture books: animal, nature/environment. Young readers: nature/environment. Middle readers and young adults: animal, nature/environment. Recently published *The Big Book for Peace*, collected by Ann Duvell and Marilyn Fachs (illustrated collection, ages 7-12); *B is for Bethlehem*, by Isabel Wilner, illustrated by Elise Kleven (all ages; illustrated alphabet); *Backyard Hunt, Praying Mantis*, by Bianca Lavies (photo essay, ages 7-10).
How to Contact/Writers: Fiction/nonfiction: query. Reports on queries in 2 months; on mss in 2-3 months. Publishes a book 12-18 months after acceptance. Will consider simultaneous electronic submissions via disk or modem.
Illustration: Number of illustrations used for fiction: picture books—14-28; easy readers—30; middle readers—15. Editorial will review ms/illustration packages submitted by authors/artists and ms/illustration packages submitted by authors with illustrations done by separate artists. Design department will review illustrator's work for possible use in separate texts.
How to Contact/Illustrators: Ms/illustration packages: Query first. Illustrations only: Resume, tearsheets, slides—no original art please. Reports on art samples in 2 months. Original artwork returned at job's completion.
Terms/Writers & Illustrators: Pays authors in royalties based on retail price. Book catalog, manuscript guidelines for SAE.
Tips: Writers: "We publish high-quality trade books and are interested in well-written manuscripts with fresh ideas and child appeal. We recommend spending time in bookstores and libraries to get an idea of the books on the market. Find out what topics have been treated again and again and should thus be avoided. Dutton has a complete publishing program—we are looking for good writing and strong quality in all categories of fiction. We would be interested in nonfiction including preschool and middle-grade nonfiction, including U.S. history, general biography (ages 7-10), science and photo essays." Illustrators: Be aware of which style of illustration would be of interest to which publishing house—is your work best suited for mass market or trade? We're interested in seeing samples or portfolios from potential illustrators of picture books (full color), young novels (black and white), and jacket artists."

EAKIN PUBLICATIONS, INC., Box 90159, Austin TX 78709. (512)288-1771 FAX: (512)288-1813. Book publisher. Estab. 1978. President: Ed Eakin. Publishes 2 picture books/year; 3 young reader titles/year; 10 middle reader titles/year; 2 young adult titles/year. 50% of books by first-time authors; 5% of books from agented writers.
Fiction: Picture books: animal. Middle readers: history, sports. Young adults: history, sports. Average word length: picture books—3,000; young readers—10,000; middle readers—15,000-20,000; young adults—20,000-30,000. "90 percent of our books relate to Texas and the Southwest."
Nonfiction: Picture books: animal. Middle readers and young adults: history, sports. Recently published *Build the Alamo*, (ages 4-10, picture book).
How to Contact/Writers: Fiction/nonfiction: Query. Reports on queries in 2 weeks; on mss in 6 weeks. Publishes a book 1 year after acceptance. Will consider simultaneous and electronic submissions via disk or modem.

Illustration: Number of illustrations used for fiction/nonfiction: picture books—40; young readers—40; middle readers—5; young adults—5. Editorial will review all varieties of ms/illustration packages.

How to Contact/Illustrators: Ms/illustration packages: Query. Illustrations only: Tearsheets. Reports on art samples in 2 weeks.

Terms/Writers & Illustrators: Pays authors in royalties of 10-15% based on wholesale price. Pay for separate authors and illustrators: "Usually share royalty." Pay for illustrators: Royalty 10-15% based on wholesale price. Sends galleys to authors. Book catalog, manuscript/artist's guidelines for SASE.

Tips: Writers: "Be sure all elements of manuscript are included—include vitae of author or illustrator." Looks for: "books relating to Texas and the Southwest or ethnic groups."

*WM. B. EERDMANS PUBLISHING COMPANY, 255 Jefferson Avenue S.E., Grand Rapids MI 49503. (616)459-4591. Book publisher. Children's Book Editor: Amy Eerdmans. Publishes 6 picture books/year; 4 young reader titles/year; 4 middle reader titles/year.

Fiction: All levels: fantasy and history; middle readers and young adults: problem novels.

Nonfiction: All levels: biography, history, nature/environment, religion.

How to Contact/Writers: Fiction/nonfiction: Query; submit complete manuscript. Reports on queries in 1-2 weeks; mss in 4 weeks.

Illustration: Reviews all varieties of manuscript packages. Art director, Willem Mineur, will review illustrator's work for possible use in separate author's text.

How to Contact/Illustrators: Illustrations only: Submit résumé, slides or color photocopy. Reports on ms/art samples in 1 month. Original artwork returned at job's completion.

Terms/Writers & Illustrators: Pays authors in royalties of 5-10%. Pays in royalty for the author. The illustrator receives royalty or permission fee. Sends galleys for review; dummies to illustrators. Book catalog free on request; manuscript and/or artist's guidelines free on request.

ENSLOW PUBLISHERS INC., Bloy St. & Ramsey Ave., Box 777, Hillside NJ 07205. (201)964-4116. Vice President: Mark Enslow. Estab. 1978. Publishes 15 middle reader titles/year; 15 young adult titles/year. 30% of books by first-time authors; 10% of books from agented writers.

Nonfiction: Middle readers: biography, history, sports. Young adults: biography, history, sports. Average word length: middle readers—10,000; young adults—20,000. Published *Learning about AIDS*, by Alvin Silverstein (grades 4-6, health); *Archbishop Tutu*, by Judith Bentley (grades 7-9, biography).

How to Contact/Writers: Nonfiction: Query. Reports on queries/mss in 2 weeks. Publishes a book 12 months after acceptance. Will consider simultaneous submissions.

Illustration: Number of illustrations used for nonfiction: middle readers—28; young adults—28.

Terms/Writers & Illustrators: Pays authors in royalties of 6-10% based on retail price. Sends galleys to authors. Book catalog/manuscript guidelines available for SAE.

*ESOTERICA PRESS, P.O. Box 170, Barstow CA 92312-0170. Book publisher. "We have not published any children's books yet, but are eager to attract submissions in this area." Editorial contact person in any category: Y. Zentella.

Fiction: Picture books and young readers: contemporary (ethnic), easy-to-read, fantasy, history.

Nonfiction: Picture books and young readers: biography, education, history, music/dance, ethnic.

How to Contact/Writers: Fiction/nonfiction: Query; submit outline/synopsis and sample chapters; submit complete manuscript. Reports on queries in 2-4 weeks; 2-3 months on mss. Publishes a book "About 6-9 months depending on editing needed and technical

problems that can arise." Will consider simultaneous submissions.
Illustration: Editorial will review all varieties of illustration packages. Publisher, Yoly Zentella, will review illustrator's work for possible use in separate texts. "Illustrator must be aware that we will reduce/enlarge to fit our needs."
How to Contact/Illustrators: Query first or submit manuscript and sketches. Submit photocopies. Reports on ms/art samples in 2-3 months. Original artwork returned at job's completion.
Terms/Writers & Illustrators: Expenses paid first. Author gets 60% of profits and 10% of print run. (Additional payment for artwork.) Pay for illustrators: by the project. Sends galleys to author; dummies to illustrators. Book catalog for legal SAE and 2 first class stamps. Manuscript/artist's guidelines for legal SAE and 2 first class stamps.
Tips: Wants "Humanist themes. We are especially interested in Latino, Native-American, Black, Arab-Muslim and Asian themes."

FABER AND FABER, INC., Faber and Faber, Ltd. (London), 50 Cross Street, Winchester MA 01890. (617)721-1427. Book publisher. Editor: Betsy Uhrig. Publishes 5 middle reader titles/year; 5 young adult titles/year. 20% of books by first-time authors; 50% of books from agented writers.
Fiction: Middle readers: animal, contemporary, fantasy, spy/mystery/adventure. Young adults: contemporary and spy/mystery/adventure. Recently published *The Moon in the Cloud* by Harris (ages 8-12, novel); *Ellis & the Hummick* by Gibson (ages 8-12, fantasy).
How to Contact/Writers: Fiction: Submit outline/synopsis and sample chapters. Reports on queries 6 weeks; mss 2 months. Publishes a book 6-12 months after acceptance. Will consider simultaneous submissions.
Illustration: Number of illustrations used for fiction and nonfiction: Middle readers— 12. Editorial will review ms/illustration packages submitted by authors/artists and ms/ illustration packages submitted by authors with illustrations done by separate artists.
How to Contact/Illustrators; Ms/illustration packages: "Query first." Illustrations only: "Send résumé, samples—not slides, not originals." Reports only if interested. Original artwork returned at job's completion.
Terms/Writers & Illustrators: Pays authors in royalties. Pay for illustrators: by the project. Sends galleys to authors; dummies to illustrators. Book catalog for 8 ½×11 SAE; manuscript guidelines free on request.
Tips: "Timeless novels of fantasy and adventure for mid-older readers, simple pen-and-ink illustrations."

FACTS ON FILE, 460 Park Ave. S., New York NY 10016. (212)683-2244. Book publisher. Editorial Contacts: James Warren and Helen Flynn. Publishes 45 young adult titles/ year. 5% of books by first-time authors; 25% of books from agented writers; additional titles through book packagers, co-publishers and unagented writers.
Nonfiction: Young adults: animal, biography, science, education, history, music/dance, nature/environment, religion, sports. Published *Martin Luther King, Jr.*, by Lillie Patterson; *The CIA*, by Graham Yost; *Opening the Space Frontier*, by Drake Moser and Ray Spangenburg. (All-ages 11-16).
How to Contact/Writers: Nonfiction: Submit outline/synopsis and sample chapters. Reports on queries in 4 weeks. Publishes a book 10 months after acceptance. Will consider simultaneous submissions. Sends galleys to authors. Book catalog free on request.
Tips: "Nothing too cutesy. We do a lot of books series in series."

FARRAR, STRAUS & GIROUX, 19 Union Square West, New York NY 10003. (212)741-6934. Book publisher. Children's books Editor-in-Chief: Margaret Ferguson. Estab. 1946. Publishes 21 picture books/year; 6 middle reader titles/year; 5 young adult titles/ year. 5% of books by first-time authors; 5% of books from agented writers.

Fiction: "Original and well-written material for all ages." Published *Valentine & Orson*, by Nancy Ekholm Burkert (all ages); *Carl Goes Shopping*, by Alexandra Day (ages 3 up); *An Acceptable Time*, by Madeleine L'Engle (young adult).

How to Contact/Writers: Fiction/nonfiction: Query; submit outline/synopsis and sample chapters. Reports on queries in 6 weeks; on mss in 12 weeks. Publishes a book 18 months after acceptance. Will consider simultaneous submissions.

Illustration: Number of illustrations used for fiction: picture books—32; middle readers—10. Number of illustrations used for nonfiction: middle readers—15. Will review ms/illustration packages submitted by authors/artists and an illustrator's work for possible use in author's texts.

How to Contact/Illustrators: Ms/illustration packages: Ms with 1 piece of final art, remainder roughs. Illustrations only: Tearsheets. Reports on art samples only if interested. Original artwork returned at job's completion.

Terms/Writers & Illustrators: "We offer an advance against royalties for both authors and illustrators." Sends galleys to authors; dummies to illustrators. Book catalog available for 6½×9½ SAE and 56¢ postage; manuscript guidelines for 1 first-class stamp.

Tips: "Study our catalog before submitting. We will see illustrator's portfolios by appointment."

FOUR WINDS PRESS, imprint of Macmillan Publishing Co., 866 Third Ave., New York NY 10022. Book publisher. Editor-in-Chief: Cindy Kane. 15-20% of books by first-time authors; 80% of books from agented writers.

Fiction: Picture books: animal, contemporary, humor, fantasy. Middle readers: history, family, contemporary. Average word length: picture books—750-1,500; middle readers—10,000-30,000. Recently published: *Mrs. Toggle's Zipper*, by Robin Pulver; and *Crow Moon, Worm Moon*, by James Skofield (picture books); *Moxie*, by Phyllis Rossiter (novel). "YA books are no longer being considered."

Nonfiction: Picture books: animal, nature/environment, biography, history, concepts. Middle readers: animal, biography, history, hobbies, music/dance, nature/environment, sports. Average word length: picture books—750-1,500; middle readers—10,000-30,000.

How to Contact/Writers: Fiction: Submit outline/synopsis and complete ms. Nonfiction: Query. Reports on queries/mss in 12 weeks. "Due to volume of submissions received, we cannot guarantee a quick response time or answer queries about manuscript status." Publishes a book 18-24 months after acceptance. "We are *not* reviewing simultaneous submissions."

Illustration: Number of illustrations used for fiction and nonfiction: picture books—24-40 full page illustrations; middle readers—15-20 mostly full page illustrations. Editorial will review all varieties of ms/illustration packages.

How to Contact/Illustrators: Picture books: Submit full ms or dummy with art samples (not originals!). Illustrations only: "Illustration portfolios are reviewed every Thursday on a drop-off basis. If you cannot drop off your portfolio, you should mail tearsheets. Your portfolio should contain samples of work that best reflect your technical and creative ability to illustrate a text for children. These samples should include two or three different scenes of animals and/or children rendered in a setting. These should show your ability to handle composition, create interesting characters, and maintain consistency between scenes. Use whatever medium is best suited to your technique. Generally, still life, three dimensional artwork and abstract compositions do not translate well to children's book illustrations." Reports on ms/art samples in 6-8 weeks; art samples only if interested. Original artwork returned at job's completion.

Terms/Writers & Illustrators: Pays authors in royalties of 5-10% based on retail price (depends on whether artist is sharing royalties). Factors used to determine payment for ms/illustration package include "complexity of artwork, number of pieces, color vs. black-and-white." Pay for separate authors and illustrators: "Each has separate contract and is paid by royalty or flat fee." Pay for illustrators: by the project; royalties range

from 2-5%; "fees and royalties vary widely according to budget for book." Sends galleys to authors; dummies to illustrators. Manuscript and/or artist's guidelines for 1 first-class stamp and a business-size envelope. "No calls, please."
Tips: "The length of your story depends on the age of the child for whom it is intended. There are no fixed lengths. A good story is almost always the right length or can easily be made so." (See also Aladdin Books/Collier Books for Young Adults, Atheneum Publishers, Bradbury Press, Margaret K. McElderry Books.)

FREE SPIRIT PUBLISHING, Ste. 616, 400 First Ave. N., Minneapolis MN 55401. (612)338-2068. Book publisher. Publisher/President: Judy Galbraith. Publishes 1-2 middle reader titles/year; 1-2 young adult titles/year. 80% of books by first-time authors.
Nonfiction: Young readers: education, psychology/self-help, reference. Middle readers: education, psychology/self-help, reference. Young adults: education, psychology/self-help, reference. Published *Directory of American Youth Organizations*, by Judith Erickson (grades 3-12, reference); *Perfectionism: What's Bad About Being Too Good*, by Miriam Adderholdt-Elliott (young adults, psychology/self-help).
How to Contact/Writers: Nonfiction: Submit outline/synopsis and sample chapters. Reports on queries in 3 months. Publishes a book 12-18 months after acceptance.
Illustration: Number of illustrations for nonfiction: young readers—15; middle readers—15; young adults—10. Editorial will review all varieties of ms/illustration packages.
How to Contact/Illustrators: Submit 3 chapters of ms with 1 piece of final art. Prefers to see: "B&w cartoon illustrations, graphic treatments." Illustrations only: résumé, tearsheets. Reports on art samples only if interested. Original artwork returned at job's completion if requested.
Terms/Writers & Illustrators: Pays authors in royalties of 8-12% based on wholesale price. Offers advance payment of $500-$1,000. Factors used to determine final payment for ms/illustration is color art vs. black-and-white and number of illustrations used. Pay for illustrations: by the project, $50-500. Sends galleys to authors; dummies to illustrators. Book catalog free on request.
Tips: Illustrations: "Hustle your work as much as possible. I've hired illustrators 'off the street.' " Looks for: "A truly helpful, informative, pro-kid, and good-humored book."

DAVID R. GODINE, PUBLISHER, 300 Massachusetts, Boston MA 02115. (617)536-0761. Book publisher. Estab. 1970. Editor: Audrey Bryant. Publishes 3-4 picture books/year; 2 young reader titles/year; 3-4 middle reader titles/year. 10% of books by first-time authors; 20% of books from agented writers.
Fiction: Picture books: animal. Young readers: animal, easy-to-read, fantasy, mystery/adventure, folk or fairy tales. Middle readers: animal, fantasy, folk or fairy tales. Recently published *Cuckoo Clock*, by Mary Stolz (ages 9-11, middle readers); *Sea Gifts*, by George Shannon (ages 8-10, early readers); *A Natural Man*, by Steve Sanfield (ages 8-10, early readers).
How to Contact/Writers: Fiction: Submit complete ms. Reports on queries in 2 weeks; on mss in 3 weeks. Publishes a book 18 months after acceptance. Will consider simultaneous submissions.
Illustration: Number of illustrations used for fiction: picture books—16; young readers—12; middle readers—10. Editorial will review all varieties of ms/illustration packages.
How to Contact/Illustrators: Ms/illustration packages: "Roughs and 1 finished art plus either sample chapters for very long works or whole ms for short works." Illustrations only: "Slides, with one full-size blow-up of art." Reports on art samples in 3 weeks. Original artwork returned at job's completion.
Terms/Writers & Illustrators: Pays authors in royalties based on retail price. Number of illustrations used to determine final payment. Pay for separate authors and illustrators: "differs with each collaboration." Illustrators paid by the project. Sends galleys to

authors; dummies to illustrators. Book catalog/manuscript guidelines free on request.

GOLDEN BOOKS, Western Publishing Co., 850 Third Ave., New York NY 10022. (212)753-8500. Editorial Directors: Margo Lundell, Selma Lanes. Book publisher.
Fiction: Picture books: animal, easy-to-read. Young readers: easy-to-read. Middle readers: history, sports. Young adult titles: contemporary, sports.
Nonfiction: Picture books: education, history, nature/environment, sports. Young readers: animal, education, history, nature/environment, sports. Middle readers: animal, education, history, nature/environment, sports.
How to Contact/Writers: "Not accepting any solicitations for at least a year." Fiction/nonfiction: query.
Illustration: Art directors David Werner and Linda Neilson will sometimes review ms/illustration packages submitted by authors/artists or ms/illustration packages submitted by authors with illustrations done by separate artists; will review an illustrator's work for possible use in authors' texts.
How to Contact/Illustrators: Ms/illustration packages: query first.
Terms/Writers & Illustrators: Pays authors in royalties based on retail price.

GREEN TIGER PRESS, INC., 435 E. Carmel St., San Marcos CA 92069. (619)744-7575. Book, calendar and card publisher. Estab. 1970. Publishes 10-15 picture books/year. Also publishes 2-4 calendars and assorted notecards annually.
Fiction: Juvenile and adult picture books. Word length: 250-2,000. Recently published *Shell of Wonder*, by Harwich and Hay; *Sugar Ships*, by Parsley; *A Visit to the Art Galaxy*, by Reiner.
How to Contact/Writers: Fiction: Submit complete ms to Editorial Committee. Reports on queries/mss in 6 months. Publishes a book 12 months after acceptance. Will consider simultaneous submissions.
Illustration: Number of illustrations used for fiction: picture book 12-20. Editorial will review all varieties of ms/illustration packages.
How to Contact/Illustrators: Ms/illustration packages: Send entire ms, prints, slides or color photocopies of illustrations and dummy. Illustrations only: Send prints, slides or color photocopies. Do not send originals of art work. Reports only if interested. Original art work returned at job's completion.
Terms/Writers & Illustrators: Usually pays authors and illustrators a royalty based on retail price. Royalty percentages vary. Book catalog, ms/artist's guidelines free on request.
Tips: "Study the publisher's catalog before submitting." Looking for "32-60 page books — one illustration and one concise paragraph per spread. 'Dreams, visions and fantasies' — not religious or necessarily educational material."

GREENHAVEN PRESS, 10907 Technology Place, San Diego CA 92127. (619)485-7424. Book publisher. Estab. 1970. Senior Editors: Terry O'Neill and Bonnie Szumski. Publishes 40-50 young adult titles/year. 35% of books by first-time authors.

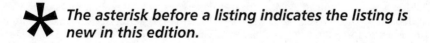 **The asterisk before a listing indicates the listing is new in this edition.**

Nonfiction: Middle readers: biography, history, controversial topics, issues. Young adults: biography, history, nature/environment. Other titles "to fit our specific series." Average word length: young adults—15,000-18,000. Recently published *Custer's Last Stand*, by Deborah Bachrach (grades 8-11); , by Debbie Hitzeroth (grades 7-9); *Irish Potato Famine*, by Don Nardo (grades 7-9).

How to Contact/Writers: Nonfiction: Query. Reports on queries generally in 1-2 weeks. Publishes a book 12-15 months after acceptance.

Terms/Writers: Buys ms outright for $1,500-$2,500. Offers average advance payment of ⅓-½. Sends galleys to authors. Books catalog available for 9 × 12 SAE and 65¢ postage.

Tips: "Get our guidelines first before submitting anything."

HARBINGER HOUSE, INC., 2802 North Alvenon Way, Tucson AZ 85712. (602)326-9595. Publisher: Laurel Gregory. Editor, Children's Books: Jeffrey H. Lockridge. Publishes 4 picture books/year; 2 young reader titles/year; 2-3 middle reader titles/year. 40% of books by first-time authors; 10% of books from agented writers.

Fiction: Picture books: "all kinds." Young readers: adventure, fantasy, history. Middle readers: animal, fantasy, problem novels, science fiction, sports, spy/mystery/adventure. Published *The Marsh King's Daughter*, by Andersen/Gentry (all ages, classic fantasy); *One Green Mesquite Tree*, by Jernigan (ages 3-5, counting rhyme); *Mystery on Mackinac Island*, (ages 8-11).

Nonfiction: Picture books: "all kinds." Young readers: animal, history, nature/environment, geography. Middle readers: animal, biography, history, music/dance, nature/environment, space science, geography. Published *The Reef & the Wrasse*, by Steere & Ring (ages 8-11, natural history); *Out in the Night*, by Liptak (ages 8-11, natural history); *Zoot Zoot Zaggle Splot or, What to Do With A Scary Dream*, (ages 4-8).

How to Contact/Writers: Fiction/nonfiction: Submit outline/synopsis and sample chapters. Reports on queries in 3-4 weeks; on mss in 6-8 weeks. Publishes a book 12-18 months after acceptance. Will consider simultaneous submissions.

Illustration: Average number of illustrations used for fiction: picture books—14; young readers—12; middle readers—12. Number of illustrations used for nonfiction: picture books—14; young readers—20; middle readers—18. Editorial will review all varieties of ms/illustration packages.

How to Contact/Illustrators: "For picture books and young readers only: Minimum of 3 pieces of finished art." Illustrations only: Tearsheets and slides. Reports on art samples in 4 weeks. Original artwork returned at job's completion.

Terms/Writers & Illustrators: Pays authors in royalties based on net receipts. Average advance payment $800-1,000. Factors used to determine final payment for ms/illustration package include "color art vs. black-and-white, and number of illustrations for outright purchase of illustrations for middle titles." Pay for separate authors and illustrators: "royalties split between author and artist." Pay for illustrators: "royalties based on net receipts." Sends galleys to authors; sometimes sends dummies to illustrators. Book catalog free on request.

Tips: Looks for "manuscripts with a particular, well-articulated message or purpose." Illustrators: Looks for "art of imagination and skill that has something special." In children's book publishing there has been "a gradual improvement in the standards of quality in both the ideas and their presentation."

HARCOURT BRACE JOVANOVICH, Children's Books Division which includes: HBJ Children's Books, Gulliver Books, Voyager Paperbacks, Odyssey Paperbacks, Jane Yolen Books, 1250 Sixth Ave., San Diego CA 92101. (619)699-6810. Book publisher. Attention: Manuscript Submissions, Children's Books Division. Publishes 40-45 picture books/year; 15-20 middle reader titles/year; 8-12 young adult titles/year. 20% of books by first-time authors; 50% of books from agented writers.

Fiction: Picture books: animal, contemporary, fantasy, history. Young readers: animal, contemporary, fantasy, history. Middle readers: animal, contemporary, fantasy, history, problem novels, romance, science fiction, sports, spy/mystery/adventure. Young adults: animal, contemporary, fantasy, history, problem novels, romance, science fiction, sports, spy/mystery/adventure. Average word length: picture books—"varies greatly;" middle readers—20,000-50,000; young adults—35,000-65,000.

Nonfiction: Picture books, young readers: animal, biography, history, hobbies, music/dance, nature/environment, religion, sports. Middle readers, young adults: animal, biography, education, history, hobbies, music/dance, nature/environment, religion, sports. Average word length: picture books—"varies greatly;" middle readers—20,000-50,000; young adults—35,000-65,000.

How to Contact/Writers: Fiction/nonfiction: Query; submit outline/synopsis and sample chapters; submit complete ms for picture books only. "Only HBJ Children's Books accepts unsolicited manuscripts." Reports on queries/mss in 6-8 weeks.

Illustration: Number of illustrations used for fiction and nonfiction: picture books—25-30; middle readers—6-12; young adults—jacket. Editorial will review all varieties of ms/illustration packages. Art Director, Children's Books, Michael Farmer, will review an illustrator's work for possible use in separate texts.

How to Contact/Illustrators: Ms/illustration packages: picture books ms—complete ms acceptable. Longer books—outline and 2-4 sample chapters. Send several samples of art; no original art. Illustrations only: Résumé, tearsheets, color photocopies, color stats all accepted. Please DO NOT send original artwork or transparencies. Include SASE for return,.please. Reports on art samples in 6-10 weeks. Original artwork returned at job's completion.

Terms/Writers & Illustrators: Pays authors in royalties based on retail price. Pay for separate writers and illustrators: "separately, usually on advance/royalty basis. Situations vary according to individual projects." Pay for illustrators: by the project. Sends galleys to authors; dummies to illustrators. Book catalog available for 8½×11 SASE; manuscript/artist's guidelines for business-size SASE.

Tips: "Study the field of children's books—go to your local library and book stores. Become acquainted with HBJ's books in particular if you are interested in submitting proposals to us. Our current needs include young adult fiction, nonfiction for all ages, and picture books for the very young."

HARPERCOLLINS CHILDREN'S BOOKS, (formerly Harper & Row Junior Books Group), 10 E. 53rd St., New York NY 10022. (212)207-7044. Contact: Submissions editor. Book publisher.

Fiction: Picture books: animal, sports. Young readers: easy-to-read, sports. Middle readers: adventure, fantasy, history, sports. Young adult titles: contemporary, history, problem novels, sports.

Nonfiction: Picture books, young readers, middle readers, young adult titles: animal, biography, history, music/dance, nature/environment, sports.

How to Contact/Writers: Fiction/nonfiction: query, submit outline/synopsis and sample chapters.

Illustration: Will review ms/illustration packages submitted by authors/artists (preferable to see picture books without art); ms/illustration packages submitted by authors with illustrations done by separate artists; illustrator's work for possible use in authors' texts (no original art, please).

How to Contact/Illustrators: Ms/illustrations packages: query first.

Terms/Writers & Illustrators: Pays authors in royalties based on retail price. Additional payment for ms/illustration packages: if the work is done by one person, he/she will get the full amount of royalty; otherwise it is split between the two.

HARVEST HOUSE PUBLISHERS, 1075 Arrowsmith, Eugene OR 97402. (503)343-0123. Book publisher. Manuscript Coordinator: LaRae Weikert. Publishes 5-6 picture books/year; 3 young reader titles/year; 3 young adult titles/year. 25% of books by first-time authors.

Fiction: Christian theme. Picture books: animal, easy-to-read. Young readers: contemporary, easy-to-read. Middle readers: contemporary, fantasy. Young adults: fantasy, problem novels, romance. Recently published *Sleep Sound in Jesus*, by Michael Card (lullabies/devotions for parents); *God's Little Dreamer*, by Ann Kiemel Anderson (ages 2-12, picture book); *The Lost Princess*, by Karen Mezek (all ages, picture book); *The Great Bible Adventure*, by Sandy Silverthrone (all ages, search-and-find Bible story illustrations).

Nonfiction: Religion: picture books, young readers, middle readers, young adults.

How to Contact/Writers: Fiction/nonfiction: Query; submit outline/synopsis and sample chapters; submit complete ms. Publishes a book 12 months after acceptance. Will consider simultaneous submissions.

Illustration: Number of illustrations used for fiction: picture books—32. Editorial will review all varieties of ms/illustration packages.

How to Contact/Illustrators: Ms/illustration packages: "3 chapters of ms with 1 piece of final art and any approximate rough sketches." Illustrations only: "résumé, tearsheets." Reports on art samples in 2 months. Original artwork returned at job's completion.

Terms/Writers & Illustrators: Pays authors in royalties of 10-15%. Average advance payment: "negotiable." Additional payment for ms/illustration packages. Factors used to determine final payment for ms/illustration package include "color art vs. black-and-white, number of illustrations used, experience of the illustrator, time-frame for completion of work." Pay for separate authors and illustrators: "Shared royalty with illustrator often times receiving an advance." Pay for illustrators: "Sometimes paid by project." Sends galleys to authors; sometimes dummies to illustrators. Book catalog, manuscript/artist's guidelines free on request.

*HAYPENNY PRESS, 211 New St., West Paterson NJ 07424. Book publisher. Publishes 1-2 young adult titles/year. 50% of books by first-time authors.

Fiction: Young adults: anthology (short stories), animal, contemporary, easy-to-read, fantasy, problem novels, science fiction, spy/mystery/adventure. Will also consider middle readers. Recently published *Cooper Street*, by P.D. Jordan (young adult, contemporary problem novel); *Nighthawk!*, by P.D. Jordan (young adult, contemporary adventure).

Nonfiction: Middle readers and young adults/teens: animal, biography, hobbies, music/dance. Average word length: young adults—25,000. Recently published *The Missing Link Guitar Book*, by Tommy Lee Curtis (young adult, music/how-to/hobby).

How to Contact/Writers: Fiction and nonfiction: Query. Reports on queries in 2 weeks; 1 months on mss. Publishes a book up to 1 year after acceptance. Will consider simultaneous submissions.

Illustrations: Reviews all varieties of ms/illustrations packages.

How to Contact/Illustrators: Query first with synopsis and one to three photocopies of artwork. Reports on ms/art samples in 6 weeks. Original artwork returned at job's completion.

"Picture books" are geared toward the preschool—8 year old group; "Young readers" to 5-8 year olds; "Middle readers" to 9-11 year olds; and "Young adults" to those 12 and up.

Terms/Writers & Illustrators: Pays authors in royalties of 20-50% based on wholesale price. Pay for separate authors and illustrators: Separately, usually by royalty but not always. Sends galleys to authors. Manuscript guidelines for 1 first class stamp and #10 SAE.

Tips: "Never talk down to your readers, whatever the age. Get your art out there in as many ways as you can, whether you're paid for it or not. Look into charity, library, school projects. Contact lots of publishers and get your name and samples into their files!"

*HENDRICK-LONG PUBLISHING COMPANY, P.O. Box 25123, Dallas TX 75225. Book publisher. Contact: Joann Long, Vice President. Publishes 1 picture book/year; 4 young reader titles/year; 4 middle reader titles/year. 20% of books by first-time authors.

Fiction: All levels: history books on Texas and the Southwest. Recently published *The Ghost at the Old Stone Fort*, by M.T. Jones (grades 4 and up, mystery with historical background); *Behind Bess, Buddy, and Me*, by Ruby Tolliver (grades 4 and up, adventure with historical background); *Adventure of Jason Jackrabbit*, by M.M. Dee (grades 1-4, nature with factual background).

Nonfiction: All levels: history books on Texas and the Southwest. Recently published *Clues from the Past*, by Texas Archaeological Society (grades 3 to 8, resource book on archaeology); *Dinosaur Deep in Texas*, by Allen and Walker (grades 3 and up, study with pictures of dinosaurs); *Indian Who Lived in Texas*, by Betsy Warren (elementary and junior high, study of the 10 native Texas tribes).

How to Contact/Writers: Fiction and nonfiction: Query with outline/synopsis and sample chapter. Reports on queries in 1 month; mss in 6 weeks. Publishes a book 18 months after acceptance. No simultaneous submissions.

Illustration: Number of illustrations used for fiction and nonfiction: picture books-22; middle readers-11; young readers-11. Editorial will review ms/illustration packages submitted by authors/artists. Will review illustrator's work for possible use in separate author's text.

How to Contact/Illustrators: Query first. Submit résumé, photocopy or tearsheets— no original work sent unsolicited. Reports on ms/art samples in 1 month.

Terms/Writers & Illustrators: Pays authors in royalty based on selling price. Advances vary. Sends galleys to author; dummies to illustrators. Book catalog for $1, 45¢ postage and large SAE; manuscript and artist's guidelines for 1 first class stamp and #10 SAE.

HERALD PRESS, Mennonite Publishing House, 616 Walnut Ave., Scottsdale PA 15683. (412)887-8500. Estab. 1908. Publishes 1 young reader title/year; 2-3 middle reader titles/year; 1-2 young adult titles/year; no picture storybooks. Editorial Contact: S. David Garber. 20% of books by first-time authors; 10% of books from agented writers.

Fiction: Young readers: religious, social problems. Middle readers: religious, social problems. Young adults: religious, social problems. Recently published *The Hard Life of Seymour F. Newton* by Anne Bixby Herald (grades 2-4, coping with learning difficulties); *A Life Apart*, by Shirlee Evans (teen and up, adoption); *Fear Strikes at Midnight*, by Linda K. Jones (grades 3-7, coping with fear of storms; relationships).

Nonfiction: Young readers: religious, social concerns. Middle readers: religious, social concerns. Young adults: religious, social concerns. Recently published *That Very Special Person—Me!*, by Margaret Houk (teen, self-esteem); *A Leap of Faith*, by Peter J. Dyck (teen and up, true stories of service and peace).

How to Contact/Writers: Fiction/nonfiction: Submit outline/synopsis and sample chapters. Reports on queries in 3 weeks; ms in 2 months. Publishes a book in 12 months. Will consider simultaneous submissions but prefer not to.

Illustration: Will review all varieties of ms/illustration packages. Art Director, Jim Butti, will review an illustrator's work for possible use in separate texts.

How to Contact/Illustrators: Illustrations only: Send tearsheets and slides.

Terms/Writers & Illustrators: Pays authors in royalties of 10-12% based on retail price. Pay for illustrators: by the project; $220-600. Sends galleys to authors. Book catalog for 3 first-class stamps; manuscript guidelines free on request.

HOLIDAY HOUSE INC., 425 Madison Ave., New York NY 10017. (212)688-0085. Book publisher. Editorial Contacts: Shannon Maughan, Margery Cuyler. Publishes 30 picture books/year; 7 young reader titles/year; 7 middle reader titles/year; 3 young adult titles/year. 20% of books by first-time authors; 10% from agented writers.

Fiction: Picture book: animal, sports. Young reader: contemporary, easy-to-read, history, sports, spy/mystery/adventure. Middle reader: contemporary, fantasy, history, sports, spy/mystery/adventure. Recently published *Ma and Pa Dracula*, by Ann M. Martin (middle reader, novel); *No Bean Sprouts, Please!*, by Connie Hiser (young reader, chapter book); and *Awfully Short for the 4th Grade*, by Elvira Woodruff (young reader/ middle reader, short novel).

Nonfiction: Picture books: biography, history, sports. Young reader: biography, history, nature/environment, sports. Middle reader: biography, history, nature/environment, sports. Recently published *The White House*, by Leonard E. Fisher (middle reader, historical); *Buffalo Hunt*, by Russell Freedman (middle reader, historical).

How to Contact/Writers: Fiction/nonfiction: Submit complete ms. Reports on queries in 4-6 weeks; on mss in 8-10 weeks. Publishes a book 10 months after acceptance. Will consider simultaneous submissions.

Illustration: Editorial will review all varieties of ms/illustration packages. David Rogers, art director, will review an illustrator's work for possible use in separate texts.

How to Contact/Illustrators: Ms/illustration packages: Query first. Illustrations only: send résumé, and tearsheets. Reports within 6 weeks with SASE or only if interested (if no SASE). Original art work returned at job's completion.

Terms/Writers & Illustrators: Manuscript/artist's guidelines for #10 SAE and 25¢ postage.

HENRY HOLT & CO., INC., 115 W. 18th St., New York NY 10011. (212)886-9200. Book publisher. Editor-in-Chief: Brenda Bowen. Publishes 15-20 picture books/year; 40-60 young reader titles/year; 6 middle reader titles/year; 6 young adult titles/year. 5% of books by first-time authors; 40% of books from agented writers.

Fiction: Recently published *The Empty Pot*, by Demi (ages 4-7, picture book); *The Mozart Season*, by Virginia Euwer Wolff (ages 9-12, fiction).

How to Contact/Writers: Fiction/nonfiction: Submit complete ms. Reports on queries/ mss in 2 months. Publishes a book 12-18 months after acceptance. Will consider simultaneous submissions.

Illustration: Editorial will review all varieties of ms/illustration packages.

How to Contact/Illustrators: Ms/illustration packages: Random samples OK. Illustrations only: Tearsheets, slides. Do *not* send originals. Reports on art samples only if interested. If accepted, original art work returned at job's completion.

Terms/Writers & Illustrators: Pays authors in royalties based on retail price. Pay for illustrators: royalties based on retail price. Sends galleys to authors; dummies to illustrators.

Always include a self-addressed stamped envelope (SASE) or International Reply Coupon (IRC) with submissions.

HOMESTEAD PUBLISHING, Box 193, Moose WY 83012. Book publisher. Editor: Carl Schreier. Publishes 8 picture books/year; 2 young reader titles/year; 2 middle reader titles/year; 2 young adult titles/year. 30% of books by first-time authors; 1% of books from agented writers.

Fiction: Picture books: animal. Young readers: animal. Middle readers: animal. Average word length: young readers—1,000; middle readers—5,000; young adults—5,000. Recently published *The Great Plains: A Young Reader's Journal*, by Bullock (ages 1-8, nature).

Nonfiction: Picture books: animal, biography, history, nature/environment. Young readers: animal, nature/environment. Middle readers: animal, biography, history, nature/environment. Young adults: animal, history, nature/environment. Average word length: young readers—1,000; middle readers—5,000; young adults—5,000. Recently published *Yellowstone: Selected Photographs 1870-1960*, by Simpson (ages 1-adult, history); *Looking at Flowers*, by O'Connor (ages 1-adult, nature); *Yellowstone's Geyser's Hot Springs and Fumaroles*, by Schreier (ages 1-adult, nature).

How to Contact/Writers: Fiction/nonfiction: Query; submit outline/synopsis and sample chapters. Reports on queries/mss in 4 weeks. Publishes a book 1 year after acceptance. Will consider simultaneous submissions.

Illustration: Number of illustrations used for fiction: picture books—70; young readers—50; middle readers—50; young adults—50. Number of illustrations used for nonfiction: picture books—150; young readers—50; middle readers—50; young adults—50. Editorial will review all varieties of ms/illustration packages. Prefers to see "watercolor, opaque, oil" illustrations.

How to Contact/Illustrators: Ms/illustration packages: "Query first with sample writing and art style." Illustrations only: "Resumes, style samples." Reports on art samples in 4 weeks. Original artwork returned at job's completion.

Terms/Writers & Illustrators: Pays authors in royalties of 5-10% based on wholesale price. Outright purchase: "depends on project." Average advance payment: "depends on project." Factors used to determine final payment: "quality and price." Pay for separate authors and illustrators: "split." Pay for illustrators: $50-$10,000/project; 3-10% royalty based on wholesale price. Sends galleys to authors; dummies to illustrators.

HOUGHTON MIFFLIN CO., Children's Trade Books, 2 Park St., Boston MA 02108. Book Publisher. VP/Director: Walter Lorraine. Senior Editor: Matilda Welter; Editor: Mary Lee Donovan. Averages 50-55 titles/year. Publishes hardcover originals and trade paperback reprints (some simultaneous hard/soft).

Fiction: Recently published *The Coolest Place in Town*, by Kathy Caple (ages 4-8, picture book); *Just Plain Penny*, by Pamela Jane (ages 8-12, novel); *Enter Three Witches*, by Kate Gilmore (ages 10-14, young adult novel).

Nonfiction: Recently published *Mummy Took Cooking Lessons and Other Poems*, by John Ciardi (ages 7-12, poetry, illustrated); *Families*, by Aylette Jenness (ages 8-10, social studies, illustrated with photographs); *The Other Victims: First Person Stories of Non-Jews Persecuted by the Nazis*, by Ina Friedman (ages 10-14, history).

How to Contact/Writers: Fiction: Submit complete ms. Nonfiction: Submit outline/synopsis and sample chapters. Reports on queries in 1 month; on mss in 2 months.

How to Contact/Illustrators: Review artwork/photos as part of ms package.

Terms/Writers & Illustrators: Pays standard royalty; offers advance. Book catalog free on request.

Tips: "The growing independant-retail book market will no doubt affect the number and kinds of books we publish in the near future. Booksellers are more informed about children's books today than ever before."

HUMANICS CHILDREN'S HOUSE, Humanics Limited, 1389 Peachtree St., Atlanta GA 30309. (404)874-1930. Book publisher. Acquisitions Editor: Robert Grayson Hall. Publishes 4 picture books/year; 4 young reader titles/year. 85% of books by first-time authors; 30% subsidy published.

Fiction: Picture books: contemporary, easy-to-read, fantasy, spy/mystery/adventure, self-image concentration. Average word length: picture books—250-350. Published *Home at Last*, by Mauro Magellan (ages 1-7, fantasy/fiction); *Max the Apt. Cat*, by Mauro Magellan (ages 1-7, self-image); *Creatures of an Exceptional Kind*, by Dorothy Whitney (ages 1-7).

Nonfiction: "Educational materials, Author-Ph.D, M.A. level, activities, project books." Average word length: picture books—500-600. Published *Lessons From Mother Goose*, by E. Commins (grades 1-6, teacher's aid); *Learning Through Color*, by Penn and Peacock, (grades 1-6, teacher's aid).

How to Contact/Writers: Fiction: Submit outline/synopsis and sample chapters or submit complete ms. Nonfiction: Query; submit outline/synopsis and sample chapters or submit complete ms. Reports on queries/mss in 6 months. Publishes a book 12-18 months after acceptance. Will consider simultaneous and electronic submissions via disk or modem.

Illustration: Number of illustrations used for fiction: picture books—16. Number of illustrations used for nonfiction: picture books—25-80. Editorial will review all varieties of ms/illustration packages.

How to Contact/Illustrators: Ms/illustration packages: Preferably complete ms with 3-4 illustrations. Illustrations only: Résumé, tearsheets. Original artwork returned at job's completion "depending on contract."

Terms/Writers & Illustrators: Pays authors in royalties of 3-10% based on wholesale price. Outright purchase "dependent on ms, previous work." Factors used to determine final payment: "overall ms quality." Pay for separate authors and illustrators: "equally, or through prior agreement between the two. Ideally, prefer authors to be the illustrator for the work." Sends galleys to authors; dummies to illustrators. Book catalog free on request; manuscript/artist's guidelines for regular SAE and 1 first-class stamp.

Tips: Writers: "Have some academic educational background. Ms should be creative, innovative, and have an approach geared toward self-image social, and intellectual development." Illustrators: "Take chances! I like abstract, thought provoking illustrations as well as simple line drawings. (Actually, we prefer the more fantastic, abstract illustrations)."

IDEALS PUBLISHING CORPORATION, Box 140300, Nashville TN 37214. (615)885-8270. Book publisher. Children's Book Editor: Peggy Schaefer. Publishes 50-60 picture books/year; 15-20 young reader titles/year. 5-10% of books by first-time authors; 5-10% of books from agented writers.

Fiction: Picture books: adventure, animal, contemporary, easy-to-read, fantasy, history, problem novels, sports. Young readers: animal, contemporary, easy-to-read, history, sports, spy/mystery/adventure. Average word length: picture books—200-1,200; young readers—1,200-2,400. Recently published *The Easter Story*, by Carol Heyer (ages 4-7, 8×10, hardcover with jacket); *The Moonrat and the White Turtle*, by Helen Ward (ages 4-8, 9½×9½, hardcover with jacket); *Where Has Daddy Gone*, by Trudy Osman, illus. by Joanna Care (ages 2-6, 7¾×8¼, hardcover with jacket).

Nonfiction: Picture books: animal, biography, history, hobbies, music/dance, nature/environment, religion, sports. Young readers: animal, biography, history, hobbies, music/dance, nature/environment, religion, sports. Average word length: picture books—

Refer to the Business of Children's Writing & Illustrating for up-to-date marketing, tax and legal information.

200-1,000; young readers—1,000-2,400. Recently published *The Survival Series: Frog, Mouse, Deer, Fox, Otter, or Squirrel*, (ages 7-12, 7½×10, hardcover); *Let's Build a House*, by Russ Flint (ages 5-10, 8×10, hardcover with jacket).

How to Contact/Writers: Fiction/nonfiction: Submit complete ms. Report on queries/mss in 3-6 months. Publishes a book 18-24 months after acceptance.

Illustration: Number of illustrations used for fiction and nonfiction: picture books—12-18; young readers—12-18. Editorial will review all varities of ms/illustration packages. Preference: No cartoon—tight or loose, but realistic watercolors, acrylics.

How to Contact/Illustrators: Ms/illustration packages: Ms with 1 color photocopy of final art and remainder roughs. Illustrations only: Resume and tearsheets showing variety of styles. Reports on art samples only if interested. "No original artwork, please."

Terms/Writers & Illustrators: "All terms vary according to individual projects and authors/artists."

Tips: "Trend is placing more value on nonfiction and packaging. (i.e., We are not interested in young adult romances.)" Illustrators: "Be flexible in contract terms—and be able to show as much final artwork as possible."

INCENTIVE PUBLICATIONS, INC., 3835 Cleghorn Ave., Nashville TN 37215. (615)385-2934. Editor: Sherri Y. Lewis. 20% of books by first-time authors.

Nonfiction: Young reader/middle reader/young adult: education.

How to Contact/Writers: Nonfiction: Submit outline/synopsis and sample chapters. Reports on queries/mss in 4 weeks. Publishes a book 18 months after acceptance. Will consider simultaneous submissions.

Illustration: Editorial will review all varieties of ms/illustration packages. Susan Eaddy, art director, will review an illustrator's work for possible use in separate texts.

How to Contact/Illustrators: Ms/illustration packages: "Query first." Illustrations only: send "résumé." Reports on ms/art samples in 4 weeks.

Terms/Writers & Illustrators: Pays in royalties or outright purchase. Illustrators paid by the project. Book catalog for SAE and 90¢ postage; ms/artist's guidelines for legal-size SASE.

JALMAR PRESS, Subsidiary of B.L. Winch and Associates, 45 Hitching Post Dr., Rolling Hills Estates CA 90274. (213)547-1240. FAX: (213)547-1644. Book publisher. Estab. 1971. President: B.L. Winch. Publishes 3 picture books and young reader titles/year. 25% of books by first-time authors.

Fiction: Picture book/young readers: animal, fantasy. Average text length: picture book/young reader—80 pages. Recently published *Do I Have To Go To School Today*, *Aliens in My Nest* and *Hoots and Toots and Hairy Brutes*, by L. Shles (picture books/young readers, self-esteem).

How to Contact/Writers: Fiction/nonfiction: Query or submit outline/synopsis and sample chapters. Reports on queries in 4 weeks; on mss in 3 months. Publishes a book 12 months after acceptance. Will consider simultaneous submissions.

Illustration: Editorial will review all varieties of ms/illustration packages.

How to Contact/Illustrators: Ms/illustration packages: Query first. Illustrations only: Send résumé.

Terms/Writers & Illustrators: Pays authors 7-15% royalty based on a combination of wholesale and retail prices. Average advance "varies." Pay for separate authors and illustrators: "split royalty." Pay for illustrators: 7-15% royalty based on combination of wholesale and retail prices. Book catalog free on request.

Tips: Looks for a "positive self-esteem type of book that deals with feelings."

JEWISH PUBLICATION SOCIETY, Room 1339, 60 E. 42 St., New York NY 10165. (212)687-0809. Editor: Alice Belgray. Book publisher.
Fiction: "All must have Jewish content." Picture books: animal, contemporary, easy-to-read. Young readers: contemporary, easy-to-read, problem novels. Middle readers: contemporary, history, problem novels, sports. Young adult titles: contemporary, history, romance (occasionally).
Nonfiction: "All must have Jewish theme." Picture books: history, religion. Young readers: biography, history, religion. Middle readers: biography, history, religion, sports. Young adult titles: biography, history, music/dance, religion.
How to Contact/Writers: Fiction/nonfiction: query, submit outline/synopsis and sample chapters. Will consider simultaneous submissions (please advise).
Illustration: Will review all varieties of ms/illustration packages.
How to Contact/Illustrators: Ms/illustration packages: query first or send three chapters of ms with one piece of final art, remainder roughs. Illustrations only: prefers photocopies of art.
Terms/Writers & Illustrators: Pays authors in royalties based on retail price.

*BOB JONES UNIVERSITY PRESS/LIGHT LINE BOOKS, 1500 Wade Hampton Blvd. Greenville SC 29614. (803)242-5100 ext. 4315. Book publisher. Contact: Gloria Repp, Editor. Publishes 4 picture books/year; 4 young reader titles/year; 4 middle reader titles/year; 2 young adult titles/year. 50% of books by first-time authors.
Fiction: Picture books: animal, contemporary, easy-to-read. Young readers: animal, contemporary, easy-to-read, history, sports, spy/mystery/adventure. Middle readers: animal, contemporary, history, problem novels, sports, spy/mystery/adventure. Young adults/teens: contemporary, history, problem novels, sports, spy/mystery/adventure. Average word length: picture books—1,000-5,000; young readers—20,000; middle readers—30,000; young adult/teens—50,000. Recently published *The Cranky Blue Crab*, by Dawn Watkins (ages 0-6, picture book—animal); *The Treasure of Pelican Cove*, by Milly Howard (grades 2-4, adventure story); *Best of Friends*, by Susan Walley (grades 5-8, contemporary)
Nonfiction: Picture books: animal, nature/environment. Young readers: animal, biography, nature/environment. Middle readers: animal, biography, history, nature/environment. Young adults/teens: biography, history, nature/environment. Average word length: picture books—2,000; young readers—20,000; middle readers—30,000; young adult/teens—50,000. Recently published *With Daring Faith*, by Becky Davis (grades 5-8, biography); *Morning Star of the Reformation*, by Andy Thomson (grades 9-12, biography).
How to Contact/Writers: Fiction: "Send the complete manuscript for these genres: Christian biography, modern realism, historical realism, regional realism and mystery/adventure. Query with a synopsis and five sample chapters for these genres: Fantasy and science fiction (no extra-terrestrials). We do not publish these genres: Romance, poetry and drama." Nonfiction: Query, submit complete manuscript or submit outline/synopsis and sample chapters. Reports on queries in 3 weeks; mss in 2 months. Publishes book "approximately one year" after acceptance. Will consider simultaneous and electronic submissions via disk or modem.
Terms/Writers & Illustrators: Buys ms outright for $500-1,000. Sends galleys to author. Book catalog and ms guidelines free on request.
Tips: "Write something fresh and unique to carry a theme of lasting value. We publish only books with high moral tone, preferably with strong evangelical Christian content. Stories for the *Light Line* should reflect the highest Christian standards of thought, feeling and action. The text should make no reference to drinking, smoking, profanity or minced oaths. Other unacceptable story elements include unrelieved suspense, sensationalism and themes advocating secular attitudes of cynicism, rebellion or materialism."

■**JORDAN ENTERPRISES PUBLISHING CO.**, (formerly Scojtia Publishing Co., Inc.), 6457 Wilcox Station, Box 38002, Los Angeles CA 90038. Book publisher. Estab. 1989. Managing Editor: Patrique Quintahlen. Publishes 2 picture books/year; 1 young reader title/year; 1 middle reader title/year; 1 young adult title/year. 90% of books by first-time authors; 50% of books from agented writers; 1% subsidy published.

Fiction: Picture books: animal, contemporary, easy-to-read. Young adults: history, problem novels, romance, science fiction, sports, spy/mystery/adventure. Average word length: picture books—2,000; young readers—3,000; middle readers—2,500; young adults—20,000. Recently published *Reuben, The Boy Who Opened Doors* (ages 7-14, novel—juvenile); *The Boy Who Opened Doors* (picture book); The Boy and the Boss' Breakfast (ages 7-14, novel—juvenile); all by Prentiss Van Daves.

How to Contact/Writers: Fiction/nonfiction: Query; submit outline/synopsis and sample chapters. Reports on queries/mss in 4 months. Publishes a book 12 months after acceptance. Will consider simultaneous and electronic submissions via disk or modem.

Illustration: Number of illustrations used for fiction and nonfiction: picture books—25; young readers—25; middle readers—8; young adults—8. Editorial will review ms/ illustration packages.

How to Contact/Illustrators: Ms/illustration packages: Query first. Illustrations only: Résumé, tearsheets. Reports on art samples in 4 months. Original artwork returned at job's completion.

Terms/Writers & Illustrators: Pays authors in royalties of 4-8% based on retail price. Buys ms outright for $20-$200. Offers average advance payment of $500. Factors used to determine final payment include number of illustrations. Pay for separate authors and illustrators: According to the terms of contract for each, author's contract, illustrator's contract, for project. Pay for illustrators: By the project, $60-$600 or 1 to 2% royalties for juvenile novels. Sends galleys to authors; dummies to illustrators.

Tips: Writers: "Children love action, characters that touch on emotions that they feel but cannot explain, except by play; and by pretending to be, for a moment, such likeable characters. Create realistic characters that children will love, even the child in all of us. There is a growing need for children's books for 12 and up that deal more with acceptable roles for children in the new American family." Illustrators: "Here it is necessary to remember that with your imagination you can do anything; but it is also important to be organized with a stock of your best work that you perfect and keep in a portfolio."

JOY STREET BOOKS, Imprint of Little, Brown and Company, 34 Beacon St., Boston MA 02108. (617)227-0730. Editor-in-Chief: Melanie Kroupa. Publishes 20-25 picture books/year; 5-10 young reader/middle reader/young adult titles/year.

How to Contact/Writers: Fiction/nonfiction: Submit outline/synopsis and sample chapters or submit complete ms. Reports on queries in 2-4 weeks; on mss in 4-8 weeks. Publishes a book 18 months after acceptance. Will consider simultaneous submissions.

Terms/Writers: Pays authors in royalties or outright purchase. Book catalog for 8 × 10 SASE; ms guidelines for legal-size SASE.

JUST US BOOKS, INC., Imprint of Afro-Bets Series, Suite 22-24, 301 Main St., Orange NJ 07050. (201)672-7701. FAX: (201)677-7570. Book publisher; "for selected titles" book packager. Estab. 1987. Vice President/Publisher: Cheryl Willis Hudson. Publishes 3-4 picture books/year; "projected 4" young reader/middle reader titles/year. 33% books by first-time authors.

 The solid block before a listing indicates the market subsidy publishes manuscripts.

Fiction: Picture books: easy-to-read, African-American themes. Young readers: contemporary, history, African-American themes. Middle reader: history, sports. Average word length: "varies" per picture book; young reader—500-2,000; middle reader—5,000. Recently published *Afro-Bets Coloring & Activity Book*, by Dwayne Ferguson (pre-kindergarten-3rd, picture/concept); *Bright Eyes, Brown Skin*, illus. by George Ford (ages 6-9, picture book); *Jamal's Busy Day*, illus. by Wade Hudson, (ages 6-9, picture book).

Nonfiction: Picture book: African-American themes; young reader: biography, history, African-American themes; middle reader: biography, history, African-American themes. Recently published *Book of Black Heroes from A to Z*, by Wade Hudson and Valerie Wilson Wesley (biography for young and middle readers); *Black History Handbook*, by Just Us Books editors (grades 3-12).

How to Contact/Writers: Fiction/nonfiction: Query or submit outline/synopsis for proposed title. Include Social Security number with submission. Reports on queries in 2-3 weeks; on ms in 8 weeks "or as soon as possible." Publishes a book 12-18 months after acceptance. Will consider simultaneous submissions (with prior notice).

Illustration: Number of illustrations used for fiction: picture book—12-24; for nonfiction: young reader—25-30. Editorial department will review ms/illustration packages submitted by authors/artists and illustrator's work for possible use in separate texts.

How to Contact/Illustrators: Ms/illustration packages: "Query first." Illustrations only: Send résumé, tearsheets, and slides. Reports in 2-3 weeks. Original artwork returned at job's completion "depending on project."

Terms/Writers & Illustrators: Pays authors a "flat fee and royalty depending on project." Royalties based on retail price. Factors to determine final payment include color art vs. black-and-white and number of illustrations used. Separate authors and illustrators are paid via "negotiated fees." Sends galleys to author; dummies to illustrator. Book catalog for business-size SAE and 25-65¢ postage; ms/artist's guidelines for business-size SAE and 25¢ postage.

Tips: Writers: "Keep the subject matter fresh and lively. Avoid "preachy" stories with stereotyped characters. Rely more on authentic stories with sensitive three-dimensional characters." Illustrators: "Submit 5-10 good, neat samples. Be willing to work with an art director for the type of illustration desired by a specific house and grow into larger projects."

KAR-BEN COPIES, INC., 6800 Tildenwood Lane, Rockville MD 20852. (301)984-8733. Book publisher. Estab. 1975. Editor: Madeline Wikler. Publishes 10 picture books/year; 10 young reader titles/year. 20% of books by first-time authors.

Fiction: Picture books: Jewish Holiday, Jewish storybook. Average word length: picture books—2,000. Recently published *My Brother's Bar Mitzvah*, by Janet Gallant (ages 6-8); *Sophie's Name*, by Phyllis A Grode (ages 5-8); *Bible Heroes I Can Be*, by Ann Eisenberg (ages 5-8); all picture books.

Nonfiction: Picture books: religion-Jewish interest. Average word length: picture books—2,000. Recently published *All About Hanukkah*, by Groner/Wikler (grades K-5, picture book); *Kids Love Israel*, by Barbara Sofer (adult, family travel guide); *Alef Is One*, by Katherine Kahn (grades K-3, a Hebrew counting book).

How to Contact/Writers: Fiction/nonfiction: Submit complete ms. Reports on queries in 3 weeks; ms in 6 weeks. Publishes a book 1 year after acceptance. Will consider simultaneous submissions. "We don't like them, but we'll look at them—as long as we *know* it's a simultaneous submission."

Illustration: Number of illustrations used for fiction: picture books—15. Number of illustrations used for nonfiction: picture books—10. Editorial will review all varieties of ms/illustration packages. Prefers "4-color art to any medium that is scannable."

How to Contact/Illustrators: Ms illustration packages: Send whole ms and sample of art (no originals). Illustrations only: Tearsheets, photocopies or anything representative that does *not* need to be returned. Reports on art samples in 4 weeks.

Terms/Writers & Illustrators: Pays authors in royalties of 5-10% based on net sales. Offers average advance payment of $1,000. Pay for separate authors and illustrators: "both get advance and equal royalties." Sends galleys to authors. Book catalog free on request. Ms guidelines for #10 SAE and 1 first class stamp.

Tips: Looks for "books for young children with Jewish interest and content, modern, non-sexist, not didactic. Fiction or nonfiction with a *Jewish* theme—can be serious or humorous, life cycle, Bible story, or holiday—related."

KENDALL GREEN PUBLICATIONS, imprint of Gallaudet University Press, 800 Florida Ave. NE, Washington DC 20002. (202)651-5488. Book publisher. Estab. 1980. Editor, Children's Books: Robyn D. Twito. Publishes 2-3 picture books/year; 2-3 young reader titles/year; 1-2 middle reader titles/year; 1-2 young adult titles/year. 75% of books by first-time authors. All titles deal with hearing loss or deafness.

Fiction: Picture books, young readers: contemporary. Middle readers, young adults: contemporary, problem novels, spy/mystery/adventure. Average word length: picture books—50; young readers—1,300; middle readers—26,000; young adults—52,000. Recently published *Little Red Riding Hood Told in Signed English*, by Harry Bornstein and Karen L. Saulnier (picture book); *Hasta Luego, San Diego*, by Jean Andrews (middle readers, mystery); *Annie's World*, by Nancy Smiler Levinson (young adults, problem).

Nonfiction: Picture books; young readers: sign language. Middle readers; young adults: biography, history, sign language. Average word length: picture books—50; young readers—1,300; middle readers—26,000; young adults—52,000. Recently published *My Signing Book of Opposites*, by Pamela Baker, forthcoming (picture book, sign language); *Buffy's Orange Leash*, by Stephen Golder and Lise Memling (young readers, informational); *Clerc: Portrait of a Deaf Teacher as a Youth*, by Cathryn Carroll (young adults, biography).

How to Contact/Writers: Fiction/nonfiction: submit outline/synopsis and sample chapters; submit complete ms. Reports on queries/mss in 4-8 weeks. Publishes a book 10-18 months after acceptance. Will consider simultaneous submissions.

Illustration: Number of illustrations used for fiction: young readers—32; middle readers—1-5; young adults—1-5. Number of illustrations used for nonfiction: picture books—30-40; young readers—32; middle readers—20; young adults—5. Editorial will review all varieties of ms/illustration packages.

How to Contact/Illustrators: Ms/illustration packages: Full ms with 2 finished pieces, remainder roughs. Illustrations only: Tearsheets, finished art, résumé. Reports on art samples in 4 weeks. Original artwork returned at job's completion.

Terms/Writers & Illustrators: Pays authors in royalties of 10-15% based on net price. Factors used to determine final payment: number of illustrations, color vs. black and white. Pay for separate authors and illustrators: Split royalty. Pay for illustrators: by the project; royalties of 5% based on net price. Send galleys to authors; sometimes dummies to illustrators. Manuscript guidelines free with SASE.

Tips: "All books published by Kendall Green Publications have to be related to hearing loss. This includes sign language books, books explaining hearing loss, and fiction with hearing-impaired character(s)."

KINGSWAY PUBLICATIONS, 1 St. Anne's Rd., Eastbourne, E. Sussex BN21 3UN England. (011-44)323-410930. Book publisher. Managing Editor: Elizabeth Gibson. Editorial contact (picture books): T. Collins. Editorial contact (young reader titles): R. Herkes. Editorial contacts (middle reader/young adult titles): R. Herkes/E. Gibson. Publishes 4-6 picture books/year; 1-2 young reader titles/year; 6 middle reader titles/year; 2-4 young adult titles/year. 25% of books by first-time authors; very few through agents.

Fiction: Picture book: contemporary, easy-to-read, "religious content." Young reader: animal, contemporary, easy-to-read, "religious content." Middle reader: animal, contemporary, easy-to-read, fantasy, science fiction, "religious content." Young adult: contemporary, easy-to-read, fantasy, problem novels, romance, science fiction, spy/mystery/adventure, "religious content." Average word length: picture book—700; young reader—20,000-60,000; middle reader—20,000-60,000; young adult—60,000. Recently published *The Will of Dargan*, by Phil Allcock (middle reader/young adult, fantasy—UK orig.); *Summer Promise*, by Robin Gunn (young adult, romance—US orig.); *The Book & the Phoenix*, by Cherith Baldry (middle reader/young adult, fantasy—UK orig.).

Nonfiction: Picture book/young reader/middle reader/young adult: religion. Young adult: biography, music/dance. Recently published *AIDS and Young People*, by P. Dixon (young adult, medical/ethics/faith); *Knowing God's Will*, by P. Miller (young adult, faith journey); *When Your Rope Breaks*, by S. Brown (young adult, self-help/psych/humor).

How to Contact/Writers: Fiction/nonfiction: Submit outline/synopsis and sample chapters. Reports on queries/mss in 2-8 weeks. Publishes a book 12-24 months after acceptance.

Illustration: Number of illustrations used for fiction: young readers—8+; middle readers—8+; young adult—0-6. Editorial will review ms/illustration packages submitted by authors with illustrations done by separate artists.

KNOPF BOOKS FOR YOUNG READERS, Random House, Inc., 8th Floor, 225 Park Ave., South, New York NY 10003. (212)254-1600. Book publisher. Estab. 1915. Publisher: J. Schulman; Associate Publisher: S. Spinner. 90% of books published through agents.

Fiction: Upmarket picture books: retellings of folktales, original stories. Middle-grade readers: realistic fiction, some fantasy, science fiction, Young adult titles: Very selective; few being published currently. Recently published titles: *Mirandy and Brother Wind*, by Patricia McKissack (ages 4-8, picture book); *There's a Boy in the Girl's Bathroom*, by Louis Sachar (ages 9-11, middle-grade novel); *Shabanu*, by Suzanne Staples (ages 11-15, young adult novel).

Nonfiction: Middle grade social studies books. Recently published titles: *Viet Nam: Why We Fought*, by D.T. Hoobler (10 and up, middle grade); *Round Buildings, Square Buildings*, and *Buildings that Wiggle Like a Fish*, by Philip Issaacson (8 and up, middle grade, architecture).

How to Contact/Writers: Fiction/nonfiction: submit through agent only. Publishes a book in 12-18 months. Will consider simultaneous submissions.

Illustration: Will review ms/illustration packages submitted by authors/artists (through agent only); ms/illustration packages submitted by authors with illustrations done by separate artists (through agent only). Art Director will review an illustrator's work for possible use in separate texts.

Terms/Writers & Illustrators: Pays authors in royalties. Book catalog free on request.

KRUZA KALEIDOSCOPIX, INC., Box 389, Franklin MA 02038. (508)528-6211. Book publisher. Picture Books Editor: Jay Kruza. Young/middle readers editorial contact: Russ Burbank. Publishes 8 picture books/year; 1 young reader title/year; 1 middle reader title/year. 50% of books by first-time authors.

Fiction: Picture books: animal, fantasy, history. Young readers: animal, fantasy, history. Average word length: picture books—200-500; young readers—500-2,000; middle readers—1,000-10,000.

Nonfiction: Picture books: animal, history, nature/environment. Young readers: animal, history, nature/environment, religion. Middle readers: biography, sports.

How to Contact/Writers: Fiction/nonfiction: Query; submit outline/synopsis and sample chapters; submit complete ms. Reports on queries/mss in 2-8 weeks.

Illustration: Number of illustrations used for fiction: 20-36. Art Editor, Brian Sawyer, will review an illustrator's work for possible use in separate texts. Prefers to see "realistic" illustrations.

How to Contact/Illustrators: Illustrations only: "actual work sample and photos." Reports on art samples only if interested.
Terms/Writers & Illustrators: Pays authors in royalties of 3-5% based on wholesale price; buys ms outright for $250-$500. Additional payment for ms/illustrations package. Pay for illustrators: $25-$200/illustration. Manuscript/artist's guidelines available for #10 SASE.
Tips: Writers: "Rework your story several times before submitting it without grammatical or spelling mistakes. *Our company charges a $3 reading fee per manuscript* to reduce unprepared manuscripts." Illustrators: "Submit professional looking samples for file. The correct manuscript may come along." Wants ms/illustrations "that teach a moral. Smooth prose that flows like poetry is preferred. The story will be read aloud. Vocabulary and language should fit actions. Short staccato words connote fast action; avoid stories that solve problems by the 'wave of a wand' or that condone improper behavior. Jack of Beanstalk fame was a dullard, a thief and even a murderer. We seek to purchase all rights to the story and artwork. Payment may be a lump sum in cash. For stronger mss., a royalty arrangement based on actual books sold for a period of seven years may be the payment."

LERNER PUBLICATIONS CO., 241 First Ave. N., Minneapolis MN 55401. (612)332-3344. Book publisher. Editor: Jennifer Martin. Publishes 15 young reader titles/year; 25 middle reader titles/year; 30 young adult titles/year. 20% of books by first-time authors; 5% of books from agented writers.
Fiction: Middle readers: contemporary, history, science fiction, sports, mystery. Young adults: contemporary, history, science fiction, sports, mystery. "Especially interested in books with ethnic characters." Recently published *A Flight of Angels*, by Geoffrey Trease (grades 4-8, mystery).
Nonfiction: Young readers: animal, biography, history, nature/environment, sports, science, social studies, geography, social issues. Middle readers: animal, biography, history, nature/environment, sports, science, social studies, geography, social issues. Young adults: animal, biography, history, nature/environment, sports, science, social studies, geography, social issues. Average word length: young readers—3,000; middle readers—7,000; young adults—12,000. Recently published *Understanding Mental Illness*, by Julie Johnson (grades 6 and up, social issues); *Here's to Ewe*, by Diane Burns and Dan Scholten (grades 1-4, riddles/reading skills); *Wayne Gretzky*, by Thomas R. Raber (grades 4-9, sports).
How to Contact/Writers: Fiction: Submit outline/synopsis and sample chapters. Nonfiction: Query; submit outline/synopsis and sample chapters. Reports on queries in 1 month; on mss in 2 months. Publishes a book 12 months after acceptance. Will consider simultaneous submissions.
Terms/Writers: Sends galleys to authors. Book catalog available for 9×12 SAE and $1 postage; manuscript guidelines for 4×9 SAE and 1 first-class stamp.
Tips: "Before you send your manuscript to us, you might first take a look at the kinds of books that our company publishes. We specialize in publishing high-quality educational books for children from preschool through high school. Avoid sex stereotypes (e.g., strong, aggressive, unemotional males/weak, submissive, emotional females) in your writing, as well as sexist language." (See also Carolrhoda Books, Inc.)

LIGUORI PUBLICATIONS, 1 Liguori Dr., Liguori MO 63057-9999. (314)464-2500. FAX: (314)464-8449. Book publisher. Estab. 1947. Editor-in-Chief: Rev. David Polek, C.S.S.R. Managing Editor: Audrey Vest. Publishes 1 middle reader title/year; 3 young adult titles/year. 10% of books by first-time authors.
Nonfiction: Young readers, middle readers, young adults: religion. Average word length: young readers—10,000; young adults—15,000. Recently published *In My Heart Room, Book II*, by Mary Therese Donze (primary, prayer/spirituality); *150 Fun Facts Found in the Bible*, by Bernadette Snyder (middle grade/young adult, scripture).

How to Contact/Writers: Nonfiction: Query; submit outline/synopsis and sample chapters. Include Social Security number with submission. Reports on queries in 6 weeks; on mss in 6-8 weeks. Publishes a book 12 months after acceptance. Will consider electronic submissions via disk or modem.
Illustration: Number of illustrations used for nonfiction: young readers—40. Editorial will review ms/illustration packages submitted by authors/artists and ms/illustration packages submitted by authors with illustrations done by separate artists.
How to Contact/Illustrators: Ms/illustration packages: Query first.
Terms/Writers & Illustrators: Pays authors in royalties of 9% based on retail price. Book catalog available for 9×12 SAE and 3 first-class stamps; manuscript guidelines for #10 SAE and 1 first-class stamp.
Tips: Ms/illustrations "must be religious and suitable to a Roman Catholic audience."

LION BOOKS, PUBLISHER, Imprint of Sayre Ross Co., Suite B, 210 Nelson, Scarsdale NY 10583. (914)725-2280. Book publisher. Editorial contact: Harriet Ross. Publishes 2 picture books/year; 5 middle reader titles/year; 10 young adult titles/year. 50-70% of books by first-time authors.
Fiction: History, sports. Average word length: middle reader—30,000-35,000; young adult—40,000-50,000.
Nonfiction: Biography, history, sports, black nonfiction. Average word length: young adult—50,000. Recently published *Ghosts and Scary Stories*, by Liss; *Great Black Inventors*, by Liss.
How to Contact/Writers: Fiction/nonfiction: Query, submit complete ms. Reports on queries in 1 month; on ms in 2 months.
How to Contact/Illustrators: Reports in 2 weeks.
Terms/Writers and Illustrators: Pays in outright purchase—$250-5,000. Average advance: $750-4,000. Separate authors and illustrators work "for hire or paid a royalty arrangement, unless contracted independent of each other." Illustrators paid $250-5,000. Sends galleys to author. Book catalog is free on request.

LION PUBLISHING CORPORATION, 1705 Hubbard Ave., Batavia IL 60510. (708)879-0707. Book publisher. Estab. 1971. Editorial Contact: Bob Bittner. Publishes 2 picture books/year; 2-4 young reader titles/year; 2-4 middle reader titles/year; 2-4 young adult titles. 1% of books by first-time authors.
Fiction: Picture books: animal, contemporary, fantasy. Young readers: animal, contemporary, fantasy. Middle readers: contemporary, fantasy, history. Young adults: contemporary, fantasy, history, problem novels, science fiction. Average word length: picture books and young readers—1,000; middle readers—25,000; young adults—40,000. Recently published *The Tale of Three Trees,* by Angela Hunt, (4 and up, picture book, folktale); *Midnight Blue*, by Pauline Fisk (10-16, young adults, fantasy); *The Tale of Anabelle Hedgehog*, by Stephen Lawhead (9-14, middle readers, fantasy).
Nonfiction: Picture books: animal, nature/environment, religion. Middle readers: biography, history, nature/environment, religion. Young readers: nature/environment, religion. Young adults: nature/environment, religion. Average word length: picture books and young readers—1,000; middle readers and young adults—"varies." Recently published *Caring for Planet Earth* by Lucas/Holland (8-12, ecological concerns); *365 Children's Prayers* by Carol Watson (4-12, prayers).
How to Contact/Writers: Fiction: Submit complete ms. Nonfiction: Submit outline/synopsis and sample chapters. Reports on queries in 4 weeks; mss in 8 weeks. Publishes a book 18 months after acceptance.
Illustration: Editorial will review ms/illustration packages submitted by authors/artists and ms/illustration packages submitted by authors with illustrations done by separate artists.

How to Contact/Illustrators: Ms/illustration packages: "Query first."
Terms/Writers & Illustrators: Pays authors in variable royalties based on wholesale price. Sometimes buys ms outright. Book catalog/manuscript guidelines for 2 first-class stamps.
Tips: "Lion publishes Christian books for the general reader. A writer should carefully study our guidelines before submitting manuscripts or querying. We are always looking for well-written nonfiction for children. We see too many retold Bible stories, evergreens that want to be Christmas trees, allegories using 'cutesy' animals and rhyming stories. Nonfiction for middle readers and young adults would be most welcome."

LITTLE, BROWN AND COMPANY, 34 Beacon St., Boston MA 02108. (617)227-0730. Book publisher. Editor-in-Chief: Maria Modugno. Editor: Stephanie O. Lurie. Estab. 1837. Publishes 30% picture books/year; 10% young reader titles/year; 30% middle reader titles/year; 10% young adult titles/year. 10% of books by first-time authors; 50% of books from agented writers.
Fiction: Picture books: animal, contemporary, fantasy, history, problem novels, sports, spy/mystery/adventure. Young readers: contemporary, fantasy, history, problem novels, sports, spy/mystery/adventure. Middle readers: animal, contemporary, fantasy, history, problem novels, sports, spy/mystery/adventure. Young adults: animal, contemporary, fantasy, history, problem novels, sports, spy/mystery/adventure. Average word length: picture books—1,000; young readers—6,000; middle readers—15,000-25,000; young adults—20,000-40,000. Recently published *Ruby*, by Michael Emberley (ages 3-8, picture book); *The Tinderbox*, by Barry Moser (all ages, picture book); *The Dragonling*, by Jackie Koller (ages 7-9, first chapter book); *The Day That Elvis Came to Town*, by Jan Marino (ages 10 and up, young adult novel).
Nonfiction: Average word length: picture books—2,000; young readers—4,000-6,000; middle readers—15,000-25,000; young adults—20,000-40,000. Recently published *Make Your Own Animated Movies and Videotapes*, by Yvonne Andersen (ages 10 and up, young adult); *Dawn to Dusk in the Galapagos*, by Rita Gelman (ages 3-8, picture book).
How to Contact/Writers: Fiction: Submit complete ms. Nonfiction: Submit outline/synopsis and 3 sample chapters. Reports on queries in 6 weeks; on mss in 6-8 weeks. Publishes a book 18 months after acceptance. Will consider simultaneous submissions.
Illustration: Number of illustrations used for fiction: picture books—32; young readers—8-10; middle readers—1-5; young adults—1. Number of illustrations used for nonfiction: picture books—32; young readers—32-48; middle readers—1; young adults—1. Editorial will review ms/illustration packages submitted by authors/artists and ms/illustration packages submitted by authors with illustrations done by separate artists. Art director will review illustrator's work for possible use in author's texts.
How to Contact/Illustrators: Ms/illustration packages: complete ms with 1 piece of final art. Illustrations only: Slides. Reports on art samples in 6-8 weeks. Original art work returned at job's completion.
Terms/Writers & Illustrators: Pays authors in royalties based on retail price. Offers average advance payment of $2,000-10,000. Sends galleys to authors; dummies to illustrators. Book catalog, manuscript/artist's guidelines free on request.

LODESTAR BOOKS, Affiliate of Dutton Children's Books, a division of Penguin Books, USA, Inc., 375 Hudson St., New York NY 10014. (212)366-2627. FAX: (212)366-2011. Estab. 1980. Editorial Director: Virginia Buckley. Senior Editor: Rosemary Brosnan. Publishes 5 picture books/year; 15-20 middle reader titles/year; 5 young adult titles/year (30 books a year). 5-10% of books by first-time authors; 50% through agents.
Fiction: Picture books: animal, contemporary, history. Middle reader: contemporary, fantasy, history, science fiction, sports, spy/mystery/adventure. Young adult: contemporary, fantasy, history, science fiction, sports, spy/mystery/adventure. Recently published *A Promise to Keep*, by Eileen Van Kirk (ages 12 and up, novel about WWII); *Fast Talk*

on a Slow Track, by Rita Williams-Garcia (ages 12 and up, novel about young Black man); and *Among the Volcanoes*, by Omar Castaneda (ages 12 and up, novel set in Guatemala).

Nonfiction: Picture books: animal, history, nature/environment. Young reader: animal, history, nature/environment, sports. Middle reader: biography, history, nature/environment, sports. Young adult: biography, history, nature/environment, sports. Recently published *Stamps! A Young Collector's Guide*, by Brenda Lewis (ages 10-14, guide to stamp collecting); *Vietnam: A War on Two Fronts*, by Sidney Lens (ages 12 and up, history of war in Vietnam); and *Behind the Blue and Gray: The Soldier's Life in the Civil War*, by Delia Ray (ages 10-14, Civil War series).

How to Contact/Writers: Fiction: submit outline/synopsis and sample chapters or submit complete ms. Nonfiction: Query or submit outline/synopsis and sample chapters. Reports on queries in 4 weeks; on mss in 8-12 weeks. Publishes a book 12 months after acceptance. Will consider simultaneous submissions.

Illustration: Number of illustrations used for fiction: picture book—16-20; middle reader—10. Number of illustrations (photographs) used for nonfiction: 30-50. Editorial will review illustrator's work for possible use in separate texts.

How to Contact/Illustrators: Ms/illustration packages: Send "manuscript and copies of art (no original art, please)." Illustrations only: Send tearsheets. Reports back only if interested. Original art work returned at job's completion.

Terms/Writers & Illustrators: Pays authors and illustrators in royalties of 5% each for picture books; 8% to author, 2% to illustrator for illustrated novel; and 10% for novel based on retail price. Factors used to determine final payment forms/illustration package include "color art vs. black-and-white and number of illustrations used." Pays for separate authors and illustrators: separate advances and royalties. Sends galleys to author. Book catalog for SASE; manuscript guidelines for #10 SAE and 1 first class stamp.

LOTHROP, LEE & SHEPARD BOOKS, div. and imprint of William Morrow Co. Inc., Children's Fiction and Nonfiction, 105 Madison Ave., New York NY 10016. (212)889-3050. Editor-in-Chief: Susan Pearson. Publishes 60 total titles/year.

Fiction: Picture books: across the board. Young and middle readers: contemporary, easy-to-read, fantasy, history, mystery, humor. Young adults: contemporary, fantasy, history, mystery, humor.

Nonfiction: Picture books, young readers, middle readers, young adults: animal, biography, science, history, music/dance, nature/environment.

How to Contact/Writers: Fiction and nonfiction: Query, "no unsolicited mss."

Illustration: Editorial will review ms/illustration packages submitted by authors/artists and ms/illustration packages submitted by authors with illustrations done by separate artists.

How to Contact/Illustrators: Ms/illustration packages: Write for guidelines first.

Terms/Writers & Illustrators: Methods of payment: "varies." Manuscript/artist's guidelines free for SASE.

LUCAS/EVANS BOOKS, 1123 Broadway, New York NY 10010. (212)929-2583. Executive Director: Barbara Lucas. Estab. 1984. Book packager specializing in children's books, preschool to high school age. Books prepared from inception to camera-ready mechanicals for all major publishers.

Fiction/Nonfiction: Particularly interested in series ideas, especially for middle grades and beginning readers. Recently published fiction titles: *Sing for a Gentle Rain*, by Alison James (YA, fantasy (Atheneum)); *Rosie Runs Away*, by Maryann MacDonald (preschool, picture book (series) Atheneum). Recently published nonfiction titles: *And Then There Was One* (series), by Margery Facklam (middle, nonfiction—Sierra Club); *Los Navidads*, by Lulu Dulacre (preschool, nonfiction—Scholastic).

Close-up

Maria Modugno
Editor-in-Chief
(Children's Division) Little, Brown & Co
Boston, Massachusetts

"I have friends who are children and I talk to all kinds of children to see what their concerns and interests are," says Maria Modugno as she explains her unorthodox market research system. As a general rule, no formal market research is done for children's book publishing, so Modugno does her own research to be aware of what children like to read. "When I look at manuscripts, I look to see what personally interests me now and what would have interested me as a child," she adds.

Despite this departure from conventional practice in the area of marketing, steps taken in reviewing manuscripts and editing material for children are similar to those employed with adult works. "When reading a manuscript I look for good writing," insists Modugno. "The writing needs to be good for the intended audience. In this respect evaluating a children's manuscript is no different than evaluating an adult manuscript."

Modugno began her career in publishing working on adult books at Harcourt Brace Jovanovich. Eventually, to her great surprise, she was asked to establish their children's division. "Working with children's books came to me more by accident than design," says Modugno.

"The young adult market is not very strong now. I want to get away from the 'problem' novels," says Modugno. "I am very selective about novels I take on for children. I look for strong characters, real texture and depth of literary merit. I look for manuscripts that will amuse and entertain children, but if it happens to teach them something along the way, that's fine.

"Specifically I look for authentic books with multi-cultural themes," says Modugno. "I look for people writing from their own cultural experiences, especially from the Mexican-American or Asian-American perspective. For beginning readers, trends are leaning toward featuring a variety of multi-ethnic children as casts of characters are becoming more varied within each book."

Modugno says an unfortunate trend in young children's picture books is very beautiful art work with a so-so story. "Children crave stories, not just a mood piece or an isolated incident."

Usually intrigued by everything she sees in children's bookstores, Modugno doesn't see any areas in the market that are overdone. However, she maintains that writers should study the market a bit to make sure they are not sending inappropriate material.

"I love to see writers striving to send us something that is fresh and different," says Modugno. "If writers write from memories of their own experiences, the good writing will translate from their experiences to the kids of the 90's.

"Artists should work on developing a strong portfolio to show off their different styles," says Modugno. "It would be helpful to see illustrators who have made up a book dummy to show their style. If an illustrator practices a series of illustrations and shows them to me I can see how these same drawings would translate into a children's book. Too often artists don't demonstrate their ability to keep within character throughout the entire book."

Modugno declines to express a preference for any one particular style of book, noting, "As many different books as there are out there, there are as many different readers. As long as kids get hooked into a reading habit, eventually they will gravitate to the 'good stuff.' "

—Marcy Knopf

How to Contact/Writers: Query. SASE for return of ms.
Illustration: Portfolios reviewed (bring, do not mail, original art). Color photo copies of art welcome for our file. Art not necessary to accompany mss unless artist professionally trained.
Terms/Writers & Illustrators: Royalty-based contracts with advance.
Tips: Prefer experienced authors and artists but will consider unpublished work. "There seems to be an enormous demand for early chapter books, although we will continue our efforts to sell to publishers in all age groups and formats. We are interested in series since publishers look to packagers for producing time-consuming projects."

LUCENT BOOKS, Sister Company to Greenhaven Press, Box 289011, San Diego CA 92128-9009. (619)485-7424. Book publisher. Editor: Bonnie Szumski. "We published 32 books for 1990 and are projecting over 60 in 1991." 50% of books by first-time authors; 10% of books from agented writers.
Nonfiction: Middle readers (grades 5-8): education, topical history, nature/environment, sports, "any overviews of specific topics—i.e., political, social, cultural, economic, criminal, moral issues." Average word length: 15,000-20,000. Recently published *Garbage*, by Karen O'Connor (grades 5-8, overview); *Special Effects in the Movies*, by Tom Powers (grades 5-8, overview); *Smoking*, by Lila Gano.
How to Contact/Writers: Nonfiction: Query. Reports on queries in 2 weeks. Publishes a book 6 months after acceptance. Will consider simultaneous submissions.
Illustration: "We use photos, mostly." Will review ms/illustration packages submitted by authors with illustrations done by separate artists. Preference: "7×9 format—4-color cover."
How to Contact/Illustrators: Ms/illustration packages: Query first.
Terms/Writers & Illustrators: "Fee negotiated upon review of manuscript." Sends galleys to authors. Manuscript guidelines free on request.
Tips: "Know the publisher's needs and requirements. Books must be written at a 7-8 grade reading level. There's a growing market for quality nonfiction. Tentative titles: free speech, tobacco, alcohol, discrimination, immigration, poverty, the homeless in America, space weapons, drug abuse, terrorism, MAD, arms race, animal experimentation, etc. Currently working on books addressing endangered species, AIDS, pollution, gun control, etc. Both the above lists are presented to give writers an example of the kinds of titles we are seeking. If you are interested in writing about a specific topic, please query us by mail before you begin writing to be sure we have not assigned a particular topic to another author. The author should strive for objectivity. There obvi-

ously will be many issues on which a position should be taken—e.g. discrimination, tobacco, alcoholism, etc. However, moralizing, self-righteous condemnations, maligning, lamenting, mocking, etc. should be avoided. Moreover, where a pro/con position is taken, contrasting viewpoints should be presented. Certain moral issues such as abortion and euthanasia, if dealt with at all, should be presented with strict objectivity."

MARGARET K. McELDERRY BOOKS, imprint of Macmillan Publishing Co., 866 Third Ave., New York NY 10022. (212)702-7855. Book publisher. Publisher: Margaret K. McElderry. Publishes 10-12 picture books/year; 2-4 young reader titles/year; 8-10 middle reader titles/year; 3-5 young adult titles/year. 33% of books by first-time authors; 33% of books from agented writers.
Fiction: Picture books: contemporary, traditional. Young readers: contemporary, beginning chapter books. Middle readers: contemporary, fantasy, science fiction, mystery/adventure. Young adults: contemporary, fantasy, science fiction. Average word length: picture books—500; young readers—2,000; middle readers—10,000-20,000; young adults—45,000-50,000. Recently published *Who Said Red?*, by Mary Serfozo, illustrated by Keiko Narahashi (ages 3-6, an unusual concept book about colors); *False Face*, by Welwyn Katz (ages 10-14, a contemporary fantasy involving an Iroquois god); *Another Shore*, by Nancy Bond (ages 12 and up, time travel story).
Nonfiction: Picture books: animal, history, nature/environment, science. Young readers: animal, history, nature/environment, science, sports. Middle readers: animal, biography, history, music/dance, nature/environment, science, sports. Young adults: biography, music/dance, nature/environment. Average word length: picture books—500-1,000; young readers—1,500-3,000; middle readers—10,000-20,000; young adults—30,000-45,000. Recently published *Searches in the American Desert*, by Sheila Cowing (ages 10 and up); *Dilly Dilly Piccadilli*, edited by Myra Cohn Livingston (ages 8-12, poetry); *Story of The Seashore*, by John S. Goodall (all ages, pictorial social history).
How to Contact/Writers: Fiction/nonfiction: Submit complete ms. Reports on queries in 2-3 weeks; on mss in 8 weeks. Publishes a book 12-18 months after acceptance. Will consider simultaneous (only if indicated as such) submissions.
Illustration: Number of illustrations used for fiction: picture books—"every page"; young readers—15-20; middle readers—15-20. Number of illustrations used for nonfiction: picture books—"every page"; young readers—20-30; middle readers—20-30. Editorial will review ms/illustration packages submitted by authors/artists; ms/illustration packages submitted by authors with illustrations done by separate artist (2 or 3 samples only); and an illustrator's work for possible use in separate texts (2 or 3 samples only).
How to Contact/Illustrators: Ms/illustration packages: Ms (complete) and 2 or 3 pieces of finished art. Illustrations only: Résumé and slides or sketches. Reports on art samples in 6-8 weeks. Original artwork returned at job's completion.
Terms/Writers & Illustrators: Pays authors in royalties based on retail price. Pay for separate authors and illustrators: "50-50 as a rule for picture books." Pay for illustrators: by the project. Sends galleys to authors; dummies to illustrators, "they make the dummies for picture books." Book catalog, manuscript/artist's guidelines free on request.
Tips: Illustrators: There is an "emphasis on books for babies and young children; on nonfiction." (See also Aladdin Books/Collier Books for Young Adults, Atheneum Publishers, Bradbury Press, Four Winds Press.)

*MAGINATION PRESS, Brunner/Mazel, Inc., 19 Union Square West, New York NY 10003. (212)924-3344. Book publisher. Editor-in-Chief: Susan Kent Cakars. Publishes 4-8 picture books and young reader titles/year.
Fiction: Picture Books and young readers: contemporary. "Books dealing with the therapeutic resolution of children's psychological problems." Recently published: *Jessica and the Wolfe: A Story for Children Who Have Bad Dreams*, by Ted Lobby (picture book); *Double-Dip Feelings: A Book to Help Children Understand Emotions*, by Barbara Cain

(picture book); *Gran-Gran's Best Trick: A Story for Children Who Have Lost Someone They Love*, by Dwight Holden (picture book).

Nonfiction: Picture Books and Young Readers: psychotherapy.

How to Contact/Writers: Fiction/nonfiction: Submit complete manuscript. Reports on queries/mss: "up to 2 months max (may be only days)." Publishes a book 1 year after acceptance.

Illustration: Number of illustrations used for fiction and nonfiction: picture books — 24-29. Reviews all varieties of illustration packages. Art director, Millicent Fairhurst, will review illustrator's work for possible use in separate author's text. Prefers black and white for text, full-color for cover.

How to Contact/Illustrators: Original artwork returned at job's completion.

Terms/Writers & Illustrators: Pays authors in royalties. Offers varied advance but low. Pay for illustrators: by the project, $2,000 max. Pays royalty, 2% max. Sends galleys to authors. Book catalog and manuscript guidelines free on request.

MARCH MEDIA, INC., #256, 7003 Chadwick, Brentwood TN 37027. (615)370-3148. FAX: (615)370-0530. Independent book producer/agency. President: Etta G. Wilson. 25% of books by first-time authors.

Fiction: Picture books, young readers and middle grade fiction. Recently published *God's Tough Guys*, by Denise Williamson (8-12, biographical fiction); *The Thong Tree*, by Dick Haynes (8-12, historical fiction).

Nonfiction: Young reader: religion. Middle reader: social studies and values.

How to Contact/Writers: Fiction: Submit outline/synopsis and sample chapters. Nonfiction: submit complete ms. Reports on queries in 2 weeks, on ms in 8 weeks. Will consider simultaneous submissions.

Illustration: Editorial will review ms/illustration packages submitted by authors'/artists' or illustrators' work for possible use in author's texts.

How to Contact/Illustrators: Ms/illustration packages: "query first." Illustrations only: send "résumé and samples." Reports back only if interested. Original art work returned at job's completion.

Terms/Writers and Illustrators: Method of payment: "Either royalty or fee, depending on project and publisher's requirements."

Tips: Illustrators: "Be certain you can draw children and study book design." Looking for "series of board books or middle-grade titles, either fiction or nonfiction." There is "more need for nonfiction and middle-grade fiction."

MARYLAND HISTORICAL PRESS, 9205 Tuckerman St., Lanham MD 20706. (301)577-5308. Book publisher. Independent book producer/packager. Publisher: Vera Rollo. Publishes 1 young reader title/year; 1 middle reader title/year. 15% of books by first-time authors.

Nonfiction: Young readers, middle readers: biography, history. Published *The American Flag*, by Vera F. Rollo (young adults); *Indians of the Tidewater Country of Maryland, Virginia, North Carolina, and Delaware*, by Thelma G. Ruskin (elementary students); *Maryland: Its Past and Present*, by Dr. Richard Wilson and Dr. E. L. Bridner, Jr. (4th-grade level).

How to Contact/Writers: Nonfiction: Query. Reports on queries in 1 month. Publishes a book 9 months after acceptance. Will consider simultaneous submissions.

Terms/Writers & Illustrators: Pays authors in royalties, buys artwork outright. Factor used to determine final payment: Time spent. Pay for illustrators: By the project. Sends galley to authors. Book catalog free on request.

Tips: "Subjects stressed: Maryland, nonfiction; Americana, nonfiction; and Aviation, college-level texts."

MEADOWBROOK PRESS, 18318 Minnetonka Blvd., Deephaven MN 55391. (612)473-5400. Book publisher. Editorial Contact: Elizabeth Weiss. Publishes 7 young reader titles/year; 4 middle reader titles/year; 2 young adult titles/year. 25% of books by first-time authors; 8% of books from agented writers.
Nonfiction: Young readers: education, hobbies, activity books. Middle readers: education, hobbies, activity books. Young adults/teens: education, hobbies, activity books. Average word length: Young readers—8,200; Middle readers—8,200. Recently published *Free Stuff for Kids,* by Free Stuff Eds. (6 and older, activity); *Science in the Kitchen,* by James Lewis (5 and older, activity); *It's My Party,* by Laurine Croasdale and Carole Davis (5 and older, activity).
How to Contact/Writers: Nonfiction: Query, submit outline/synopsis and sample chapters or submit complete ms. Reports on queries/mss in 4 weeks. Publishes a book 9 months after acceptance. Will consider simultaneous submissions.
Illustration: Number of illustrations used for nonfiction: young readers—100; middle readers—100. Editorial will review all varieties of ms/illustration packages. Jennifer L. Nelson and Anne Marie Hoppe, Art Directors, will review an illustrator's work for possible use in separate texts.
How to Contact/Illustrators: Ms/illustration packages: Send "three sample chapters of ms with 1 piece of final art." Illustrations only: Send résumé and samples. Reports back in 6 weeks. Original art work returned at job's completion.
Terms/Writers & Illustrators: Pays authors in royalties of 5-7½% based on retail price. Offers average advance payment of $1,000-5,000. Factors used to determine final payment for ms/illustration package include sales potential and number and type of illustrations. Pay for separate authors and illustrators: "either they can split the advance/royalty, or if there are few illustrations, the illustrator might receive a fee." Pay for illustrators: $100-10,000; ¼-¾% of total royalties. Sends galleys for review to authors "sometimes." Book catalog, manuscript/artist's guidelines free on request.
Tips: Illustrators: "Develop a commercial style—compare your style to that of published authors, and submit your work when it is judged 'in the ball park.'" Looking for: "A children's book by objective observers, aimed at early elementary aged kids which explains how to get into, e.g., science, astronomy, magic, collecting, hobbies."

MERIWETHER PUBLISHING LTD., 885 Elkton Dr., Colorado Springs CO 80907. Book publisher. Estab. 1969. "We do most of our artwork in house; we do not publish for the children's elementary market." 75% of books by first-time authors; 5% of books from agented writers.
Nonfiction: Young adults: how-to, how-to church activities. Average length: 200 pages. Recently published *Double Talk,* by Bill Majeski (50 comedy duets for actors, high school); *Christmas on Stage* (an anthology of Christmas plays for children and adults); *The Youth in Action Book,* by Shirley Pollack (a go-power guide for teens, junior and senior high).
How to Contact/Writers: Nonfiction: Query or submit outline/synopsis and sample chapters. Include Social Security number with submission. Reports on queries in 4 weeks. Publishes a book 6-12 months after acceptance. Will consider simultaneous submissions.
Illustration: Number of illustrations used for nonfiction: young adults—15. Art Director, Michelle Zapel, will review an illustrator's work for possible use in separate texts.
How to Contact/Illustrators: Ms/illustration packages: Query first. Illustrations only: Slides. Reports on art samples in 4 weeks.
Terms/Writers & Illustrators: Pays authors in royalties based on retail and wholesale price. Pay for illustrators: by the project; royalties based on retail or wholesale price. Sends galleys to authors. Book catalog for SAE and $1 postage; manuscript guidelines for SAE and 1 first-class stamp.
Tips: Plans "more nonfiction on communication arts subjects."

■**METAMORPHOUS PRESS**, Box 10616, Portland OR 97210. (503) 228-4972. Book publisher. Editorial Contact: Anita Sullivan. Estab. 1982. Publishes 1 picture book/year; 1 young reader title/year; 1 middle reader title/year; 1 young adult title/year. 90% of books by first-time authors; 10% of books from agented writers. Subsidy publishes 10%.
Fiction: "Metaphors for positive change."
Nonfiction: Picture books: education. Young readers: education, music/dance. Middle readers: education, music/dance, self-help/esteem. Young adults: education, music/dance, self-help/esteem. Recently published *Thinking, Changing, Rearranging*, by Anderson (ages 10 and up, workbook to improve self-esteem); *Classroom Magic*, by Lloyd (lesson plans for elementary grades).
How to Contact/Writers: Fiction: Query. Nonfiction: Query; submit outline/synopsis and sample chapters. Reports on queries in 3-4 months; on mss in 4-6 months. Publishes a book 12-24 months after acceptance. Will consider simultaneous and electronic submissions via disk or modem.
Illustration: Number of illustrations used for fiction/nonfiction: "varies." Editorial will review all varieties of ms/illustration packages. Children's Editor, Janele Gantt, will review an illustrator's work for possible use in separate texts.
How to Contact/Illustrators: Ms/illustrations: Query. Illustrations only: "vitae with samples of range and style." Reports on art samples only if interested.
Terms/Writers & Illustrators: Other methods of pay: "varies, negotiable." Pay for separate authors and illustrators: "Individually negotiated usually between author and illustrator." Sends galleys to authors; dummies to illustrators. Book catalog free on request.
Tips: Looks for "Books that relate and illustrate the notion that we create our own realities, self-reliance and positive outlooks work best for us—creative metaphors and personal development guides given preference."

MISTY HILL PRESS, 5024 Turner Rd., Sebastopol CA 95472. (707)823-7437. Book publisher. Editor-in-Chief: Sally Karste. Publishes 2 middle reader titles/year. 100% of books by first-time authors.
Fiction: Middle readers: history. Young adults: history.
Nonfiction: Middle readers: history. Young adults: history. Recently published *Trails to Poosey*, by Olive Cooke (young adults, historical fiction).
How to Contact/Writers: Fiction/nonfiction: Submit outline/synopsis and sample chapters. Reports on queries in 1 week; on mss in 4 weeks. Publishes a book 8 months after acceptance. Will consider simultaneous submissions.
Terms/Writers & Illustrators: Illustrators paid by the project. Sends galleys to authors.
Tips: "Historical fiction: substantial research, good adventure or action against the historical setting. Historical fiction only."

■**MOREHOUSE PUBLISHING CO.**, 78 Danbury Rd., Wilton CT 06897. (203)762-0721. FAX: (203)762-0727. Book publisher. Estab. 1884. Juvenile Books Editor: Stephanie Oda. Publishes 10 picture books/year. 75% of books by first-time authors. Subsidy publishes 25%.
Fiction: All levels: religion. Recently published *Meet the Alphabuddies*, by Jill Weaver (ages 5-9, picture book); *Betsy Bigmouth*, by Felicity Hoffecker (ages 7-10, picture book).
Nonfiction: All levels: religion, moral message, family values. Picture books and young readers: religion. Recently published *Maria Montessori*, by Beverly Birch; *John Muir*, by Sally Tolan; *Sojourner Truth*, by Susan Taylor-Boyd; *Desmond Tutu*, by David Winner; all titles young adults, bios.
How to Contact/Writers: Fiction/nonfiction: Submit outline/synopsis and sample chapters. Include Social Security number with submission. Reports on queries in 4-6 weeks. Publishes a book 12 months after acceptance. Will consider computer printout

and electronic submissions via disk or modem. Editorial will review all varieties of ms/illustration packages.

How to Contact/Illustrators: Ms/illustration packages: 3 chapters of ms with 1 piece of final art. Illustrations only: Résumé, tearsheets. Reports on art samples in 4-6 weeks. Original artwork returned at job's completion.

Terms/Writers & Illustrators: Pays authors "both royalties and outright." Offers average advance payment of $500. Additional payment for ms/illustration packages. Sends galleys to authors. Book catalog free on request.

Tips: Writers: "Prefer authors who can do own illustrations. Be fresh, be fun, not pedantic, but let your work have a message." Currently expanding juvenile list. Illustrators: "Work hard to develop original style." Looks for ms/illustrations "with a religious or moral value while remaining fun and entertaining."

MOSAIC PRESS, 358 Oliver Rd., Cincinnati OH 45215. (513)761-5977. Miniature book publisher. Publisher: Miriam Irwin. Publishes less than 1 young reader title/year. 50% of books by first-time authors.

Fiction: Middle readers: animal, contemporary, history, problem novels, sports, spy/mystery/adventure. Average word length: middle readers—under 2,000.

Nonfiction: Middle readers: animal, biography, education, history, hobbies, music/dance, nature/environment, religion, sports. Average word length: middle readers—2,000. Published *Plain Jane Vanilla*, by Missy McConnell (10-11 year olds, story-poem); *Miriam Mouse's Survival Manual*, by Miriam Irwin (ages 6-10, story); *The Grandparent Book*, by Christopher Irwin (ages 8-10, story). "We have done 4 children's books in 10 years. None of our recent books were for children."

How to Contact/Writers: Fiction: Query; submit complete ms. Nonfiction: Submit complete ms. Reports on queries/mss in 2 weeks. Publishes a book 4 years after acceptance. Will consider simultaneous submissions.

Illustration: Number of illustrations used for fiction: middle readers—12. Number of illustrations used for nonfiction: middle readers—8. Editorial will review all varieties of ms/illustration packages. Prefers to see "pen and ink under 5″ tall."

How to Contact/Illustrators: Illustrations only: "photocopies of pen and ink work with SASE." Reports on art samples in 2 weeks. Original artwork returned at job's completion "after several years if requested."

Terms/Writers & Illustrators: Buys ms outright for $50 and 5 copies of book. Additional payment for ms/illustration package is $50 and 5 copies of book. Final payment is a "flat fee." Pay for separate authors and illustrators: "by check when the book goes to press. The first completed copies are sent to artist and author." Pay for illustrators: $50 and 5 copies. Book catalog is available for $3. Manuscript/artist's guidelines for business-size SAE and 45¢.

Tips: Looks for "any type of writing that has something to say worth preserving in the form of a miniature book; that says it beautifully in very few words. Most of our children's books are bought by adults for *themselves*. Most of our books are in the $24 range, and people won't pay that much for a little book for children."

*JOHN MUIR PUBLICATIONS, INC., P.O. Box 613, Santa Fe NM 87504-0613. (505)982-4078. Book publisher. Editorial Contact: Ken Luboff. Publishes 6 picture books/year; 10-15 middle reader titles/year.

Nonfiction: Middle Readers: animal, biography, hobbies, nature/environment. Average word length: middle readers—12,000-15,000. Recently published *Indian Way*, by Gary Mclain (middle readers); *Kidding Around Series* (12 titles), by different authors (middle readers).

How to Contact/Writers: Query. Reports on queries/mss in 4-6 weeks. Publishes a book 8 months after acceptance. Will consider simultaneous submissions.

Illustration: Number of illustrations used for fiction and nonfiction: picture books—25; middle readers—40-60. Reviews all varieties of illustration packages. Production Director, Harry Wich, will review illustrator's work for possible use in separate author's text.

How to Contact/Illustrators: Ms/illustration packages: query, outline and 1 chapter for illustration; 4 original finished pieces and roughs of ideas. Illustrations only: submit résumé and samples of art that have been reproduced or samples of original art for style. Original artwork returned at job's completion.

Terms/Writers & Illustrators: Pays authors in royalties based on wholesale price. Offers advance of $750 for 50-60 illustrations, 2 color and cover 4 color. "Advance for each and 6% royalty, however some books are paid by flat fee for illustration. Pay for Illustrators: by the project when they work on our authors' titles. Royalty. Sends galleys to authors; dummies to illustrators. Book catalog free on request."

MULTNOMAH PRESS, 10209 SE Division, Portland OR 97266. (503)257-0526. Book publisher. Editor: Al Janssen. Publishes 1-2 young reader titles/year; 3-4 middle reader titles/year. 60% of books by first-time authors.

Fiction: Young readers: animal, contemporary, easy-to-read, spy/mystery/adventure. Middle readers: contemporary, fantasy, history, sports, spy/mystery/adventure. Average word length: young readers—5,000-6,000; middle readers 15,000-25,000. Published *T. J. Flopp,* by Stephen Cosgrove, (ages 5-9, picture book); *Brown Ears,* by Stephen Lawhead, (ages 5-9, young reader); *I Know the World's Worst Secret,* by Doris Sanford, (ages 5-9, picture book/young reader); *The Purple Door,* (ages 8-12, middle reader).

Nonfiction: Picture books: animal, nature/environment, religion. Young readers: animal, biography, nature/environment, religion, sports. Middle readers: animal, biography, history nature/environment, sports. Average word length: picture books—2,000-3,000; young readers—5,000-6,000; middle readers—15,000-25,000. Published *Destination: Moon,* by Jim Irwin, (8-12, middle readers).

How to Contact/Writers: Fiction: Submit complete ms. Nonfiction: Submit outline/synopsis and sample chapters. Reports on queries in 2-3 weeks; on mss in 6 weeks. Publishes a book 9-12 months after acceptance. Will consider simultaneous submissions. "Computer printouts must be letter quality so scanner machine can read the manuscripts."

Illustration: Number of illustrations used for fiction: picture books—16; young readers—7-10; middle readers—7-10. Nonfiction: picture books—16. Editorial will review an illustrator's work for possible use in separate texts.

How to Contact/Illustrators: Ms/illustration packages: "Send 3 chapters with 1 finished piece of art; pencil sketches of rest." Illustrations only: Send "résumé and either tear sheets, slides or photographs. Also, need to see that artist can follow a story line. So, if possible, submit illustrations of a well-known story, such as a fairy tale, etc." Original artwork returned at job's completion.

Terms/Writers & Illustrators: Pays author in royalty; percentage "depends on type of book; first time or well known author." Factors used to determine final payment are "type of illustration and number of illustrations." "Split royalty if well-known or work is equal. Generally the illustrator receives a flat fee." Pay for illustrators: by the project-negotiable fee. Sends galleys to authors. Book catalog/manuscript guidelines are free on request.

Tips: Illustrators: "Put only the work that you do well in your portfolio. Be willing to concept an entire story (well-known fairy tale) so editor can see how you follow a story and the kind of creativity you would bring to the story." Looking for "series format for both fiction and nonfiction. In fiction, a well-developed main character. Multnomah is an evangelical publishing house, so we desire wholesome fiction with a Christian world view, although not necessarily an overt one."

*NAR PUBLICATIONS, P.O. Box 233, Barryville NY 12719. (914)557-8713. Book publisher. 50% of books by first-time authors; 5% of books from agented writers.
Fiction: Recently published *Poems for Young Children*, by Mimi Roes (preschool-11, poems and finger plays).
How to Contact/Writers: Fiction/nonfiction: Query. Reports on queries in 3 weeks; mss in 1 month. Publishes book 9 months after acceptance. Will consider simultaneous and electronic submissions via disk.
Terms/Writers: Buys ms outright. Book catalog for 1 first class stamp and #10 SAE.
Tips: "We have only published two books for children. Preschool to age 8 has best chance of acceptance."

*NATUREGRAPH PUBLISHER, INC., P.O. Box 1075, Happy Camp CA 96039. (916)493-5353. Contact: Barbara Brown. Publishes 4 young adult titles/year. 100% of books by first-time authors.
Nonfiction: Young adults/teens: animal, nature/environment, native American. Average word length: young adult/teens—70,000. Recently published *Beaver Behavior*, by Morrell Allred (young adult, natural history); *Mystery Tracks in the Snow*, by Hap Gilliland (young adult, natural history); *Give Peas a Chance*, by Peter Barbarow (young adult, outdoors/edibles); *Run to Glory*, by William Soars (young adult, animal).
How to Contact/Writers: Nonfiction: Query. Reports on queries/mss in 2 weeks. Publishes book 18 months after acceptance.
Terms/Writers: Pays authors in royalties of 10% based on wholesale price. Sends galleys to authors. Book catalog is free on request.

NEW DAY PRESS, 2355 E. 89, Cleveland OH 44106. (216)795-7070. Book publisher. Editorial Contact: Carolyn Gordon. Publishes 1 middle reader title/year; 1 young adult title/year. 75% of books by first-time authors.
Fiction: Middle readers, young adults: history. Published *Fireside Tales*, by Mary S. Moore (5th grade to adult, stories from the oral traditional folk tales).
Nonfiction: Middle readers, young adults: biography, history. Published *Black Image Makers*, by E. Gaines et al. (middle readers-young adults, biographical narratives).
How to Contact/Writers: Fiction/nonfiction: Query. Reports on queries in 4 weeks; on mss in 12 weeks. Publishes a book a year or more after acceptance.
Illustration: Number of illustrations used for fiction and nonfiction: middle readers—5; young adults—5. Editorial will review ms/illustration packages submitted by authors/artists and ms/illustration packages submitted by authors with illustrations done by separate artists.
How to Contact/Illustrators: Reports on art samples in 3 months. Buys ms outright for $100. Book catalog free on request.

ODDO PUBLISHING, INC., Box 68, Fayetteville GA 30214. (404)461-7627. Book publisher. Estab. 1964. Contact: Editor. Publishes 3-6 picture books/year; 1-2 young reader titles/year; 1-2 middle reader titles/year. 10% of books by first-time authors.
Fiction: Picture books: animal, contemporary, easy-to-read, science fiction, sports, spy/mystery/adventure. Young readers: animal, contemporary, easy-to-read, fantasy, science fiction, sports, spy/mystery/adventure. Middle readers: animal, contemporary, fantasy, science fiction, sports, spy/mystery/adventure. Average word length: picture books—500; young readers—1,000; middle readers—2,000. Recently published *Bobby Bear's Magic Show*, by Marilue Johnson (grades 1 and 2, picture book); *Bobby Bear at the Circus*, by Marilue Johnson (grades 1 and 2, picture book); *Timmy Tiger and Too Many Twins*, by Alvin Westcott (grade 2, picture book).

Nonfiction: Picture books: animal, nature/environment, sports. Young readers: animal, biography, hobbies, nature/environment, sports. Middle readers: animal, biography, hobbies, nature/environment, sports. Average word length: picture books—500; young readers—1,000; middle readers—2,000.

How to Contact/Writers: Fiction/nonfiction: Query; submit outline/synopsis and sample chapters. Reports on queries 1-2 weeks; on mss 8-12 weeks. Publishes a book 24 months after acceptance. Will consider simultaneous submissions.

Illustration: Number of illustrations used for fiction and nonfiction: picture books—33; young readers—33; middle readers—33. Editorial will review all illustration packages.

How to Contact/Illustrators: Ms/illustration packages: Query first. Illustrations only: Sample art or slides. Reports on art samples only if interested, or if required to review slides.

Terms/Writers & Illustrators: Buys ms outright, "negotiable" price. Additional payment for ms/illustration packages "negotiable." Factors used to determine final payment include number of illustrations. Pay for separate authors and illustrators: separate contracts. Illustrators paid by the project. Sends galleys to authors "only if necessary." Book catalog available for 9 × 12 SAE and $2.25.

Tips: "Send simultaneous submissions. Do not be discouraged by 'no.' Keep sending to publishers." Looks for: "Books/art with a 'positive' tone. No immorality or risque subjects. Books must have an underlying theme or concept. 'Coping' subjects are accepted. We want children who read our books to learn something and feel good when they are finished."

ORCHARD BOOKS, div. and imprint of Franklin Watts, Inc., 387 Park Ave. S., New York NY 10016. (212)686-7070. Book publisher. Vice President and Publisher: Norma Jean Sawicki. "We publish between 50 and 60 books, fiction, poetry, picture books, and photo essays." 10-25% of books by first-time authors.

Nonfiction: "We publish very selective nonfiction."

How to Contact/Writers: Fiction: Submit outline/synopsis and sample chapters; submit complete ms. Nonfiction: Submit outline/synopsis and sample chapters. Reports on queries in 2 weeks; on mss in 1 month. Average length of time between acceptance of a book-length ms and publication of work "depends on the editorial work necessary. If none, about 8 months." Will not consider simultaneous submissions.

Illustration: Editorial will review ms/illustration packages submitted by authors/artists and ms/illustration packages submitted by authors with illustrations done by separate artists. "But it is better to submit ms and illustration separately unless they are by the same person, or a pairing that is part of the project such as husband and wife."

How to Contact/Illustrators: Ms/illustration packages: 3 chapters of ms with 1 piece of final art, remainder roughs. Illustrations only: "tearsheets or photocopies or photostats of the work." Reports on art samples in 4 weeks. Original artwork returned at job's completion.

Terms/Writers & Illustrators: Pays authors in royalties "industry standard" based on retail price. Additional payment for ms/illustration packages. Factors used to determine final payment for ms/illustration package include number of illustrations, and experience. "We never buy manuscripts outright. An author/illustrator gets the whole royalty. The royalty is shared between writer and artist." Sends galleys to authors; dummies to illustrators. Book catalog free on request.

*OUR CHILD PRESS, 800 Maple Glen Ln., Wayne PA 19087. (215)964-0606. Book publisher. Contact: Carol Hallenbeck, President. 90% of books by first-time authors.

Fiction/Nonfiction: All levels: adoption. Average word length: Open. Recently published *Oliver,* by Lois Wickstrom (preschool, adoption story); *Don't Call Me Marda,* by Sheila Kelly Welch (middle readers and up, novel).

How to Contact/Writers: Fiction/Nonfiction: Query or submit complete manuscript. Include Social Security number with submission or unsolicited manuscripts not returned. Reports on queries/mss in 2 months. Publishes a book 6-12 months after acceptance.

Illustration: Reviews all varieties of ms/illustration packages. Carol Hallenbeck will review illustrator's work for possible use in separate author's text.

How to Contact/Illustrators: Query first. Submit résumé, tearsheets and photocopies. Reports on art samples in 2 months. Original artwork returned at job's completion.

Terms/Writers & Illustrators: Pays authors in royalties of 5% based on wholesale price. Pay for separate authors and illustrators: Royalty percentage. Book catalog for SAE (business envelope) and 45¢ postage.

PANDO PUBLICATIONS, 540 Longleaf Dr., Roswell GA 30075. (404)587-3363. Book publisher. Estab. 1988. Owner: Andrew Bernstein. Publishes 2-6 middle reader titles/year; 2-6 young adult titles/year. 20% of books by first-time authors.

Nonfiction: Middle readers: animal, biography, education, history, hobbies, music/dance, nature/environment, sports. Young adults: animal, biography, education, history, hobbies, music/dance, nature/environment, sports. Average length: middle readers—175 pages; young adults—200 pages. Recently published *Teach Me to Play: A First Bridge Book*, by Jude Goodwin (ages 8-14, how-to, about card game of bridge).

How to Contact/Writers: Fiction/nonfiction: Prefers full ms. Reports on queries in 4 weeks; on mss in 6 weeks. Publishes a book 9 months after acceptance. Will consider simultaneous submissions. "Prefers" electronic submissions via disk or modem.

Illustration: Number of illustrations used for nonfiction: middle readers—125; young adults—125. Editorial will review all illustration packages.

How to Contact/Illustrators: Ms/illustrations: Query first. Illustrations only: Tearsheets. Reports on art samples in 1 month. Original artwork returned at job's completion.

Terms/Writers & Illustrators: Offers average advance payment of "⅓ royalty due on first run." Pay for separate authors and illustrators is "according to contract." Illustrators paid "according to contract." Sends galleys to authors; dummies to illustrators. "Book descriptions available on request." Manuscript/artist's guidelines are free on request.

Tips: Writers: "Find an untapped market then write to fill the need." Illustrators: "Find an author with a good idea and writing ability. Develop the book with the author. Join a professional group to meet people—ABA, publisher's groups, as well as writer's groups and publishing auxiliary groups. Talk to printers." Looks for "how-to books, but will consider anything."

PARENTING PRESS, INC., Box 75267, Seattle WA 98125. (206)364-2900. Book publisher. Estab. 1979. Editorial Director: Shari Steelsmith. Publishes 2-3 picture books/year; 1-2 young reader titles/year; 1-2 middle reader titles/year. 40% of books by first-time authors.

Fiction: "We rarely publish straight fiction." Recently published *A Horse's Tale,* by Nancy Luenn (ed.), (middle readers, collection of 10 short stories on children in history). "No other fiction titles on our list."

Nonfiction: Picture books: biography, education, social skills building. Young readers: education, nature/environment, social skills building books. Middle readers: social skills building. Average word length: picture books—500-800; young readers—1,000-2,000; middle readers—up to 10,000. Published *Bully on the Bus,* by Carl Bosch, (middle readers, how to deal with bullies); *Ellie's Day,* by Conlin/Friedman, (picture book); *Harriet Tubman,* by Linda Meyer, (picture book, biography).

How to Contact/Writers: Fiction: "We publish educational books for children in story format. NO STRAIGHT FICTION." Nonfiction: Query. Reports on queries 4-6 weeks; mss in 1-2 months, "after requested." Publishes a book 10-11 months after acceptance. Will consider simultaneous submissions.

Illustrations: Number of illustrations used for fiction and nonfiction: picture books—14; young readers—50. Will review ms/illustration packages submitted by authors/artists. "We do reserve the right to find our own illustrator, however." Editorial will review an illustrator's work for possible use in separate texts.

How to Contact/Illustrators: Ms/illustration packages: Query. Illustrations only: Send "résumé, samples of art/drawings (no original art); photocopies or color photocopies okay." Original art work returned at job's completion for illustrators under contract.

Terms/Writers & Illustrators: Pays authors in royalties of 4% based on retail price. Outright purchase of ms, "negotiated on a case-by-case basis. Not common for us." Offers average advance of $150. Additional payment for ms/illustration package: "We offer an 8% royalty on list price. This royalty is split 50/50 with the illustrator and author." Pay for separate authors and illustrators: "split royalty." Pay for illustrators: by the project; 4% royalty based on retail price. Sends galleys to authors; dummies to illustrators. Book catalog/manuscript guidelines for #10 SAE and 1 first-class stamp.

Tips: Writers: "Query publishers who already market to the same audience. We often get manuscripts (good ones) totally unsuitable to our market." Illustrators: "We pay attention to artists who are willing to submit an illustration on speculation." Looking for "social skills building books for children, books that empower children, books that encourage decision making, books that are balanced ethnically and in gender. Since 1983 there has been a proliferation of children's-only bookstores. Publishers are producing more children's titles."

PAULIST PRESS, 997 Macarthur Blvd., Mahwah NJ 07430. (201)825-7300. FAX: (201)825-8345. Book publisher. Estab. 1865. Editor: Georgia J. Christo. Publishes 8-10 picture books/year; 5 young reader titles/year; 5 middle reader titles/year. 70% of books by first-time authors; 30% of books from agented writers.

Fiction: Picture books, young readers, middle readers: religious/moral. Average length: picture books—24 pages; young readers—24-32 pages; middle readers—64 pages. Recently published *Feliz Navidad, Pablo,* by Teri Martini (ages 6-9, picture book); *Silvester and the Oogaloo Boogaloo,* by Teddi Doleski (ages 7-10, picture book); *Where is God?,* by Daniel O'Leary (ages 3-7, children's poem).

Nonfiction: Young readers, middle readers: religion. Recently published *Saint Joan the Girl in Armour,* by Dorothy Smith (ages 9-12, biography); *Thomas More: A Man for All Seasons,* by Dorothy Smith (ages 9-12, biography).

How to Contact/Writers: Fiction/nonfiction: Submit complete ms. Reports on queries in 1-2 weeks; on mss in 4 weeks. Publishes a book 12-16 months after acceptance. Will consider simultaneous submissions, "prefer original, typed, double-spaced mss."

Illustration: Number of illustrations used for fiction and nonfiction: picture books—12-16; young readers—12; middle readers—6-8. Editorial will review all varieties of ms/illustration packages.

How to Contact/Illustrators: Ms/illustration packages: Complete ms with 1 piece of final art, remainder roughs. Illustrations only: Résumé, tearsheets. Reports on art samples in 2-3 weeks. Original artwork returned at job's completion, "if requested by illustrator."

Terms/Writers & Illustrators: Outright purchase: $30-$45/illustration. Offers average advance payment of $450-$650. Factors used to determine final payment: Color art, b&w, number of illustrations, complexity of work. Pay for separate authors and illustrators: Author paid by royalty rate; illustrator paid by flat fee. Sends galleys to authors; dummies to illustrators.

Tips: "We are looking for manuscripts that deal with morals and values in everyday childhood situations."

The newest picture book by Paulist Press, **Silvester and the Oogaloo Booga-** *loo, written by Teddi Doleski, "is a story about feeling different and not fitting in, and about taking time to lis- ten," according to editor Georgia Christo. The story was illustrated by Pa- mela T. Keating, who received a $500 advance against royalties for her draw- ings.*

PELICAN PUBLISHING CO. INC., 1101 Monroe St., Gretna LA 70053. (504)368-1175. Book publisher. Estab. 1926. Editor: Nina Kooij. Publishes 2 picture books/year; 4 mid- dle reader titles/year; 1-2 young adult titles/year. 25% of books by first-time authors; 5% of books from agented writers.
Fiction: Picture books, middle readers, young adult titles: animal, contemporary, fan- tasy, history, problem novels, sports. Average word length: picture books—32 pages; middle readers—112 pages; young adults—112+ pages. Recently published *Louisiana Indian Tales*, by Elizabeth Moore/Alice Couvillon (fiction collection); *The Magic Box*, by Olga Cossi (12 and up, young adult fiction).
Nonfiction: Picture books, middle readers, young adult titles: biography, education, hobbies, music/dance, nature/environment, religion.
How to Contact/Writers: Fiction/Nonfiction: Query. Reports on queries in 4-6 weeks; mss in 12-16 weeks. Publishes a book 12-18 months after acceptance.
Illustration: Number of illustrations used for fiction and nonfiction: picture books—16- 32; middle readers—1 per chapter. Will review all varieties of ms/illustration packages. Production Manager, Dana Bilbray, will review an illustrator's work for possible use in separate texts.
How to Contact/Illustrators: Ms/illustration packages: Query first.
Illustrations: Send résumé, samples (preferably photocopies). Reports on ms/art sam- ples only if interested.
Terms/Writers & Illustrators: Pays authors in royalties; buys ms outright "rarely." Pay for separate authors and illustrators: "By arrangement; can either be through contract or between author and artist." Send galleys to authors.
Tips: Writers: "Be as original as possible. Develop characters that lend themselves to series and always be thinking of new and interesting situations for those series. Give your story a strong hook—something that will appeal to a well-defined audience. There is a lot of competition out there for general themes." Looks for: "Series, preferably with

anthropomorphic animals or other humorous characters. Stories that reflect high moral values."

PERSPECTIVES PRESS, P.O. Box 90318, Indianapolis IN 46290. (317)872-3055. Book publisher. Estab. 1982. Publisher: Pat Johnston. Publishes 1-3 picture books/year; 1-3 young reader titles/year; 1-3 middle reader titles/year. 95% of books by first-time authors.
Fiction: Picture books, young readers, middle readers, young adults: adoption, foster care. Recently published *Real For Sure Sister*, by Angel (middle readers); *Where the Sun Kisses the Sea*, by Gabel (young/middle readers).
Nonfiction: Picture books, young readers, middle readers, young adults: adoption, foster care. Recently published *Filling in the Blanks*, by Gabel (middle/young adults, self-help); *Our Baby: A Birth & Adoption Story*, by Janice Koch (picture book, young reader).
How to Contact/Writers: Fiction/nonfiction: Query or submit outline/synopsis and sample chapters. Reports on queries in 2 weeks; on mss in 6 weeks. Publishes a book 6-10 months after acceptance. Will consider simultaneous submissions.
Illustration: Number of illustrations used for fiction/nonfiction: picture books—16-32; young readers—10-24; middle readers—5-8. Editorial will review ms/illustration packages submitted by authors/illustrators. Publisher, Pat Johnston, will review illustrator's work for possible use in separate texts.
How to Contact/Illustrators: Reports on art samples only if interested.
Terms/Writers & Illustrators: Pays authors in royalties of 5-15% based on net sales. Sends galleys to authors; dummies to illustrators. Book catalog, manuscript guidelines available for #10 SAE and 2 first-class stamps.
Tips: "Do your homework! I'm amazed at the number of authors who don't bother to check that we have a very limited interest area and subsequently submit unsolicited material that is completely inappropriate for us. For children, we focus exclusively on issues of adoption and interim (foster) care; for adults we also include infertility issues."

PHILOMEL BOOKS, imprint of The Putnam & Grosset Group, 200 Madison Ave., New York NY 10016. (212)951-8700. Book publisher. Editor-in-Chief: Patricia Lee Gauch (picture books). Editorial Contact: Paula Wiseman (young reader titles). Publishes 20 picture books/year; 5-10 young reader titles/year. 20% of books by first-time authors; 80% of books from agented writers.
Fiction: Picture books: animal, fantasy, history. Young readers: animal, fantasy, history. Middle readers: fantasy, history. Young adults: contemporary, fantasy, history. "Any well written book." Average word length: "Books of quality, varying length." Recently published *Lon Po Po*, by Ed Young.
Nonfiction: Picture books, young readers, middle readers, young adults: animal, biography, history. "Creative nonfiction on any subject." Average length: "not to exceed 150 pages." Published *Elephant Crossing*, by Yoshida (middle reader).
How to Contact/Writers: Fiction/nonfiction: Query; submit outline/synopsis and sample chapters; all other unsolicited mss returned unopened. Reports on queries/mss in 3 months. Publishes a book 2 years after acceptance.
Illustration: Number of illustrations used for fiction: picture books—24. Will review ms/illustration packages submitted by authors/artists "if requested." Art Director, Nanette Stevenson, will review an illustrator's work for possible use in separate texts.
How to Contact/Illustrators: Ms/illustration packages: Query first. Illustrations only: "appointment to show portfolio." Reports on art samples in 2 months. Original art work returned at job's completion.
Terms/Writers & Illustrators: Pays authors in advance royalties. Average advance payment "varies." Illustrators paid by advance and in royalties. Sends galleys to authors; dummies to illustrators. Books catalog, manuscript/artist's guidelines free on request.

Tips: "Discover your own voice and own story—and persevere." Looks for "something unusual, original, well-written. Fine art. Our needs change, but at this time, we are interested in receiving young fiction for the 4- to 10-year-old child. The genre (fantasy, contemporary, or historical fiction) is not so important as the story itself, and the spirited life the story allows its main character. We are also interested in receiving adolescent novels, particularly novels that contain regional spirit, such as a story about a young boy or girl written from a southern, southwestern, or northwestern perspective."

PIPPIN PRESS, 229 E. 85th St., Gracie Station, Box 92, New York NY 10028. (212)288-4920. Children's book publisher. Estab. 1987. Publisher/President: Barbara Francis. Publishes 6-8 picture books/year; 3 young reader titles/year. "Not interested in young adult books."

Fiction: Picture books: animal, fantasy, humorous. Young readers: fantasy, spy/mystery/adventure, humorous. Middle readers: fantasy, spy/mystery/adventure, humorous. Average word length: picture books—750-1,500; young readers—2,000-3,000; middle readers—3,000 +. Recently published *Seven Times Eight*, by David Updike (grades 2 and up, fantasy); *Lost in the Amazon*, by Robert Quackenbush (grades 2 and up, fantasy); *A Spring Story*, by David Updike (grades 2 and up).

Nonfiction: Picture books: animal. Young readers: biography, humorous. Recently published *Pass the Quill, I'll Write a Draft: A Story of Thomas Jefferson*, by Robert Quackenbush.

How to Contact/Writers: Fiction/nonfiction: Query. Include Social Security number with submission. Reports on queries in 2-3 weeks; on mss in 6-8 weeks. Publishes a book 9-18 months after acceptance. Will consider simultaneous submissions.

Illustration: Number of illustrations used for fiction: picture books—25-30; young readers—15-20; middle readers—8-10. Number of illustrations used for nonfiction: picture books—25-30; young readers—15-20; middle readers—15-20. Editorial will review an illustrator's work for possible use in separate texts.

How to Contact/Illustrators: Illustrations only: "Tearsheets or Xeroxes would be fine. I see illustrations by appointment." Reports on art samples only if interested. Original artwork returned at job's completion.

Terms/Writers & Illustrators: Pays authors in royalties. Pay for illustrators: Royalty. Sends galleys to authors; dummies to illustrators. "The illustrator prepares the dummy on picture books; dummies for longer books prepared by the designer are submitted to the illustrator." Book catalog available for 6 × 9 SAE; manuscript/artist's guidelines for #10 SAE.

Tips: "Be thoroughly familiar with the market, what is being published and what sells. Visits to children's room at local libraries and to children's bookstores would be helpful. Read reviews in *The New York Times Book Review*, *The Booklist*, *Publishers Weekly*, *School Library Journal*." Looks for "humorous picture book story, humorous fiction for young readers, middle group. Children's books almost across the board are the fastest growing segment of the publishing industry. Exceptions include young adult problem novels, historical fiction." We will be publishing more transitional books, i.e. picture storybooks for ages 7 and up and more nonfiction.

"Picture books" are geared toward the preschool—8 year old group; "Young readers" to 5-8 year olds; "Middle readers" to 9-11 year olds; and "Young adults" to those 12 and up.

PLAYERS PRESS, INC., Box 1132, Studio City CA 91614. (818)789-4980. Book publisher. Estab. 1965. Vice President/Editorial: R. W. Gordon. Publishes 2-10 young readers dramatic plays and musicals titles/year; 2-10 middle readers dramatic plays and musicals titles/year; 4-20 young adults dramatic plays and musicals titles/year. 35% of books by first-time authors; 1% of books from agented writers.

Fiction: "We use all categories (young readers, middle readers, young adults) but only for dramatic plays and/or musicals." Recently published *Nessie The Musical*, by William Hezlep (grades 5-8, musical play).

Nonfiction: "Any children's nonfiction all pertaining to the entertainment industry, performing arts and how-to for the theatrical arts only." Published *Clown Makeup*, by C. Strutter, (ages 5-15, theater).

How to Contact/Writers: Fiction/nonfiction: Submit plays or outline/synopsis and sample chapters of entertainment books. Reports on queries in 2-4 weeks; on mss in 12-16 weeks. Publishes a book 10 months after acceptance. No simultaneous submissions.

Illustration: Number of illustrations used for fiction: young readers—1-10; middle readers—1-8. Number of illustrations used for nonfiction: young readers—15; middle readers—2; young adults—20. Associate Editor will review an illustrator's work for possible use in separate texts.

How to Contact/Illustrators: Ms/illustration packages: Query first. Illustrations only: Resume, tearsheets, slides. Reports on art samples only if interested.

Terms/Writers & Illustrators: Pays authors in royalties of 2-20% based on retail price. Other method(s) of payment: "Negotiable." Factors used to determine final payment include color art, number of illustrations used. Pay for illustrators: by the project; royalties range from 2-5%. Sends galleys to authors; dummies to illustrators. Book catalog available for $1.

Tips: Looks for "plays/musicals and books pertaining to the performing arts only."

■*POCAHONTAS PRESS, INC.,** 2805 Wellesley Ct., Blacksburg VA 24060-4126. (703)951-0467. Book Publisher. Editorial contact: Mary C. Holliman. Publishes 1-2 middle readers/year. Subsidy publishes 50%.

Fiction: All levels: history and sports. Recently published *From Massacre to Matriarch*, by Clara T. Fugate (middle/young adult, biographical fiction); *From Lions to Lincoln*, by Fran Hartman (middle/young adult, biographical fiction); *The Legend of Natural Tunnel*, by Clara T. Fugate (middle/young adult, historical fiction).

Nonfiction: All levels: biography, history, hobbies, nature/environment, sports. Recently published *Quarter-Acre of Heartache*, by C.C. Smith (young adult, Indian battle to save reservation).

How to Contact/Writers: Fiction/nonfiction: Query; submit outline/synopsis and sample chapters. Reports on queries in 3-4 weeks; mss in 1-2 months. Publishes a book "probaly as much as a year" after acceptance.

Illustrations: Will review all varieties of manuscript illustration packages. Prefers "black ink, though will sometimes accept pencil drawings. No color."

Terms/Writers & Illustrators: Pays authors in royalties of 10% based on actual receipts. Pays illustrators either by the project $20/hour or in royalties of 5-10% based on actual receipts. Authors see galleys for review; illustrators see dummies for review. Book catalog free on request. Manuscript guidelines not available.

Tips: "Have respect for your child reader, and remember that the actual reader is often an adult. Don't talk down and make jokes or references that are beyond the child's experience. Please, avoid the caricature and the scary." Looks for "a story, well told,

The solid block before a listing indicates the market subsidy publishes manuscripts.

about a real person, not necessarily well known, who has done something interesting or unusual or achieved something from a poor start."

CLARKSON N. POTTER INC., Random House, 201 E. 50th St., New York NY 10022. (212) 572-6166. Editor: Shirley Wohl. Book publisher.
Fiction: "We do nature and picture books for children through age 11."
Nonfiction: "We rarely do nonfiction for children."
How to Contact/Writers: Fiction/nonfiction: Agented work only. Query with SASE only.
Illustrations: Will not accept unagented artwork.
Terms/Writers: Pays authors in royalties based on retail price.

THE PRESS OF MACDONALD & REINECKE, imprint of Padre Productions, Box 840, Arroyo Grande CA 93420-0840. (805)473-1947. Book publisher. Estab. 1974. Editor: Lachlan P. MacDonald. 80% of books by first-time authors; 5% of books from agented writers.
Fiction: Middle readers: fantasy, history, nature. Average length: middle reader—120-140 pages. Published *Joel in Tananar*, by Robert M. Walton (ages 8-14, fantasy adventure).
Nonfiction: Middle readers: biography, history, hobbies, nature/environment. Average length: middle readers—120 pages. Published *Pioneer California*, by Margaret Roberts (grades 4-9, history).
How to Contact/Writers: Fiction: Submit outline/synopsis and sample chapters. Nonfiction: Submit complete ms. Reports on queries in 2 weeks; on mss in 16 weeks. Publishes a book 36 months after acceptance. Will consider simultaneous submissions.
Illustration: Number of illustrations used for fiction: middle readers—8. Number of illustrations used for nonfiction: middle readers—12. Editorial will review all varieties of ms/illustration packages.
How to Contact/Illustrators: Illustrations only: Tearsheets. Reports on art samples only if interested.
Terms/Writers & Illustrators: Pays authors in royalties based on retail price. Other method(s) of payment: "Advance plus royalty." Average advance payment "varies." Additional payment for ms/illustration packages. Factors used to determine final payment include color art vs. black-and-white. Pay for separate authors and illustrators: "Separate contracts." Illustrators paid by the project. Sends galleys to authors; dummies to illustrators. Book catalogs for 9×12 SAE and 45¢ in first-class stamps. Manuscript guidelines/artist's guidelines for #10 SASE.
Tips: Writers: "Concentrate on nonfiction that recognizes changes in today's audience and includes minority and gender considerations without tokenism. The Press of MacDonald & Reinecke is devoted to highly selected works of drama, fiction, poetry and literary nonfiction. Juveniles must be suitable for 140-page books appealing to both boys and girls in the 8-14 year range of readers." Illustrators: "There is a desperate lack of realism by illustrators who can depict proportionate bodies and anatomy. The flood of torn-paper and poster junk is appalling." Looks for: "A book of historical nonfiction of U.S. regional interest with illustrations that have 19th Century elegance and realistic character representations, about topics that still matter today."

PRICE STERN SLOAN, 360 N. LaCienega Blvd., Los Angeles CA 90048. (213)657-6100. FAX: (213)855-8993. Book publisher. Publishes 6 picture books/year; 10 young reader titles/year; 15 middle reader titles/year. 65-70% of books by first-time authors; 35% of books from agented writers.
Fiction: Picture books: animal, contemporary, easy-to-read, spy/mystery/adventure. Young readers: animal, contemporary, easy-to-read, spy/mystery/adventure. Middle readers: animal, contemporary, easy-to-read, spy/mystery/adventure. Published *Adven-*

tures in the Solar System, by Geoffrey Williams (ages 7-12, space adventure book and cassette); *Elephant Ann & How the First Circus Began*, by Jon Madian (ages 0-7, storybook); *Good Night Sleep Tight*, by Mary Cron (ages 0-7, storybook).

Nonfiction: Picture books, young readers, middle readers: animal, educational, history, hobbies, nature/environment, sports. Young adults: biography. Published *Since 1776*, by Paul C. Murphy (ages 11 and up, history); *Collecting Bugs & Things*, by Julia Moutran (ages 5 and up, science activities).

How to Contact/Writers: Fiction/nonfiction: Query. Reports on queries/mss in 3 months. Publishes a book 6-8 months after acceptance. Will consider simultaneous submissions.

Illustration: Editorial will review all varieties of ms/illustration packages.

How to Contact/Illustrators: Ms/illustration: Query first. Illustrations only: Resume, tearsheets, slides. Reports on art samples only if interested.

Terms/Writers & Illustrators: Pays authors in royalties based on net price. Sends galleys to authors; dummies to illustrators. Book catalog available for 9×12 SAE and 6 first-class stamps; manuscript guidelines for legal-size SASE; artist's guidelines for letter-size SAE and 1 first-class stamp.

Tips: "Avoid writing stories with themes that have been done over and over again. We are looking for books that teach as well as entertain. Subject areas include nature, science, how-to, wordplay for early readers, book and cassette ideas, activity books, and original storybooks."

*PROMETHEUS BOOKS, 700 E. Amherst St., Buffalo NY 14215. (716)837-2475. Book publisher. Editor: Jeanne O'Day. Publishes 1 young reader title/year; 3 middle reader titles/year; 1 young adult title/year. 40% of books by first-time authors; 50% of books from agented writers.

Fiction: Picture books: sex education, moral education, magic. Young readers, middle readers and young adults/teens: sex education, moral education, critical thinking, magic, skepticism, science. Average word length: picture books—2,000; young readers—10,000; middle readers—20,000; young adult/teens—60,000. Recently published *Bellybuttons Are Navels*, by Mark Schoen (ages 3-8, sex education); *The Snark Puzzle Book*, by Martin Gardner (ages 9 and up, critical thinking).

Nonfiction: Picture books: sex education, moral education, magic. Young readers, middle readers and young adults/teens: sex education, moral education, critical thinking, magic, skepticism, science. Average word length: picture books—2,000; young readers—10,000; middle readers—20,000; young adult/teens—60,000. Recently published *The Magic Detectives*, by Joe Nickell (ages 9-15, skepticism); *It's Magic*, by Henry Gordon (ages 9 and up, magic); *Smart Moves*, by Dick De Venzio (young adult, how to succeed).

How to Contact/Writers: Fiction/nonfiction: Submit complete manuscript. Reports on queries in 2 weeks; mss in 2-3 months. Publishes a book 1 year after acceptance.

Illustration: Number of illustrations used for fiction and nonfiction: picture books—40; young readers—20. Editorial will review all varieties of illustration packages. Editor, Jeanne O'Day, will review illustrator's work for possible use in separate texts.

How to Contact/Illustrators: "Prefer to have full work (manuscript and illustrations); will consider any proposal." Include résumé, photocopies. Reports on ms/art samples

 The asterisk before a listing indicates the listing is new in this edition.

in 1-2 months. Original artwork returned at job's completion.
Terms/Writers & Illustrators: "Contact terms vary with projects." Sends galleys to author; dummies to illustrators. Book catalog is free on request. Manuscript/artists guidelines not available.

RANDOM HOUSE BOOKS FOR YOUNG READERS, Random House, Inc., 8th Floor, 225 Park Ave. South, New York NY 10003. (212)254-1600. Book publisher. Editor-in-Chief: Kate Klimo. 100% of books published through agents; 2% of books by first-time authors.
Fiction: Picture books: animal, easy-to-read, history, sports. Young readers: animal, easy-to-read, history, sports, spy/mystery/adventure. Middle readers: history, science, sports, spy/mystery/adventure. Recently published titles: *No Mail for Mitchell*, by Catherine Siracusa (K-1, step into reading); *The Adventures of Rat Man*, by Ellen Weiss (grades 2-3, stepping stones); *The Little Quiet Book*, by Katharine Ross (ages 1-3, chunky book).
Nonfiction: Picture books: animal. Young readers: animal, biography, hobbies. Middle readers: biography, history, hobbies, sports. Recently published *The First Thanksgiving*, by Linda Hayward (grades 1-3); *Make Way for Trucks*, by Gail Herman (grades 1-3, picture book).
How to Contact/Writers: Fiction/nonfiction: submit through agent only. Publishes a book in 12-18 months. Will consider simultaneous submissions.
Illustration: Will review ms/illustration packages submitted by authors with illustrations done by separate artists (through agent only); ms/illustration packages submitted by authors with illustrations done by separate artists (through agent only). Executive Art Director, Cathy Goldsmith, will review an illustrator's work for possible use in separate texts.
Terms/Writers & Illustrators: Pays authors in royalties; sometimes buys mss outright. Sends galleys to authors. Book catalog free on request.
Tips: There is a "trend away from licensed characters" in book publishing.

■*READ'N RUN BOOKS,** Subsidiary of Crumb Elbow Publishing, P.O. Box 294, Rhododendron OR 97049. (503)622-4798. Book publisher. Publisher: Michael P. Jones. Publishes 3 picture books/year; 5 young reader titles/year; 2 middle reader titles/year; 5 young adult titles/year. 50% of books by first-time authors; 2% of books from agented writers. Subsidy publishes 10%.
Fiction: Will consider all categories for all age levels. Average word length: "Open." Recently published *Nightrider*, by Michael P. Jones (horror).
Nonfiction: Will consider all categories for all age levels. Average word length: "Open." Recently published *Fitting Out for the Oregon Trail*, by Joel Palmer (elementary/secondary, history on Oregon Trail); *Wagons with Covers on the Oregon Trail*, by Grace Butterfield (elementary/secondary, history of Oregon Trail); *The Old Emmigrant Road*, by G.W. Kennedy (elementary/juvenile, history of Oregon Trail).
How to Contact/Writers: For fiction and nonfiction: Query. Reports on queries/mss in 2 months "or sooner depending upon work load." Publishes a book about 8 months to a year depending on workload and previously committed projects. Will consider simultaneous submissions.
Illustration: Number of illustrations used for fiction and nonfiction: picture books—15; young readers—15; middle readers—20; young adult/teens—20. Reviews all varieties of ms/illustration packages. Publisher, Michael P. Jones, will review illustrator's work for possible use in separate author's text. "Black and white, 8×10 or 5×7 illustrations. No color work for finished artwork, but color work is great to demonstrate the artist's talents."
How to Contact/Illustrators: Query with sample chapter and several pieces of the artwork. "Artists should submit a good selection of their work, a résumé and a letter

outlining their goals. Photocopies are fine." Reports on ms/art samples in 1-2 months. Original artwork returned at job's completion.

Terms/Writers & Illustrators: Pays in published copies only. Sends galleys to authors; dummies to illustrators. Book catalog available in February 1991 for $1. Manuscript or artists' guidelines for 1 first class stamp and #10 SAE.

Tips: "Don't give up. The field can seem cruel and harsh when trying to break into the market. Roll with the punches. We love history books (i.e., Oregon Trail, Native Americans), nature, environmental and something with a message, like saving the earth and its resources and creatures."

THE ROCKRIMMON PRESS, INC., Imprint of Industrial Printers of Colorado, Inc., 110 E. Enterprise, Colorado Springs CO 80918. (719)594-6337. Book publisher. Editor: Toni Knapp. Publishes 2 young reader titles/year; 2 middle reader titles/year.

Fiction: "If an idea is good, we'll consider it."

Nonfiction: Young reader/middle reader: animal, history, nature/environment.

How to Contact/Writers: Query or submit outline/synopsis and sample chapters. Reports on queries in 1 month; on ms in 2 months. Publishes a book 1 year after acceptance. Will consider simultaneous submissions.

Illustration: Number of illustrations used in fiction: young reader—10-15; middle reader—8-10. Editorial will review ms/illustration packages submitted by authors/artists. Editor, Toni Knapp, will review illustrator's work for possible use in authors' texts.

How to Contact/Illustrators: "Query first except for picture books." Illustrations only: submit résumé, tearsheets. Reports in 2 months. Originals sometimes returned to artist at job's completion.

Terms/Writers & Illustrators: Pays authors in royalties based on wholesale price. Advance payment varies. Pay for illustrators: by the project; royalties based on wholesale price. Sends galleys to author; dummies to illustrator. Book catalog and ms/artists guidelines free on request.

Tips: Illustrators should "have an excellent professional portfolio as well as outstanding examples for queries. Try the major trade houses, but don't overlook the small, high quality presses. The trend is toward nonfiction, a higher language level, excellence in illustration and writing."

ROSEBRIER PUBLISHING CO., 1510 Perkinsville Dr., Box 106, Boone NC 28607. Independent book producer/packager. Editorial Contact: Beverly Donadio. Publishes 1 picture book/year. 50% of books by first-time authors.

Fiction: Picture books: animal, fantasy. Published *The Rosebrier Collection, Mis' Luci, The Rabbit Family, Montgomery Mole* and *Quincy Quail*, by Beverly Rose (K-5th grades, fantasy).

How to Contact/Writers: Fiction: submit complete ms. Include Social Security number with submission. Reports on queries/ms in 6 months. Publishes a book 6 months after acceptance.

Illustration: Number of illustrations used in fiction: picture book—20. Editorial will review ms/illustration packages submitted by authors/artists; ms/illustration packages submitted by authors with illustrations done by separate artists.

How to Contact/Illustrators: Submit 3 chapters of ms with 1 piece of art.

Terms/Writers & Illustrators: Pays authors in royalties.

THE ROSEN PUBLISHING GROUP, 29 E. 21st St., New York NY 10010. (212)777-3017. Book publisher. Estab. 1950. Editorial Contact: Ruth Rosen. Publisher: Roger Rosen. Publishes 8 middle reader titles/year; 50 young adult titles/year. 35% of books by first-time authors; 3% of books from agented writers.

Nonfiction: Young readers: contemporary, easy-to-read, sports. Middle readers: contemporary, easy-to-read, sports, psychological self-help. Young adults: contemporary, easy-to-read, sports, careers, psychological self-help. Average word length: young readers—8,000; middle readers—10,000; young adults—40,000. Recently published *Coping with Depression*, by Sharon Carter (grades 7-12, self-help); *Coping with a Dysfunctional Family*, by Diane Bosley Taylor and Paul Michael Taylor (grades 7-12, self-help); *Coping with Your Sexual Orientation*, by Deborah A. Miller, Ph.D (grades 7-12, self-help).

How to Contact/Writers: Nonfiction: Submit outline/synopsis and sample chapters. Publishes a book 9 months after acceptance.

Illustration: Number of illustrations used for nonfiction: young readers—20; middle readers—10. Editorial will review all varieties of ms/illustration packages. Roger Rosen will review an illustrator's work for possible use in separate texts.

How to Contact/Illustrators: Ms/illustration packages: 3 chapters of ms with 1 piece of final art. Illustrations only: Résumé, tearsheets. Original artwork returned at job's completion.

Terms/Writers & Illustrators: Pays authors in royalties. Sends galleys to authors. Book catalog free on request.

Tips: "Target your manuscript to a specific age group and reading level and write for established series published by the house you are approaching."

ST. ANTHONY MESSENGER PRESS, 1615 Republic St., Cincinnati OH 45210. (513)241-5615. FAX: (513)241-0399. Book publisher. Managing Editor: Lisa Biedenbach. 25% of books by first-time authors.

Fiction: "Very few titles published." Middle readers and young adults: religious. Published *Saints of the Seasons for Children*, by Ethel Pochocki Marbach, (middle readers, lives of saints).

Nonfiction: Young readers, middle readers and young adults: religion. Recently published *What's A Kid to Do? Practicing Moral Decision-Making with 10- to 13-Year Olds*, by John A. Flanagan, (middle readers, 39 exercises for moral development); *What's a Teen to Do? Developing Helping Skills with 14- to 16-Year Olds*, by John A. Flanagan, (young adults, 40 stories with discussion questions to lead teens to growth in awareness of needs and to satisfaction of helping others).

How to Contact/Writers: Fiction/nonfiction: Query, submit outline/synopsis and sample chapters. Reports on queries in 2-4 weeks; mss in 4-6 weeks. Publishes a book 12-18 months after acceptance.

Illustration: Editorial will review ms/illustration packages submitted by authors/artists. "We design all covers and do most illustrations in-house."

Terms/Writers & Illustrators: Pays authors in royalties of 10-12% based on net receipts. Offers average advance payment of $600. Sends galleys to authors. Book catalog, manuscript guidelines free on request.

Tips: "We're looking for programs to be used in Catholic schools and parishes, programs that have successful track record."

ST. PAUL BOOKS AND MEDIA, Daughters of St. Paul, 50 St. Paul's Ave., Jamaica Plain, Boston MA 02130. (617)522-8911. Book publisher. Estab. 1934. Editor: Sister Anne Joan, fsp. Publishes 1-2 picture books/year; 1-2 young reader titles/year; 1-2 middle reader titles/year; 1-3 young adult titles/year. 20% of books by first-time authors.

Fiction: Picture books: contemporary, religion, devotionals. Young readers: anthology, contemporary, history, religion, saints, devotionals. Middle readers: anthology, contemporary, history, problem novels, saints, devotionals. Young adults: anthology, contemporary, history, problem novels, religion. Average word length: picture books—150-300; young readers—1,500-5,000; middle readers—10,000; young adults—20,000-50,000. Published *Hoover Wants to Help*, by Price (picture book, animal/toys); *Best Gift of All*, by Wilkeshvis (young reader, religion).

Nonfiction: All levels: religion. Average word length: picture books—200; young readers—1,500-5,000; middle readers—10,000; young adults—20,000-50,000. Recently published *Little Lights in the Darkness*, by Wever (young reader, devotional); *That's Me in Here*, by Darby (picture book, education); *On the Way to Bethlehem*, by deVries (picture book, religion).

How to Contact/Writers: Fiction/nonfiction: Submit outline/synopsis and sample chapters. Reports on queries in 3-8 weeks; on mss in 12 weeks. Publishes a book 2-3 years after acceptance. No simultaneous submissions.

Illustration: Number of illustrations used for fiction/nonfiction: picture books—8-12; young readers—8; middle readers—5; young adults—2-5. Editorial will review all varieties of ms/illustration packages. Style/size of illustration "varies according to the title. Re: colors, our scanner will not take fluorescents."

How to Contact/Illustrators: Ms/illustration packages: "Outline first with art samples." Illustrations only: Résumé, slides and tearsheets. Reports on art samples in 3-8 weeks.

Terms/Writers & Illustrators: Pays authors in royalties of 4-12% based on gross sales. Additional payment for ms/illustrations packages: "negotiable." Pay for separate authors and illustrators: Varies by job. Illustrations paid by the project. Book catalog for 9×12 SAE and 4 first class stamps. Manuscript guidelines for legal-size SAE and 1 first class stamp.

Tips: "We are a Roman Catholic publishing house looking for manuscripts (whether fiction or nonfiction) that communicate high moral, religious and family values. Lives of saints, Bible stories welcome, as well as historical or contemporary novels for children. In Catholic circles, a renewed interest in saints. In general, high interest in allegorical fantasy, as well as stories that reflect attitudes and life situations children are deeply familiar with."

SANDLAPPER PUBLISHING CO., INC., 281 Amelia St., Box 1932, Orangeburg SC 29116. (803)531-1658. Book publisher. Editor: Frank Handal. 10% of books by first-time authors.

Fiction: Middle readers: easy-to-read, spy/mystery/adventure. Young adults: contemporary, history. Published *Whopper!*, by Idella Bodie (middle readers).

Nonfiction: Young adults: biography, education, history, hobbies, nature/environment, sports. Published *The South Carolina Story*, by Anne Osborne (young adults to adults, history); *SC's Lowcountry: A Past Preserved*, by Halcomb/Messmer (adults, pictorial/history); *Dorn: Of the People*, by Dorn/Derks (adults, political/history).

How to Contact/Writers: Fiction/nonfiction: Submit outline/synopsis and sample chapters. Reports on queries in 1 week; on mss in 24 weeks. Publishes a book 24 months after acceptance. Will consider simultaneous submissions.

Illustration: Number of illustrations used for fiction: picture books, young readers, middle readers, young adults—6/category. Number of illustrations used for nonfiction: picture books, young readers, middle readers, young adults—20/category. Editorial will review all varieties of ms/illustration packages.

How to Contact/Illustrators: Illustrations only: Resume, tearsheets, slides. Reports on art samples in 2 weeks. Original artwork returned at job's completion.

Terms/Writers & Illustrators: Pays authors in royalties. Illustrator paid by the project. Sends galleys to authors. Book catalog, manuscript guidelines free on request.

Tips: Looks for: "regional works on the south; history, literature, cuisine and culture."

SCHOLASTIC HARDCOVER, Imprint of Scholastic Inc., 730 Broadway, New York NY 10003. (212)505-3000. Book publisher. Editorial Director, Jean Feiwel. Senior Editor: Dianne Hess. Editorial contacts are as follows: picture books: Jean Feiwel, Dianne Hess, Grace Maccarone; young readers: Dianne Hess; middle readers: Jean Teivel and Regina Griffin; young adult tales: Jean Feiwel and Regina Griffin. Publishes 40+ (in hardcover) picture books/year; 20+ young reader titles/year; 20+ middle reader titles/

Close-up

Johanna Hurwitz
Writer
Great Neck, New York

"When I started writing, I did not realize that I would become involved with so many series," says Johanna Hurwitz. "However, I have discovered that the more I write about a particular character and his or her family, the better I know them all and the more eager I become to write still more about them."

Intentional or not, Hurwitz has been writing series since her first book, *Busybody Nora* was published in 1976. Since then, seven additional books featuring Nora and her clan have been published.

Hurwitz says she has been making up stories since she was 8 years old, and always knew she wanted to be a writer. At 38, she finally sold her first book; that's why when children ask her how long it takes to write a book, she says *Busybody Nora* took her whole life. Fortunately, she has been publishing books regularly ever since. She enjoys writing especially for 7 to 9-year-olds.

Hurwitz also writes books for two other series. Her books slated for publication in 1991 include *School's Out*, a continuation of the adventures of *Class Clown*'s Lucas Cott, and *E is for Elisa*. These books will bring her total number of published books up to 31. In the series featuring Lucas Cott, she says she almost made her characters too old for her audience. With each of the three books, the characters became a year older. To keep the series from outgrowing her readers, she has backtracked with *School's Out*. This book starts "five minutes after *Class Clown* (the first book in the series) ends."

Hurwitz says she gets her ideas from real life incidents. However, she points out these incidents don't necessarily have to be experienced. Rather, merely observing the actions of other people can spark ideas for stories. She cites one case where she once witnessed a woman in a public restroom who took her ring off and held it in her mouth while washing her hands. Her initial reaction to watching this was concern the woman would swallow the ring. Though in real life the woman didn't swallow the ring, that didn't stop Hurwitz from having Cricket Kaufman swallow it in *Teacher's Pet*.

Eavesdropping is another effective tool in getting story ideas. Having once overheard two women talking about using mayonnaise in their hair, Hurwitz thought it would be interesting to have one of her characters do it. She wrote about it in *Tough Luck Karen*. Whether it is from her own experiences or those of others, Hurwitz says in every one of her books there is a hint of real life.

In addition to being a writer, Hurwitz has been a children's librarian for over 30 years and holds an MS in Library Science from Columbia University. Though she now only works a few hours a week as a librarian, she says she loves doing it because it gives her a chance to keep up with what's new in children's books. "Best of all," she says, "I love working with the young readers." One thing she does to promote reading by children is mention the names of other books within her own, her logic being that the kids reading the book will be interested in reading the same thing the characters are reading. One trend she notices is that kids are reading less fantasy, though "those who do are the brightest." Also, she notes historical fiction is not as popular as it used to be.

Though known primarily as a writer of middle-grade fiction, Hurwitz is definitely not restricted to just that. Her first picture book is scheduled to be published in the spring of 1992. Hurwitz has also written two biographies, one on Anne Frank and the other about Astrid Lindgren (the woman who created the character of Pippi Longstocking). Currently she is working on her third biography, this one about Leonard Bernstein. "I enjoy the change from fiction to biography because in the latter the story is all there waiting for me to research and shape into a book. I love doing research and the temptation is to read and read and read about the subject and postpone the actual writing. Fortunately, there are publishing deadlines or I might never finish writing."

Hurwitz submitted manuscripts for three years before she finally got published, and she feels a new writer's first book almost has to be better than anything published *after* the first. "Too many beginning writers believe they can send a manuscript out and that if an editor is interested, he or she will make any necessary changes. This is not the way it works. Because so many manuscripts come into a publishing house daily, an editor has to read something that is quite perfect if he or she is going to take the risk of publishing it. Once one has been published, editors are more willing to take the time to discuss why a manuscript does not work and give the writer a chance to improve it.

"If you want to write, you must believe in yourself and not give up. I am certain that some truly wonderful manuscripts have been torn up or buried in the bottom drawer of a desk because the writer became discouraged after only two or three or ten rejections. Some of the best known children's book writers have the worst horror stories of near misses and rejections. Luckily for their readers, they did not give up."

When asked how one should go about writing a children's book, Hurwitz says all writers must find the steps that best suit them. Some feel it is necessary to take a slew of writing classes before they even attempt to sit down and write. Others depend on nothing other than an active imagination. She says some authors outline every detail of what they will write, while others sit down, start writing and allow the story to develop as it goes along. Hurwitz says she uses a combination of the two and likens it to "taking a trip and leaving the map at home. I know in what general direction I'm going. I may get lost at times, but the detours I take are most memorable."

—Lisa Carpenter

year; 20+ young adult titles/year. 5% of books by first-time authors; 50% of books through agents.

Fiction: Picture books/young readers/middle readers/young adult: animal, contemporary, humor, easy-to-read, fantasy, history, problem novels, romance, science fiction, sports, spy/mystery/adventure, etc. Published *Fallen Angels*, by Walter Dean Meyers (young adult, Vietnam War, historic fiction); *The Trouble with the Johnsons*, by Mark Teague (picture book, humor/fantasy); and *Time for School, Nathan*, by Lulu Delaune (picture book, friendship/contemporary fantasy).

Nonfiction: Picture books/young readers/middle readers/young adult: animal, biography, education, history, hobbies, music/dance, nature/environment, religion, sports. Published *Sarah Morton's Day: A Day in the Life of a Pilgrim Girl*, by Kate Waters (picture book/young reader, historic nonfiction); *The Magic School Bus*, by Joanna Cole (picture book/young reader, humorous science-fantasy); *Exploring the Titanic*, by Robert D. Ballard (middle reader/young adult, history/social studies).

How to Contact/Writers: Fiction (for picture book and young reader): Submit complete mss with SASE; (for young adult and middle reader); query or submit outline/synopsis and sample chapters. Nonfiction: Query or submit outline/synopsis and sample chapters. Reports on queries in 2-4 weeks; on mss in 6-8 weeks. Publishes a book 1 year after acceptance.

Illustrations: Editorial will review ms/illustration packages submitted by authors/artists; ms/illustration packages submitted by authors with illustrations done by separate artists. "It is not necessary for authors to supply art." Dianne Hess, senior editor, or Claire Counihan, Art Director, will review an illustrator's work for possible use in separate texts.

How to Contact/Illustrators: Illustrations only: Send tearsheets or slides. Reports in 6-8 weeks. Original art work returned at job's completion.

Terms/Writers & Illustrators: Pays authors in royalties of 10% (5% if split with artist) based on retail price. Sends galleys to author; dummies to illustrator. Book catalog for postage and mailing label.

Tips: Writers: "Attend writing workshops, learn your craft, don't be afraid to revise. Illustrators: Create a finished dummy of any story and one piece of finished art to show an editor how you work."

SCHOLASTIC, INC., 730 Broadway, New York NY 10003. (212)505-3000. Book publisher. Editorial Contact: Dianne Hess, Senior Editor (picture books); Eva Moore (young readers). Executive Editor: Ann Reit (middle readers/young adult titles). 5-25% of books by first-time authors; 50% of books from agented writers.

Fiction: Picture books, middle readers: contemporary, fantasy, mystery/adventure. Young adults/teens: contemporary, romance, mystery/adventure. Average word length: middle readers—35,000; young adult/teens—45,000. Recently published *Is Your Mama a Llama?*, by Deborah Guanno (pre-school-grade 3, picture book); *How Many Sports Does a Leopard Have?*, by Julius Lester (grades 3-8, picture book); *Fallen Angels*, by Walter Dean Meyers (grades 6-12, novel).

Nonfiction: Middle readers: biography, nature/environment. Published *Jesse Jackson*, by Patricia McKissack (middle reader, hard/paper).

How to Contact/Writers: Fiction/nonfiction: Submit outline/synopsis and sample chapters or submit complete ms. Reports on queries 1 month; mss 3 months. Publishes a book 12-18 months after acceptance.

Terms/Writers & Illustrators: Pays in royalties.

Tips: Writers: "Know the firm you are sending a submission to—what they publish, what they don't publish." Trends in book publishing: "Emphasis is on quality middle readers, young readers and picture books."

CHARLES SCRIBNER'S SONS, Imprint of Macmillan Publishing Co., 866 Third Ave., New York NY 10940. (212)702-7885. Book publisher. Senior Vice President/Editorial Director: Clare Costello. 25% of books from agented writers.
Fiction: Picture books: animal, contemporary, folk material. Young readers: animal, contemporary. Middle readers: animal, contemporary, fantasy, history, science fiction, mystery/adventure. Young adults/teens: animal, contemporary, fantasy, history, science fiction. Recently published *Animals of the Night*, by Banks/Himler (picture book); *Secret City, U.S.A.*, by Holman (contemporary, young adult fiction); *The Man in the River*, by Duffy (intermediate, mystery novel).
Nonfiction: Picture books: animal. Young readers: animal, nature/environment. Middle readers: animal, biography, history, nature/environment. Young adults/teens: animal, biography, history, nature/environment. Recently published *Ellis Island*, by Jacobs (young readers, history); *Shifting Shores*, by Hecht (young adult, environment); *The Other 1492*, by Finkelstein (intermediate, Jewish American history).
How to Contact/Writers: Fiction: Submit outline/synopsis and sample chapters. Nonfiction: Query. Reports on queries in 4 weeks; mss in 10-14 weeks. Publishes a book 12-18 months after acceptance, "picture books longer." Will consider simultaneous (if specified when submitted) submissions.
Illustrations: Editorial will review ms/illustration packages submitted by authors/artists.
How to Contact/Illustrators: Ms/illustration packages: "Query first." Illustrations only: Send tearsheets. Reports back only if interested. Original artwork returned at job's completion.
Terms/Writers & Illustrators: Pays authors in royalties based on retail price. Sends galleys to authors; dummies to illustrators. Book catalog for 8×10 SAE; manuscript guidelines are for legal-size SASE.

HAROLD SHAW PUBLISHERS, 388 Gundersen Dr., Box 567, Wheaton IL 60189. (708)665-6700. Book publisher. Estab. 1967. Dir. of Editorial Services: Ramona Cramer Tucker. Publishes 4 young adult titles/year. 10% of books by first-time authors; 5% of books from agented writers.
Fiction/Nonfiction: Young adults: fiction and teen devotionals. Average length: young adults—112-250 pages. Recently published *Dark Is A Color*, by Fay S. Lapka (ages 13 and up, novel); *All the King's Horses*, by Jeffrey Asher Nesbit (ages 13 and up, novel); *One in a Zillion*, by Annette Heinrich (ages 13 and up, young adult devotional); *A Safe Place: Beyond Sexual Abuse*, by Jan Morrison (ages 13 and up, nonfiction self-help).
How to Contact/Writers: Nonfiction: Query. Reports on queries in 2-4 weeks; on mss in 4-6 weeks. Publishes a book 12 months after acceptance. Will consider simultaneous submissions.
Illustration: Number of illustrations used for nonfiction: young adults—1. Editorial will review ms/illustration packages submitted by authors with illustrations done by separate artists and an illustrator's work for possible use in separate texts.
How to Contact/Illustrators: Ms: Query first. Illustrations only: Résumé, sample of work (2-3). Reports on art samples in 4 weeks. Original artwork returned at job's completion.
Terms/Writers & Illustrators: Pays authors in royalties of 5-10% based on retail price. Buys ms outright for $500-$1,500. Factors used to determine final payment include color art vs. b&w and number of illustrations used. Pay for separate authors and illustrators: royalty or ms payment is split. Illustrators paid by the project. Sends pages to authors. Book catalog available for SAE and $1.25; manuscript guidelines for SAE and 1 first-class stamp.
Tips: Writers: "Visit your bookstore. Read your stories to children and to adults. You'll find children are the most honest." Illustrators: "Show your illustrations to children and see if they appeal to them first before contacting a publisher." Looks for "a study guide

or a very unusual story which would make us change our minds about not picking up any more children's books! It (the children's book market) is growing bigger, but at the same time the quality has been going down (quality of writing and illustrations). Lasting books are being replaced by more chapbook-flimsy paperbooks."

SHOE TREE PRESS, Imprint of Betterway Publications, Inc., Box 219, Crozet VA 22932. (804)823-5661. Book publisher. Editor: Susan Lewis. Published 3 middle reader titles in 1989. 70% of books by first-time authors.
Fiction: Middle readers and young adults: history, problem novels. Middle readers—20,000-35,000; young adults—50,000-75,000. Published *Melvil and Dewey in the Fast Lane*, by Pamela Curtis Swallow (middle readers, contemporary fiction); *Summer Captive*, by Penny Pollock (young adults, contemporary); *By George Bloomers!*, by Judith St. George (easy reader for young readers).
Nonfiction: Middle readers and young adults: animal, biography, history, hobbies, music/dance, nature/environment, reference. Average word length: middle readers—30,000-45,000; young adults—35,000-75,000. Recently published *Market Guide for Young Writers*, by Kathy Henderson (ages 10 and up, reference); *Devoted Friends: Amazing True Stories about Animals Who Cared*, by Gretchen Alday (10 and up, animals/nonfiction).
How to Contact/Writers: Fiction/nonfiction: Query first please. Reports on queries in 4 weeks; on mss in 12 weeks. Publishes a book 6-12 months after acceptance. Will consider simultaneous submissions.
Illustration: Number of illustrations used for fiction and nonfiction: young readers—12-30; middle readers—12-30. Editorial will review all varieties of ms/illustration packages.
How to Contact/Illustrators: Ms/illustration packages: Query first. Illustrations only: Resume/tearsheets. Reports on art samples only if interested. Original artwork returned at job's completion.
Terms/Writers & Illustrators: Pays authors in royalties based on wholesale prices. Sends galleys to authors; dummies to illustrators.
Tips: "Avoid getting caught up in market trends." Looks for "middle years and young adult nonfiction. We do *not* publish picture books. Our focus has shifted to mainly nonfiction along with biographies and historical fiction. We want books that kids ages 10 and up can learn from, but also enjoy."

SKYLARK/BOOKS FOR YOUNG READERS, Imprint of Bantam Books Inc., 666 Fifth Ave., New York NY 10103. Editorial Contact: Judy Gitenstein.
Fiction: Middle readers: chapter books for ages 5-8. Contemporary, fantasy, historical, mystery, adventure. No short stories.
How to Contact/Writers: Fiction: Submit outline/synopsis and sample chapters; "You will get a form rejection if your ms is not for us. The number of submissions received does not allow us time to comment on them all."
Terms/Writers & Illustrators: Pays authors in royalties of 6-8% based on retail price.

*THE SPEECH BIN, INC., 1766 Twentieth Ave., Vero Beach FL 32960. (407)770-0007. Book publisher. Contact: Jan J. Binney, Senior Editor. Publishes 10-12 books/year. 50% of books by first-time authors; less than 15% of books from agented writers. "Nearly all our books deal with treatment of children (as well as adults) who have communication disorders of speech or hearing or children who deal with family members who have such

Always include a self-addressed stamped envelope (SASE) or International Reply Coupon (IRC) with submissions.

disorders (example, a grandparent with Alzheimer's or stroke)."
Fiction: Picture books: animal, easy-to-read, fantasy. Young readers: easy-to-read. Recently published *The Many Voices of Paws*, by Julie Dzewaltkowski Reville (preschool-grade 2, picture book with teacher's edition).
Nonfiction: Recently published *Calendar Capers*, by Pamela Meza Steckbeck, Illustrated by Marie M. Long (preschool-grade 5, activity book); *Acquire*, by Linda B. Collins & Sandra Sayre Chadwell (grades 4-12, word games); *Spotlight on Speech-Language Services*, by Janet M. Shaw (grades K-12, activity book).
How to Contact/Writers: Fiction/nonfiction: Query. Include Social Security number with submission. Reports on queries in 4-6 weeks; 2-3 months on mss. Publishes a book 10-12 months after acceptance. "Will consider simultaneous submissions only if notified; too many authors fail to let us know if ms is simultaneously submitted to other publishers! We *strongly* prefer sole submissions."
Illustration: Number of illustrations used for fiction and nonfiction: picture books— 50; young readers—50; middle readers—50; young adult/teens—less than 10. Editorial will review ms/illustration packages submitted by authors/artists and authors with illustrations done by separate artists.
How to Contact/Illustrators: "Query first!" Submit résumé; tearsheets or copies also OK. Original art work returned at job's completion.
Terms/Writers & Illustrators: Pays authors in royalties of 8% (without art). Additional payment for ms/illustration package is 10% royalty. Pay for separate authors and illustrators: writer—royalty; illustrator—purchase. Pay for illustrators: by the project when they work on your author's title. Sends galleys to authors. Book catalog for 3 first class stamps and 9×12 SAE; manuscript guidelines for 1 first class stamp and #10 SAE.

SRI RAMA PUBLISHING, Box 2550, Santa Cruz CA 95063. (408)426-5098. Book publisher. Estab. 1975. Secretary/Manager: Karuna K. Ault. Publishes 1 or fewer young reader titles/year.
Fiction: Published *Mystic Monkey*, Hari Dass (ages 7-13, storybook).
Nonfiction: Published *A Child's Garden of Yoga*, by Hari Dass (ages 3-12, Yoga instruction).
Illustration: 40 illustrations used for fiction. Graphic Design Director, Josh Gitomer, will review illustrators' work for possible use in separate texts.
How to Contact/Illustrators: Submit several samples. Reports on art samples in 2 months. Original art work returned at job's completion.
Terms/Writers & Illustrators: "We are a nonprofit organization. Proceeds from our sales support an orphanage in India, so we encourage donated labor, but each case is worked out individually." Pay for illustrators: $200 minimum, $1,000 maximum. Sends galleys to authors; dummies to illustrators. Book catalog and manuscript guidelines free on request.

STANDARD PUBLISHING, 8121 Hamilton Ave., Cincinnati OH 45231. (513)931-4050. Book publisher. Director: Mark Plunkett. Publishes 25 picture books/year; 4 young reader titles/year; 8 middle reader titles/year; 4 young adult titles/year. 25% of books by first-time authors; 1% of books from agented writers.
Fiction: Picture books: animal. Young readers: easy-to-read. Middle readers: contemporary, sports. Young adults: contemporary, problem novels. Average word length: picture books—400; young readers—1,000; middle readers—25,000; young adults—40,000. Published *Summer's Quest*, by Susanne Elliott (young adults, contemporary); *Wheeler's Big Break*, by Daniel Schantz (middle readers, contemporary); *Runaway*, by Janet Willig (ages 12-15).
Nonfiction: Picture books: animal, religion. Young readers, middle readers, young adults: religion. Average word length: picture books—400; young readers—1,000; middle readers—25,000; young adults—40,000. Published *The Little Lost Sheep*, by Marilyn

Lindsay (picture book, religious); *Thank You God, for Christmas*, by Henrietta Gambill (picture book, religious); *Seven Special Days*, by Henrietta Gambill (picture book, religious).

How to Contact/Writers: Fiction/nonfiction: Query. Reports on queries in 3 weeks; on mss in 12 weeks. Publishes a book 18 months after acceptance. Will consider simultaneous and electronic submissions via disk or modem.

Illustration: Number of illustrations used for fiction: picture books—24; young readers—24; middle readers—12; young adults—12. Number of illustrations used for nonfiction: picture books—24. Editorial will review all varieties of ms/illustration packages. Art Director, Frank Sutton, will review an illustrator's work for possible use in separate texts.

How to Contact/Illustrators: Ms/illustration packages: Query. Illustrations only: "Tearsheets and résumé." Reports on art samples in 3 weeks.

Terms/Writers & Illustrators: Pays authors in royalties of 5-12% based on wholesale price. Buys ms outright for $250-$1,000. Offers average advance payment of $250. Sends galleys to authors. Book catalog available for 8½×11 SAE; manuscript guidelines for letter-size SASE.

Tips: "When writing children's books, make the vocabulary level correct for the age you plan to reach. Watch spelling and sentence structure. Keep your material true to the Bible. Be accurate in quoting Scriptures and references." Looks for picture books.

STAR BOOKS, INC., 408 Pearson St., Wilson NC 27893. (919)237-1591. Editorial Contact: Irene Burk Harrell. "We are still a new and growing company."

Fiction/Nonfiction: "Manuscripts must be somehow strongly related to the good news of Jesus Christ." Recently published *The Galactic Rocking Chair*, by Crystal Zapata; *The Adventures of Captain Rhema*, by Barbara Grady; *Black Lizard's Startling Encounter*, by Chip Hill.

How to Contact/Writers: Submit complete ms. Include Social Security number. Reports on queries in 1-2 weeks; mss in 4-8 weeks. Publishes a book 6 months after acceptance ("longer if extensive editing needed"). *No* simultaneous submissions.

Illustration: Editorial will review all varieties of ms/illustration packages. "At present, we prefer informal black and white line art. As finances improve, we'll be interested in color."

How to Contact/Illustrators: Ms/illustration packages: send whole ms, 1-3 roughs of art. Reports on art samples within a month. Original artwork returned at job's completion.

Terms/Writers & Illustrators: Pay: "We issue contract for the whole (ms/illustration) package." Sends galleys to authors. Book catalog/guidelines available for #10 SAE and 2 first-class stamps.

Tips: "We want biblical values, conversation that sounds real, characters that come alive, stories with 'behavior modification' strengths."

STEMMER HOUSE PUBLISHERS, INC., 2627 Caves Rd., Owings Mills MD 21117. (301)363-3690. Book publisher. Estab. 1975. President: Barbara Holdridge. Publishes 1-3 picture books/year. "Sporadic" numbers of young reader/middle reader/young adult titles/year. 60% of books by first-time authors.

Fiction: Picture books: animal, ecology. Young reader/middle reader: history. Recently published *The Pied Piper*, by Sharon Chmielarz (ages 4-8, picture book); *Grandma's Band*, by Brad Bowles (4-8 years old, picture book).

Nonfiction: Picture book: animal, music/dance. Young reader: music/dance.

How to Contact/Writers: Fiction/nonfiction: Query, submit outline/synopsis and sample chapters. Reports on queries in 6 weeks. Publishes a book 18 months after acceptance. Will consider simultaneous submissions.

Illustration: Number of illustrations used for fiction: picture books—48; young readers—24; middle readers—12. Number of illustrations used for nonfiction: picture book—48; young reader—24; middle reader—24. Will review all varieties of ms/illustration packages.

How to Contact/Illustrators: Ms/illustration packages: "Query first, with several photocopied illustrations." Illustrations only: Send "tearsheets and/or slides (with SASE for return)." Reports in 2 weeks.

Terms/Writers & Illustrators: Pays authors in royalties of 4-6% based on wholesale price. Offers average advance payment of $300. Additional payment for ms/illllustration packages is 6-10% royalty. Factors used to determine payment for ms/illustration package include "permissions fees and/or other authors." Pay for illustrators: 4-5% royalty based on wholesale price. Sends galleys to authors. Book catalog for 9×12 SASE.

Tips: Writers: "simplicity, literary quality and originality are the keys."

STERLING PUBLISHING CO., INC., 387 Park Ave. South, New York NY 10016. (212)532-7160. Book publisher. Acquisitions Editor: Sheila Anne Barry. Publishes 30 middle reader titles/year. 10% of books by first-time authors.

Nonfiction: Middle readers: animal, hobbies, nature/environment, sports, humor. "Since our books are highly illustrated, word length is seldom the point. Most are 96-128 pages." Recently published *Riddlemania*, by Lori Miller Fox (middle readers, humor); *World's Strangest "True" Ghost Stories*, by John Macklin (middle readers-young adults, very short anecdotes); *Simple Weather Experiments*, by Muriel Mandell (middle readers).

How to Contact/Writers: Reports on queries in 2 weeks; on mss in 6-8 weeks. Publishes a book 6-12 months after acceptance. Will consider simultaneous submissions.

Illustration: Number of illustrations used for nonfiction: middle readers—approximately 60. Editorial will review all varieties of ms/illustration packages.

How to Contact/Illustrators: Ms/illustration packages: "Query first." Illustrations only: "Send sample photocopies of line drawings." Original artwork returned at job's completion "if desired, but usually held for future needs."

Terms/Writers & Illustrators: Pays authors in royalties of up to 10% "standard terms, no sliding scale, varies according to edition." Sends galleys to authors; dummies to illustrators. Manuscript guidelines for SASE.

Tips: Looks for: "Humor, hobbies, science books for middle-school children." Also, "mysterious occurrences, activities and fun and games books."

*TAB BOOKS, a division of McGraw-Hill,Inc., Blue Ridge Summit PA 17294-0850. (717)794-2191. Book Publisher. Editorial contact: Kim Tabor. Publishes 6 young reader titles/year; 6 young adult titles/year. 50% of books by first-time authors. 10% of books by agented authors.

Nonfiction: All levels: animal, hobbies, nature/environment, science, crafts. Recently published *Computers: 49 Science Fair Projects*, by Robert Bonnet/Daniel Keen (6th grade, science experiments); *Physics for Kids; 49 Easy Experiments with Heat*, by Robert Wood (4th grade, science experiments); *Holiday Crafts: More Year-Round Crafts Kids Can Make*, by Alan and Gill Bridgewater (ages 2-10, crafts).

How To Contact/Writers: Nonfiction: Query; submit outline/synopsis and sample chapters. Reports on queries in 4 weeks; mss in 3 months. Publishes a book 9-12 months after acceptance.

Illustration: Will review all varieties of manuscript illustration packages.

How To Contact/Illustrators: Query first; submit resume, tearsheets, photocopies. Reports back only if interested. Originals returned to artist at job's completion.

Refer to the Business of Children's Writing & Illustrating for up-to-date marketing, tax and legal information.

Terms/Writers & Illustrators: "Terms vary from project to project." Book catalog and manuscript guidelines are free on request.

Tips: Looks for "science and craft topics that are fun and educational that include activities that adult and children can work on together. Projects should be designed around inexpensive, household materials and should require under two hours for completion."

*TEXAS CHRISTIAN UNIVERSITY PRESS, Box 30783, Fort Worth TX 76129. (817)921-7822. Book Publisher. Editorial contact: Judy Alter. Publishes 1 young adult title/year. 75% of books by first-time authors.

Fiction: Young adults/teens: history. Average word length: 35,000-50,000 words. Recently published *The Last Innocent Summer*, by Fowler (Y/A, novel); *Letters To Oma*, by Gurasich (Y/A, novel); *Muddy Banks*, by Tulliver (Y/A, novel).

Nonfiction: Young adults/teens; biography, history. Average word length: 35,000-50,000 words.

How To Contact/Writers: Fiction/nonfiction: Query. Reports on queries in 2 weeks; mss in 2 months. Publishes a book 1-2 years after acceptance.

Illustration: Number of illustrations used for fiction: young adults/teens-6. Editor/Art Director Tracy Row will review an illustrator's work for possible use in authors' texts.

How To Contact/Illustrators: Reports back to artists within 1 week. Originals returned to artist at job's completion.

Terms/Writers & Illustrators: Pays in royalty of 10% based on wholesale price. Illustrators are paid flat fee. Book catalog is free on request. Manuscript guidelines free on request.

Tips: "We look only at historical novels set in Texas."

*THISTLEDOWN PRESS LTD., 633 Main St., Saskatoon, Saskatchewan S7H 0J8 Canada. (306)244-1722. Book publisher. Contact: Patrick O'Rourke. Publishes 1 middle reader title/year; 1 young adult title/year. "Thistledown originates books by Canadian authors only, although we have co-published titles by authors outside Canada."

Fiction: Middle readers and young adults: anthology (short stories), spy/mystery/adventure. Average word length: middle readers—35,000; young adult/teens—40,000. Recently published *Paradise Café and Other Stories*, by Martha Brooks (young adult, short stories anthology); *The Mystery of the Turtle Lake Monster*, by Jeni Mayer (middle reader, mystery novel).

How to Contact/Writers: Query first. Fiction and nonfiction: Submit outline/synopsis and sample chapters. Reports on queries/mss in 3 months. Publishes a book one year after acceptance. No simultaneous submissions. Will consider electronic submissions via disk or modem.

Terms/Writers: Pays authors in royalties based on retail price. Sends galleys to authors. Book catalog free on request. Manuscript guidelines for #10 envelope and IRC.

TRILLIUM PRESS, Box 209, Monroe NY 10950. (914)783-2999. Book publisher. Editorial Contact: William Neumann. Publishes 70 picture books, young readers, middle readers, young adult titles/year. 50% of books by first-time authors.

How to Contact/Writers: Fiction: Submit complete ms. Nonfiction: Query; submit complete ms. Reports on queries in 1 week; on mss in 8 weeks. Publishes a book 6 months after acceptance.

Illustration: Editorial will review all varieties of ms/illustration packages.

Terms/Writers & Illustrators: Pays authors in royalties. Buys ms outright. Sends galleys to authors; dummies to illustrators. Book catalog available for 9 × 12 SAE and 65¢ first-class stamp; manuscript guidelines for #10 SAE and 1 first-class stamp.

TYNDALE HOUSE PUBLISHERS, 351 Executive Dr., P.O. Box 80, Wheaton IL 60189. (708)668-8300. Book publisher. Children's editorial contact: Lucille Leonard. Children's illustration contact: Marlene Muddell. Publishes approximately 25 children's titles a year. 10% of books by first-time authors. Accepts approximately 2% of solicited and unsolicited manuscripts.
Fiction/Nonfiction: Picture books, early readers, middle reader series fiction and nonfiction.
How to Contact/Writers: "For manuscripts under 10,000 words, submit complete manuscript. Longer manuscripts, submit query, outline/synopsis and at least two sample chapters — or entire manuscript." Reports on queries/mss in 6-8 weeks. Publishes a book 12-18 months after acceptance. Will consider simultaneous submissions.
Illustration: Full-color for picture books, black and white for paperbacks, some spot illustrations for nonfiction, covers. Number of illustrations used for fiction and nonfiction: picture books — "varies." Will review all varieties of ms/illustration packages.
How to Contact/Illustrators: Ms/illustration packages: Send 3 chapters of ms with 1 piece of final art. Illustrations only: Send photocopies (color or b&w) of samples, résumé.
Terms/Writers & Illustrators: Pays authors fee (for some series) or royalty of 10% net for manuscript with illustrations, higher for unillustrated ms. Pay for illustrators: variable fee or royalty.
Tips: "All accepted mss will appeal to evangelical Christian children and parents."

VOLCANO PRESS, Box 270, Volcano CA 95689. (209)296-3345. FAX: (209)296-4515. Book publisher. President: Ruth Gottstein. Published 1 picture book 1989; 3 in 1990.
Fiction: Will consider feminist, social issues, Pacific rim-related (Asian) material for picture books, young readers and middle readers. Recently published *Berchick,* by Blanc (5-11 year olds, illustrated); *Mighty Mountain and The Three Strong Women*, by Irene Hedlund (originally published in Denmark).
Nonfiction: Will consider feminist, social issues, Pacific-rim related (Asian) material for picture books, young readers and middle readers. Published *Period*, by Gardner-Loulan et al (10-15 year olds, illustrated health book); *Periodo* (Spanish edition of *Period*, by Gardner-Loulan et al).
How to Contact/Writers: Fiction: Query. Nonfiction: Submit outline/synopsis and sample chapters. Include Social Security number with submission. Reports on queries in approximately one month. Publishes a book 12 months after acceptance.
Terms/Writers and Illustrators: Sends galleys to authors; dummies to illustrators. Book catalog for #10 SASE.

*VOYAGEUR PUBLISHING CO., INC., 4506 Beacon Dr., Nashville TN 37215. (615)665-2623. Book publisher. Contact: Eric Youngfuist, President. Publishes 2 middle reader titles/year; 3 young adult titles/year. 50% of books by first-time authors; 50% of books from agented writers.
Fiction: Middle readers and young adults/teens: animal, history, sports. Recently published *The Thong Tree*, by Haynes (grades 3-7, fiction/history); *Kentucky Frontiersmen*, by Altsheler (grades 5-10, fiction/history).
Nonfiction: Middle readers and young adults/teens: animal, biography, history, nature/environment, sports.
How to Contact/Writers: Fiction and nonfiction: Query. Submit outline/synopsis and sample chapters. SASE. Reports on queries in 1-3 weeks. Publishes a book 6 months after acceptance.
Illustration: Number of illustrations used for fiction and nonfiction: middle readers-10; young adult/teens — 6. Editorial will review ms/illustration packages submitted by authors/artists. Eric Youngfuist, President, or Nathaniel Kenton, Editor, will review illustrator's work for possible use in separate author's text.

How to Contact/Illustrators: Query first. SASE. "We will work with first time illustrators if they have a style that appeals to us." Submit résumé (list books that the artist has illustrated), tearsheets and "anything that will show an artist's use of color." Reports on art samples in 3 weeks. Originals "not returned if we have purchased the art."
Terms/Writers & Illustrators: Pays authors in royalties of 15% based on wholesale price. Additional payment for ms/illustration package. "Generally, we would pay royalty to the writer and purchase the artwork." Pay for illustrators: by the project. "We agree on price, then illustrator gets half of price when finished art delivered; remainder when book is released. But this is open for negotiation." Book catalog for #10 SAE and one first-class stamp. Manuscript guidelines for 1 first-class stamp and #10 SAE.

■*W.W. PUBLICATIONS, Subsidiary of American Tolkien Society, Box 373, Highland MI 48031-0373. (813)585-0985. Independent book producer. Editorial Contact: Phil Helms. 75% of books by first-time authors. Subsidy publishes 75%.
Fiction: All ages: easy-to-read, fantasy, history, science fiction, spy/mystery/adventure, Tolkien/middle-earth related.
How to Contact/Writers: Fiction: Query. Submit outline/synopsis of complete ms. Reports on queries in 4-6 weeks; 2-3 months mss. Publishes a book 3-6 months after acceptance. Will consider simultaneous submissions.
Illustrations: Reviews all illustration packages. Prefers 8½ × 11 b&w and ink.
How to Contact/Illustrations: Query with samples. Reports on ms/art samples in 3 months. Original art work returned at job's completion if requested.
Terms/Writers & Illustators: Pays author free copies. Sends galleys to author if requested; dummies to illustrators. Book catalog for 1 first class stamp and #10 SAE.
Tips: "Tolkien oriented only."

WALKER AND CO., div. of Walker Publishing Co. Inc., 720 Fifth Ave., New York NY 10019. (212)265-3632. Book publisher. Estab. 1959. Editor-in-Chief: Amy C. Shields. Publishes 2-3 picture books/year; 10 young reader titles/year; 10 middle reader titles/year; 15 young adult titles/year. 10-15% of books by first-time authors; 65% of books from agented writers.
Fiction: Picture books: animal, contemporary, easy-to-read, fantasy, history. Young readers: animal, contemporary. Middle readers: animal, contemporary, fantasy, science fiction, sports, spy/mystery/adventure. Young adults: animal, contemporary, fantasy, history, problem novels, romance, science fiction, sports, spy/mystery/adventure. Recently published *Reluctant Hero*, by Brady (young adult, history); *Bert*, by Skulavik (picture book); *My Grandfather the Spy*, by Gersen (middle reader).
Nonfiction: Picture books, young readers, middle readers, young adults: animal, biography, education, history, hobbies, music/dance, nature/environment, religion, sports. Recently published *Shaker Inventions*, by Randolph/Bolick (middle readers, history); *American Music Makers*, by Nichols (young adult, music/dance); *A Long Hard Journey: The Story of the Pullman Porter*, by Mekissach (young adult, history).
How to Contact/Writers: Fiction/nonfiction: Submit outline/synopsis and sample chapters. Report on queries/mss in 8-12 weeks. Publishes a book 12 months after acceptance. Will consider simultaneous submissions.
Illustration: Number of illustrations used for fiction: picture books—32-48; young readers—30; middle readers—30. Number of illustrations used for nonfiction: picture books—32-48; young readers—20-30; middle readers—20-30; young adults—20-30. Editorial will review all varieties of ms/illustration packages.
How to Contact/Illustrators: Ms/illustration packages: 5 chapters of ms with 1 piece of final art, remainder roughs. Illustrations only: "Tearsheets." Reports on art samples only if interested. Original artwork returned at job's completion.
Terms/Writers & Illustrators: Pays authors in royalties of 5-10% based on wholesale price "depends on contract." Offers average advance payment of $2,000-$4,000. Factors

used to determine final payment include "quality and name recognition." Pay for separate authors and illustrators: "If a picture book, royalty is split 50/50. Beyond that we try to make equitable arrangements." Pay for illustrators: By the project, $500-$2,000; royalties from 10%. Sends galleys to authors. Book catalog available for 8½×11 SASE; manuscript guidelines for SASE.

Tips: Writers: "Keep writing, keep trying. Don't take rejections personally and try to consider them objectively. If 10 publishers reject a work, put it aside and look at it again after a month. Can it be improved?" Illustrators: "Have a well-rounded portfolio with different styles." Looks for: "Science and nature series for young and middle readers. Good contemporary young adult fiction."

WARNER JUVENILE BOOKS, Warner Publishing Inc., 666 Fifth Ave., New York NY 10103. (212)484-2900. Associate editor: Alison Weir. Book publisher.
Fiction: Picture books, young readers: animal, easy-to-read, history, sports, seasonal books.
How to Contact/Writers: Agented work only. Fiction: submit complete ms. Will consider simultaneous submissions.
Illustrations: Will review all varieties of ms/illustrations packages.
How to Contact/Illustrators: Ms/illustration packages: query first, no original art. Illustrations only: send slides or photocopies.
Terms/Writers & Illustrators: Pays authors in royalties based on retail price. Additional payment for ms/illustrations packages varies.

WATERFRONT BOOKS, 98 Brookes Ave., Burlington VT 05401. (802)658-7477. Book publisher. Publisher: Sherrill N. Musty. 100% of books by first-time authors.
Fiction: Picture books, young readers, middle readers, young adults: mental health, family/parenting, health, special issues involving barriers to learning in children. Recently published *Luke Has Asthma, Too,* by Alison Rogers (ages 8-12, paperback).
Nonfiction: Picture books, young readers, middle readers, young adults: education, guidance, health, mental health, social issues. "We publish books for both children and adults on any subject that helps to lower barriers to learning in children: mental health, family/parenting, education, and social issues. We are now considering books for children on bettering the environment." Recently published *My Kind of Family, About Kids in Single-Parent Homes,* by David Fassler, M.D., Michele Lash, M.E.D., A.T.R., Sally Ives Loughridge, Ph.D. (ages 4-12, paper and plastic comb binding).
How to Contact/Writers: Fiction/nonfiction: Query. Reports on queries in 2 weeks; on mss in 6 weeks. Publishes a book 6 months after acceptance.
Illustration: Editorial will review ms/illustration packages submitted by authors/artists and ms/illustration packages submitted by authors with illustrations done by separate artists.
How to Contact/Illustrators: Ms/illustration packages: Query first. Illustrations only: Resume, tearsheets. Reports on art samples only if interested.
Terms/Writers & Illustrators: Pays authors in royalties of 10-15% based on wholesale price. Pays illustrators by the job. Additional payment for ms/illustration packages: Negotiable. Factors used to determine final payment: Number of illustrations used. Pay for separate authors and illustrators: "amount is negotiable but it would be within industry standards." Sends galleys to authors; dummies to illustrators. Book catalog available for #10 SAE and 1 first-class stamp.
Tips: "Have your manuscript thoroughly reviewed and even copy edited, if necessary. If you are writing about a special subject, have a well-qualified professional in the field review it for accuracy and appropriateness. It always helps to get some testimonials before submitting it to a publisher. The publisher then knows she/he is dealing with something worthwhile."

*FRANKLIN WATTS, INC., a subsidiary of Grolier Inc., 95 Madison Ave., 11th Floor, New York NY 10016. (212)686-7070. Book publisher. Editorial contact person: Jeanne Vestal. 5% of books by first-time authors; 40% of books from agented writers.
Nonfiction: Young readers, middle readers, young adults: open categories. Average word length: middle readers—5,000; young adult/teens—16,000-35,000. Recently published *George Washington Carver*, by Suzanne M. Coil (ages 5-8, first book biography); *Water Pollution*, by Kathyln Gay (ages 9-12, impact—discussion of issues); *Famous Experiments You Can Do*, by Robert Gardner (ages 9-12, experimental science ideas for projects).
How to Contact/Writers: Query. Reports in 1 month. Publishes book 1 year after acceptance. Editorial will review ms packages submitted by authors; will review illustrators work for possible use in separate author's text.
How to Contact/Illustrators: Query first. Original artwork returned at job's completion.
Terms/Writers & Illustrators: Book catalog for 10×13 SASE.
Tips: Looks for children's nonfiction grades 5-8 or 9-12.

WEIGL EDUCATIONAL PUBLISHERS, 2114 College Ave., Regina Saskatchewan S4P 1C5 Canada. (306)569-0766. Book publisher. Editor: Catherine Pritchard.
Nonfiction: Young reader/middle reader/young adult: education, history, social studies. Average word length: young reader/middle reader/young adult—64 pages. Published *Links Between Canadian Communities*, by Wilma Birchill (grades 2-4, social studies); *Canadian Neighbours*, by Carlotta Hacker (grades 1-3, social studies); and *Early Canada*, by Emily Odynak (grades 4-6, history).
How to Contact/Writers: Nonfiction: Submit query and résumé. Reports on queries in 4 weeks. Publishes a book 24 months after acceptance. Will consider simultaneous submissions.
Illustration: Number of illustrations used in nonfiction: young reader/middle reader/ young adult—20. Editorial will review all varieties of ms/illustration packages.
How to Contact/Illustrators: Ms/illustration packages: "Query first." Illustrations only: Send "résumé and photocopies of completed works." Reports back only if interested or when appropriate project comes in.
Terms/Writers and Illustrators: Pays "either royalty or fee." Separate authors and illustrators: "royalty or fee." Illustrators paid by the project. Sends galleys to author; sends dummies to illustrator. Book catalog free on request.
Tips: Looks for "educational material suited to a specific curriculum topic."

■WINSTON-DEREK PUBLISHERS, INC., Box 90883, Nashville TN 37209. (615)321-0535. Book publisher. Estab. 1972. Editorial contact as follows: picture books: Matalyn Rose Peebles; young reader titles: Maggie Ella Sims; middle reader/young adult titles: Candi Williams. Publishes 35-40 picture books/year; 25-30 young reader titles/year; 10-15 middle reader titles/year; 10-15 young adult titles/year. 50% of books by first-time authors; 5% through agents. Subsidy publishes 20% of books/year.
Fiction: Picture books: animal, easy-to-read, fantasy. Young reader: contemporary. Middle reader: problem novels, science fiction, African-American. Young adult: history, romance, spy/mystery/adventure, African-American. Average word length: picture book—600-1200; young reader—3,000-5,000; middle reader—2,000; young adult—10,000-40,000. Recently published *Matthew's Allowance*, by Christine White (ages 5-7, educational); *Saturn Storm's Broccoli Adventure*, by D. James Harrison (ages 5-7, adventure); and *Jamako and the Beanstalk*, by Fred Crump, Jr. (ages 3-6, fairy tale).
Nonfiction: Picture books: animal. Young reader: history, religion, African American biographies. Middle reader: African-American biographies. Young adult: biography, education, history, nature/environment, religion, African-American biographies. Average word length: picture book—600-800; young readers—2,500-4,000; middle reader—

1,000-2,500; young adult—10,000-30,000. Recently published *First Black Doctor in America*, by Benjamin E. Holt (grades 4-6, African-American studies); *Sprinter in Life*, by Dorothy Croman (grades 4-6, African-American studies); and *Kizito*, by Elaine M. Stone (grades 4-6, African-American studies).

How to Contact/Writers: Fiction: Query or submit outline/synopsis and sample chapters. Nonfiction: Submit complete ms. Reports on queries in 6 weeks; on mss in 8 weeks. Publishes a book 10 months after acceptance. Will consider simultaneous submissions.

Illustration: Number of illustrations used in fiction/nonfiction: picture book—20; young reader—10; middle reader—5. Editorial will review all varieties of ms/illustration packages. Editor, Robert Earl, will review an illustrator's work for possible use in authors' texts.

How to Contact/Illustrators: Ms/illustration packages: 3 chapters of ms with 1 piece of final art. Illustrations only: Send résumé and tearsheets. Reports in 3 weeks. Original art work returned at job's completion.

Terms/Writers & Illustrators: Pays authors in royalties of 10-15% based on wholesale price. Also pays in copies. Factors to determine final payment: "color art vs. black-and-white, and number of illustrations used." Separate authors and illustrators: 12½% royalty to writer and 2½% royalty to illustrator. Illustrators paid $30-150 or 2½-8½ royalty. Sends galleys to author; dummies to illustrator. Book catalog for SASE; ms/artist's guidelines free on request.

Tips: Illustrators: Use "action illustrations plus send good work and variety of subjects such as male/female; b&w." Looks for: "educational, morally sound subjects, multiethnic; historical facts."

*WOMEN'S PRESS, 233-517 College Street, Toronto, Ontario M6G 4A2 Canada. (416)921-2425. Book publisher. Editorial contact people: Ann Decter and Angela Robertson. Publishes 1-2 picture books/year; 0-1 middle reader titles/year; 0-1 young adult titles/year. 60% of books by first-time authors. "We give preference to authors who are Canadian citizens or those living in Canada."

Fiction: Picture books: contemporary, social issues, health and family problems. Young Readers, Middle Readers and Young Adults/Teens: contemporary, problem novels. Average word length: picture books—24 pages; young readers—70-80 pages; middle readers—60-70 pages; young adult/teens—80-150 pages. Recently published *Come Sit by Me*, by Merrifield (ages 4-8, picture-issue); *Asita's Mums*, by Elwin & Paulse (4-8, picture-issue); *SP Likes AD*, by Brett (12 and up, problem novel).

Nonfiction: Picture books: environment. Young Adults/Teens: sex, health.

How to Contact/Writers: Fiction/Nonfiction: Query. Reports on queries in 1 month; reports on mss in 3-6 months. Publishes a book 1 year after acceptance.

Illustration: Number of illustrations used for fiction: picture books—20+; young readers—3; middle readers—2; young adult/teens—1. Editorial will review ms/illustration packages submitted by authors/artists (Canadian only).

Terms/Writers & Illustrators: Pays authors in royalties of 10% min. based on retail price. Pay for separate authors and illustrators: split royalty 5% author, 5% illustrator. Sends galleys to authors; dummies to illustrators. Book catalog and/or manuscript guidelines free on request.

Other Book Publishers

The following book publishers are not included in this edition of *Children's Writer's & Illustrator's Market* for the reasons indicated. The phrase "did not respond" means the publishers was in the 1990 *Children's Writer's & Illustrator's Market* but did not respond to our written and phone requests for updated information for a 1991 listing.

African American Images (did not respond)

Albatross Books Pty. Ltd. (deleted per request)

Alegra House Publishers (currently overstocked)

Bookmaker's Guild, Inc. (did not respond)

Breakwater Books (did not respond)

Carnival Enterprises (did not respond)

The Child's World (did not respond)

Coteau Books Ltd. (did not respond)

Dundurn Press Ltd. (out of juvenile market)

Exposition Phoenix Press (complaints)

Fiesta City Publishers (did not respond)

Friendship Press (did not respond)

Mage Publishers Inc. (did not respond)

Julian Messner (deleted per request)

National Press Inc. (deleted per request)

New Seed Press (deleted per request)

Odyssey Press (deleted per request)

Proforma Books (did not respond)

Starfire (did not respond)

TSM Books, Inc. (did not respond)

Weekly Reader Books (overstocked)

Western Producer Prairie Books (did not respond)

Magazine Publishers

Books usually come to mind when considering reading resources for children. But magazines also provide a valuable educational tool. Like adult magazines, today there is a diverse selection of juvenile periodicals. There's a magazine for almost every interest.

It's simply logical to expect magazines to become more popular as the audience increases, but there are other reasons besides the baby boom for the current growth in children's magazines:

Kids' magazines are better today. In our visually-oriented society, many juvenile periodicals find it a necessity to print in four-color in order to compete with television and movies. The tendency toward increased production quality has resulted in glitzier, glossier and flashier magazines for children.

Magazines are timelier than books. Children, like adults, want to know what is going on in the world around them. Magazines provide exposure to current events in less time than it would take to produce a book. As you will notice in this section, many of the markets listed are fact-based educational magazines which seek to teach kids about managing their own lives and the world around them.

Children have subscriptions to magazines in order to have something to call their own. When kids see their parents reading magazines, they tend to emulate those actions. Perhaps that is why kids like to read about characters the same age or older than they are. Putting subscriptions in kids' names makes the magazines their "own."

More adult magazines are developing magazines for kids as spinoffs. Magazines such as *Consumer Reports* and *National Geographic* have published their own junior editions. The logic is loyal adult readers will purchase subscriptions for their kids.

Working parents feel guilty. Magazines are a way for parents to keep their latchkey kids reading while they are working. Unlike books, magazines are more inviting to browsers who just want to flip through the pages to see what's there. Because of this, magazines are able to compete with the passiveness of today's visual-oriented activities, such as watching television.

Magazines are cheaper than books. For the price of one hardcover picture book, a year's subscription to a juvenile magazine can be purchased.

Children have more purchasing power. Because of increased allowances and part-time jobs, children now have more expendable income than ever before and are buying magazines that appeal to them.

Magazines tend to be preferred over books in the "hurry up" environment we live in. It doesn't take as long to look through a magazine as it does to read a book. And the variety of articles and stories found in a magazine allows the reader to choose what he reads. Short stories and articles are not nearly as intimidating as a thick book, especially to a child who does not read much.

Magazines are used as supplements in schools.

The markets

Manuscripts needed by the listed periodicals include student-read pieces, church-oriented material, general interest, as well as special interest articles. There are many children's magazines that are not much more than promotions for toys, movies or television shows. You're not likely to find any of these magazines in this book, for they rely more on advertising than literary content and have limited needs for freelancers.

The larger-circulation, ad-carrying publications will generally offer a better pay rate than denominational or nonprofit magazines. But, for beginning writers and artists, remember smaller magazines may be more open to reviewing the work of newcomers. They can provide an excellent vehicle for you to compile clipping files as you work your way toward the more lucrative markets.

Be sure to obtain a sample copy of any magazine you're interested in submitting to. Perusing a magazine is really the only way you can determine what that magazine needs. Becoming familiar with the "slant" of each publication will save valuable time in submitting appropriate articles or artwork. The traditional distribution for juvenile magazines is through home subscriptions and schools; so don't be surprised if you can't find a particular magazine in the bookstore or at the newsstand. Most of the listings in this section offer sample copies that a writer can send for.

Once you have determined which magazines you are interested in contacting, take another look at the listing to review their preferred method of receiving submissions. Some may wish to see an entire manuscript; others may wish to see a query letter and outline, especially for nonfiction articles. In all situations, you can count on the editor appreciating any graphics you can provide with the piece.

AIM MAGAZINE, America's Intercultural Magazine, Box 20554, Chicago IL 60620. (312)874-6184. Articles Editor: Ruth Apilado. Fiction Editor: Mark Boone. Art Director: Bill Jackson. Quarterly magazine. 8½ × 11; 48 pages; slick paper. Circ. 8,000. Readers are high school and college students, teachers, adults interested in helping, through the written word, to create a more equitable world. 15% of material aimed at juvenile audience.

Fiction: Young adults: history, "stories with social significance." Wants stories that teach children that people are more alike than they are different. Does not want to see religious fiction. Buys 20 mss/year. Average word length: 1,000-4,000. Byline given.

Nonfiction: Young adults: interview/profile, "stuff with social significance." Does not want to see religious nonfiction. Buys 20 mss/year. Average word length: 500-2,000. Byline given.

How to Contact/Writers: Fiction: Send complete ms. Nonfiction: Query with published clips. Reports on queries/mss in 1 month. Will consider simultaneous submissions.

Illustration: Buys 20 illustrations/issue. Preferred theme or style: Overcoming social injustices through nonviolent means. Will review all varieties of ms/illustration packages.

How to Contact/Illustrators: Ms/illustration packages: Query first. Illustrations only: "Send examples of art, ask for a job." Reports on art samples in 2 months. Original art work returned at job's completion "if desired."

Terms/Writers & Illustrators: Pays on publication. Buys first North American serial rights. Pays $5-25 for assigned/unsolicited articles. Pays in contributor copies if copies are requested. Pays $5-25/b&w cover illustration. Sample copy $3.50.

Tips: "We need material of social significance, stuff that will help promote racial harmony and peace and the stupidity of racism."

ANIMAL TALES, 2113 W. Bethany, Phoenix AZ 85015. Articles/Fiction Editor and Art Director: Berta I. Cellers. Bimonthly magazine 8½ × 11; 32 pages. Estab. 1989. Circ. 1,000. Publishes "stories about animals and the people who love them." 25% of material aimed at juvenile audience."

Fiction: Young adult: animal, contemporary, humorous. Does not want to see dedications to a deceased pet. Buys 75 mss/year. Average word length: 2,000-6,000. Byline given.

Nonfiction: Young adult: animal, humorous. Buys 6 mss/year. Average word length: 2,000-6,000. Byline given.

Poetry: Reviews "light verse and traditional poems about animals." Will accept 5 submissions/author.

How to Contact/Writers: Fiction/nonfiction: Send complete ms. Include Social Security number with submission. Reports on queries in 8 weeks. Will consider simultaneous submissions.

Illustrations: Buys 10-15 illustrations/issue; buys 70 illustrations/year. Prefers "sketches used to illustrate a story and decorate front cover." Will review all varieties of ms/ illustration packages.

How to Contact/Illustrators: Ms/illustrations packages: Complete ms with final artwork. Illustrations only: Samples of artwork. Reports on art samples in 8 weeks. Original art work returned at job's completion.

Terms/Writers & Illustrators: Pays on publication. Buys first rights. Pays $5-50 for unsolicited articles. Additional payment for ms/illustration packages is $10-75. Pays $5-25/b&w cover illustration or inside illustration. Sample copy $4.95. Writer's/illustrator's guidelines free with SAE and 1 first class stamp.

Tips: "We are looking for unique material that communicates the animal/human relationship. Should be easy to read but not childish. Especially seeking illustrations that accompany a manuscript."

ATALANTIK, 7630 Deer Creek Dr., Worthington OH 43085. (614)885-0550. Articles/ Fiction Editor: Prabhat K. Dutta. Art Director: Tanushree Bhattacharya. Quarterly magazine. Estab. 1980. Circ. 400. "*Atalantik* is the first Bengali (Indian language) literary magazine published from the USA. It contains poems, essays, short stories, translations, interviews, opinions, sketches, book reviews, cultural information, scientific articles, letters to the editor, serialized novels and a children's section. The special slant may be India and/or education." 10% of material aimed at juvenile audience.

Fiction: Young reader: animal. Middle readers: history, humorous, problem solving, math puzzles, travel. Young adult/teens: history, humorous, problem solving, romance, science fiction, sports, spy/mystery/adventure, math puzzles, travel. Does not want to see: "religious, political, controversial or material without any educational value." Buys 20-40 mss/year. Average word length: 300-1,000. Byline given, "sometimes."

Nonfiction: Middle readers: history, how-to, humorous, problem solving, travel. Young adults/teens: history, how-to, humorous, interview/profile, problem solving, travel puzzles. Does not want to see: "religious, political, controversial or material without any educational value." Buys 20-40 mss/year. Average word length: 300-1,000. Byline given, "sometimes."

 The asterisk before a listing indicates the listing is new in this edition.

Poetry: Reviews 20 line humorous poems that rhyme; maximum of 5 submissions.
How to Contact/Writers: Fiction/nonfiction: Send complete ms. Reports on queries in 2 weeks; mss in 4 weeks. Will consider simultaneous submissions.
Illustration: Buys 4-20 illustrations/year. Prefers to review juvenile education, activities, sports, culture and recreations. Will review all varieties of ms/illustration packages, including illustrator's work for possible use with fiction/nonfiction articles and columns by other authors.
How to Contact/Illustrators: Ms/illustration packages: Send "complete manuscript with final art." Illustrations only: Send "résumé with copies of previous published work." Reports only if interested.
Terms/Writer & Illustrators: Pays on publication. Buys all rights. Usually pays in copies for all circumstances. Sample copy $6. Writer's/illustrator's guidelines free with 1 SAE and 1 first class stamp.
Tips: Writers: "Be imaginative, thorough, flexible and educational. Most importantly, be a child."

BOYS' LIFE, Boy Scouts of America, 1325 W. Walnut Hill Ln., Box 152079, Irving TX 75015-2079. (214)580-2000. Editor-in-Chief: William McMorris. Managing Editor: Scott Stuckey. Columns Editor: Jeffrey Csatari. Fiction Editor: William Butterworth. Director of Design: Joseph P. Connolly. Monthly magazine. Estab. 1911. Circ. 1,300,000. *Boys' Life* is "primarily for boys 8 to 18 who are members of the Cub Scouts, Boy Scouts or Explorers. A general interest magazine for all boys." 100% of material aimed at juvenile audience.
Fiction: Middle readers: animal, contemporary, fantasy, history, humorous, problem-solving, science fiction, sports, spy/mystery/adventure. Does not want to see "talking animals and adult reminiscence. All short stories feature a boy or boys." Buys 12 mss/year. Average word length: 500-1,500. Byline given.
Nonfiction: "Articles, columns and special features (how-tos). Articles are 500-1,200 words. Each issue contains at least one full-length piece about a Scout activity—mountain climbing, canoeing, hiking, bike touring, camping, etc. Depending on season, we also use athlete profiles (adults and children), how-to's (fishing, camping, money-making, game playing), history, humor, hobbies, etc. Special features are up to 500 words. Hobby how-tos such as wood carving, model building, painting and crafts. Descriptive writing that's clear and simple is a must; step-by-step photos or sketches helpful. An occasional how-to crosses over to a full-length article—i.e., building a robot, a model train layout, using remot-controlled cars. Columns are 350-500 words. Each issue uses seven columns, on average. A partial category list: Science, Outdoors, Health, Cars, Bicycling, Electronics, Sports, Computers, Entertainment. See actual issues for others." Byline given.
How to Contact/Writers: Fiction/nonfiction: Send complete ms/query. Reports on queries/mss in 2-3 weeks.
Illustration: Buys 5-7 illustrations/issue; buys 23-50 illustrations/year. Will review all varieties of ms/illustration packages. Works on assignment only.
How to Contact/Illustrators: Ms/illustration packages: "Query first." Illustrations only: Send tearsheets. Reports on art samples only if interested. Original artwork returned at job's completion. Buys first rights.
Terms/Writers: $350 and up for articles; $200 and up for special features; $250 for columns; $750 and up for fiction; $150 for 1 page comic scripts. Writer's guidelines available for SASE.
Tips: "No set of guidelines can substitute for careful reading of as many back issues as possible. *Boys' Life* can be found in the children's section of most libraries."

*MARION ZIMMER BRADLEY'S FANTASY MAGAZINE, Box 245A, Berkeley CA 94701. (415)601-9000. Fiction Editor: Marion Bradley. Art Director: Jan Burke. Quarterly magazine. 8½×11; 64 pp.; glossy cover stock. Estab. 1988. Circ. 2,000+. Publishes fantasy stories. "We are not a kiddie magazine but most of our work should not be unsuitable for bright children."

Fiction: Middle readers: fantasy, science fiction. Young adults/teens: comtemporary, fantasy, science fiction. Buys 50+ mss/year. Average word length: 500-5,000. Byline given. "No pen names - if a story isn't good enough to put real name on it, it's not good enough to print."

How To Contact/Writers: Query or send complete manuscript. Include social security number and phone number with submission. Reports on queries in 2 weeks; mss in 2-3 weeks. Average length of time between acceptance of mss and publication of work is 4 months. "No simultaneous submissions. I know noone can afford to have stuff tied up so I try to report by return mail if I can't use it."

Illustration: "Must be professional illustrators, I'm occassionally willing to work with amateurs but I have limited time." Preferred theme/style: full page; double page spreads; 4 sided bleeds; ½, ⅓, ¼ page; illustration of the stories. Will not review manuscript illustration packages submitted by authors/artists.

How To Contact/Illustrators: For information on submissions, query to P.O. Box 11095, Oakland CA 94611-9991. Include return address and phone number. Reports back on art samples within 2 weeks. Originals returned to artist at job's completion.

Terms/Writers & Illustrators: Pays on acceptance. Buys first North American serial rights. Pays 3-10 cents/word for stories. Sample copies for $3.50. Writer's guidelines free on request.

Tips: "Our short-story section looks for good plot, likeable characters. Put art on a postcard - that way I can't fail to see it!"

CAREERS, E.M. Guild, 1001 Avenue of the Americas, New York NY 10018. (212)354-8877. Editor-in-Chief: Mary Dalheim. Senior Editor: Don Rauf. Art Director: Ore Li-Bretto. Magazine published 4 times during school year (Sept., Nov., Jan., March). Circ. 600,000. This is a magazine for high school juniors and seniors, designed to prepare students for their futures.

Nonfiction: Young adults: how-to, humorous, interview/profile, problem solving. Buys 30-40 mss/year. Average word length: 1,000-1,250. Byline given.

How to Contact/Writers: Nonfiction: Query. Reports on queries/mss in 6 weeks. Will consider electronic submissions via disk or modem.

Illustration: Buys 10 illustrations/issue; buys 40 illustrations/year. Will review all varieties of ms/illustration packages. Works on assignment "mostly."

How to Contact/Illustrators: Ms/illustration packages: Query first. Illustrations only: Send tearsheets, cards. Reports on art samples only if interested. Original artwork returned at job's completion.

Terms/Writers & Illustrators: Pays 90 days after publication. Buys first North American serial rights. Pays $250-300 assigned/unsolicited articles. Additional payment for ms/illustration packages "must be negotiated." Pays $500-1,000/color illustration; $300-700 b&w/color (inside) illustration. Sample copy $1 with SAE and $1 postage; writer's guidelines free with SAE and 1 first-class stamp.

"Picture books" are geared toward the preschool—8 year old group; "Young readers" to 5-8 year olds; "Middle readers" to 9-11 year olds; and "Young adults" to those 12 and up.

*CAT FANCY, The Magazine for Responsible Cat Owners, Fancy Publications, P.O. Box 6050, Mission Viejo CA 92690. (714)855-3045. Articles Editor: K.E. Segnar. Monthly magazine. 8 × 11; 88 pp. Estab. 1965. Circ. 317,000. "Our magazine is for cat owners who want to know more about how to care for their pets in a responsible manner." 3% of material aimed at juvenile audience.

Fiction: Middle readers: animal (cat). Does not want to see stories in which cats talk. Buys 3-9 mss/year. Average word length: 750-1,100. Byline given.

Nonfiction: Middle readers: animal (cat). Buys 3-9 mss/year. Average word length: 450-1,100. Byline given.

Poetry: Reviews maximum of 64 short lines poems. "No more than 10 poems per submission please."

How To Contact/Writers: Fiction/nonfiction: Send complete manuscript, query is okay too. Reports on queries in 2 weeks; mss in 6 weeks. Average length of time between acceptance and publication of work: 4 months for juvenile material.

Illustration: Buys 3-6 illustrations/year. "Most of our illustrations are assigned or submitted with a story. We look for realistic images of cats done with pen and ink (no pencil)." Will review all varieties of manuscript illustration packages.

How To Contact/Illustrators: Query first or send complete manuscript with final art. "We only work with local artists on assignment. Ideally, the artist needs to reside in Orange County. Submit photocopies of work." Originals returned to artist at job's completion.

Terms/Writers & Illustrators: Pays on publication. Buys first rights and one-time rights. Pays $20-50/juvenile articles. Pays additional $45-75 for manuscript/illustration packages. $20-50/black and white (inside). Sample copies for $3.50. Writer's/Artist's Guidelines free for #10 SAE and 1 first class stamp.

Tips: "Our 'kids for cats' department is most open. Perhaps the most important tip I can give is: consider what 9 to 11 year olds want to know about cats and what they enjoy most about cats, and address that topic in a style appropriate for them. The entire magazine is open to freelance illustrators. We have a tremendous need for spot art."

CHICKADEE, for Young Children from OWL, Young Naturalist Foundation, 56 The Esplanade, Ste. 306, Toronto Ontario M5E 1A7 Canada. (416)868-6001. Editor: Catherine Ripley. Art Director: Tim Davin. Publishes 10 times/year, magazine. Estab. 1979. 8³⁄₁₆ × 10¾; 32 pages; 60 lb. gamma paper and cover stock. Circ: 160,000. *Chickadee* is a "hands-on" publication designed to interest 4-9 year olds in the world and environment around them.

Fiction: Picture material, young readers: animal, contemporary, history, humorous, sports, spy/mystery/adventure. Does not want to see religious, anthropomorphic animal, romance material. Buys 8 mss/year. Average word length: 200-800. Byline given.

Nonfiction: Picture material, young readers: animal, how-to, interview/profile, travel. Does not want to see religious material. Buys 2-5 mss/year. Average word length: 20-200. Byline given.

How to Contact/Writers: Fiction/nonfiction: Send complete ms. SAE and $1 money order for answer to query and return of ms. Report on queries/mss in 8 weeks. Will consider simultaneous submissions.

Illustration: Buys 3-5 illustrations/issue; buys 40 illustrations/year. Preferred theme or style: Gentle realism/humor (but not cartoons). Will review all varieties of ms/illustration packages. Works on assignment only.

How to Contact/Illustrators: Ms/illustration packages: Story with sample of art. Illustrations only: Tearsheets. Reports on art samples only if interested.

Terms/Writers & Illustrators: Pays on publication. Buys all rights. Pays $25-200 for assigned/unsolicited articles. Additional payment for ms/illustration packages is $25-600. Pays $500 color (cover) illustration, $50-500 b&w (inside), $50-650 color (inside). Sample copy $3.25. Writer's guidelines free.

Tips: "Study the magazine carefully before submitting material. 'Read-to-me selection' most open to freelancers. Uses fiction stories. Kids should be main characters and should be treated with respect." (See listing for *Owl.*)

CHILD LIFE, Children's Better Health Institute, 1100 Waterway Blvd., Indianapolis IN 46202. (317)636-8881. Articles Fiction Editor: Steve Charles. Art Director: Janet Moir. Magazine published 8 times/year. Estab. 1923. Circ. 80,000. "Adventure, humor, fantasy and health-related stories with an imaginative twist are among those stories we seek. We try to open our readers' minds to their own creative potential, and we want our stories and articles to reflect and encourage this." 100% of material aimed at juvenile audience.

Fiction: Young readers: animal, contemporary, fantasy, history, humorous, problem-solving, science fiction, sports, spy/mystery/adventure. Middle readers: fantasy, history, humorous, science fiction. Buys 30-35 mss/year. Average word length: 1,000. Byline given.

Nonfiction: Middle readers: animal, history, how-to, humorous, interview/profile, problem solving, travel. Average word length: 800. Byline given.

Poetry: Reviews poetry.

How to Contact/Writers: Fiction/nonfiction: Send complete ms. Reports on queries/mss in 8-10 weeks. Will consider simultaneous submissions.

Illustration: Buys 8-10 illustrations/issue; buys 65-80 illustrations/year. Preferred theme: "Need realistic styles especially." Will review an illustrator's work for possible use with fiction/nonfiction articles and columns by other authors. Works on assignment only.

How to Contact/Illustrators: Illustrations only: Send "résumé, tearsheets, photocopies and/or slides. Samples must be accompanied by SASE for response and/or return of samples." Reports on art samples in 4-6 weeks.

Terms/Writers & Illustrators: Editorial: Pays on publication; minimum 8¢/word; buys all rights. Pays 3 weeks prior to publication. Pays $250/color cover; $30-70/b&w inside; $65-140 color inside. Writer's/illustrator's guidelines free with SAE and 1 first class stamp.

Tips: Illustrators: "Make sure you can draw children well and draw them accurately as far as age. Be able to illustrate a story situation. I assign poems, fiction stories and factual articles about health subjects and animals. I look for samples that portray a story, that involve children interacting with others in a variety of situations. Most of my assignments are for realistic styles, but I also use humorous, cartoony styles and unusual techniques like cut-paper, collage and woodcut." (See listings for *Children's Digest, Children's Playmate, Humpty Dumpty's Magazine, Jack and Jill, Turtle Magazine.*)

CHILDREN'S DIGEST, Children's Better Health Institute, Box 567, Indianapolis IN 46206. (317)636-8881. Articles/Fiction Editor: Elizabeth Rinck. Art Director: Lisa Nelson. Magazine published eight times/year. 6½×9; 48 pages; 35 lb. uncoated, 40 lb. coated paper; 40 lb. coated self-cover stock. Estab. 1950. Circ. 125,000. For preteens; approximately 33% of content is health-related.

Fiction: Middle readers: animal, contemporary, fantasy, history, humorous, problem solving, science fiction, sports, spy/mystery/adventure. Buys 25 mss/year. Average word length: 500-1,500. Byline given.

Always include a self-addressed stamped envelope (SASE) or International Reply Coupon (IRC) with submissions.

Nonfiction: Middle readers: animal, history, how-to, humorous, problem solving. Buys 16-20 mss/year. Average word length: 500-1,200. Byline given.

How to Contact/Writers: Fiction/nonfiction: Send complete ms. Include Social Security number with submission. Reports on mss in 10 weeks.

Illustration: Will review an illustrator's work for possible use with fiction/nonfiction articles and columns by other authors. Works on assignment only.

How to Contact/Illustrators: Ms/illustration packages: Query first. Illustrations only: Send résumé and/or slides or tearsheets to illustrate work. Reports on art samples in 8-10 weeks.

Terms/Writers & Illustrators: Pays on acceptance for illustrators, publication for writers. Buys all rights. Pays 10¢/word for accepted articles. Pays $225/color (cover) illustration; $24-100/b&w (inside); $60-125/color (inside). Sample copy 75¢. Writer's/illustrator's guidelines for SAE and 1 first-class stamp. (See listings for *Child Life, Children's Playmate, Humpty Dumpty's Magazine, Jack and Jill, Turtle Magazine.*)

CHILDREN'S PLAYMATE, Children's Better Health Institute, Box 567, Indianapolis IN 46206. (317)636-8881. Articles/Fiction Editor: Elizabeth Rinck. Art Director: Steve Miller. Magazine published 8 times/year. 6½ × 9; 48 pages; 35 lb. uncoated, 40 lb. coated paper; 40 lb. coated self-cover stock. Estab. 1929. Circ. 135,000. For children between 6 and 8 years; approximately 33% of content is health-related.

Fiction: Young readers: animal, contemporary, fantasy, history, humorous, problem solving, science fiction, sports, spy/mystery/adventure. Buys 25 mss/year. Average word length: 200-700. Byline given.

Nonfiction: Young readers: animal, history, how-to, humorous, problem solving. Buys 16-20 mss/year. Average word length: 200-700. Byline given.

How to Contact/Writers: Fiction/nonfiction: Send complete ms. Include Social Security number with submission. Reports on mss in 8-10 weeks.

Illustration: Will review an illustrator's work for possible use with fiction/nonfiction articles and columns by other authors. Works on assignment only.

How to Contact/Illustrators: Ms/illustration packages: Query first. Illustrations only: "Resume and/or slides or tearsheets to illustrate work." Reports on art samples in 8-10 weeks.

Terms/Writers & Illustrators: Pays on acceptance for illustrators, publication for writers. Buys all rights. Pays 10¢/word for assigned articles. Pays $225/color (cover) illustration; $25-100/b&w (inside); $60-125/color (inside). Sample copy 75¢. Writer's/illustrator's guidelines for SAE and 1 first-class stamp. (See listings for *Child Life, Children's Digest, Humpty Dumpty's Magazine, Jack and Jill, Turtle Magazine.*)

*CHOICES, The Magazine for Personal Development and Practical Living Skills, Scholastic, Inc. 730 Broadway, New York NY 10003-9538. Articles Editor: Karen Glenn. Art Director: Joan Michaels. Monthly magazine. 8½ × 11; 32 editorial pages. Estab. 1986 as *Choices* (formerly called *Coed*). "We go to teenagers in home economics and health classes. All our material has curriculum ties: Personal Development, Family Life, Careers, Food & Nutrition, Consumer Power, Child Development, Communications, Health."

Nonfiction: Buys 30 mss/year. Word length varies. Byline given (except for short items).

How to Contact/Writers: Nonfiction: Query with published clips "We don't want unsolicited manuscripts." Reports on queries in 2 weeks. Sample copy for 9 × 12 SAE and 2 first class stamps.

"Pictures of kids having fun in the snow are consistent with both the month of the issue (December), and our ongoing emphasis on fitness," says editor Elizabeth Rinck. "This cover illustrates a variety of winter exercises and reinforces the idea that fitness is fun." Len Ebert has illustrated many features and covers for Children's Digest *and is one of the magazine's most popular artists.*

Illustration: Works on assignment only. "All art is *assigned* to go with specific articles."
Tips: "*Read* the specific magazines. We receive unsolicited manuscripts and queries that do not in any way address the needs of our magazine. For example, we don't publish poetry, but we get unsolicited poetry in the mail."

CLUBHOUSE, Your Story Hour, Box 15, Berrien Springs MI 49103. (616)471-3701. Articles/Fiction Editor, Art Director: Elaine Trumbo. Bimonthly magazine. 6×9; 32 pages; 50 lb. offset paper. Estab. 1949. Circ. 12,000.
Fiction: Middle readers, young adults: animal, contemporary, history, humorous, problem solving, religious. Does not want to see science fiction/fantasy/Halloween or Santa-oriented fiction. Buys 50 mss/year. Average word length: 800-1,300. Byline given.
Nonfiction: Middle readers, young adults: how-to. "We do not use articles except 200-500 word items about good health: anti—drug, tobacco, alcohol; pro—nutrition." Buys 10-12 mss/year. Average word length: 200-400. Byline given.
How to Contact/Writers: Fiction/nonfiction: Send complete ms. Reports on queries/mss in 6 weeks. Will consider simultaneous submissions.
Illustration: Buys 20-25 illustrations/issue; buys 120+ illustrations/year. Preferred theme or style: "variety." Will review an illustrator's work for possible use with fiction/nonfiction articles and columns by other authors. Works on assignment only.
How to Contact/Illustrators: Illustrations only: Send photocopies or prints of work which we can keep on file. Reports on art samples in 6 weeks. Originals usually not returned at job's completion, but they can be returned if desired.
Terms/Writers & Illustrators: Pays on acceptance. Buys first North American serial rights and one-time rights. Pays $25-35 for articles. "Writers and artists receive 2 copies free in addition to payment." Pays $30/b&w (cover) illustration; $7.50-25/b&w (inside).

Refer to the Business of Children's Writing & Illustrating for up-to-date marketing, tax and legal information.

Sample copy for business SAE and 3 first-class stamps; writers/illustrator's guidelines free for business SAE and 1 first class stamp.

Tips: Writers: "Take children seriously—they're smarter than you think! Respect their sense of dignity, don't talk down to them and don't write stories about 'bad kids.' Illustrators: "Keep it clean, vigorous, fresh—whatever your style. Send samples we can keep on file. Black and white line art is best."

COBBLESTONE, The History Magazine for Young People, Cobblestone Publishing, Inc., 30 Grove St., Peterborough NH 03458. (603)924-7209. Articles/Fiction Editor: Carolyn P. Yoder. Art Directors: Jim Fletcher and Marilyn Moran. Monthly magazine. Circ. 45,000. "*Cobblestone* is theme-related. Writers should request editorial guidelines which explain procedure and list upcoming themes. Queries must relate to an upcoming theme. Fiction is not used often, although a good fiction piece offers welcome diversity. It is recommended that writers become familiar with the magazine (sample copies available)."

Fiction: Middle readers, young adults: history. Does not want to see pieces that do not relate to an upcoming theme. Buys 6-10 mss/year. Average word length: 750. Byline given.

Nonfiction: Middle readers, young adults: history, interview/profile, travel. Does not want to see material that does not relate to an upcoming theme. Buys 120 mss/year. Average word length: 300-1,000. Byline given.

How to Contact/Writers: Fiction/nonfiction: Query with published clips. Reports on queries in 5-6 months before publication; mss in 2 months before publication.

Illustration: Buys 3 illustrations/issue; buys 36 illustrations/year. Preferred theme or style: Material that is simple, clear and accurate but not too juvenile. Sophisticated sources are a must. Will review all varieties of ms/illustration packages. Works on assignment only.

How to Contact/Illustrators: Ms/illustration packages: Illustrations are done by assignment. Roughs required. Illustrations only: Send samples of black and white work. "Illustrators should consult issues of *Cobblestone* to familiarize themselves with our needs." Reports on art samples in 1-2 months. Original artwork returned at job's completion.

Terms/Writers & Illustrators: Pays on publication. Buys all rights. Pays 10-15¢ word for assigned articles. Pays $10-125/b&w (inside) illustration. Sample copy $3.95 with 7½×10½ SAE and 5 first-class stamps; writer's/illustrator's guidelines free with SAE and 1 first-class stamp.

Tips: Writers: "Submit detailed queries which show attention to historical accuracy and which offer interesting and entertaining information. Be true to your own style. Study past issues to know what we look for. All feature articles, recipes, activities, fiction and supplemental nonfiction are freelance contributions." Illustrators: "Submit black and white samples, not too juvenile. Study past issues to know what we look for. The illustration we use is generally for stories, recipes and activities." (See listing for *Faces, The Magazine About People*.)

COCHRAN'S CORNER, Cochran's Publishing Co., Box 2036, Waldorf MD 20604. (301)843-0485. Articles Editor: Ada Cochran. Fiction Editor/Art Director: Debby Thompkins. Quarterly magazine. Estab. 1985. Circ. 1,000. "Our magazine is open to most kinds of writing that is wholesome and suitable for young children to read. It is a 52 page, 8½×11 devoted to short stories, articles and poems. Our children's corner is reserved for children up to the age of 14." 30% of material aimed at juvenile audience.

Fiction: Picture-oriented material: religious. Young readers: animal, fantasy, humorous, problem solving, religious. Middle readers: religious. Young adults/teens: contemporary, history, religious, romance, science fiction. Does not want to see "anything that contains bad language or violence." Buys 150 mss/year. Average word length: 1,000 words maximum.

Nonfiction: Picture-oriented material: religious, travel. Young readers: animal, how-to, problem solving, religious, travel. Middle readers: religious, travel. Young adults/teens: history, humorous, interview/profile, religious, travel. Does not want to see "editorials or politics." Buys 100 mss/year. Average word length: 150. Byline given.

Poetry: Reviews 20-line poetry on any subject.

How to Contact/Writers: Fiction/nonfiction: Send complete ms. Reports on mss in 3 months. Will consider simultaneous submissions.

Terms/Writers: Sample copy $3 with 6×9 SASE. Writer's guidelines free for SASE.

CRICKET MAGAZINE, Carus Corporation, P.O. Box 300, Peru IL 61354. (815)224-6656. Articles/Fiction Editor: Marianne Carus. Art Director: Ron McCutchan. Monthly magazine. Estab. 1973. Circ. 130,000. Children's literary magazine for ages 6-14.

Fiction: Picture-oriented material: animal, contemporary, fantasy, history, humorous, problem solving, science fiction, sports, spy/mystery/adventure. Middle readers: animal, contemporary, fantasy, history, humorous, problem solving, science fiction, sports, spy/mystery/adventure. Buys 180 mss/year. Average word length: 1,500. Byline given.

Nonfiction: Picture-oriented material: animal, history, how-to, humorous, interview/profile, problem solving, travel. Middle readers: animal, history, how-to, humorous, interview/profile, problem solving, travel. Buys 180 mss/year. Average word length: 1,000. Byline given.

Poetry: Reviews 1 page maximum length poems.

How to Contact/Writers: Send complete ms. Include Social Security number with submission. Reports on mss in 3 months. Will consider simultaneous submissions.

Illustration: Buys 50 (18 separate commissions)/issue; 600 illustrations/year. Preferred theme or style: "strong realism; strong people, especially kids; good action illustration; no cartoons." Will review ms/illustration packages submitted by authors/artists "but reserve option to re-illustrate." Will review an illustrator's work for possible use with fiction/nonfiction articles and columns by other authors.

How to Contact/Illustrators: Ms/illustrations packages: complete manuscript with sample and query. Illustrations only: tearsheets or good quality photocopies. Reports on art samples in 8 weeks. Original art work returned at job's completion.

Terms/Writers & Illustrators: Pays on publication. Buys first North American serial rights. Pays up to 25¢/word for unsolicited articles; up to $3/line for poetry. Pays $500/color cover; $75-150/b&w inside. Writer's/illustrator's guidelines free with SAE and 1 first class stamp.

Tips: "Nonfiction, historical articles and how-to's" most open to freelancers. (See listing for *Ladybug*.)

CRUSADER, Calvinist Cadet Corps, Box 7259, Grand Rapids MI 49510. (616)241-5616. Editor: G. Richard Broene. Art Director: Robert DeJonge. Magazine published 7 times/year. Circ. 13,000. Our magazine is for members of the Calvinist Cadet Corps—boys aged 9-14. Our purpose is to show how God is at work in their lives and in the world around them.

Fiction: Middle readers: contemporary, humorous, problem solving, religious, sports. Does not want to see fantasy, science fiction. Buys 12 mss/year. Average word length: 800-1,500.

Nonfiction: Middle readers: animal, how-to, humorous, interview/profile, problem solving, religious. Buys 6 mss/year. Average word length: 400-900.

How to Contact/Writers: Fiction/nonfiction: Send complete ms. Reports on queries in 1-3 weeks; mss in 1-5 weeks. Will consider simultaneous submissions.

Illustration: Buys 1 illustration/issue; buys 6 illustrations/year. Works on assignment only.

Terms/Writers & Illustrators: Pays on acceptance. Buys first rights; one-time rights; second serial (reprint rights). Pays 4-5¢/word for assigned articles; 2-5¢/word for unsolicited articles. Sample copy free with 9 × 12 SAE and 3 first-class stamps.
Tips: Publication is most open to fiction: write for a list of themes (available yearly in January).

*CURRENT HEALTH I, The Beginning Guide to Health Education, General Learning Corporation, 60 Revere Dr., Northbrook IL 60062-1563. (708)205-3000. Monthly (during school year Sept.-May) magazine. 7 × 10; 32 pages. "For classroom use by students, this magazine is curriculum specific and requires experienced educators who can write clearly and well at fifth grade reading level."
Nonfiction: Middle readers: nature/environment, problem solving, health. Buys 60-70 mss/year. Average word length: 1,000. "Credit given in staff box."
How to Contact/Writers: Nonfiction: Query with published clips and résumé. Reports on queries in 2 months. Publishes ms 6-7 months after acceptance.
Terms/Writers: Pays on publication. Buys all rights. Pays $100-150 ("More for longer features.") Writer's guidelines available only if writer is given an assignment.
Tips: Needs material about drug education, nutrition, fitness and exercise.

*CURRENT HEALTH II, The Continuing Guide to Health Education, General Learning Corporation, 60 Revere Dr., Northbrook IL 60062-1563. (708)205-3000. Monthly (during school year Sept.-May). 7 × 10; 32 pages. "For classroom use by students, this magazine is curriculum specific and requires experienced educators who can write clearly and well at a ninth grade reading level."
Nonfiction: Young adults/teens: nature/environment, problem solving, sports, health. Buys 70-90 mss/year. Average word length: 1,000-2,500. Byline given.
How to Contact/Writers: Nonfiction: Query with published clips and résumé. Reports on queries in 2 months. Publishes ms 6-7 months after acceptance.
Terms/Writers: Pays on publication. Buys all rights. Pays $100-150 for assigned articles, more for longer features. Writer's guidelines available only if writers are given an assignment.
Tips: Needs articles on drug education, nutrition, fitness and exercise.

DAY CARE AND EARLY EDUCATION, Human Sciences Press, 233 Spring St., New York NY 10013. (212)620-8000. Articles/Fiction Editor: Randa Nachbar. Art Director: Bill Jobson. Quarterly magazine. Circ. 2,500. Magazine uses material "involving children from birth to age 7." 5% of material aimed at juvenile audience.
Fiction: Picture material, young readers: contemporary, fantasy, humorous, problem solving. Average word length: 1,000-3,000. Byline given.
Nonfiction: Picture material, young readers: animal, how-to, humorous, problem solving. Average word length: 1,000-3,000. Byline given.
How to Contact/Writers: Fiction/nonfiction: Send complete ms. Reports on queries in 1 month; mss in 2-3 months.
Illustration: Will review all varieties of ms/illustration packages.
How to Contact/Illustrators: Ms/illustration packages: Send complete ms with final art. Reports on art samples only if interested. Original artwork returned at job's completion.
Terms/Writers & Illustrators: Pays in 2 copies. Free sample copy; free writer's guidelines.

*DELIRIUM, Muggwart Press, Route One-Box 7X, Harrison ID 83833. Fiction and Art Editor: Judith Shannon Paine. Quarterly magazine. 6½ × 8; 28-38 pages; 50 lb. paper; 50 lb. cover stock. Estab. 1989. Circ. 200. "Our publication is a joyous publication and we reach an international audience. Our theme is open." 5% of material aimed at juvenile audience.

Fiction: Young adults: animal, contemporary, humorous. Does not want to see science fiction or religious. Buys 24 mss/year. Average word length: 300. Byline given.

Poetry: Reviews "30 line maximum length poems. Will accept 10 submissions/author.

How to Contact/Writers: Fiction: Send complete manuscript. Reports on queries in 2 weeks; mss 2-12 weeks. Publishes ms 6 months to 1 year after acceptance. Will consider electronic submissions via disk or modem.

Illustration: Buys 2 illustrations/year from freelancers. "Black and white with any colors indicated on overlays, Avant Garde, clean, surreal, with each line counting—no cluttered/busy stuff. Should *never* be violent or ugly." Works on assignment only.

How to Contact/Illustrators: Query first with résumé, photocopies. Reports on art samples in 3 months (only if interested). Original artwork returned at job's completion.

Terms/Writers & Illustrators: Pays on publication. Buys one-time rights. Pay writers with contributor's copies or other premiums rather than a cash payment. "Cash is not in our vocabulary, yet!" Sample copy for $4 "and SASE sufficient to send a chap-sized 'zine of 24 pages—45 cents postage, please." Writer's guidelines free for 3⅝ × 6½ and 2 first class stamps. All checks should be made out to Frank L. Nicholson.

Tips: "Remember what it was like to be a child. Indulge that memory and write as cleanly and clearly as you can. Please send me material (fiction or poetry) that has to do with nature."

DISCOVERIES, Children's Ministries, 6401 The Paseo, Kansas City MO 64131. (816)333-7000. Editor: Molly Mitchell. Executive Editor: Mark York. Weekly tabloid. *Discoveries* is a leisure reading piece for third through sixth graders. It is published weekly by the Department of Children's Ministries of the Church of the Nazarene. "The major purposes of *Discoveries* are to: provide a leisure reading piece which will build Christian behavior and values; provide reinforcement for Biblical concepts taught in the Sunday School curriculum. The focus of the reinforcement will be life-related, with some historical appreciation. *Discoveries'* target audience is children ages 8-12 in grades three through six. The readability goal is fourth to fifth grade."

Fiction: "Fiction—stories should vividly portray definite Christian emphasis or character-building values, without being preachy. The setting, plot and action should be realistic." Average word length: 400-800. Byline given.

How to Contact/Writers: Fiction: Send complete ms. Report on mss in 4-6 weeks.

Illustration: Preferred theme or style: Cartoon—humor should be directed to children and involve children. It should not simply be child-related from an adult viewpoint. Some full color story illustrations are assigned. Samples of art may be sent for review.

Terms/Writers & Illustrators: Pays on acceptance. Buys first rights; second serial (reprint rights). Pays 3.5¢/word (first rights). Contributor receives complimentary copy of publication. Writer's guidelines free with #10 SAE.

Tips: "*Discoveries* is committed to reinforcement of the Biblical concepts taught in the Sunday School curriculum. Because of this, the themes needed are mainly as follows: faith in God, obedience to God, putting God first, choosing to please God, accepting Jesus as Savior, finding God's will, choosing to do right, trusting God in hard times, prayer; trusting God to answer, Importance of Bible memorization, appreciation of Bible as God's Word to man, Christians working together, showing kindness to others, witnessing." (See listing for *Together Time*.)

DOLPHIN LOG, The Cousteau Society, 8440 Santa Monica Blvd., Los Angeles CA 90069. (213)656-4422. Articles Editor: Pamela Stacey. Bimonthly magazine. Circ. 100,000. Subject matter encompasses all areas of science, history and the arts which can be related to our global water system. The philosophy of the magazine is to delight, instruct and instill an environmental ethic and understanding of the interconnectedness of living organisms, including people. Of special interest are articles on ocean- or water-related themes which develop reading and comprehension skills. 100% of material aimed at juvenile audience.

Nonfiction: Picture material, middle readers: animal, environmental, ocean. Does not want to see talking animals. Buys 15 mss/year. Average word length: 500-1,200. Byline given.

How to Contact/Writers: Nonfiction: Query. Include Social Security number with submission. Reports on queries in 4 weeks; mss in 8 weeks.

Illustration: Buys 1 illustration/issue; buys 6 illustrations/year. Preferred theme or style: Biological illustration. Will review ms/illustration packages by authors/artists; ms/illustration packages submitted by authors with illustrations done by separate artists; illustrator's work for possible use with nonfiction articles.

How to Contact/Illustrators: Ms/illustration packages: No original artwork, copies only. Illustrations only: Send tearsheets, slides. Reports on art samples in 8 weeks only if interested. Original artwork returned at job's completion.

Terms/Writers & Illustrators: Pays on publication. Buys first North American serial rights; "translation rights." Pays $25-150 for assigned/unsolicited articles. Additional payment for ms/illustration packages is in the $25-150 range. Pays $25-150/b&w illustration; $25-200/color (cover); $25-200/color (inside). Sample copy $2 with SAE and 2 first-class stamps. Writer's/illustrator's guidelines free with SAE and 1 first-class stamp.

Tips: Writers: "Write simply and clearly and don't anthropomorphize." Illustrators: "Be scientifically accurate and don't anthropomorphize. Some background in biology is helpful, as our needs range from simple line drawings to scientific illustrations which must be researched for biological and technical accuracy."

*DYNAMATH, Scholastic Inc., 730 Broadway, New York NY 10003. Fiction Editor: Jackie Glasthall. Monthly magazine. 8½ × 11; 16 pp. Estab. 1981. Circ. 356,000. Purpose is "to make learning math fun, challenging and uncomplicated for young minds in a very complex world."

Fiction/nonfiction: All levels: anything related to math and science topics. Byline given sometimes.

Poetry: Does review poetry.

How To Contact/Writers: Fiction/nonfiction: Query with published clips, send manuscript. Reports on queries in 6 weeks. Average length of time between acceptance and publication of work: 4 months. Will consider simultaneous submissions and electronic submissions via disk or modem.

Illustration: Buys 4 illustrations/issue. Reviews all varieties of manuscript illustration packages.

How To Contact/Illustrators: Query first. Reports back in 2 months on submissions. Originals returned to artist at job's completion.

Terms/Writers & Illustrators: Pays on acceptance. Buys first North American serial rights.

EXPLORING, Boy Scouts of America, Box 152079, 1325 West Walnut Hill Ln., Irving TX 75015-2079. (214)580-2365. Executive Editor: Scott Daniels. Art Director: Joe Connally. Magazine published "4 times a year—not quarterly." *Exploring* is a 12 page, 4-color magazine published for members of the Boy Scouts of America's Exploring program. These members are young men and women between the ages of 14-21. Interests include careers, computers, camping, hiking, canoeing.

Nonfiction: Young adults: interview/profile, problem solving, travel. Buys 12 mss/year. Average word length: 600-1,200. Byline given.

How to Contact/Writers: Nonfiction: Query with published clips. Reports on queries/mss in 1 week.

Illustration: Buys 3 illustrations/issue; buys 12 illustrations/year. Will review an illustrator's work for possible use with fiction/nonfiction articles and columns by other authors. Works on assignment only.

How to Contact/Illustrators: Reports on art samples in 2 weeks. Original art work returned at job's completion.

Terms/Writers & Illustrators: Pays on acceptance. Buys first North American serial rights. Pays $300-500 for assigned/unsolicited articles. Pays $500-800/b&w (cover) illustration; $800-1,000/color (cover); $250-500/b&w (inside); $500-800/color (inside). Sample copy with 8½ × 11 SAE and 5 first-class stamps. Free writer's/illustrator's guidelines.

Tips: Looks for "short, crisp career profiles of 1,000 words with plenty of information to break out into graphics."

FACES, The Magazine About People, Cobblestone Publishing, Inc., 30 Grove St., Peterborough NH 03458. (603)924-7209. Articles/Fiction Editor: Carolyn P. Yoder. Art Director: Coni Porter. Magazine published 9 times/year (Sept.-May). Circ. 13,500. "Although *Faces* operates on a by-assignment basis, we welcome ideas/suggestions in outline form. All manuscripts are reviewed by the American Museum of Natural History in New York before being accepted. *Faces* is a theme-related magazine; writers should send for theme list before submitting ideas/queries."

Fiction: Middle readers, young adults: contemporary, history, religious, anthropology. Does not want to see material that does not relate to a specific upcoming theme. Buys 9 mss/year. Average word length: 750. Byline given.

Nonfiction: Middle readers, young adults: history, interview/profile, religious, travel, anthropology. Does not want to see material not related to a specific upcoming theme. Buys 63 mss/year. Average word length: 300-1,000. Byline given.

How to Contact/Writers: Fiction/nonfiction: Query with published clips. Reports on queries in 5-6 months before publication; mss 2 months before publication.

Illustration: Buys 3 illustrations/issue; buys 27 illustrations/year. Preferred theme or style: Material that is meticulously researched (most articles are written by professional anthropologists); simple, direct style preferred, but not too juvenile. Will review all varieties of ms/illustration packages. Works on assignment only.

How to Contact/Illustrators: Ms/illustration packages: Illustration is done by assignment. Roughs required. Illustrations only: Send samples of black and white work. Illustrators should consult issues of *Faces* to familiarize themselves with our needs. Reports on art samples in 1-2 months. Original artwork returned at job's completion.

Terms/Writers & Illustrators: Pays on publication. Buys all rights. Pays 10-15¢/word for assigned articles. Pays $10-125/b&w (inside) illustration. Sample copy $3.95 with 7½ × 10½ SAE and 5 first-class stamps. Writer's/illustrator's guidelines free with SAE and 1 first-class stamp.

Tips: "Writers are encouraged to study past issues of the magazine to become familiar with our style and content. Writers with anthropological and/or travel experience are particularly encouraged; *Faces* is about world cultures. All feature articles, recipes and activities are freelance contributions." Illustrators: "Submit black and white samples, not too juvenile. Study past issues to know what we look for. The illustration we use is generally for retold legends, recipes and activities." (See listing for *Cobblestone, The History Magazine for Young People.*)

FRIEND, Wesleyan Publishing House, 6060 Castleway W. Dr., Box 50434, Indianapolis IN 46250. (317)842-0444, ext. 196. Articles/Fiction Editor/Art Director: Kathy Weaver. Quarterly magazine. Circ. 31,000. "*Friend* is a Sunday School take-home paper for children ages 6-8 years old. All contributors need to keep in mind the ages of the children this publication is for."

Fiction: Young readers: animal, contemporary, history, humorous, problem solving, sports, spy/mystery/adventure. Does not want to see animals praying, romance, science

fiction, fantasy. Buys 4 mss/year. Average word length: 450-600. Byline given.
Nonfiction: Young readers: animal, history, humorous, problem solving, religious, travel. Does not want to see animals praying, science fiction, fantasy. Buys 4 mss/year. Average word length: 450-600. Byline given.
How to Contact/Writers: Fiction/nonfiction: Send complete ms. Include Social Security number with submission. Report on mss in 1-2 months.
Illustration: Will review all varieties of ms/illustration packages.
How to Contact/Illustrators: Ms/illustration packages: Send complete ms and final art. Illustrations only: Send color slides. Reports on art samples in 1-2 months.
Terms/Writers & Illustrators: Pays on publication. Buys first rights. Sample copy free with #10 SAE and 1 first-class stamp. Writer's/illustrator's guidelines free with #10 SAE and 1 first-class stamp.
Tips: "The following are turn-offs: a letter of recommendation from a teacher, a letter of recommendation from a pastor, tearsheets. The ability of the writer will be apparent. A résumé might be a way for the editor to become acquainted with the writer without the use of a letter of recommendation." Advice to new writers: "Be yourself. Don't copy someone else's writing technique. Use a technique that is you—not your teacher's or your friend's. Remember your childhood and how it was for you to be a child. Have the children in your stories act in a developmentally appropriate manner." Advice to new artists: "Use bright, clear colors which captivate the action and attract reader interest. Draw children (not little adults)."

THE FRIEND MAGAZINE, The Church of Jesus Christ of Latter-day Saints, 50 E. North Temple, Salt Lake City UT 84150. (801)240-2210. Managing Editor: Vivian Paulsen. Art Director: Dick Brown. Monthly magazine. 8¼ × 10½; 48 pages. Estab. 1971. Circ. 225,000. Magazine for 3-11 year olds.
Fiction: Uses history, humorous, religious, ethnic, mainstream, nature, adventure pieces. Does not want to see controversial issues, political, horror, fantasy. Average word length: 400-1,000. Byline given.
Nonfiction: Uses animal, how-to, religious. Does not want to see controversial issues, political, horror, fantasy. Buys 20 mss/year. Average word length: 400-1,000. Byline given.
How to Contact/Writers: Fiction/nonfiction: Send complete ms. Reports on mss in 2 months.
Terms/Writers & Illustrators: Pays on acceptance. Buys all rights. Pays 8¢/word for unsolicited articles. Contributors are encouraged to send for free sample copy with 9 × 11 envelope and 85¢ postage. Free writer's guidelines.
Tips: "The *Friend* is published by The Church of Jesus Christ of Latter-day Saints for boys and girls up to twelve years of age. All submissions are carefully read by the *Friend* staff, and those not accepted are returned within two months when a self-addressed stamped envelope is enclosed. Submit seasonal material at least eight months in advance. Query letters and simultaneous submissions are not encouraged. Authors may request rights to have their work reprinted after their manuscript is published."

GROUP, Thom Schultz Publications, Box 481, Loveland CO 80537. (303)669-3836. Articles Editor: Rick Lawrence. "We are a religious publication for Christian youth ministers. Our readers are adult youth leaders."
Fiction/Nonfiction: Young adults: religious.
How to Contact/Writers: Fiction/nonfiction: query with published clips. Will consider simultaneous and electronic submissions.
Illustration: Will review ms/illustration packages by authors/artists.
How to Contact/Illustrators: Ms/illustration packages: query first with SASE.
Terms/Writers & Illustrators: Pays on acceptance. Buys all rights. Pays $20-200/assigned or unsolicited article.

GUIDE MAGAZINE, Review and Herald Publishing Association, 55 West Oak Ridge Dr., Hagerstown MD 21740. (301)791-7000. Articles Editor: Jeannette Johnson. Art Director: Stephen Hall. Weekly magazine. Estab. 1953. Circ. 42,000. "Ours is a weekly Christian journal written for 10- to 14-year-olds, presenting true stories relevant to the needs of today's young person, emphasizing positive aspects of Christian living. 100% of material aimed at juvenile audience."

Fiction: Young adults: Animal, contemporary, history, humorous, problem solving, religious, character-building. "We like 'true-to-life,' that is, based on true happenings."

Nonfiction: Young adults: animal, history, how-to, humorous, interview/profile, problem solving, religious, character-building. Does not want to see violence, hunting nonfiction. Buys 300+ mss/year. Average word length: 500-600 minimum, 1,200-1,500 maximum. Byline given.

How to Contact/Writers: Nonfiction: Send complete ms. Include Social Security number with submission. Reports in 1-2 weeks. Will consider simultaneous and electronic submissions via disk or modem. "We can only pay half of the regular amount for simultaneous submissions."

Illustration: Buys 4-6 illustrations/issue; buys 350+ illustrations/year. Works on assignment only.

How to Contact/Illustrators: Ms/illustration packages: "art is by assignment only. Glad to look at portfolios." Artists interested in illustrations only: "Send tearsheets and slides." Original artwork returned at job's completion.

Terms/Writers & Illustrators: Pays on acceptance. Buys first North American serial rights; first rights; one-time rights; second serial (reprint rights) simultaneous rights. Pays 4¢/word/assigned articles; 3-4¢/word/unsolicited articles. "Writer receives several complimentary copies of issue in which work appears." Pays $150-250/b&w (cover) illustration; $175-300/color (cover); $125-175/b&w (inside); 150-175/color (inside). Sample copy free with 5×9 SAE and 2 first-class stamps; writer's/illustrator's guidelines for SASE.

HICALL, Gospel Publishing House, 1445 Boonville Ave., Springfield MO 65802-1894. (417)862-2781, ext. 4349. Articles/Fiction Editor, Art Director: Deanna Harris. Quarterly newsletter (Sunday school take-home paper). Estab. 1920. Circ. 80,000. "Slant articles toward the 15-to 17-year-old teen. We are a Christian publication, so all articles should focus on the Christian's responses to life. Fiction should be realistic, not syrupy nor too graphic. Fiction should have a Christian slant also." 100% of material aimed at teen audience.

Fiction: Young adults/teens: contemporary, fantasy, history, humorous, problem-solving, religious, romance. Buys 100 mss/year. Average word length 1,000-1,500. Byline given.

Nonfiction: Young adults/teens: animal, history, humorous, problem solving, religious. Buys 25 mss/year. Average word length: 1,000. Byline given.

Poetry: Reviews 40-line poetry.

How to Contact/Writers: Fiction/nonfiction: Send complete ms. Do *not* send query letters. Include Social Security number with submission. Reports on mss in 4-6 weeks. Will consider simultaneous submissions.

Illustration: Buys 10-30 illustrations/year. "Freelance art used only when in-house art department has a work overload." Prefers to review "realistic, cartoon, youth-oriented styles." Will review an illustrator's work for possible use with fiction/nonfiction articles and columns by other authors. Works on assignment only. "Any art sent will be referred to the art department. Art department will assign freelance art."

How to Contact/Illustrators: Illustrations only: Send "tearsheets, slides, photos. Résumé helpful." Reports in 4-6 weeks.

Terms/Writers & Illustrators: Pays on acceptance. Buys first North American serial rights, first rights, one-time rights, second serial (reprint rights), simultaneous rights.

Pays 4¢/word/assigned articles; 2-3¢/word unsolicited articles. Pays $35/b&w cover photo; $50 color cover photo; $25/b&w inside photo; $35 color inside photo. Sample copy free with 6×9 SASE. Writer's guidelines free with SASE.

HIGH ADVENTURE, Assemblies of God, 1445 Boonville Ave., Springfield MO 65802. (417)862-2781, Ext. 4181. FAX: (417)862-8558. Editor: Marshall Bruner. Quarterly magazine. Circ. 86,000. Estab. 1971. Magazine is designed to provide boys with worth-while, enjoyable, leisure reading; to challenge them in narrative form to higher ideals and greater spiritual dedication; and to perpetuate the spirit of Royal Rangers through stories, ideas and illustrations. 75% of material aimed at juvenile audience.
Fiction: Buys 100 mss/year. Average word length: 1,000. Byline given.
Nonfiction: Articles: Christian living, devotional, Holy Spirit, salvation, self-help; biography; missionary stories; news items; testimonies.
How to Contact/Writers: Fiction/nonfiction: Send complete ms. Include Social Security number with submission. Reports on queries in 6-8 weeks. Will consider simultaneous submissions. Will review all varieties of ms/illustration packages.
How to Contact/Illustrators: Ms/illustration packages: Send complete ms with final art. Illustrations only: "Most of our artwork is done in-house."
Terms/Writers & Illustrators: Pays on acceptance. Buys first rights. Pays 2-3¢/word for unsolicited articles. Sample copy free with 8½×11 SASE. Free writer's/illustrator's guidelines.

HIGHLIGHTS FOR CHILDREN, 803 Church St., Honesdale PA 18431. (717)253-1080. Manuscript Coordinator: Beth Troop. 8½×11; 42 pages; cover stock slick. Art Director: Rosanne Guararra. Monthly (July-August issue combined) magazine. Estab. 1964. Circ. 2.8 million. Our motto is "Fun With a Purpose." We are looking for quality fiction and nonfiction that appeals to children, will encourage them to read, and reinforces positive values. All art is done on assignment. 100% of material aimed at juvenile audience.
Fiction: Picture-oriented material: animal, contemporary, fantasy, history, humorous, problem solving. Young readers, middle readers: animal, contemporary, fantasy, history, humorous, problem solving, science fiction, sports, mystery/adventure. Does not want to see: war, crime, violence. Buys 150+ mss/year. Average word length: 400-800. Byline given.
Nonfiction: Picture-oriented material: animal, history, how-to, humorous, problem solving. Young readers, middle readers: animal, history, how-to, humorous, interview/profile, problem solving, foreign, science, nature, arts, sports. Does not want to see: trendy topics, fads, personalities who would not be good role models for children, guns, war, crime, violence. Buys 75+ mss/year. Average word length: 900. Byline given.
How to Contact/Writers: Fiction: Send complete ms. Nonfiction: Include Social Security number with submission. Reports on queries in 4 weeks; mss in 4 weeks.
Illustration: Preferred theme or style: Realistic, some stylization, cartoon style acceptable. Works on assignment only.
How to Contact/Illustrators: Ms/illustration packages: Art is done on assignment only. Illustrations only: Photocopies, tearsheets, or slides. Résumé optional. Reports on art samples in 4 weeks.

 The asterisk before a listing indicates the listing is new in this edition.

Terms/Writers & Illustrators: Pays on acceptance. Buys all rights. Pays 14¢/word and up for unsolicited articles. Pays $400-$550 color (cover) illustration; $200-$350 color (inside) illustration. Writer's/illustrator's guidelines free on request.

Tips: Writers: "Study the market. Analyze several issues of the magazines you want to write for. Send for writer's guidelines. Send in professional-looking work." Illustrators: "Fresh, imaginative work presented in a professional portfolio encouraged. Flexibility in working relationships a plus. Illustrators in presenting their work need not confine themselves to just children's illustrations as long as work can translate to our needs. We also use animal illustrations, real and imaginary. We need party plans, crafts and puzzles—any activity that will stimulate children mentally and creatively. We are always looking for imaginative cover subjects."

*THE HOME ALTAR, Meditations for Families with Children, Augsburg Fortress, 426 S. Fifth St., Box 1209, Minneapolis MN 55440. Articles/Fiction Editor: M. Elaine Dunham, Box 590179, San Francisco CA 94159-0179. Quarterly magazine. 5¼×7¼; 64 pages. Quality newsprint. Cover Stock coated. Circ. approx. 70,000. This is a booklet of daily devotions, used primarily by Lutheran families. Each day's reading focuses on a specific Bible passage. 98% of material aimed at juvenile audience.

Fiction: Young readers, middle readers: religious. Buys 365 mss/year. Average word length: 125-170. Byline given.

Nonfiction: Young readers, middle readers: religious. Average word length: 125-170. Byline given.

How to Contact/Writers: Fiction/nonfiction: Query with published clips.

Illustration: Buys 100 illustrations/year. Works on assignment only.

How to Contact/Illustrators: Reports on art samples only if interested.

Terms/Writers & Illustrators: Pays on acceptance. Buys all rights. Pays $10 for assigned articles. Free writer's guidelines for 6×9 SAE and 85¢ in first-class stamps.

*HOPSCOTCH, The Magazine for Girls, Hopscotch, Inc., Box 1292, Saratoga Springs NY 12866. (518)587-2268. Articles/Fiction/Art Director: Donald P. Evans. Bimonthly magazine. 7×9 ; 44-48 pp; 45 lb. 5 enamel paper stock; 80 lb. 3 enamel cover stock. Estab. 1989. Circ. 7,000. For girls from 6 to 12 years, featuring traditional subjects— pets, games, hobbies, nature, science, sports etc.—with an emphasis on articles that show girls actively involved in unusual and/or worthwhile activities."

Fiction: Young Readers and Middle Readers: animal, contemporary, fantasy, history, humorous, problem solving, science fiction, sports, spy/mystery/adventure. Does not want to see stories dealing with dating, sex, fashion, hard rock music. Buys 24 mss/year. Average word length: 300-1,100. Byline given.

Nonfiction: Young Readers and Middle Readers: animal, biography, education, history, how-to, humorous, interview/profile, nature/environment, problem solving, travel, sports. Does not want to see pieces dealing with dating, sex, fashion, hard rock music. Buys 36 mss/year. Average word length: 400-1,100. Byline given.

Poetry: Reviews traditional, wholesome, humorous poems. Maximum word length: 400; maximum line length: 40. Will accept 6 submissions/author.

How to Contact/Writers: Fiction: Send complete manuscript. Nonfiction: Query, send complete manuscript. Include social security number with submission. Reports on queries/mss in 2 weeks. Publishes ms 6 months after acceptance. Will consider simultaneous submissions.

Illustration: Buys 4-8 illustrations/issue; buys 24-48 illustrations/year. "Generally, the illustrations are assigned after we have purchased a piece (usually fiction). Occasionally, we will use a painting—in any given medium—for the cover, and these are usually seasonal." Will review all varieties of ms/illustration packages.

Close-up

Donald Evans
Editor
Hopscotch
Saratoga Springs, New York

According to Donald Evans, editor of *Hopscotch*, his wife was the main force behind the creation of the magazine. He explains she is an elementary school librarian and, "she had looked for a magazine like *Hopscotch* for years and could not find such an animal. She told me this and kept urging me to create one." He says at first he was doubtful and could not believe there was not a magazine for pre-teen girls on the market. "I did some research and found out, low and behold, she was totally correct."

Considering Evans' credentials, it's no wonder his wife solicited his help. In addition to being a freelance writer for 30 years, he is quite familiar with magazine publishing, as he was involved with association and corporate magazines when he was employed in publicity and public relations.

"We assumed there was a vast market for the magazine," says Evans. "We just had to determine the demand. Part of determining that is putting out a quality product, and you *have* to do that, because you can't fool children, you can't fool librarians, and you can't fool parents."

Evans says the hardest task involved in the groundwork was coming up with a name for the magazine, as well as determining the logo and format. One of the first format questions was whether to use fiction or nonfiction. "We thought a combination of the two was the most workable," says Evans, noting they prefer to publish mostly nonfiction. *Hopscotch* also accepts submissions of poetry, crafts and columns. The ultimate purpose of the magazine, says Evans, is to encourage reading among pre-teen girls. "We want an editorially-pointed magazine as opposed to graphics."

Since the first issue was printed in June, 1989, the operation has grown steadily, but still remains small. Currently the circulation is around 7,000. "We're so small we'd be overwhelmed by huge success all at once," says Evans. Though four people are on staff, Evans is the only one that is full time.

Hopscotch receives about 2,500 submissions a year, says Evans, and every one of them is read. Out of that number, about 1,500-1,700 are fiction manuscripts, which are not high in demand. "The story we rarely get and cherish the most is the (nonfiction) story about a girl or several girls who are directly involved in an interesting and/or worthwhile activity. That is by far the easiest story to sell to us. If there are some photos or artwork, it becomes even easier to sell to us.

"I can't imagine someone writing for a magazine without at least having seen its guidelines," says Evans. Though *Hopscotch* looks for articles, fiction and poetry likely to interest young girls ages 6-12, certain subjects such as dating, romance, human sexuality, cosmetics and fashion are off limits. "Yet I see stories like that all the while. They simply have no chance in our magazine."

Usually Evans deals with a small stable of illustrators across the country, but he says he is always willing to receive submissions from artists. Pen and ink sketches are best, but "I'm always open to color painting or drawing for the cover." He says eventually he would like to incorporate the use of color through the entire magazine.

Finally, Evans says he tries to write as many personal notes as possible to people who submit to him. He writes the notes so writers won't get discouraged. "If we return the story, it's not necessarily because it's not good. It's just we get so much material and use so little. Writers should not get down on themselves."

—Lisa Carpenter

How to Contact/Illustrators: Query first or complete manuscript with final art. Illustrations only: send photocopies. Reports on art samples in 2 weeks. Original artwork returned at job's completion.

Terms/Writers & Illustrators: Pays on acceptance. Buys first North American serial rights; second serial (reprint rights). Pays $40-100 for assigned articles; $30-80 for unsolicited articles. "We always send a copy of the issue to the writer or illustrator." Text and art are treated separately. Pays $100-200/color/cover; $25-50 b&w/inside. Sample copy for $3. Writer's/Illustrators guidelines free for #10 SAE.

Tips: "Please look at our guidelines and our magazine ... and remember, we use far more non-fiction than fiction. Most welcome is the article that has a girl or girls directly involved in an interesting and/or worthwhile activity. If decent photos accompany the piece, it stands an even better chance of being accepted. We believe it is the responsibility of the contributor to come up with photos. Please remember, our readers are 6-12 years—most are 7-10—and your text should reflect that."

HUMPTY DUMPTY'S MAGAZINE, Children's Better Health Institute (div. Benjamin Franklin Literary & Medical Soc.), 1100 Waterway Blvd., Box 567, Indianapolis IN 46206. (317)636-8881. Articles/Fiction Editor: Christine French Clark. Art Director: Larry Simmons. Magazine published 8 times/year—Jan/Feb; Mar; April/May; June; July/Aug; Sept; Oct/Nov; Dec. *HDM* is edited for kindergarten children, approximately ages 4-6. It includes fiction (easy-to-reads; read alouds; rhyming stories; rebus stories), nonfiction articles (some with photo illustrations), poems, crafts, recipes and puzzles. Much of the content encourages development of better health habits. We especially need material promoting fitness. "All but 2 pages aimed at the juvenile market. The remainder may be seasonal and/or more general."

Fiction: Picture-oriented material: animal, contemporary, fantasy, humorous, sports, health-related. Young readers: animal, contemporary, fantasy, humorous, science fiction, sports, spy/mystery/adventure, health-related. Does not want to see bunny-rabbits-with-carrot-pies stories! Also, talking inanimate objects are very difficult to do well. Beginners (and maybe everyone) should avoid these. Buys 35-50 mss/year. Maximum word length: 700. Byline given.

Nonfiction: Picture-oriented material, young readers: animal, how-to, humorous, interview/profile, health-related. Does not want to see long, boring, encyclopedia rehashes. "We're open to almost any subject (although most of our nonfiction has a health angle), but it must be presented creatively. Don't just string together some facts." Looks for a fresh approach. Buys 6-10 mss/year. Prefers very short nonfiction pieces—500 words maximum. Byline given.

How to Contact/Writers: Send complete ms. Nonfiction: Send complete ms with bibliography if applicable. Include Social Security number with submission. "No queries, please!" Reports on mss in 8-10 weeks.

Illustration: Buys 13-16 illustrations/issue; buys 90-120 illustrations/year. Preferred theme or style: Realistic or cartoon. Will review all varieties of ms/illustration packages. Works on assignment only.

How to Contact/Illustrators: Ms/illustration packages: Send slides, printed pieces, or photocopies. Illustrations only: Send slides, printed pieces or photocopies. Reports on art samples only if interested.

Terms/Writers & Illustrators: Writers: Pays on publication. Artists: Pays within 6-8 weeks. Buys all rights. "One-time book rights may be returned if author can provide name of interested book publisher and tentative date of publication." Pays about 10¢/word for unsolicited stories/articles; payment varies for poems and activities. Up to 10 complimentary issues are provided to author with check. Pays $250/color cover illustration; $30-70 per page b&w (inside); $55-110/2-color (inside); $65-140/color (inside). Sample copy for 75¢. Writer's/illustrator's guidelines free with SASE.

Tips: Writers: "Study current issues and guidelines. Observe, especially, word lengths and adhere to requirements. It's sometimes easier to break in with recipe or craft ideas, but submit what you do best. Don't send your first, second, or even third drafts. Polish your piece until it's as perfect as you can make it." Illustrators: "Please study the magazine before contacting us. Your art must have appeal to three- to seven-year-olds." (See listings for *Child Life*, *Children's Digest*, *Children's Playmate*, *Humpty Dumpty's Magazine*, *Jack and Jill*, *Turtle Magazine*.)

INSIGHTS, NRA News for Young Shooters, National Rifle Assoc. of America, 1600 Rhode Island Ave. NW, Washington DC 20036. (202)828-6290. Articles Editor: John Robbins. Monthly magazine. 8⅛ × 10⅞; 24 pp; mid grade 4 paper, 60 lb. cover stock. Establ 1980. Circ. 33,000. "*InSights* promotes the shooting sports. We teach the safe and responsible use of firearms for competition shooting, hunting or recreational shooting. Our articles are instructional yet entertaining. We teach but don't preach. We emphasize safety."

Fiction: Young adults: animal, history, humorous, sports. "Fiction that does not relate to the shooting sports or positively promote the safe and ethical use of firearms will not be considered." Buys 12 mss/year. Average word length: 600-1,500. Byline given.

Nonfiction: Young adults: animal, history, how-to, humorous, interview/profile, "all these categories must involve the shooting sports." Buys 40 mss/year. Average word length: 600-1,500. Byline given.

How to Contact/Writers: Fiction/nonfiction: Query, send complete ms. Include Social Security number with submission. Reports on queries/mss in 2 months.

Illustration: Buys 1 illustration/issue; buys 7 illustrations/year. Will review ms/illustration packages submitted by authors with illustrations done by separate artists. Works on assignment only.

How to Contact/Illustrators: Ms/illustration packages: Query first. Illustrations only: Tearsheets or slides would be great! Illustrator should have technical knowledge of firearms and shooting.

Terms/Writers & Illustrators: Pays on acceptance. Buys first North American serial rights, second serial (reprint rights). Pays $200 for assigned/unsolicited articles. Additional payment for ms/illustration packages: $300. Pays $150-200 b&w (inside) illustration. Sample copy free with 10×12 SAE and 3 first class stamps; writer's/illustrator's guidelines free with business SAE and 1 first-class stamp.

Tips: Writers: "You have to know your subject. Kids are smart and quickly pick up on inaccuracies. As an authority, your credibility is then zilch. Material should instruct without sounding preachy. We do not buy material that shows shooting in a bad light. We show our readers the correct, safe and ethical way to use a firearm." Illustrators: "When illustrating a story, stick to the description in the plot. We find young readers don't like illustrations when they differ from the story. Forego creative license this time. Wildlife art must be anatomically and environmentally correct. Shooting scenes must be safe and instructionally correct. We will be sponsoring a wildlife art contest for our readers. Entrants must be in 12th grade or below."

INTERNATIONAL GYMNAST, Sundbysports, Inc., 225 Brooks, Box G, Oceanside CA 92054. (619)722-0030. Editor: Dwight Narmile. Monthly publication. "We are a magazine about gymnasts for ages up to 17."

Nonfiction: Gymnastics material only.

How to Contact/Writers: Nonfiction: query, query with published clips. Will consider simultaneous submissions (please advise).

Illustration: Will review all varieties of ms/illustration packages.

How to Contact/Illustrators: Ms/illustration packages: query first. Illustrations only: send slides or prints.

Terms/Writers & Illustrators: Pays on publication by arrangement. Buys one-time rights. Pay "varies; negotiated." Additional payment for ms/illustration packages or illustrations only also "varies; negotiated."

JACK AND JILL, Children's Better Health Institute, 1100 Waterway Blvd., Indianapolis IN 46206. (317)636-8881. Articles Fiction Editor: Steve Charles. Art Director: Ed Cortese. Magazine published 8 times/year. Estab. 1938. Circ. 360,000. "Write entertaining and imaginative stories *for* kids, not just *about* them. Writers should understand what is funny to kids, what's important to them, what excites them. Don't write from an adult "kids are so cute" perspective. We're also looking for health and healthy lifestyle stories and articles, but don't be preachy."

Fiction: Young readers: animal, contemporary, fantasy, history, humorous, problem solving. Middle readers: contemporary, humorous. Buys 30-35 mss/year. Average word length: 900. Byline given.

Nonfiction: Young readers: animal, history, how-to, humorous, interview/profile, problem solving, travel. Buys 8-10 mss/year. Average word length: 1,000. Byline given.

Poetry: Reviews poetry.

How to Contact/Writers: Fiction/nonfiction: Send complete ms. Reports on queries in 2 weeks; mss in 8-10 weeks. Will consider simultaneous submissions.

Terms/Writers: Pays on publication; minimum 10¢/word. Buys all rights. (See listings for *Child Life, Children's Digest, Children's Playmate, Humpty Dumpty's Magazine, Turtle Magazine.*)

JUNIOR TRAILS, Gospel Publishing House, 1445 Boonville Ave., Springfield MO 65802. (417)862-2781. Articles/Fiction Editor: Sinda S. Zinn. Quarterly magazine. Circ. 70,000. Junior Trails is a 4-page take-home paper for fifth and sixth graders. Its articles consist

"Picture books" are geared toward the preschool — 8 year old group; "Young readers" to 5-8 year olds; "Middle readers" to 9-11 year olds; and "Young adults" to those 12 and up.

of fiction stories of a contemporary or historical nature. The stories have a moral slant to show how modern-day people can work out problems in acceptable ways, or give examples in history from which we can learn.

Fiction: Middle readers: contemporary, history, humorous, problem solving, religious, sports, spy/mystery/adventure. Does not want to see science fiction, mythology, ghosts and witchcraft. Buys 80 mss/year. Average word length: 800-1,200. Byline given.

Nonfiction: Middle readers: animal, history, how-to, humorous, problem solving, religious, travel. Buys 30 mss/year. Average word length: 300-800. Byline given.

How to Contact/Writers: Fiction/nonfiction: Send complete ms. Reports on queries in 2 weeks; mss in 4-6 weeks. Will consider simultaneous submissions.

Terms/Writers & Illustrators: Pays on acceptance. Buys first rights; one-time rights; second serial (reprint rights); simultaneous rights. Pays 2-3¢/word for unsolicited articles. Sample copy free with 9 × 12 SASE.

Tips: "Submit stories with which children can identify. Avoid trite, overused plots and themes. Make children be children—not babies or super, adult-like people. Let your characters weave the story. Don't fill up space with unnecessary details. We are always in need of good fiction stories. We tend to get a lot of very long stories that will not fit in our available space." Looks for: "fiction that presents believable characters working out their problems according to Bible principles; present Christianity in action without being preachy; articles with reader appeal, emphasizing some phase of Christian living, presented in a down-to-earth manner; biography or missionary material using fiction technique; historical, scientific or nature material with a spiritual lesson; fillers that are brief, purposeful, usually containing an anecdote, and always with a strong evangelical emphasis."

KEYNOTER, Key Club International, 3636 Woodview Trace, Indianapolis IN 46268. (317)875-8755. Articles Editor: Tamara P. Burley. Art Director: James Patterson. Monthly magazine. 8¼ × 10⅞; 16 pp; #4 offset paper. Estab. 1915. Circ. 133,000. As the official magazine of the world's largest high school service organization, we publish nonfiction articles that interest teenagers and will help our readers become better students, better citizens, better leaders.

Nonfiction: Young adults: how-to, humorous, problem solving. Does not want to see first-person accounts; short stories. Buys 15 mss/year. Average word length: 1,800-2,500. Byline given.

How to Contact/Writers: Nonfiction: Query. Include Social Security number with submission. Reports on queries/mss in 1 month. Will consider simultaneous submissions.

Illustration: Buys 2-3 illustrations/issue; buys 15 illustrations/year. Will review all varieties of ms/illustration packages. Works on assignment only.

How to Contact/Illustrators: Ms/illustration packages: "Because of our publishing schedule, we prefer to work with illustrators/photographers within Indianapolis market." Illustrators only: Send résumé, tearsheets, slides, samples or photos. Reports on art samples only if interested. Original artwork returned at job's completion if requested.

Terms/Writers & Illustrators: Pays on acceptance. Buys first North American serial rights. Pays $75-300 for assigned/unsolicited articles. Sample copy free with 8½ × 11 SAE and 65¢ postage. Writer's guidelines free with SAE and 1 first-class stamp.

Tips: "We are looking for light or humorous nonfiction, self help articles." Also looking for articles about education reform, national concerns, trends, teen trends in music, fashion, clothes, ideologies, etc.

KID CITY, Children's Television Workshop, 1 Lincoln Plaza, New York NY 10023. (212)595-3456. Articles editor: Maureen Hunter-Bone; Fiction editor: Lisa Rao; Art director: Michele Weisman. Monthly magazine. 8×11; 36 pp; 40 lb. glossy paper and 60 lb. glossy cover stock. Estab. 1971. Circ. 330,000+.

Fiction: Middle readers: animal, contemporary, history, humorous, science fiction, sports, spy/mystery/adventure. Does not want to see "cutsie, overly moralistic, preachy material." Buys 3-4 mss/year. Average word length: 200-500. Byline given.

Nonfiction: Middle readers: animal, nature/environment, sports. Does not want to see puzzle and games submissions. Buys 12 mss/year. Average word length: 200-500. Byline given.

How to Contact/Writers: Fiction: Send complete ms. Nonfiction: Query or send complete ms. Reports on queries/mss in 4 weeks. Will consider simultaneous submissions (if notified).

Illustration: Buys 5+ illustrations/issue; 50-60 illustrations/year. Works on assignment only.

How to Contact/Illustrators: Artists send samples. Reports back only if interested. Originals returned to artist at job's completion.

Terms/Writers & Illustrators: Pays on acceptance. Buys all rights. Pays $75-300 for assigned/unsolicited articles. Pays $300-400 per page for inside color illustrations. Writer's guidelines free with SASE. Sample copy with 8×11 SASE and $1.50.

Tips: Writers: "Write about what you know. Don't try to talk down to kids. Know your audience. Use concrete, colorful, direct language. We use short-short stories—2 pages, 100 lines at 45 characters per line." Illustrators: "Avoid the cute. Use hot colors. Don't make kids you illustrate look like kewpie dolls. Don't be afraid of detail. Use a sense of humor. Send lots of sample cards to art directors. Write or call to bring in portfolios." (See listing for *3-2-1 Contact.*)

*LADYBUG, THE MAGAZINE FOR YOUNG CHILDREN, P.O. Box 300, 315 Fifth Street, Peru IL 61354. (815)224-6643. Editor-in-Chief: Marianne Carus. Managing Editor: Theresa Gaffey. Art Director: Ron McCutchan. Monthly magazine. 8×9¼; 36 pp plus 4-page activity pullout; 70 lb. paper and 100 lb. cover stock. Estab. 1990. Circ. 130,000. Literary magazine for children 2-7, with stories, poems, activities, songs and picture stories.

Fiction: Picture-Oriented Material, Young Readers: animal, contemporary, fantasy, humorous, spy/mystery/adventure. "Open to any fiction stories." Buys 200 mss/year. Average word length 300-750 words. Byline given.

Nonfiction: Picture-Oriented and Young Readers: how-to, nature/environment. "Nonfiction in *Ladybug* will not be in article form, but rather in pictures." Buys 35 mss/year. Average word length: 750 words.

Poetry: Reviews 20 line maximum length poems; "no limit, but recommend no more than 5."

How to Contact/Writers: Fiction/nonfiction: Send complete manuscript. Queries not accepted. Include social security number with submission. Reports on mss in 3 months. Publishes ms 2 years after acceptance. Will consider simultaneous submissions.

Illustration: Buys 12 illustrations/issue; buys 145 illustrations/year. Prefers "Bright colors; all media, but use watercolor and acrylics most often; same size as magazine is preferred but not required." Reviews all varieties of ms/illustration packages.

How to Contact/Illustrators: Ms/illustrations packages: "Manuscript with one or two rough sketches and some examples of finished artwork from other projects." Illustrations only: "Tearsheets, good quality photocopies, C-prints; slides are somewhat less useful, but OK." Reports on art samples in 2 months. Original artwork returned at job's completion.

Terms/Writers & Illustrators: Pays on publication. Buys first North American serial rights; one-time rights; second serial (reprint rights). Pays up to 25¢/word. Pays $750 for color (cover) illustration, $200-300 for color (inside) illustration. Sample copy for $2. Writers/illustrator's guidelines free for #10 SAE and 1 first class stamp.

Tips: Writers: "Read copies of back issues and current issues. Set a manuscript aside for a few weeks, then reread before sending it off. Keep to specified word limits." Illustrators: "Include examples, where possible, of children, animals, and—mostly important—action and narrative (i.e., several scenes from a story, showing continuity and an ability to maintain interest)." Has a need for "well-written read-aloud stories." (See listing for *Cricket Magazine*.)

Ladybug, a new magazine for children, is aimed at toddlers, preschoolers and beginning readers. This cover illustration, entitled "To Market, to Market, to Buy a Fat Pig," was done by Cyndy Szekeres, who lives in Vermont and has been writing and illustrating books for children for over 25 years.

LIGHTHOUSE, Lighthouse Publications, Box 1377, Auburn WA 98071-1377. Fiction Editor: Lynne Trindl. Bimonthly magazine. 5½ × 8½; 56 pp; 20 lb. paper and cover stock. Estab. 1986. Circ. 500. Magazine contains timeless stories and poetry for family reading. 15-20% of material aimed at juvenile audience.

Fiction: Young readers, middle readers: animal, contemporary, humorous, sports, spy/mystery/adventure. Young adults: animal, contemporary, humorous, problem solving, romance, sports, spy/mystery/adventure. Does not want to see anything not "G-rated," any story with a message that is not subtly handled. Buys 15 mss/year. Average word length: 2,000. Byline given.

How to Contact/Writers: Fiction: Send complete ms. Include Social Security number with submission. Reports on mss in 2 months.

Terms/Writers: Pays on publication. Buys first North American serial rights; first rights. Sample copy for $2 (includes guidelines). Writer's guidelines free with regular SAE and 1 first-class stamp.

Tips: "All sections are open to freelance writers—just follow the guidelines and stay in the categories listed above."

LISTEN, Celebrating Positive Choices, 1350 North Kings Rd., Nampa ID 83687. (208)465-2500. Monthly magazine. Circ. 100,000. *Listen* offers positive alternatives to drug use for its teenage readers.

Fiction: Young adults: contemporary, humorous, problem solving. Buys 12 mss/year. Average word length: 1,200-1,500. Byline given.

Nonfiction: Young adults: how-to, interview/profile, problem solving. Buys 50 mss/year. Average word length: 1,200-1,500. Byline given.

How to Contact/Writers: Fiction/nonfiction: Send complete ms. Reports on queries/mss in 2 months.

Terms/Writers: Pays on acceptance. Buys first North American serial rights. Pays $150 for assigned articles; $100 for unsolicited articles. Sample copy for $2 and SASE. Writer's guidelines free with SASE.

Tips: *Listen* is a magazine for teenagers. It encourages development of good habits and high ideals of physical, social and mental health. It bases its editorial philosophy of primary drug prevention on total abstinence from alcohol and other drugs. Because it is used extensively in public high school classes, it does not accept articles and stories with overt religious emphasis. Four specific purposes guide the editors in selecting materials for *Listen*: 1) To portray a positive lifestyle and to foster skills and values that will help teenagers deal with contemporary problems, including smoking, drinking and using drugs. This is *Listen*'s primary purpose. 2) To offer positive alternatives to a lifestyle of drug use of any kind. 3) To present scientifically accurate information about the nature and effects of tobacco, alcohol and other drugs. 4) To report medical research, community programs and educational efforts which are solving problems connected with smoking, alcohol and other drugs. Articles should offer their readers activities that increase one's sense of self-worth through achievement and/or involvement in helping others. They are often categorized by three kinds of focus: 1) Hobbies—Recent subjects have been model railroading, autograph collecting, remote-control aircraft, amateur radio, photography, genealogy. 2) Recreation—*Listen* has recently featured articles on canoeing, orienteering, amateur golf, horseback riding, ice-boating. 3) Community Service—Recent subjects have been caring for injured raptor birds, working at summer camps for children with cancer, serving as teenage police cadets, volunteering for rescue work. Cartoons: May be slanted against using tobacco, alcohol and other drugs; or may be of general interest to teenagers. Pays $15 each.

MAD MAGAZINE, E.C. Publications, Inc., 485 Madison Ave., New York NY 10022. (212)752-7685. Articles Editor: John Ficarra. Art Director: Lenny Brenner. Magazine published every 6 weeks. Estab. 1952. Circ. 1.2 million. *MAD* deals with humor and satire.

Nonfiction: Satire. Picture-oriented material/middle readers/young adult/teens. No text pieces. "Buy all our work from freelancers." Byline given.

How to Contact/Writers: Fiction/nonfiction: Query with 3 or 4 examples of premise. Reports on queries in 4 weeks.

Illustration: Buys all illustrations/issue from freelancers. "Every submission is welcomed and considered! Look at a current issue for idea of styles we prefer." Will review all varieties of ms/illustration packages.

How to Contact/Illustrators: Ms/illustration packages: "Query with 3 or 4 examples of artwork." Illustrators only: Send tearsheets. Reports back in 4 weeks.

Terms/Writers & Illustrators: Pays on acceptance. Buys all rights. Pay: "Starts $350/page of art or writing." Additional payment for ms/illustration packages, "starts $350 art and $350 script/per page." Writer's/illustrator's guidelines free with SAE and 1 first class stamp.

Tips: "Don't write down! Be funny! Be original! Have fun and let that fun show through in your writing!"

Always include a self-addressed stamped envelope (SASE) or International Reply Coupon (IRC) with submissions.

MY FRIEND, A Magazine for Children, Daughters of St. Paul/St. Paul Books and Media, 50 St. Paul's Ave., Jamaica Plain, Boston MA 02130. (617)522-8911. Articles/Fiction Editor: Sister Anne Joan, fsp. Art Director: Sister M. Joseph, fsp/re. Magazine published 10 times/year. 8½ × 10¾; 32 pp; glossy paper and self cover stock. Estab. 1979. Circ. 10,000. *"My Friend* is a magazine of inspiration and entertainment for a predominantly Catholic readership. We reach ages 6-12."

Fiction: Picture-oriented material: animal, contemporary, religious. Young readers: contemporary, fantasy, history, humorous, problem solving, religious, sports, adventure. Middle readers: contemporary, history, humorous, problem solving, religious, science fiction, sports, adventure. Young adults: religious. Does not want to see poetry, animals as main characters in religious story, stories whose basic thrust would be incompatible with Catholic values. Buys 50 mss/year. Average word length: 450-750. Byline given.

Nonfiction: Picture-oriented material: animal, religious. Young readers: history, how-to, humorous, interview/profile, science religious. Middle readers: history, interview/profile, problem solving, science religious. Does not want to see material that is not compatible with Catholic values; "new age" material. Buys 10 mss/year. Average word length: 450-750. Byline given.

How to Contact/Writers: Fiction/nonfiction: Send complete ms. Reports on queries in 3 weeks; mss in 3-4 weeks.

Illustration: Buys 8 illustrations/issue; buys 60-80 illustrations/year. Preferred theme or style: Realistic depictions of children, but open to variety! "We'd just like to hear from more illustrators who can do *humans*! (We see enough of funny cats, mice, etc.)" Looking for a "Bible stories" artist, too. Will review all varieties of ms and illustration.

How to Contact/Illustrators: Ms/illustration packages: Send complete ms with copy of final art. Reports on art samples in 3-4 weeks. Original artwork not returned at job's completion "unless previously requested and arranged."

Terms/Writers & Illustrators: Pays on publication. Buys one-time rights. Pays $5-25 per story. Sample copy free with 9 × 12 SAE and 4 first-class stamps. Writer's/illustrator's guidelines free with SAE and 1 first-class stamp,

Tips: Writers: "Right now, we're especially looking for science articles and stories that would appeal to boys. We are not interested in poetry unless it is humorous." Illustrators: "Please contact us! For the most part, we need illustrations for fiction stories; usually one 'main' illustration and a second supporting picture."

NATIONAL GEOGRAPHIC WORLD, National Geographic Society, 17th and M Streets NW, Washington DC 20036. (202)857-7000. Editor: Pat Robbins. Submissions Editor: Eleanor Shannahan. Photo Editor: Chuck Herron. Art Director: Ursula Vosseler. Monthly magazine. Circ. 1.3 million. "National Geographic *World* features factual stories on outdoor adventure, natural history, sports, science and history for children ages 8 and older. Full-color photographs are used to attract young readers and the text easily guides them through the story. "Does not publish fiction.

Nonfiction: *"World* does not publish manuscripts from outside writers. Story ideas that lend themselves to photo stories will be considered. All writing is done by staff." Picture material: animal, history, how-to, travel. Middle readers: animal, history, how-to, travel. Average word length: 90-600.

How to Contact/Writers: Nonfiction: Query only—no ms please. Reports on queries in 6-8 weeks.

Illustration: Assignment only.

How to Contact/Illustrators: Ms/illustration packages: Query story idea first. Illustrations only: Submit samples in slide form or tearsheets. Reports on art samples only if interested. Original artwork returned at job's completion; NGS retains copyright.

Terms/Writers & Illustrators: Pays on publication. Buys one-time rights. Pays $75-350 for assigned articles. Free sample copy; contributor's guidelines available free.

Tips: "All *World* stories are written by staff. For *World,* the story proposal is the way to break in. Think through the focus of the story and outline what action photos are available. Keep in mind that *World* is a visual magazine. A story will work best if it has a very tight focus and if the photos show children interacting with their surroundings as well as with each other."

NATURE FRIEND MAGAZINE, Pilgrim Publishers, 22777 State Road 119, Goshen IN 46526. (219)534-2245. Articles Editor: Stanley Brubaker. Monthly magazine. 6½ × 9⅜; 36 pp; 50# offset paper and 10 pt. coated cover stock. Estab. 1983. Circ. 11,000. "See our writers guide *before* submitting articles."
Nonfiction: Picture-oriented material: animal, nature. Young readers: animal, nature. Middle readers: animal, nature. Young adult/teens: animal, nature. Does not want to see evolutionary material. Buys 50-80 mss/year. Average word length: 350-1,500. Byline given.
How to Contact/Writers: Nonfiction: Send complete ms. Reports on mss in 4-16 weeks. Will consider simultaneous submissions.
Illustration: Buys 10 illustrations/year. See samples of magazine for styles of art used. Will review ms/illustration packages submitted by authors/artists; ms/illustration packages submitted by authors with illustrations done by separate artists.
Terms/Writers & Illustrators: Pays on publication. Buys one-time rights. Pays $15-45. Payment for ms/illustration packages: $15-40. Payment for illustrations: $15-40/b&w inside. Two sample copies for $2 with 7 × 10 SAE and 85¢ postage. Writer's/illustrator's guidelines for $1.
Tips: "Study the magazine to get their mood." Looks for "main articles, puzzles and simple nature and science projects."

*NEW ERA MAGAZINE, Official publication for youth of the Church of Jesus Christ of Latter-Day Saints, 50 E. North Temple Street, Salt Lake City UT 84150. (801)240-2951. Articles/Fiction Editor: Richard M. Romney. Art Director: B. Lee Shaw. Monthly magazine 8 × 10½; 51 pp; Estab. 1971. Circ. 180,000. "General interest religious publication for youth ages 12-18 who are members of The Church of Jesus Christ of Latter-day Saints ("Mormons").
Fiction: Young Adults/Teens: contemporary, fantasy, history,humorous, problem solving, religious, romance, science fiction, sports. "All material must relate to 'Mormon' point of view." Does not want to see formula pieces, articles not sensitive to an LDS audience. Buys 20 mss/year. Average word length: 250-2,500. Byline given.
Nonfiction: Young Adults/Teens: religion, "general interest articles by, about and for young Mormons. Does not want to see formula pieces, articles not adapted to our specific voice and our audience." Buys 150-200 mss/year. Average word length: 250-2,000. Byline given.
Poetry: Reviews 30 line maximum poems. Will accept 10 submissions/author.
How to Contact/Writers: Fiction/nonfiction: Query. Include Social Security number with submission. Reports on queries/mss in 6-8 weeks. Publishes ms 1 year or more after acceptance. Will consider electronic submissions via disk or modem.
Illustration: Buys 5 illustrations/issue; buys 50-60 illustrations/year. "We buy only from our pool of illustrators. We use all styles and mediums." Works on assignment only.
How to Contact/Illustrators: Send slides of portfolio or tearsheets, etc. Reports on art samples in 6-8 weeks. Original artwork returned at job's completion.
Terms/Writers & Illustrators: Pays on acceptance. Buys first rights; other rights ("right to publish again in other church usage"). Pays $25-375 for articles. Sample copy for $1. Writer's guidelines free for SAE (business envelope and 1 first class stamp).
Tips: Open to "first-person and true-life experiences. Tell what happened in a conversational style."

NOAH'S ARK, A Newspaper for Jewish Children, 8323 Southwest Freeway, #250, Houston TX 77074. (713)771-7143. Articles/Fiction Editor: Debbie Israel Dubin. Art Director: Nachman. Monthly tabloid. Circ. 450,000. All submissions must have Jewish content and positive Jewish values. The newspaper is sent to more than 400 religious schools and submissions must be appropriate for educational use as well.

Fiction: Young readers, middle readers: contemporary, history, religious, sports. Does not want to see Christian and secular material. Buys 3 mss/year. Average word length: 650. Byline given.

Nonfiction: Young readers, middle readers: history, how-to, humorous, interview/profile, problem solving, religious, travel. Does not want to see secular, Christian nonfiction. Buys 1 ms/year, "only because more not submitted." Average word length: 500. Byline given.

How to Contact/Writers: Fiction/nonfiction: Send complete ms. Report on mss 6-8 weeks.

Terms/Writers & Illustrators: Pays on acceptance. Buys first North American serial rights. Pays 5¢/word for unsolicited articles. Sample copy free with #10 SAE and 1 first-class stamp. Writer's guidelines free with SAE and 1 first-class stamp.

Tips: "Send appropriate material. We receive mostly inappropriate submissions; very few submissions have Jewish values as required."

ODYSSEY, Kalmbach Publishing Co., 21027 Crossroads Cr., Box 1612,Waukesha WI 53187. (414)796-8776. FAX: (414)796-0126. Articles Editor: Nancy Mack. Art Director: Jane Borth-Lucius. Monthly magazine. 8⅜ × 10¾; 40 pp; glossy paper and 60# cover stock. Estab. 1979. Circ. 104,148. Magazine covers astronomy and space exploration for children ages 8-14.

Nonfiction: Middle readers, young adults: how-to, humorous, astronomy, space science. Does not want to see very general or overview articles. Buys 20-30 mss/year. Average word length: 600-2,000. Byline given.

How to Contact/Writers: Nonfiction: Query. Reports in 10 weeks. Will consider simultaneous submissions.

Illustration: Buys 10-12 illustrations/year. Will review all varieties of ms and illustration packages. Works on assignment only.

How to Contact/Illustrators: Ms/illustration packages: Query first. Illustrations only: Send tearsheets and/or slides. Reports on art samples in 10 weeks. Original artwork returned at job's completion.

Terms/Writers & Illustrators: Pays on publication. Buys one-time rights. Pays $100-350 for assigned/unsolicited articles. Additional payment for ms/illustration packages is $350-1,000. Pays $100-350/color (cover/inside) illustration; $100-300/b&w (cover/inside). Sample copy free with 9 × 11 SAE and 4 first-class stamps. Writer's guidelines free with SAE and 1 first-class stamp.

Tips: "At *Odyssey*, short, offbeat articles have the best chance of acceptance. Major articles are usually handled by staff or contributing editors." Looks for "short, humorous articles and experiments. Keep the writing very simple (usually the topic will be technical)."

ON THE LINE, Mennonite Publishing House, 616 Walnut Ave., Scottdale PA 15683. (412)887-8500. Editor: Mary Clemens Meyer. "Monthly in weekly parts" magazine. 7 × 10; 8 pp; #3 grade commodity offset paper and cover. Estab. 1970. Circ. 10,000.

Refer to the Business of Children's Writing & Illustrating
for up-to-date marketing, tax and legal information.

Fiction: Buys 60 mss/year. Average word length: 900-1,200. Byline given.

Nonfiction: Middle readers: animal, history, how-to, humorous, interview/profile, problem solving, religious, environment/ecology. Does not want to see articles written from an adult perspective. Average word length: 200-900. Byline given.

How to Contact/Writers: Fiction/nonfiction: Send complete ms. Reports on queries/ mss in 1 month. Will consider simultaneous submissions.

Illustration: Buys 1-2 illustrations/issue; buys 52 illustrations/year. "Illustrations are done on assignment only, to accompany our stories and articles—our need for new artists is very limited."

How to Contact/Illustrators: Illustrations only: "Prefer samples they do not want returned; these stay in our files." Reports on art samples only if interested. Original art work returned at job's completion.

Terms/Writers & Illustrators: Pays on acceptance. Buys one-time rights; second serial (reprint rights). Pays 2-4¢/word for assigned/unsolicited articles. Pays $12-50/color (inside) illustration. Sample copy free with 7×10 SAE. Free writer's guidelines.

Tips: "We will be focusing on the 12 and 13 age group of our 10-14 audience. (Focus was somewhat younger before.)"

OWL MAGAZINE, The Discovery Magazine for Children, Young Naturalist Foundation, Suite 306, 56 The Esplanade, Toronto Ontario M5E 1A7 Canada. (416)868-6001. Editor: Debora Pearson. Managing Editor: Deena Waisberg. Art Director: Tim Davin. Magazine published 10 times/year. Circ. 160,000. "*Owl* helps children over eight discover and enjoy the world of science and nature. We look for articles that are fun to read, that inform from a child's perspective and that motivate hands-on interaction. *Owl* explores the reader's many interests in the natural world in a scientific, but always entertaining, way."

Fiction: Middle readers, young adults: animal, contemporary, fantasy, humorous, science fiction, sports, spy/mystery/adventure. Does not want to see romance, religion, anthropomorphizing. Average word length: 500-1,000. Byline given. "We publish only 3-4 pieces of fiction per year."

Nonfiction: Middle readers, young adults: animal, biology, high-tech, how-to, humor, interview/profile, travel. Does not want to see religious topics, anthropomorphizing. Buys 20 mss/year. Average word length: 200-1,500. Byline given.

How to Contact/Writers: Fiction/nonfiction: Query with published clips. Report on queries in 4-6 weeks; mss in 6-8 weeks.

Illustration: Buys 3-5 illustrations/issue; buys 40-50 illustrations/year. Preferred theme or style: lively, involving, fun, with emotional impact and appeal. Works on assignment only.

How to Contact/Illustrators: Illustrations only: Send tearsheets and slides. Reports on art samples only if interested. Original artwork returned at job's completion.

Terms/Writers & Illustrators: Pays on acceptance. Buys all rights. Pays $35-600 for assigned/unsolicited articles. Pays $600-700/color (inside) illustration. Sample copy $3.25. Free writer's guidelines.

Tips: Writers: "Talk to kids and find out what they're interested in; make sure your research is thorough and find good consultants who are doing up-to-the-minute research. Be sure to read the magazine carefully to become familiar with *Owl*'s style." Illustrators: "Talk to kids and find out what work appeals to them. Look through *Owl* to see what styles we prefer." (See listing for *Chickadee*.)

PENNYWHISTLE PRESS, Gannett, Suite 1000, 1000 Wilson Blvd., Arlington VA 22229-0002. Articles/Fiction Editor: Anita Sama. Weekly tabloid. Circ. 2.5 million. "We are an educational supplement for kids from 7 to 14 years old. We generally buy fiction from freelancers about kids in real life situations."

Fiction: Picture material, middle readers, young adults: animal, contemporary, history, humorous, problem solving, science fiction, sports, spy/mystery/adventure. Does not want to see stories that include talking animals. Buys 30 mss/year. Average word length: 200-600. Byline given.
How to Contact/Writers: Fiction: Send complete ms. Large SASE for return of ms. Reports on mss in 2-3 months.
Illustration: Buys 2 illustrations/issue; buys 4 illustrations/year. Will review all varieties of ms/illustration packages.
How to Contact/Illustrators: Illustrations only: Send tearsheets. Reports on art samples only if interested. Original artwork returned at job's completion.
Terms/Writers & Illustrators: Pays on acceptance. Buys all rights. Pays $125 for unsolicited articles. Additional payment for ms/illustration package is $250-300. Sample copy 75¢.

PIONEER, Brotherhood Commission, SBC, 1548 Poplar Ave., Memphis TN 38134. (901)272-2461. Articles Editor: Jene Smith. Monthly magazine. Circ. 30,000. Magazine contains boy interests, sports, crafts, sports personalities, religious.
Nonfiction: Young adults: animal, how-to, humorous, interview/profile, problem solving, religious, travel. Buys 15 mss/year. Average word length: 600-800. Byline given.
How to Contact/Writers: Nonfiction: Send complete ms. Include Social Security number with submission. Reports on queries in 1 month; mss in 2 months. Will consider simultaneous submissions.
Illustration: Buys 1-2 illustrations/issue; buys 12 illustrations/year. Will review all varieties of ms/illustration packages.
How to Contact/Illustrators: Ms/illustration packages: Send complete ms with final art.
Terms/Writers & Illustrators: Pays on acceptance. Buys one-time rights, simultaneous rights. Pays $25-35 for unsolicited articles. Sample copy free with #10 SAE and 2 first-class stamps. Writer's/illustrator's guidelines free with SAE and 1 first-class stamp.

POCKETS, Devotional Magazine for Children, The Upper Room, 1908 Grand, Box 189, Nashville TN 37202. (615)340-7333. Articles/Fiction Editor: Janet R. McNish. Art Director: Chris Schechner, Ste. 206, 3100 Carlisle Plaza, Dallas TX 75204. Magazine published 11 times/year. 7½×9; 32 pp; 80# coated cover stock. Estab. 1981. Circ. 68,000. Stories should help children 6 to 12 experience a Christian lifestyle that is not always a neatly wrapped moral package, but is open to the continuing revelation of God's will.
Fiction: Young readers, middle readers: contemporary, fantasy, history, religious, "retold Bible stories." Does not want to see violence. Buys 26-30 mss/year. Average word length: 800-2,000. Byline given.
Nonfiction: Young readers, middle readers: history, interview/profile, religious, "communication activities." Does not want to see how-to articles. Our nonfiction reads like a story. History is in form of role-model stories as is profile. Buys 10 mss/year. Average word length: 800-2,000. Byline given.
How to Contact/Writers: Fiction/nonfiction: Send complete ms. Report on mss in 4 weeks. Will consider simultaneous submissions.
Illustration: Buys 30 illustrations/issue. Preferred theme or style: varied; both 4-color and 2-color. Will review all varieties of ms/illustration packages. Works on assignment only.
How to Contact/Illustrators: Ms/illustration packages: No final art. Illustrations only: Send résumé, tearsheets, slides to Chris Schechner, Ste. 206, 3100 Carlisle Plaza, Dallas TX 75204. Reports on art samples only if interested. Original artwork returned at job's completion.

Terms/Writers & Illustrators: Pays on acceptance. Buys first North American rights. Pays $250 for assigned articles; 10¢/word for unsolicited articles. Pays $500/color (cover) illustration; $50-500/color (inside). Sample copy free with 7×9 SAE and 4 first-class stamps. Writer's/illustrator's guidelines free with SAE and 1 first-class stamp.
Tips: "Ask for our themes first. They are set yearly in the fall."

R-A-D-A-R, Standard Publishing, 8121 Hamilton Ave., Cincinnati OH 45231. (513)931-4050. Articles/Fiction Editor: Margaret Williams. Art Director: Frank Sutton. Weekly magazine. Circ. 110,000. *R-A-D-A-R* is a weekly take-home paper for boys and girls who are in grades 3-6. Our goal is to reach these children with the truth of God's Word, and to help them make it the guide of their lives. Many of our features, including our stories, now correlate with the Sunday school lesson themes. Send for a quarterly theme list and sample copies of *R-A-D-A-R*. Keep in mind that others will be submitting stories for the same themes – this is not an assignment.
Fiction: Middle readers: animal, contemporary, history, humorous, problem solving, religious, sports, spy/mystery/adventure. Does not want to see fantasy or science fiction. Buys 150 mss/year. Average word length: 400-1,000. Byline given.
Nonfiction: Middle readers: animal, history, how-to, humorous, interview/profile, problem solving, religious, travel. Buys 50 mss/year. Average word length: 400-1,000. Byline given.
How to Contact/Writers: Fiction/nonfiction: Send complete ms. Include Social Security number with submission. Reports on queries/mss 6-8 weeks. Will consider simultaneous (but prefer not to). Reprint submissions must be retyped.
Illustration: Will review all illustration packages. Works on assignment only; there have been a few exceptions to this.
How to Contact/Illustrators: Illustrations only: Send résumé, tear sheets; samples of art can be photocopied. Reports on art samples only if interested.
Terms/Writers & Illustrators: Pays on acceptance. Buys first rights, one-time rights, second serial; all rights to art. Pays 3-7¢/word for unsolicited articles, few are assigned. Contributor copies given "not as payment, but all contributors receive copies of their art/articles." Pays $70-150 for color illustrations; $40-60 for line art only. Sample copy and writer's/illustrator's guidelines free with 9⅜×4¼ SAE and 1 first-class stamp. (See listing for *Straight*.)

RANGER RICK, National Wildlife Federation, 8925 Leesburg Pike, Vienna VA 22184. (703)790-4000. Editor: Gerald Bishop. Art Director: Donna Miller. Monthly magazine. Circ. 950,000. "Our audience ranges from ages six to twelve, though we aim the reading level of most material at nine-year-olds or fourth graders."
Fiction: Animal, fantasy, humorous, science fiction. Buys 4-6 mss/year. Average word length: 900. Byline given.
Nonfiction: Animal, humorous. Buys 20-30 mss/year. Average word length: 900. Byline given.
How to Contact/Writers: Fiction: Query with published clips; send complete ms. Nonfiction: Query with published clips. Include Social Security number with submission. Reports on queries/mss in 6 weeks.
Illustration: Buys 6-8 illustrations/issue; buys 75-100 illustrations/year. Preferred theme or style: Nature, wildlife. Will review an illustrator's work for possible use with fiction/nonfiction articles and columns by other authors. Works on assignment only.
How to Contact/Illustrators: Illustrations only: Send résumé, tearsheets. Reports on art samples in 6 weeks. Original artwork returned at job's completion.
Terms/Writers & Illustrators: Pays on acceptance. Buys all rights (first North American serial rights negotiable). Pays up to $550 for full-length of best quality. For illustrations, buys one-time rights. Pays $250-1,000 for color (inside, per page) illustration. Sample copy $2. Writer's guidelines free with SASE.

Tips: "Fiction and nonfiction articles may be written on any aspect of wildlife, nature, outdoor adventure and discovery, domestic animals with a 'wild' connection (such as domestic pigs and wild boars), science, conservation, or related subjects. To find out what subjects have been covered recently, consult our annual indexes and the *Children's Magazine Guide*. These are available in many libraries. The National Wildlife Federation (NWF) discourages the keeping of wildlife as pets, so the keeping of such pets should not be featured in your copy. Avoid stereotyping of any group. For instance, girls can enjoy nature and the outdoors as much as boys can, and mothers can be just as knowledgeable as fathers. The only way you can write successfully for *Ranger Rick* is to know the kinds of subjects and approaches we like. And the only way you can do that is to read the magazine. Recent issues can be found in most libraries or are available from our office for $2 a copy."

SCHOLASTIC MATH MAGAZINE, Scholastic, Inc., 730 Broadway, New York NY 10003. (212)505-3135. FAX: (212)505-3377. Editor: Tracey Randinelli. Artist: Leah Bossio. Art Director: Joan Michael. Magazine published 14 times/year; September-May. Estab. 1980. Circ. 307,000. "We are a math magazine for 7, 8, 9 grade classrooms. We present math in current, relavant, high-interest topics. Math skills we focus on include whole number, fraction, and decimal computation, percentages, ratios, proportions, geometry."
Fiction: Buys 14 mss/year "in the form of word problems." Average line length 80-100.
Nonfiction: Young adult/teens: animal, history, how-to, humorous, interview/profile, problem solving, travel. Does not want to see "anything dealing with *very* controversial issues—ie, teenage pregnancy, AIDS, etc." Buys 20 mss/year. Average line length 80-100. Byline given.
How to Contact/Writers: Fiction/nonfiction: Query. Reports on queries/mss in 1 month. Will consider simultaneous submissions.
Illustration: Buys 4 illustrations/issue; 56 illustrations/year. Prefers to review "humorous, young adult sophistication" types of art. Will review all varieties of ms/illustration packages. Works on assignment only.
How to Contact/Illustrators: Ms/illustration packages: "Query first." Illustrations only: Send tearsheets. Reports back only if interested. Original art work returned at job's completion.
Terms/Writers & Illustrators: Pays on acceptance. Pays $100-350/assigned article.
Tips: "For our magazine, stories dealing with math concepts and applications in the real world are sought."

SCIENCELAND, To Nurture Scientific Thinking, Scienceland Inc., 501 Fifth Ave. #2108, New York NY 10017-6102. (212)490-2180. FAX: (212)986-2077. Editor/Art Director: Al Matano. Magazine published 8 times/year. Estab. 1977. Circ. 16,000. This is "a content reading picture-book for K-3rd grade to encourage beginning readers; for teachers and parents."
Nonfiction: Picture-oriented material: animal, how-to, humorous, problem solving. Young readers: animal, how-to, humorous, problem solving. Does not want to see "unillustrated material."
How to Contact/Writers: Not interested in stories. *Must* be picture or full color illustrated stories.
Illustration: Prefers to review "detailed, realistic, full color art. No abstracts." Will review all varieties of ms/illustration packages.
How to Contact/Illustrators: Ms/illustration packages: "Query first." Illustrations only: Send résumé and tearsheets. Reports back in 3-4 weeks. Original art work returned at job's completion, "depending on material."
Terms/Writers & Illustrators: Pays on publication. Buys first North American serial rights or all rights. Payment for ms/illustration packages: $50-500. Payment for illustra-

tions: $25-300 color cover; $25-300 color inside. Sample copy free with 9 × 12 SASE.
Tips: "Must be top notch illustrator or photographer. No amateurs."

SCOPE, Scholastic Inc., 730 Broadway, New York NY 10003. (212)505-3000. Editor:
Laura Galen. Art Director: Joy Makon. Biweekly magazine. Estab. 1964. Circ. 700,000.
"*Scope* is directed at middle-school and high school students who often wish they
weren't at school. Many are poor readers. *Scope* aims to motivate them to read and to
think about their world."
Fiction: Middle readers, young adults: animal, contemporary, fantasy, humorous, problem solving, science fiction, sports and spy/mystery/adventure. Young adults: romance.
Buys 20 mss/year. Average word length: 200-2,500. Byline given.
Nonfiction: Middle readers, young adults: animal, how-to, humorous, interview/profile
and problem solving. Buys 35 mss/year. Average word length: 200-2,000. Byline "sometimes given."
How to Contact/Writers: Fiction: Send complete ms. Nonfiction: Query with published clips. Include Social Security number with submission. Reports on queries in 1
month; mss in 2 months.
Illustration: Buys 6-10 illustrations/issue; buys 100-150 illustrations/year. Preferred
theme or style: "varies; prefer sophisticated, non-childish styles." Works on assignment
only.
How to Contact/Illustrators: Ms/illustration packages: "Submit portfolio; leave sam-
ples/tearsheets." Illustrations only: "Submit portfolio; leave samples/tearsheets. Do not
send any non-returnable materials." Original artwork returned at job's completion.
Terms/Writers & Illustrators: Pays on acceptance. Pays $75-400 for assigned articles;
$50-250 for unsolicited articles. Additional payment for ms/illustration packages. Sam-
ple copy for $1.75 with 9 × 12 SAE. Writer's guidelines free with SASE.
Tips: Illustrators: "Do not telephone art department. Submit portfolio of sample styles;
leave samples/tearsheets to keep on file."

SEVENTEEN MAGAZINE, News America, 850 Third Ave., New York NY 10022.
(212)759-8100. Articles Editor: Roberta Myers. Fiction Editor: Adrian Nicole LeBlanc.
Art Director: Annie Demchick. Monthly magazine. Estab. 1944. Circ. 1,750,000. "Gen-
eral-interest magazine for teenage girls."
Fiction: Young adults: animal, contemporary, fantasy, history, humorous, problem-
solving, religious, romance, science fiction, sports, spy/mystery/adventure, adult. "We
consider all good literary short fiction." Buys 12-20 mss/year. Average word length 900-
3,000. Byline given.
Nonfiction: Young adults: animal, history, how-to, humorous, interview/profile, problem solving, religious, travel. Buys 150 mss/year. Word length: Lengths vary from 800-
1,000 words for short features and monthly columns to 2,500 words for major articles.
Byline given.
Poetry: Reviews poetry "only by teenagers younger than 21."
How to Contact/Writers; Fiction: Send complete ms. Nonfiction: Query with published clips or send complete ms. Reports on queries/mss in 3 weeks. Will consider
simultaneous submissions. Writer's guidelines for business-size envelope and 1 first-
class stamp.
Illustration: 1 illustration per short story. Will review ms packages submitted by au-
thors/artists; ms/illustration packages submitted by authors with illustrations done by
separate artists. Illustrators paid by the project.

SHOFAR, Sr. Publications Ltd., 43 Northcote Dr., Melville NY 11747. (516)643-4598.
Articles Editor: Gerald H. Grayson. Magazine published monthly Oct. through May—
double issues Dec./Jan. and April/May. Circ. 10,000. For Jewish children ages 8-13.

Fiction: Middle readers: contemporary, humorous, religious, sports. Buys 10-20 mss/ year. Average word length: 500-1,000. Byline given.
Nonfiction: Middle readers: history, humorous, interview/profile, religious. Buys 10-20 mss/year. Average word length: 500-1,000. Byline given.
How to Contact/Writers: Fiction/nonfiction: Send complete ms. Will consider simultaneous and electronic submissions via disk or modem (only Macintosh).
Illustration: Buys 3-4 illustrations/issue; buys 15-20 illustrations/year. Works on assignment only.
How to Contact/Illustrators: Ms/illustration packages: Query first. Illustrations only: Send tearsheets. Reports on art samples only if interested. Original artwork returned at job's completion.
Terms/Writers & Illustrators: Buys one-time rights. Pays $25-125 for assigned articles. Additional payment for ms/illustration packages $50-250. Pays $25-100/b&w cover illustration; $50-150/color (cover). Sample copy free with 9 × 12 SAE and 3 first-class stamps. Free writer's/illustrator's guidelines.

SING OUT!, The Folk Song Magazine, Sing Out! Corp., Box 5253, 125 E. 3rd St., Bethlehem PA 18015-5253. (215)865-5366. Editor: Mark D. Moss. Contributing Editor: Jeff Eilenberg. Managing Director: Diane C. Petro. Quarterly magazine. Estab. 1950. Circ. 5,000 member; 1,500 newstand. Readers are "a diverse group of music lovers, who believe in preserving the folk music of America as well as the native music of all countries. Additionally, *Sing Out!* explores the new musical fusions being created daily by rising new troubadors." 20% (Kidsbeat column) of material aimed at juvenile audience.
Fiction: Middle readers, Young adult/teens: storytelling. "We have a storytelling column, Endless Tale."
Nonfiction: Picture-oriented material: music. Young readers: music. Middle readers: history, interview/profile, music. Young adult/teens: history, how-to, humorous, interview/profile, religious, music. Does not want to see "non-music material."
How to Contact/Writers: Fiction/nonfiction: "Query first." Will consider simultaneous and electronic submissions via disk or modem.
Illustration: Prefers to review "music-oriented themes—folk preferred." Will review all varieties of ms/illustration packages.
How to Contact/Illustrators: Ms/illustration packages: "Query first and foremost!" Illustrations only: Send tearsheets. Reports only if interested.
Terms/Writers & Illustrators: Pays on publication. Buys first North American serial rights or first rights. Pay is "negotiable." Writers/illustrator's guidelines free with SASE.
Tips: "Be as pertinent as possible to folk music needs and interests. We accept many freelance reviews of artists and their work."

THE SINGLE PARENT, Journal of Parents Without Partners, Inc., Parents Without Partners, Inc., 8807 Colesville Rd., Silver Spring MD 20910. (301)588-9354. FAX: (301)588-9216. Articles/Fiction Editor/Art Director: Allan Glennon. Bimonthly magazine. 8¼ × 10⅞; 48 pp; 40 basis Carolina gloss paper and self cover. Estab. 1957. Circ. 125,000. Members of PWP are single parents who are divorced, widowed or never married. "All our material is related to this basic fact. We look at the positive side of our situation and are interested in all aspects of parenting, and the particular situation of single parenting. 10% of material aimed at juvenile audience."
Fiction: Young readers, middle readers, young adults: contemporary, fantasy, humorous, problem solving, science fiction, spy/mystery/adventure. Does not want to see anthropomorphic material. Buys 12 mss/year. Average word length: 800-1,500. Byline given.
Nonfiction: Young readers, middle readers, young adults: humorous, problem solving. "We do not ordinarily use nonfiction aimed at children, but could be persuaded by a particularly good piece." Does not want to see material unrelated to single-parent chil-

dren and families. Average word length: 800-1,800. Byline given.

How to Contact/Writers: Fiction/nonfiction: Send complete ms. Reports on queries/ mss in 3 weeks. Will consider simultaneous submissions. "When material has been accepted we request disk, if available."

Illustration: Buys 4-6 illustrations/issue. Preferred theme or style: Line art, sometimes with mechanicals. No special preference for style, but lean toward realistic. Will review all varieties of ms/illustration packages. Works on assignment only.

How to Contact/Illustrators: Ms/illustration packages: Send complete ms with final art with prepaid return envelope. Illustrations only: Send nonreturnable samples in whatever form the artist prefers. Reports on art samples only if interested. Original artwork returned at job's completion.

Terms/Writers & Illustrators: Pays on publication. Buys one-time rights. Pays $35-125 for unsolicited stories. Additional payment for ms/illustration packages: $50-75. Pay $100-150/color (cover) illustration; $50-75/b&w (inside); $50-75/color (inside). Sample copy $1. Writer's/illustrator's guidelines free with SASE.

Tips: Writers: "Study your target; do not submit material if you've never seen the magazine. In stories where the protagonist undergoes a behavior change, build up a credible reason for it. 'Comes to realize' is not a credible reason. We are overstocked at the moment with children's stories, but still buy one occasionally that we're unable to resist. Our greatest need is for articles for adults, in particular, articles on parenting from the single father's perspective." Illustrators: "Get examples of your work to as many editors as possible, but remember, there are hundreds of others doing the same thing. I review all samples that are submitted, and put those that appeal to me in a separate file as potential illustrators for the magazine. To get into the 'may call on' file, provide me with nonreturnable samples that illustrate the broadest range of your work—I may not appreciate your cartoon style, but think your realistic style is super or vice versa."

SIX LAKES ARTS, (formerly *In Between*), Art and Entertainment Between the Lakes, Six Lakes Arts Communications Inc., 43 Chapel St., Seneca Falls NY 13148. (315)568-2508. Publisher: Stephen Beals. Associate Editor: Jim Porto. Art Director: Wayne Lohr. Bimonthly magazine. 8½ × 11; 32 pp. 50 lb. offset paper and coated 80 lb. cover stock. Estab. 1987. Circ. 1,500. Magazine includes "arts and entertainment, music, theatre, exhibitions, history, short stories and poetry." Annual Young Artist and Writers Contest Edition aimed at school-age audience.

Fiction: Young readers, middle readers, young adults: history, spy/mystery/adventure. Does not want to see religious, romance, sports, science fiction material. Publishes 1-2 mss/year. Byline given.

Nonfiction: Young readers, middle readers, young adults: history, how-to, interview/ profile. Does not want to see religious material. Publishes 3-5 mss/year. Average word length: 500-2,500. Byline given. "Looking for features on young artists in the Finger Lakes.

How to Contact/Writers: Fiction/nonfiction: Send complete ms. Reports on queries in 2 months; mss in 3 months. Will consider simultaneous and electronic submissions via disk or modem (Apple MacIntosh).

Illustration: Publishes 1 illustration/issue; Publishes 3-4 illustrations/year. Preferred theme or style: Pen and ink. Will review all varieties of ms/illustration packages.

How to Contact/Illustrators: Ms/illustration packages: Send complete ms with final art or samples. Illustrations only: Send samples—copies OK. Reports on art samples in 2 months. Original art work returned at job's completion.

Terms/Writers & Illustrators: $5-25/story. Sample copy and writer's guidelines for $2.25.

Tips: "We have a young writers and artists annual contest."

*SKIPPING STONES, A Multi-ethnic Children's Forum, Aprovecho Institute, 80574 Hazelton Rd., Cottage Grove OR 97424. (503)942-9434. Articles/Art Editor: Arun N. Toké. Fiction and Poetry Editor: Amy Klauke. Quarterly magazine. 8½×11; 32 pages; recycled 50 lb. paper; 80 lb. cover stock. Estab. 1988. Circ. 3,000-4,000. *"Skipping Stones* is a multi-cultural nonprofit children's magazine to encourage cooperation, creativity and celebration of cultural and environmental richness. We encourage submissions by minorities and under-represented populations."

Nonfiction: All age groups: animal, nature/environment, problem solving, religious, travel and multicultural and environmental awareness. Does not want to see preaching, or abusive language. Average word length: 300 words. Byline given.

How to Contact/Writers: Query. For nonfiction, send complete ms. Reports on queries in 2 months. Will consider simultaneous submissions.

Illustration: Prefers b&w line drawings especially by young adults. Will consider all illustration packages.

How to Contact/Illustrators: Submit complete ms with final art. Submit tearsheets. Reports back in 2 months (only if interested). Original artwork returned at job's completion.

Terms/Writers and Illustrators: No payment; just a copy of the magazine containing work. Acquires one-time rights. Sample copy for $4 with SAE and 4 first class stamps. Writer's/illustrator's guidelines for 1 first class stamp and 4×9 SAE.

Tips: Wants material "meant for children," with multi-cultural or environmental awareness theme. "Think, live and write as if you were a child. Let the 'inner child' within you speak out—naturally, uninhibited." Wants "material that gives insight on cultural celebrations, lifestyle, custom and tradition, glimpse of daily life in other countries and cultures. Photos, songs, artwork are most welcome if they illustrate/highlight the points. Translations are welcome if the submission is in a language other than English."

STARWIND, Starwind Press, Box 98, Ripley OH 45167. (513)392-4549. Editor: David F. Powell. Quarterly magazine. 8½×11; 64+ pp; 60# uncoated paper. Estab. 1974. Circ. 2,000. *"Starwind* is a science fiction magazine which also publishes science and technology-related nonfiction along with the stories. Although the magazine is not specifically aimed at children, we do number teenagers among our readers. Such readers are the type who might enjoy reading science fiction (both young adult and adult), attending science fiction conventions, using computers, be interested in such things as astronomy, the space program, etc."

Fiction: Young adult/teens: fantasy, science fiction. Buys 8-10 mss/year. Average word length 2,000-10,000.

Nonfiction: Young adult/teens: how-to (science), interview/profile, travel, informational science book review. Does not want to see crafts. Buys 8-10 mss/year. Average word length: 1,500-5,000. Byline given.

How to Contact/Writers: Fiction/nonfiction: Send complete ms. Reports on queries/mss in 2-3 months. Will consider submissions via disk (Macintosh MacWrite, WriteNow, IBM PC or compatible in Multimate or ASCII format).

Illustration: Buys 12-15 illustrations/issue; buys 20-30 illustrations/year. Prefers to review "science fiction, fantasy or technical illustration." Will review all varieties of ms/illustration packages.

How to Contact/Illustrators: Ms/illustration packages: "Would like to see clips to keep on file (black and white only, preferably photocopies)." Illustrations only: "If we have an assignment for an artist, we will contact him/her with the ms we want illustrated. We like to see roughs before giving the go-ahead for final artwork." Reports in 2-3 months. Original art work returned at job's completion, "sometimes, if requested. We prefer to retain originals, but a high-quality PMT or Velox is fine if artist wants to keep artwork."

Terms/Writers & Illustrators: Pays 50% on acceptance (for art), 50% on publication. Pays 25% on acceptance (for writing), 75% on publication. Buys first North American serial rights; first rights; second serial (reprint rights). Pays $5-100/article. Additional payment for ms/illustration packages: $5-10. Payment for illustrations: Pays $30-50/b&w cover; $25/b&w inside. Sample copy $3.50 with 9×12 SAE and 5 first class stamps; writer's/illustrator's guidelines free with business-size SAE and 1 first class stamp. "Specify fiction or nonfiction guidelines, or both."

Tips: Writers: "Read lots of children's writing in general, especially specific genre if you're writing a genre story. (SF, romance, mystery, etc.). We list upcoming needs in our guidelines; writers can study these to get an idea of what we're looking for." Illustrators: "Study illustrations in back issues of magazines you're interested in illustrating for, and be able to work in a genre style if that's the type of magazine you want to publish your work. Everything is open to freelancers, as almost all our artwork is done out-of-house. (We occasionally use public domain illustrations, copyright-free illustrations and photographs.)"

*STORY FRIENDS, Mennonite Publishing House, 616 Walnut Ave., Scottdale PA 15683. (412)887-5181. FAX: (412)887-3111. Editor: Marjorie Waybill. Art Director: Jim Butti. "Monthly in weekly issues magazine." 7¾×10¼; 4 pp. Estab. 1905. Circ. 10,000. Story paper that reinforces Christian values for children ages 4-9.

Fiction: Young Readers: contemporary, humorous, problem solving, religious, relationships. Buys 45 mss/year. Average word length: 300-800. Byline given.

Nonfiction: Picture-Oriented and Young Readers: interview/profile, nature/environment. Buys 10 mss/year. Average word length: 300-800. Byline given.

Poetry: "I like variety—some long story poems and some four-lines."

How to Contact/Writers: Fiction/nonfiction: Send complete manuscript. Reports on mss in 2-3 weeks. Will consider simultaneous submissions.

Illustration: Works on assignment only.

Terms/Writers: Writer's guidelines free with #9 SAE and 2 first class stamps.

"I needed a serious, strong style for a piece on spiritual warfare," says Staight magazine editor Carla Crane. Kevin Caddell of Indianapolis, Indiana is the illustrator.

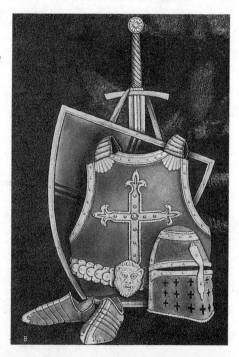

STRAIGHT, Standard Publishing, 8121 Hamilton Ave., Cincinnati OH 45231. (513)931-4050. Articles/Fiction Editor: Carla J. Crane. Art Director: Frank Sutton. "Quarterly in weekly parts" magazine. 6¼×7½; 12 pp; newsprint paper and cover stock. Circ. 60,000. *Straight* is a magazine designed for today's Christian teenagers.

Fiction: Young adults: contemporary, humorous, problem solving, religious, sports. Does not want to see science fiction, fantasy, historical. Buys 100-115 mss/year. Average word length: 1,100-1,500. Byline given.

Nonfiction: Young adults: how-to, humorous, interview/profile, problem solving, religious. Does not want to see devotionals. Buys 24-30 mss/year. Average word length: 500-1,000. Byline given.

How to Contact/Writers: Fiction/nonfiction: Query or send complete ms. Include Social Security number with submission. Report on queries in 1-2 weeks; mss in 4-6 weeks. Will consider simultaneous submissions.

Illustration: Buys 40-45 illustrations/year. Preferred theme or style: Realistic, cartoon (full-color only). Will review ms/illustration packages submitted by authors/artists "on occasion." Works on assignment only.

How to Contact/Illustrators: Ms/illustration packages: Query first. Illustrations only: Art done on assignment only. Artists must work through the art director.

Terms/Writers & Illustrators: Pays on acceptance. Buys first rights; one-time rights; second serial (reprint rights). Sample copy free with business SASE. Writer's/illustrator's guidelines free with business SASE.

Tips: "Study the copies and guidelines and get to know teenagers: how they talk, act and feel. The main characters should be contemporary teens who cope with modern-day problems using Christian principles. Stories should be uplifting, positive and character-building, but not preachy. Conflicts must be resolved realistically, with thought-provoking and honest endings. Accepted length is 1,100 to 1,500 words. Nonfiction is accepted. We use devotional pieces, articles on current issues from a Christian point of view, and humor. Nonfiction pieces should concern topics of interest to teens, including school, family life, recreation, friends, part-time jobs, dating and music." (See listing for *R-A-D-A-R*.)

*SUPERSCIENCE, Blue Scholastic, Inc., 730 Broadway, New York NY 10003. (212)505-3000. Assistant Editor: Lorraine Hopping Egan. Art Director: Susan Kass. Monthly (during school year) magazine. 8×10⅞; 32 pp. Estab. 1989. Circ. 375,000. "News and hands-on science for children in grades 4-6. Designed for use in a class setting; distributed by teacher. Articles make science fun and interesting for a broad audience of children. Issues are theme-based."

Nonfiction: Middle Readers: animal, how-to (science experiments), nature/environment, problem solving, science topics. Does not want to see "general nature stories. Our focus is science with a *news* or *hands-on* slant. Write for editorial calendar.'" Buys 10-20 mss/year. Average word length: 250-600. Byline sometimes given.

How to Contact/Writers: Nonfiction: Query with published clips. (Most freelance articles are assigned.) Reports on queries in 4-6 weeks. Publishes ms 4 months after acceptance.

Illustration: Buys 2-3 illustrations/issue; 10-12 illustrations/year. Works on assignment only.

How to Contact/Illustrators: Illustrations only: Send résumé and tearsheets. Reports on art samples only if interested. Original artwork returned at job's completion.

Terms/Writers & Illustrators: Pays on acceptance. Buys all rights. Pays $150-450. Illustrations only: $75+ b&w (inside); $150-1,200 for color/inside (complicated spreads only). Writer's guidelines free on request.

Tips: Looks for "news articles and photo essays. Good journalism means always going to *primary* sources—interview scientists in the field, for example, and *quote* them for a more lively article."

*TAKE 5, Back to the Bible, P.O. Box 82808, Lincoln NE 68501. (402)474-4567. Articles Editor: Judy Kinnaird. Art Directors: Judy Kinnaird/Kim Johnson. Quarterly devotional. Circ. approx. 25,000.

Fiction: Middle Readers: problem solving, religious, science fiction, sports, spy/mystery/adventure, scriptural emphasis. Young Adults/Teens: contemporary, fantasy, problem solving, religious, science fiction, sports, spy/mystery/adventure, scriptural emphasis. Does not want to see biographies, ultra-romance. Buys 4-6 mss/year. Average word length: 800-5,000. Byline given.

Nonfiction: Middle Readers and Young Adults/Teens: education, history, how-to, interview/profile, nature/environment, problem solving, religion, travel, sports, scriptural emphasis. Does not want to see biographies. Buys 4-6 mss/year. Average word length: 800-5,000. Byline given.

How to Contact/Writers: Fiction/nonfiction: Query. Reports on queries in 2 weeks; mss in 6-8 weeks. Publishes ms 6-12 months after acceptance.

Illustration: Buys 4-6 illustrations/year. Preferred theme or style: realistic and/or mood-capturing illustrations; size—no smaller than 8 × 10. Will review all varieties of ms/illustration packages. Works on assignment only.

How to Contact/Illustrators: Query first. Send résumé, number and address of where artist can be reached. Will probably want to see an actual printed book cover. Reports on art samples in 2 weeks.

Terms/Writers & Illustrators: Pays on acceptance. Buys first North American serial rights; first rights, one-time rights; second serial (reprint rights); all rights. Pays $500-2,000 color/cover. Writer's/illustrator's guidelines free on request.

*TEEN DREAM, Starline Publications, 63 Grand Ave., River Edge NJ 07661. Articles Editor: Anne Raso. Art Director: Stuart Roban. Monthly magazine. Estab. 1988. Publishes "teen entertainment star profiles for an audience of females, 10-14."

Nonfiction: Middle readers and young adults/teens: interview/profile; "anything except profiles from stars." Buys 100 mss/year from freelancers. Word length for articles: 500-1,000. Byline given sometimes.

How To Contact/Writers: Nonfiction: Query with published clips. Reports on queries/mss in one month. Average length of time between acceptance and publication of work: 3 months.

Terms/ Writers: Pays on acceptance. Buys first North American serial rights. Pays $50-100/assigned articles.

Tips: "I only buy stories on stars that are the most popular (i.e. New Kids On The Block). Keep stories clean and easy to understand for 13 year- olds."

'TEEN MAGAZINE, Petersen Publishing Co., 8490 Sunset Blvd., Los Angeles CA 90069. (213)854-2950. Editor: Roxanne Camron. Fiction Editor: Karle Dickerson. Art Director: Laurel Finnerty. Monthly magazine. Estab. 1957. Circ. 1,100,000. "We are a pure junior high and senior high female audience. *'TEEN* teens are upbeat and want to be informed."

Fiction: Young adults: humorous, problem-solving, romance and spy/mystery/adventure. Does not want to see "that which does not apply to our market—i.e., science fiction, history, religious, adult-oriented." Buys 12 mss/year. Length for fiction: 10-15 pages typewritten, double-spaced.

Nonfiction: Young adults: animal, how-to, humorous, interview/profile, problem solving and young girl topics. Does not want to see adult oriented, adult point of view." Buys 25 mss/year. Length for articles: 10-20 pages typewritten, double-spaced. Byline given.

How to Contact/Writers: Fiction/nonfiction: Query. Reports on queries/mss in 10 weeks. Will consider electronic submissions via disk or modem.

Illustration: Buys 0-4 illustrations/issue. Preferred theme or style: "Various styles for variation. Use a lot of b&w illustration. Light, upbeat." Will review all varieties of ms/illustration packages; illustrator's work for possible use with fiction/nonfiction articles and columns by other authors.

How to Contact/Illustrators: Ms/illustration packages: "Query first." Illustrations only: "Want to see samples whether it be tearsheets, slides, finished pieces showing the style."

Terms/Writers & Illustrators: Pays on acceptance. Buys all rights. Pays $25-400 for assigned articles. Pays $25-250/b&w inside; $100-$400/color inside. Writer's/illustrator's guidelines free with SASE.

Tips: Illustrators: "Present professional finished work. Get familiar with magazine and send samples that would be compatible with the style of publication." There is a need for artwork with "fiction/specialty articles. Send samples or promotional materials on a regular basis."

*TEEN POWER, Scripture Press Publications, Inc., Box 632, Glen Ellyn IL 60138. (708)668-3806. Editor: Amy J. Swanson. Quarterly magazine. 5½ × 8½; 8 pp.; non-glossy paper quality and cover stock. Estab. 1965. "Teen Power is an eight-page Sunday School take-home paper aimed at 11-16 year olds in a conservative Christian audience. It's primary objective is to help readers see how principles for Christian living can be applied to everyday life."

Fiction: Young Adults/teens: contemporary, humorous, problem solving, religious, sports. Does not want to see "unrealistic stories with tacked-on morals. Fiction should be true-to-live and have a clear, spiritual take-away value." Buys 50 mss/year. Average word length: 400-1,200. Byline given.

Nonfiction: Young Adults/teens: how-to, humorous, interview/profile, problem solving religion. Does not want to see "articles with no connection to Christian principles." Buys 30 mss/year. Average word length: 250-700. Byline given.

How To Contact/Writers: Fiction/nonfiction: Send complete manuscript; include social security number with submission. Reports on mss in 2 months. Average length of time between acceptance and publication of work: "at least one year." Will consider simultaneous submissions.

Terms/Writers: Pays on acceptance. Buys one-time rights. Pays $20-120/unsolicited articles. Sample copies for #10 SAE and 1 first class stamp; writer's guidelines for #10 SAE and 1 first class stamp.

3-2-1 CONTACT, Children's Television Workshop, One Lincoln Plaza, New York NY 10023. (212)595-3456. Articles Editor: Jonathan Rosenbloom. Fiction Editor: Curtis Slepian. Art Director: Al Nagy. Magazine published 10 times/year. Estab. 1979. Circ. 440,000. This is a science and technology magazine for 8-14 year olds. Features cover all areas of science and nature.

Fiction: "Our fiction piece is an on-going series called "The Time Team." So far it has been written in-house."

 The asterisk before a listing indicates the listing is new in this edition.

Nonfiction: Middle readers: animal, how-to, interview/profile. Young adults: animal, how-to, interview/profile. Does not want to see religion, travel or history. Buys 20 mss/year. Average word length: 750-1,000. Byline given.

How to Contact/Writers: Fiction/nonfiction: Query with published clips. Reports on queries in 3 weeks.

Illustration: Buys 15 illustrations/issue; buys 150 illustrations/year. Works on assignment only.

How to Contact/Illustrators: Illustrations only: Send tearsheets. Reports on art samples only if interested. Original artwork returned at job's completion.

Terms/Writers & Illustrators: Pays on acceptance. Pays $100-600 for assigned/unsolicited articles. Pays $500-1,000/color (cover) illustration; $150-300/b&w (inside); $175-350/color (inside). Sample copy for $1.75 and 8×14 SASE; writer's/illustrator's guidelines free with 8½×11 SASE.

Tips: Looks for "features. We do not want articles based on library research. We want on-the-spot interviews about what's happening in science now." (See listing for *Kid City*.)

TOGETHER TIME, Children's Ministries, 6401 The Paseo, Kansas City MO 64131. Editor: Lynda T. Boardman. Executive Editor: Mark A. York. Weekly tabloid. *"Together Time* is a take-home reading piece for 2 and 3 year-olds and their parents. It correlates with Adldersgate Graded Curriculum for two's and three's. The major purposes of *Together Time* are to provide a home-reading piece to help parents build Christian behavior and values in their children, and to provide life-related home reinforcement for Biblical concepts taught in the Sunday School curriculum."

Fiction: Picture material: religious. "Fiction stories should have definite Christian emphasis or character-building values, without being preachy. The setting, plot and action should be realistic." Average word length: 150-200. Byline given.

How to Contact/Writers: Fiction: Send complete ms. Reports on mss in 10-12 weeks.

Terms/Writers: Pays on acceptance. Buys all rights. Pays 3.5¢/word for unsolicited articles. Complimentary copy mailed to contributor. Writer's guidelines free with #10 SASE.

Tips: *"Together Time* is planned to reinforce the Biblical concepts taught in the Sunday School curriculum. Because of this, the basic themes needed are as follows: security in knowing there is a God, God is creator and giver of good gifts, Jesus is God's son, Jesus is a friend and helper, the Bible is God's special book, introduction to God's love and forgiveness, asking forgiveness (from parents, teacher, friends and God), expressing simple prayers, church is a special place where we learn about God, each person is special and loved by God, accept failure without losing self-confidence, desire to be like Jesus, desire to be helpful, appreciate God's world, appreciate community helpers." (See listing for *Discoveries*.)

TOUCH, Calvinettes, Box 7259, Grand Rapids MI 49510. (616)241-5616. Editor: Joanne Ilbrink. Managing Editor: Carol Smith. Art Director: Chris Cook. Monthly (with combined issues May/June, July/Aug.) magazine. Circ. 15,200. *"Touch* is designed to help girls ages 9-14 see how God is at work in their lives and in the world around them."

Fiction: Middle readers: animal, contemporary, history, humorous, problem solving, religious, romance. Does not want to see unrealistic stories and those with trite, easy endings. Buys 40 mss/year. Average word length: 400-1,000. Byline given.

Nonfiction: Middle readers: how-to, humorous, interview/profile, problem solving, religious. Buys 5 mss/year. Average word length: 200-800. Byline given.

How to Contact/Writers: Fiction/nonfiction: Send complete ms. Report on mss in 4 months. Will consider simultaneous submissions.

Illustration: Buys 1-2 illustrations/issue; buys 10-15 illustrations/year. Prefers illustrations to go with stories. Will review ms/illustration packages by authors/artists; ms/

Close-up

Al Nagy
Art Director
3-2-1 Contact
New York City

"We try to attract kids to science and make it fun," says Al Nagy, art director for *3-2-1 Contact*. He looks for fresh, lively, colorful illustration to combat the idea many children, and even a few adults, have that science is a confusing, complex and somewhat boring subject.

While a lot of the illustration used in the magazine is humorous, Nagy says illustrators interested in submitting to him should avoid sending overly comic or "cutesy" material. He does not want to see talking bunnies. "I see too many cute, trite images. The magazine is for children from eight to 14 years old so our art is more sophisticated than that for younger children."

On the other hand, he says, the illustration must "read" to the children. "By this I mean the work cannot be so sophisticated or avant garde that even I have trouble figuring out what it is. Illustrators should make the effort to adjust their style to the audience. Look at four or five copies of the magazine to find out what is needed."

Nagy has been a freelance designer and illustrator for book publishers for 30 years. Hired to design the prototype for *3-2-1 Contact* 12 years ago, he has stayed on as art director, although he is technically working on a freelance basis. He continues to work on freelance book jacket and text illustration jobs.

"Book and magazine illustration are different. Book illustration tends to be softer, more detailed. Magazine illustration must have punch. We use a lot of spot art and one page illustrations. We want eye-openers."

Perhaps because Nagy has "been there" himself, he is very interested in seeing the work of new freelancers. "You don't have to have a lot of printed work in your portfolio," he says. "Unpublished work is fine. It's nice to discover new talent and I try to be encouraging. I'll see potential in a portfolio and I'll ask the illustrator to work on it and come back. There's always room for more good work."

Nagy reminds freelancers "you are only as good as the worst piece in your portfolio. Edit yourself. It's better to see less but better work." Yet, ideally, Nagy would like to see 15 or 20 pieces, if available.

He also says having one basic style will make it easier for art directors to remember your work, but he understands how hard it is to follow this advice. "Art directors like to know what to expect, but for artists this can get boring. It is for me, so my style is so varied it drives other art directors nuts.

"If you are going to devote your life to illustration, you should do what you like to do. If you feel you have to compromise your style, don't do it." Real success, he says, is making a living doing what you love to do.

—Robin Gee

illustration packages submitted by authors with illustrations done by separate artists. Works on assignment only.

How to Contact/Illustrators: Ms/illustration packages: "We would prefer to consider finished art with a ms." Illustrations only: "A sample of work could be submitted in tearsheets or rough drafts." Reports on art samples only if interested.

Terms/Writers & Illustrators: Pays on publication. Buys first North American serial rights; first rights; second serial (reprint rights); simultaneous rights. Pays $20-50 for assigned articles; $5-30 for unsolicited articles. "We send complimentary copies in addition to pay." Additional payment for ms/illustration packages: $5-20. Pays $25-50/b&w (cover) illustration; $15-25/b&w (inside) illustration. Writer's guidelines free with SASE.

Tips: Writers: "The stories should be current, deal with adolescent problems and joys, and help girls see God at work in their lives through humor as well as problem solving." Illustrators: Write for guidelines and our biannual update. It is difficult working with artists who are not local."

TQ, Teen Quest, Good News Broadcasting Assoc., Box 82808, Lincoln NE 68501. (402)474-4567. FAX: (402)474-4519. Articles/Fiction Editor: Win Mumma. Art Director: Victoria Valentine. Monthly (combined July/August issue) magazine. 8⅛ × 10¾; 48 pp; 50# paper and cover stock. Estab. 1947. Circ. 55,000. "Ours is a magazine for Christian teenagers. Articles and fiction purchased from freelancers must have a Christian basis, be relevant to contemporary teen culture, and be written in a style understandable and attractive to teenagers. Artwork must be likewise appropriate."

Fiction: Young adults: contemporary, fantasy, humorous, problem solving, religious, romance, science fiction, sports, spy/mystery/adventure. Buys 40 mss/year. Average word length: 1,500-3,000. Byline given.

Nonfiction: Young adults: how-to, humorous, interview/profile, problem solving, religious, travel. Buys 30 mss/year. Average word length: 500-2,000. Byline given.

How to Contact/Writers: Fiction/nonfiction: Query. Reports on queries in 6 weeks; mss in 6-8 weeks. Will consider simultaneous (indicate so) submissions.

Illustration: Buys 5 illustrations/issue; buys 50 illustrations/year. Preferred theme or style: Realistic, somewhat contemporary, but not too far out of the mainstream. Works on assignment only.

How to Contact/Illustrators: Ms/illustration packages: Query only. Illustrations only: Send tearsheets. Reports on art samples only if interested. Original art work returned at job's completion.

Terms/Writers & Illustrators: Pays on completion of assignment. Buys one-time rights. Pays 10-15¢/word for assigned articles; 7-12¢/word for unsolicited articles. Sample copy for 10 × 12 SAE and 5 first-class stamps; writer's/illustrator's guidelines for business-size envelope and 1 first-class stamp.

Tips: Fiction: be current; Christian message without being "preachy." "Most stories we buy will center on the lives and problems of 14 to 17 year-old characters. The problems involved should be common to teens (dating, family, alcohol and drugs, peer pressure, school, sex, talking about one's faith to nonbelievers, standing up for convictions, etc.) in which the resolution (or lack of it) is true to our reader's experiences. In other words, no happily-ever-after endings, last-page spiritual conversions or pat answers to complex problems. We're interested in the everyday (though still profound) experiences of teen life—stay away from sensationalism."

TURTLE MAGAZINE, For Preschool Kids, Ben Franklin Literary & Medical Society, Children's Better Health Institute, Box 567, Indianapolis IN 46206. (317)636-8881. Editorial Director: Christine Clark. Art Director: Bart Rivers. Monthly/bimonthly magazine, Jan./Feb., March, April/May, June, July/August, Sept., Oct./Nov., Dec. Circ. approx. 650,000. *Turtle* uses bedtime or naptime stories that can be read to the child. Also

used are poems and health-related articles. All but 2 pages aimed at juvenile audience.
Fiction: Picture-oriented material: animal, contemporary, health-related. Does not want to see stories about monsters or scary things. Avoid stories in which the characters indulge in unhealthy activities like eating junk food. Buys 50 mss/year. Average word length: 200-600. Byline given.
Nonfiction: Picture-oriented material: animal, contemporary, health. Buys 20 mss/year. Average word length: 200-600. Byline given.
How to Contact/Writers: Fiction/nonfiction: Send complete ms. Include Social Security number with submission. Reports on mss in 8-10 weeks.
Illustration: Buys 20-25 illustrations/issue from freelancers; 160-200 illustrations/year from freelancers. Prefers "realistic and humorous illustration."
Terms/Writers & Illustrators: Pays $250 color (cover) illustration, $30-70/b&w (inside); $65-140/color (inside). Sample copy 75¢. Writer's/illustrator's guidelines free with SAE and 1 first-class stamp.
Tips: "We're beginning to edit *Turtle* more for the very young preschooler, so we're looking for stories and articles that are written more simply than those we've used in the past. Our need for health-related material, especially features that encourage fitness, is ongoing. Health subjects must be age-appropriate. When writing about them, think creatively and lighten up! Fight the tendency to become boringly pedantic. Nobody— not even young kids—likes being lectured. Always keep in mind that in order for a story or article to educate preschoolers, it first must be truly entertaining—warm and engaging, exciting, or genuinely funny. Understand that writing for *Turtle* is a difficult challenge." (See listings for *Children's Digest, Children's Playmate, Child Life, Humpty Dumpty's Magazine, Jack and Jill.*)

TYRO MAGAZINE, Tyro Publishing, 194 Carlbert St., Sault Ste. Marie ON P6A 5E1 Canada. (705)253-6402. Articles Editor: George Hemingway. Fiction Editor: Stan Gordon. Art Director: Lorelee. Bimonthly magazine. 5½ × 8½; 200-220 pp; 13-20 lb. bond paper and card (usually matte) cover stock. Estab. 1984. Circ. 1,000. "*Tyro* is a practice medium for developing writers and accepts almost anything worthy." 15% of material aimed at juvenile audience.
Fiction: "We have published material and will consider submissions in any area and level." Buys 80 mss/year. Average word length: 5,000. Byline given.
Nonfiction: "We will consider any of these: animal, history, how-to, humorous, interview/profile, problem solving, religious, travel." Buys 6 mss/year. Average word length: 5,000. Byline given.
How to Contact/Writers: Fiction: Send complete ms. Nonfiction: Query. Reports on queries/mss in 1 month.
Illustration: "We use only camera-ready, b&w art." Buys up to 5 illustrations/issue; buys up to 30 illustrations/year. Will review all varieties of ms/illustration packages.
How to Contact/Illustrators: Ms/illustration packages: Send complete ms with final art. Reports on art samples in 1 month. Original artwork returned at job's completion.
Terms/Writers & Illustrators: "Since we are a practice vehicle, no fees paid." Pays in contributor copies. Sample copy $10. Writer's guidelines free with SASE.
Tips: "Many believe that because children's literature is often simple it is easy to write. That's not so. It's a discipline that requires as much, if not more, skill as any writing."

"Picture books" are geared toward the preschool—8 year old group; "Young readers" to 5-8 year olds; "Middle readers" to 9-11 year olds; and "Young adults" to those 12 and up.

USKIDS®, A Weekly Reader Magazine, Field Publications, 245 Long Hill Rd., Middletown CT 06457. (203)638-2400. Editor: Gabriel Davis. Art Director: Nancy Driscoll. Monthly magazine. $8 \times 10\frac{7}{8}$; 44 pp; predominately matte paper, 110 lb. coated cover stock. Estab. 1987. Circ. 250,000. *"USKids* is a 44-page magazine with a 'real world' focus. Its objective is to teach 5 to 9-year-olds about their world in a fun and entertaining way. Publication includes news, true-life stories, science and nature stories, activities and puzzles."
Fiction: Animal, contemporary, humorous, spy/mystery/adventure. Does not want to see fantasy. No talking animals. Buys 15-20 mss/year. Average word length: 300-400. Byline given.
Nonfiction: Animal, interview/profile, true-life, lifestyles. Buys 15-20 mss/year. Average word length: 200-300. Byline usually given.
How to Contact/Writers: Fiction: Send complete ms. Nonfiction: Query with published clips. Reports on queries/mss in 6-8 weeks.
Terms/Writers & Illustrators: Pays on acceptance. Buys first North American serial rights for fiction, all rights for nonfiction. Pays $100-300 for assigned or unsolicited articles. Writer's guidelines free with SASE.
Tips: "Include intriguing title; quick beginning; fast-moving prose; clear treatment of subject matter; humor; emphasis on active response of reader; expressions that make the child want to repeat certain phrases. Write on child's reading level; in the case of *USKids*, grade 2 reading level. Magazine is much more activity-oriented. Would welcome material that lends itself to this type of presentation."

VENTURE, Christian Service Brigade, Box 150, Wheaton IL 60189. (312)665-0630. Articles/Fiction Editor: Deborah Christensen. Art Director: Robert Fine. Bimonthly magazine. $8\frac{1}{4} \times 10\frac{7}{8}$; 32 pp; 50 lb. enamel paper. Estab. 1937. Circ. 23,000. The magazine is designed "to speak to the concerns of boys from a biblical perspective. To provide wholesome, entertaining reading for boys."
Fiction: Middle readers, young adults: animal, contemporary, history, humorous, problem solving, religious, sports, spy/mystery/adventure. Does not want to see fantasy, romance, science fiction. Buys 12 mss/year. Average word length: 1,000-1,500. Byline given.
Nonfiction: Middle readers, young adults: animal, history, how-to, humorous, interview/profile, problem solving, religious, travel. Buys 3 mss/year. Average word length: 1,000-1,500. Byline given.
How to Contact/Writers: Fiction/nonfiction: Query; send complete ms. Reports on queries in 1 week; mss in 2 weeks. Will consider simultaneous submissions.
Illustration: Buys 3 illustration/issue; buys 18 illustrations/year. Will review all varieties of ms/illustration packages.
How to Contact/Illustrators: Ms/illustration packages: query first. Illustrations only: Send tearsheets, slides. Reports on art samples in 2 weeks. Original art work returned at job's completion.
Terms/Writers & Illustrators: Pays on publication. Buys first North American serial rights; first rights; one-time rights; second serial (reprint rights). Pays $75-150 for assigned articles; $30-100 for unsolicited articles. Additional payment for ms/illustration packages: $100-200. Pays $35-125/b&w (cover) illustration; $35-50/b&w (inside) illustration. Sample copy $1.85 with 9×12 SAE and 85¢ postage affixed. Writer's/illustrator's guidelines free with SAE and 1 first class stamp.

Always include a self-addressed stamped envelope (SASE) or International Reply Coupon (IRC) with submissions.

VOICE, Scholastic, Inc., 730 Broadway, New York NY 10003. (212)505-3000. Fiction Editor: Forrest Stone. Art Director: Joy Makon. Biweekly "during school year (16 issues/year)" magazine. Estab. 1946. Circ. 250,000. *Voice* is "a language-arts magazine for junior high and high school students."
Fiction: Young adults: contemporary, fantasy, history, humorous, problem-solving, romance, science fiction, sports, spy/mystery/adventure, poetry and drama. Does not want to see "anything over 3,000 words unless writer is quite established." Buys 10 mss/year. Average word length: up to 3,000. Byline given.
Nonfiction: Young adults: humorous, problem solving and travel. Buys 5 mss/year. Average word length: up to 1,000. Byline given.
Poetry: Reviews "good" poetry; send no more than 10 submissions.
How to Contact/Writers: Fiction: Send complete ms. Nonfiction: Query with published clips. Include Social Security number with submission. Reports on queries in 2-4 weeks; mss in 1-3 months. Will consider simultaneous submissions.
Terms/Writers: Pays on publication. Pays $100-500 for assigned and unsolicited articles.

WEE WISDOM MAGAZINE, Children's Magazine, Unity School of Christianity, Unity Village MO 64025. (816)524-3550, ext. 329. Editor: Judy Gehrlein. Published 10 times/year. 8½×5½; 48 pp; white penpair 45 lb. paper and White Mounty Matte 80 lb. text cover stock. Estab. 1893.
Fiction: Picture material, young readers, middle readers: animal, contemporary, fantasy, history, humorous, problem solving, science fiction, sports, spy/mystery/adventure. Does not want to see anything on war, crime; avoid negative perspective. Buys 60 mss/year. Average word length: 800. Byline given. Rarely assign stories.
How to Contact/Writers: Fiction: Send complete ms. Report on mss in 8 weeks.
Illustration: Buys 25 illustrations/issue; buys 250 illustrations/year. Preferred theme or style: "We assign according to literature." Will review all varieties of ms/illustration packages. Works on assignment only.
How to Contact/Illustrators: Ms/illustration packages: No queries, full manuscript, sample illustration package. Illustrations only: Samples. "We are interested in freelancers in children's art. We are most interested in seeing their work—perhaps their range in work." Reports on art samples in 6 weeks. "Originals returned one year after publication."
Terms/Writers & Illustrators: Pays on acceptance. Buys first North American serial rights. Pays 5-9¢/word for stories. "We pay the same rate for assigned work and unsolicited. We rarely assign stories. Contributor copies are sent at no charge." Pays $80 full page (2-color) illustration, $30-60 fraction (2-color) illustration; $100 full page (4-color) illustration, $30-60 fraction (4-color) illustration; $200 double cover illustration; $200 calendar (always 4-color, always a package). Free sample copy. Writer's/illustrator's guidelines free with SASE.
Tips: Writers: "Use dialogue in stories taken from real life rather than imagination. Develop characters that express real feelings and explore human relationships through behavior and dialogue. Do not over-describe with adjectives. We need to read your fresh, individual approach to children's fiction of no more than 800 words. We're looking for up-to-date kids with basic values. We must have positive yet plausible solutions to real situations. We select very few poems within a year. We are open to puzzles and riddles for 4-12 year olds."

WITH, Faith & Life Press, Mennonite Publishing House, Box 347, 722 Main, Newton KS 67114. (316)283-5100. Monthly magazine. Circ. 6,500. Magazine published for teenagers in Mennonite congregations. We deal with issues affecting teens and try to help them make choices reflecting an Anabaptist-Mennonite faith.
Fiction: Teenagers: contemporary, humorous, problem solving, religious, sports. Buys 30 mss/year. Average word length: 1,200-2,000. Byline given.

Nonfiction: Young adults: how-to, humorous, interview/profile, problem solving, religious. Buys 5-6 mss/year. Average word length: 1,000-1,750. Byline given.
How to Contact/Writers: Fiction: Send complete ms. Nonfiction: Query. Reports on queries in 1 month; mss in 3 months. Will consider simultaneous submissions.
Illustration: Buys 6-8 illustrations/issue; buys 70-75 illustrations/year. Preferred theme or style: Candids/interracial. Will review all varieties of ms/illustration packages.
How to Contact/Illustrators: Ms/illustration packages: Query first. Illustrations only: Send slides 8 × 10 b&w prints preferred. Reports on art samples in 1 month. Original art work returned at job's completion.
Terms/Writers & Illustrators: Pays on acceptance. Buys one-time rights; second serial (reprint rights). Pays $40-80 for assigned articles; $20-80 for unsolicited articles. Additional payment for ms/illustration packages: $30-100. Pays $25-50/b&w (cover) illustration; $25-35/b&w (inside) illustration. Sample copy $1.50 with 9 × 12 SAE and 85¢ postage. Writer's/illustrator's guidelines free with SASE.
Tips: Writers: "Fiction and poetry are most open to freelancers." Illustrators: "We use almost exclusively illustrations from freelancers. Since we can't use color photos, I appreciate submissions that are b&w. Art can be 2-color."

WONDER TIME, Beacon Hill Press, 6401 The Paseo, Kansas City MO 64131. (816)333-7000. Editor: Evelyn Beals. Weekly magazine: 8½ × 11; 4 pages; newsprint paper and cover stock. Circ. 45,000. "*Wonder Time* is a full-color story paper for first and second graders. It is designed to connect Sunday School learning with the daily living experiences and growth of the primary child. Since *Wonder Time's* target audience is children ages six to eight, the readability goal is to encourage beginning readers to read for themselves. The major purposes of *Wonder Time* are to: Provide a life-related paper which will build Christian values and encourage ethical behavior and provide reinforcement for the biblical concepts taught in the Word Action Sunday School curriculum." 100% of material aimed at juvenile audience.
Fiction: Young readers: problem solving, religious. Buys 52 mss/year. Average word length: 400-550. Byline given.
Poetry: Reviews religious poetry of 4-8 lines.
How to Contact/Writers: Fiction/nonfiction: Send complete ms. Reports on queries/mss in 6-8 weeks. Will consider simultaneous submissions.
Illustration: Buys 10-15 illustrations/year. Will review all illustration packages. Works on assignment only.
How to Contact/Illustrators: Ms/illustration packages: Ms with sketch. Illustrations only: Samples of work. Reports on art samples only if interested.
Terms/Writers & Illustrators: Pays 1 month after acceptance. Buys first rights and second serial (reprint rights). Pays 3.5¢/word for stories and a complimentary contributor's copy of publication. Additional payment for ms/illustration package. Sample copy, writer's/illustrator's guidelines with 9½ × 12 SAE and 2 first class stamps.
Tips: "These basic themes reappear regularly: faith in God; putting God first; choosing to please God; understanding that Jesus is God's Son and our Savior; choosing to do right; asking forgiveness; trusting God in hard times; prayer: trusting God to answer; appreciation of the Bible as God's word to man; importance of Bible memorization; understanding both meanings of church: a place where we worship God, a fellowship of God's people working together; understanding each person's value to God and to others; showing love and kindness to others; enriching family life, including non-traditional family units; addressing current problems which children may face."

THE WORLD OF BUSINES$ KIDS, America's Future, Lemonade Kids, Inc., Suite 330, 301 Almeria Ave., Coral Gables FL 33134. (305)445-8869. Articles Editor: Jacky Robinson. Art Director: Donn Matus. Quarterly newsletter. Estab. 1988. Circ. 75,000. "We cover stories about young entrepreneurs, how teens and preteens can become entrepreneurs, and useful information for effective business operation and management. Our goal is to help prepare America's youth for the complex and competitive world of business by sharing with them every possible business experience, the problems *and* the solutions. And while we're *serious* about business, we want them to know that business can be *fun*. 99% of material aimed at juvenile audience with one article aimed at parents in each issue."

Nonfiction: Middle readers: how-to, interview/profile, problem solving. Young adult/teens: how-to, interview/profile, problem solving. "All must relate to business;" does not want to see "any articles which do not deal with business." Buys 15 mss/year. "Our goal is 50% freelance." Average word length: 200-600. Byline: Listed as a contributing writer.

Poetry: Reviews free verse, light verse, traditional poetry; 25-50 lines.

How to Contact/Writers: Nonfiction: Send complete ms. Include Social Security number with submission. Reports on mss in 2 months.

Terms/Writers: Pays on publication. Buys all rights. Pays 15¢ word/unsolicited articles; $35-50 for puzzles/games; $15-20 for cartoons; $5-10 for b&w/8×10 photos. Sample copies available. Writer's guidelines and sample copy available.

Tips: Looking for "any nonfiction pertaining to teens in the business world. How to choose, build, improve, market or advertise a business. When, and how, to hire (or fire) employees. Lots of profiles about successful young entrepreneurs. The latest in *any* field—entertainment, sports, medicine, etc.—where teens are making megabucks (or just movie money!). New products; book reviews on children and money; motivational articles; how-to invest/save money; news releases; tax information; stock market tips; bonds; banking; precious metals; cartoons; puzzles; poetry; games also sought."

YABA FRAMEWORK, (formerly *The New YABA World*), Young American Bowling Alliance, 5301 South 76th St., Greendale WI 53129. (414)421-4700. Media Relations Manager: Mark Schaefer. Editor: Laura Plizka. Tabloid published 6 times/bowling season. Estab. 1987. Circ. 600,000. "Our audience is youth bowlers between the ages of 3-21. Our paper is predominantly nonfiction news regarding our membership, leagues and tournaments. On occasion we use puzzles, fiction and cartoons." 85% of material directed to children.

Nonfiction: Does not want to see "anything not pertaining to YABA sanctioned leagues or tournaments." Average word length: 500-1,500. Byline sometimes given.

How to Contact/Writers: Nonfiction: Query. Reports on queries in 2 weeks. Will consider simultaneous submissions.

Illustration: Buys 1 illustration/issue; 3 illustrations/year. Preferred theme or style: "Relating to youth bowling." Works on assignment only.

How to Contact/Illustrators: Ms/illustration packages: "Query first." Illustrations only: Send tearsheets. Reports on art samples only if interested. Original artwork returned at job's completion "if requested."

Terms/Writers and Illustrators: Pays on publication. Buys first North American serial rights. Pays $40-50/assigned articles. Sample copy for 9×12 SAE; writer's/illustrator's guidelines free with SASE.

YOUNG AMERICAN, America's Newspaper for Kids, Young American Publishing Co., Inc., Box 12409, Portland OR 97212. (503)230-1895. FAX: (503)236-0440. Articles/Fiction Editor: Kristina Linden. Art Director: Duane Wells. Biweekly (national) tabloid. Estab. 1983. Circ. 1,200,000+.

Fiction: Young readers, middle readers, young adults: animal, contemporary, fantasy, history, humorous, problem solving, science fiction, sports, spy/mystery/adventure. Does not want to see religious themes. Buys 12-15 mss/year. Average word length: 500-1,000. Byline given.

Nonfiction: Young readers, middle readers, young adults: animal, history, how-to, humorous, interview/profile, problem solving. Does not want to see preachy, moralistic themes. Buys 75 mss/year. Maximum word length: 350. Byline given sometimes.
How to Contact/Writers: Fiction/nonfiction: Send complete ms. Include Social Security number with submission. Reports on mss in 4 months. Will consider simultaneous submissions.
Illustration: "Future plans are to increase freelance illustrations." Will review all varieties of ms/illustration packages.
How to Contact/Illustrators: Ms/illustration packages: Submit complete ms. Illustrations only: Send examples of style. Reports on art samples in 4 months. Original art work returned at job's completion.
Terms/Writers & Illustrators: Pays on publication. Buys first North American serial rights; may buy reprint rights. Pay is "negotiable" for assigned articles. Pay for illustrations is "negotiable." Sample copy for $1.50. Writer's guidelines free with SASE.
Tips: "Know today's kids — quote them when possible. Fiction: don't be condescending."

THE YOUNG CRUSADER, National WCTU, 1730 Chicago Ave., Evanston IL 60201. (708)864-1396. Managing Editor: Michael C. Vitucci. Monthly magazine. Estab. 1900. Circ. 3,500. The magazine is geared to the 8-12 year old child. It stresses high morals and good character. Nature and informational stories are also used. Above all, the stories should not be preachy or religious as the magazine is used in public schools.
Fiction: Middle readers: contemporary, problem solving, positive character building. Does not want to see preachy, religious-type stories. Buys 4 mss/year. Average word length: 550-650. Byline given.
Nonfiction: Middle readers: animal, history, interview/profile, problem solving, travel. Buys 10 mss/year. Average word length: 550-650. Byline given.
How to Contact/Writers: Fiction/nonfiction: Send complete ms. Will consider simultaneous submissions. "I require submissions to be copies. If used, I will publish; if not used, the manuscript will be destroyed."
Terms/Writers: Pays on publication. Buys second serial (reprint rights); simultaneous rights. Pays ½¢/word for assigned/unsolicited articles. Free sample copy.
Tips: "Don't write down to the child. Writers often underestimate their audience." Looks for: "nonfiction stories stressing good character and high morals."

YOUNG JUDAEAN, Hadassah Zionist Youth Commission, 50 W. 58th St., New York NY 10019. (212)303-8250. Editor: Ira Weiss. Published 3 times a year (fall, winter, spring). Estab. 1910. Circ. 4,000. "Magazine is intended for members — age 9-12 — of Young Judaea, which is the Zionist-oriented youth movement sponsored by the Hadassah Women's Organization." 100% of material is directed to children.
Fiction: Middle readers: contemporary, fantasy, history, humorous, science fiction, sports and spy/mystery/adventure. Does not want to see "any material that does *not* relate to Jewish themes. Also, no material whose Jewishness is theological rather than cultural." Buys 10-15 mss/year. Average word length: 500-1,500. Byline given.
Nonfiction: Middle readers, young adults: history, how-to, humorous, interview/profile, problem solving and travel. Does not want to see "anything that preaches a particular theological outlook. Anything that is *not* related to Jewish life." Buys 30 mss/year. Average word length: 500-1,500. Byline given.
How to Contact/Writers: Fiction: Send complete ms. Nonfiction: Send complete ms or query.

Refer to the Business of Children's Writing & Illustrating for up-to-date marketing, tax and legal information.

Illustration: Buys 6 illustrations/issue. Preferred theme or style: "Lively and anecdotal." Will review all varieties of ms/illustration packages, including illustrator's work for possible use with fiction/nonfiction articles and columns by other authors.

How to Contact/Illustrators: Ms/illustration packages: Send complete ms with final art. Illustrations only: Send tearsheets. Original artwork returned at job's completion "if requested."

Terms/Writers & Illustrators: Pays on publication. Buys first North American serial rights. Pays $20-50 for assigned articles; $20-50 for unsolicited articles. Additional payment for ms/illustration packages is "manuscript plus $20 per illustration." Pays $20-40/b&w cover illustration, $20-30 b&w inside illustration. Sample copy $1 with SASE; free writer's/illustrator's guidelines.

YOUNG SALVATIONIST, The Salvation Army, 799 Bloomfield Ave., Verona NJ 07003. (201)239-0606. Articles Editor: Captain Robert R. Hostetler. Monthly magazine. Estab. 1984. Circ. 50,000. "We accept material with clear Christian content written for high school age teenagers. *Young Salvationist* is published for teenage members of The Salvation Army, a fundamental, activist denomination of the Christian Church." 100% of material directed to youth.

Fiction: Picture-oriented material, young adults: religious. Buys 12-20 mss/year. Average word length: 750-1,200. Byline given.

Nonfiction: Young adults: religious. Buys 40-50 mss/year. Average word length: 750-1,200. Byline given.

Poetry: Reviews 16-20 line poetry dealing with a Christian theme. Send no more than 6 submissions.

How to Contact/Writers: Query; query with published clips or send complete ms. Reports on queries in 2-3 weeks; mss in 1 month. Will consider simultaneous submissions.

Illustrations: Buys 2-3 illustrations/issue; 20-30 illustrations/year. Will review all types of illustration packages.

How to Contact/Illustrators: Ms/illustration packages: "Query or send manuscript with art." Reports on artwork in 2-3 weeks (with SASE). Original artwork returned at job's completion "if requested."

Terms/Writers & Illustrators: Pays on acceptance. Buys first North American serial rights, first rights, one-time rights, second serial (reprint rights) simultaneous rights. Pays $40/assigned articles (depends on length); $25 for unsolicited articles (depends on length). Additional payment for ms/illustration packages "depends on use." Pays $100-150 color (cover) illustration; $50-100 b&w (inside) illustration; $100-150 color (inside) illustration. Sample copy for 9×12 SAE and 3 first class stamps. Writer's/illustrator's guidelines free for #10 SASE.

Tips: Writers: "Write for our themes." Looking for "nonfiction articles to fit themes."

YOUTH UPDATE, St. Anthony Messenger Press, 1615 Republic St., Cincinnati OH 45210. (513)241-5615. Articles Editor: Carol Ann Morrow. Art Director: Julie Lonneman. Monthly newsletter. Estab. 1982. Circ. 32,000. "Each issue focuses on one topic only. *Youth Update* addresses the faith and Christian life questions of young people and is designed to attract, instruct, guide and challenge its audience by applying the gospel to modern problems and situations. The students who read *Youth Update* vary in their religious education and reading ability. Write for the average high school student. This student is 15-years-old with a C+ average. Assume that they have paid attention to religious instruction and remember a little of what 'sister' said. Aim more toward 'table talk than teacher talk.' "

Nonfiction: Young adults: religious. Does not want to see travel material. Buys 12 mss/year. Average word length: 2,300-2,400. Byline given.

How to Contact/Writers: Nonfiction: Query. Include Social Security number with submission. Reports on queries/mss in 6 weeks. Will consider computer printout and electronic submissions via disk.

Terms/Writers: Pays on acceptance. Buys first North American serial rights. Pays $325-400 for assigned/unsolicited articles. Sample copy free with #10 SAE and 1 first-class stamp.

Tips: "Read the newsletter yourself—3 issues at least. In the past, our publication has dealt with a variety of topics including: dating, lent, teenage pregnancy, baptism, loneliness, rock and roll, confirmation and the Bible. When writing, use the *New American Bible* as translation. More interest in church-related topics."

*ZILLIONS: Consumer Reports for Kids, (formerly *Penny Power*), Consumers Union, 101 Truman Ave., Yonkers NY 10703-1057. (914)667-9400. FAX: (914)667-2701. Editor: Jeanne Kiefer. Art Director: Rob Jenter. Bimonthly magazine. 8 × 11; 36 pp; 4-color glossy paper. Estab. 1990 (1980 as *Penny Power*). Circ. 200,000. "Consumer Education—advice on buying, saving, product tests, coping skills, media reviews, advertising smarts, health, ecology. Audience—kids 8-14."

Nonfiction: Middle Readers and Young Adults/Teens: how-to, environment, problem solving, sports, advice, consumer education, health. "All articles are assigned—no submissions accepted." Buys 12+ mss/year. Average word length: 1,000-1,500. Consumers Union policy.

How to Contact/Writers: Query with published clips. Publishes ms 3 months after acceptance.

Illustration: Buys 5 illustrations/issue. Prefers humorous all 4/c. Reviews all varieties of ms/illustration packages. Works on assignment only.

How to Contact/Illustrators: Ms/illustrations packages: query only. Illustrations only: send tearsheets. Reports on art samples only if interested. Original artwork returned at job's completion.

Terms/Writers & Illustrators: Pays on acceptance. Buys all rights. Pays $500-1,000 for assigned articles. Pays $1,000-1,500/color (cover); $500-1,500/color (inside). Sample copy and writer's guidelines free on request.

Other Magazine Publishers

The following magazine publishers are not included in this edition of *Children's Writer's & Illustrator's Market* for the reasons indicated. The phrase "did not respond" means the publisher was in the 1990 *Children's Writer's & Illustrator's Market* but did not respond to our written and phone requests for updated information for a 1991 listing.

Barbie Magazine (declined to be listed)
Brilliant Star (did not respond)
Calli's Tales (did not respond)
Class Act (did not respond)
Ducktales Magazine (declined to be listed)
Equilibrium (did not respond)
4 and 5 (does not accept freelance material)
Hob-Nob (overstocked)

Hobo Stew Review (did not respond)
Jackie (did not respond)
Junior Scholastic (declined to be listed)
Muppet Magazine (declined to be listed)
Sports Illustrated for Kids (declined to be listed)
Teenage (suspended publication)
Thundercats Magazines (de

clined to be listed)
Tiger Beat (suspended publication)
Tiger Beat Star (suspended publication)
Weekly Bible Reader (does not accept freelance material)
Your Big Backyard (currently no freelance needs)

Audiovisual Markets

The burgeoning children's videotape industry can be attributed to two factors: firstly, owning a video cassette recorder (VCR) is considered much more mainstream than it used to be. Secondly, new channels of distribution are being used for children's video. Whereas it used to be videos could only be purchased at video stores, book and toy stores are now finding it quite lucrative to carry videos also.

Bruce Pfander, vice-president of marketing for CBS/Fox, said in the July 27, 1990 issue of _Publishers Weekly_, "The estimated market for sell-through video in general is currently at $2.5 billion, with the children's category representing about 40 percent of that figure." Pfander went on to say sell-through is today what rental was a few years ago. People are actually buying videos now instead of renting them, and children's programming is a big part of these purchases.

It should come as no surprise that children's videotapes are selling well. When you consider the popularity of the adult video market and today's crop of TV-oriented children, the prognosis looks good for this market to grow steadily.

Video production companies are just now starting to recognize the profit potential of children's video. Many such production companies are included in this section and have a range of writing and animation needs that include educational as well as entertainment subjects.

Educational films may not pay quite as much as those destined for entertainment distribution, but once you're established as a professional who can create quality work on time, you will find steady work.

Read through each listing carefully to determine the company's needs and methods of contact. You will also notice that video isn't the only format produced by many production houses. A writer or illustrator may find himself working on a film project, film strip or multi-media production.

Be aware that audiovisual media rely more on the "visual" to tell the story. The script plays a "secondary" role and explains only what the visual message doesn't make clear to viewers. This will be a greater challenge to writers than to illustrators as the latter are already trained to think primarily in visual terms.

AERIAL IMAGE VIDEO SERVICES, #203, 101 W. 31 St., New York NY 10001. (212)279-6026, (800)237-4259. FAX: (212)279-6229. President: John Stapsy. Estab. 1979. Type of company: Video production and post production, and audio production and post production. Uses videotapes and audio. (For list of recent productions consult the Random House catalog of children's videos.)

Children's Writing: Submissions returned with proper SASE. Reports in "days."

Children's Illustration/Animation: Hires illustrators for: computer and hand animation, storyboarding, live action and comprehensives. Types of animation produced: cel animation, clay animation, stop motion, special effects, 3-D, computer animation, video graphics, motion control and live action. Submission method: send cover letter, résumé and demo tape. Art samples returned with proper SASE. Reports in "weeks." Pays "per project."

Tips: When reviewing a portfolio/samples, looks for "application to a project, general talent and interests based on examples."

KEN ANDERSON FILMS, P.O. Box 618, Winona Lake IN 46590. (219)267-5774. Contact: Margaret Mauzy. Estab. 1959. Type of company: film production facility. Audience: the evangelical market. Uses film strips, slide sets, films, videotapes.
Children's Writing: Needs: Children's adventure; teen (junior high). Submission method: query with synopsis. Submission returned with proper SASE. Reports in 1 month. Guidelines/catalog free.
Children's Illustration/Animation: Guidelines/catalog free.
Tips: "Don't get discouraged. Keep on trying. We are open to material of children's adventure stories; our slant is to the evangelical market, cannot at the moment consider full scripts. We need to see one-page gist of the story, and from this we will decide to have the material developed. Payment is by prior negotiation with the author."

CLEARVUE, 6465 N. Avondale, Chicago IL 60631. (312)775-9433. President: W.O. McDermed (for scripts); V.P. Editorial: Matthew Newman (for illustration/animation). Estab. 1969. Type of company: production house. Audience: educational pre-school through high school. Uses film strips, slide sets, videotapes. 30% of writing is by freelancers; 70% of illustrating/animating is by freelancers.
Children's Writing: Needs: educational material; preschool, 5-8, 9-11, 12 and older. Submission method: query with synopsis. Submissions are returned. Reports in 2 weeks. Guidelines/catalog free. Buys material outright.
Children's Illustration/Animation: Hires illustrators for: animation, storyboarding. Types of animation produced: cel animation. Art samples returned. Reports in 2 weeks. Guidelines/catalog free. Pay: "open."
Tips: "Programs must be designed for educational market—not home or retail."

DIMENSION FILMS, 15007 Gault St., Van Nuys CA 91405. (818)997-8065. President: Gary Goldsmith. Estab. 1962. Type of company: Production house. Audience: schools and libraries. Uses film strips, films, videotapes. Recent children's productions: *Literature to Write About*, written by Gary Goldsmith; illustrated by various artists. These subjects are comprised of filmstrips and videos dealing with books as a basis of writing for 10-12 year olds. *Legend of the Bluebonnet*, written by Gary Goldsmith, adapted from Tomie dePaola's work. This is a live-action 16mm film for 6-10 year olds. 20% of writing is by freelancers; 20% of illustrating/animating is by freelancers.
Children's Writing: Needs: educational material and documentaries for Kindergarten-12th-grade audience. Submission method: query. Submissions filed. Reports in a matter of weeks. "Prefer phone calls" for guidelines. Pays in accordance with Writer's Guild standards.
Children's Illustration/Animation: Hires illustrators for: storyboarding, comprehensives. Types of animation produced: cel animation, video graphics, live action. Submission method: send cover letter and résumé. Reports in a matter of weeks. "Call for guidelines." Pays $30-60/frame.
Tips: Illustrators/animators: looking for "imagination, clarity and purpose." Portfolio should show "strong composition; action in stillness."

 The asterisk before a listing indicates the listing is new in this edition.

EDUCATIONAL VIDEO NETWORK, 1401 19th St., Huntsville TX 77340. (409)295-5767. Editor: Gary Edmondson. Estab. 1954. Type of company: production house. Audience: educational (school). Uses film strips, videotapes. Recent children's production: *Improvising Your Self-Esteem*, written by Bill Carroll. This is a video for 12-17 year olds. 20% of writing by freelancers; 20% of illustrating/animating is by freelancers.
Children's Writing: Needs: "Educational material" for ages 9-11 and 12-18. Submission method: script with video or animation. Submissions returned with proper SASE. Reports in 1 month. Guidelines/catalog free. Pays writers in royalties or buys material outright.
Children's Illustration/Animation: Hires illustrators for: acetate cels, animation. Types of animation produced: cel animation stills, video graphics, live action. Submission method: send cover letter and VHS demo tape. Art samples returned with proper SASE. Reports in 1 month. Guidelines/catalog free.
Tips: "Materials should fill a curriculum need in grades 6-12." Writers/scriptwriters: "Work must be of professional quality adaptable to video format." Illustrators/animators: Looks for "creativity." "More live-action is being demanded. Go to school library and ask to review most popular A-V titles."

*KDOC-TV, 1730 S. Clementine, Anaheim CA 92802. (714)999-5050. FAX: (714)999-1218. Program Manager: Bill Dailey. Promotion Manager: Tricia Ward. Estab. 1982. Type of company: TV station. Audience: All viewers. Uses videotapes. "Always open to new ideas."
Children's Writing: Needs: scripts, documentaries. Submission method: query with synopsis. Submissions filed. Reports in 3-4 weeks. Writers paid in accordance with Writer's Guild standards.
Illustration: Hires illustrators for: animation (computer, video graphics). Types of animation produced: video graphics. Submission method: send ¾" demo tape. Art samples are filed. Reports in 3-4 weeks. Pay is "open."

MARSHMEDIA, 5903 Main St., Kansas City MO 64113. (816)523-1059. FAX: (816)333-7421. Production Director: Janie Fopeano. Estab. 1969. Type of company: production house. Audience: grades K-12. 100% of writing is by freelancers; 100% of illustrating/animating is by freelancers.
Children's Writing: Needs: educational materials—filmstrip and video scripts for grades K-12. Subjects include: "health, drug education, guidance, safety, nutrition." Submission method: query with synopsis and submit completed scripts, résumé. Submissions returned with proper SASE. Reports in 1 month. Buys material outright.
Children's Illustration/Animation: Submission method: send résumé and VHS demo tape. Art samples returned with proper SASE. Reports in 1 month.

NTC PUBLISHING GROUP, (formerly National Textbook Company), 4255 W. Touhy Ave., Lincolnwood IL 60646. (708)679-5500. FAX: (708)679-2494. Editorial Director: Michael Ross. Art Director: Karen Christoffersen. Estab. 1960. Type of company: publisher. Audience: all ages. Uses film strips, multimedia productions, videotapes, books and audiocassettes. Recent children's productions: *Ready for English*, written by Linda Ventriglia, illustrated by Terry Meider. These are books, tapes, videos and story cards dealing with pre-reading aimed at ages 5-7. *Hello, English*, written by Barbara Zaffran, illustrated by Alan Jansen. These are books, tapes, videos and story cards on reading and writing. *Viva el Español*, written by Linda Tibensky, illustrated by Don Wilson. These are texts, filmstrips, cassettes, flashcards and posters dealing with Spanish aimed at ages 6-14. 40% of writing is by freelancers; 50% of illustrating/animating is by freelancers.

Children's Writing: Needs educational material for ages 5-14. Subjects include: "mostly foreign language, travel and English." Submission method: submit synopsis/outline, completed script, résumé and samples. Submission returned with proper SASE only. Reports in 2 months. Guidelines/catalog free. Pays writers in royalties or buys material outright—"depends on project."

Children's Illustration/Animation: Hires illustrators for: character development, comprehensives, pencil testing. Types of animation produced: stop motion, video graphics. Submission method: send cover letter, résumé, color print samples, tearsheets, business card. Art samples returned with proper SASE. Reports in 8 weeks. Guidelines/catalog free.

Tips: Looking for "experienced professionals only with proven track record in the *educational* field."

*OLIVE JAR ANIMATION, 44 Write Pl., Brookline MA 02146. (612)566-6699. FAX: (617)566-0689. Executive Producer: Phred McDonald. Estab. 1984. Type of company: animation studio. Audience: all ages. Uses films, videotapes. 75% of writing is by freelancers; 75% of illustrating/animating is by freelancers.

Illustration: Hires illustrators for: animation (all types), storyboarding, pencil testing, design, ink paint, sculpture, illustrate. Types of animation produced: cel animation, clay animation, stop motion, special effects. Submission method: send cover letter, résumé, demo tape, black & white print samples, color print samples, tearsheets, business card. Art samples are filed. Reports back only if interested. Pays $7-12/hour for animation work; $7-12/cel for animation work; $7-15 project for animation work; $7-15/hour for specialized animation work; $7-15/frame or cel; $7-12/project for specialized animation.

Tips: Looks for "someone who is really good at a particular style or direction as well as people who work in a variety of mediums. Attitude is as important as talent. The ability to work with others is very important."

SINNOT & ASSOCIATES, INC., 676 N. LaSalle, Chicago IL 60610. (312)440-1875. Director: Tim Sinnot. Producer: Cynthia Neal. Estab. 1975. Type of company: animation studio, special effects 3-D computer graphics. Audience: television. Uses films, videotapes. Recent children's productions: *Ronald McDonald and the Adventure Machine*—a videotape for children, aimed at ages 2-10. *Return to Mocha*—educational film aimed at ages 10-16. *Cap'n Crunch*—cereal commercials aimed at ages 5-25. 75% by freelance illustrators; 25% by freelance animators.

Children's Illustration/Animation: Hires illustrators for: animation, storyboarding, character development, live action, pencil testing. Types of animation produced: cel animation, stop motion, special effects, 3-D, motion control, live action. Submission method: send cover letter, résumé, VHS demo tape. Art samples filed; returned with proper SASE. Reports only if interested.

TREEHAUS COMMUNICATIONS, INC., 906 W. Loveland Ave., Loveland OH 45140. (513)683-5716. President: Gerard A. Pottebaum. Estab. 1968. Type of company: production house. Audience: preschool through adults. Uses film strips, multimedia productions, videotapes. Recent children's productions: *The Treehouse Stories*, written by G. Pottebaum. This is a filmstrip dealing with self-esteem, for kindergarten-grade 4 children. *The Christmas Story*, written by G. Pottebaum. This is a video dealing with religion for kindergarten-grade 3 children. *The Sunday Series*, written by Christine Brusselmans and Paule Freeburg. Print leaflets for kindergarten-age 12. 30% of writing by freelancers; 30% of illustrating/animating by freelancers.

Children's Writing: Needs: educational material/documentaries, for all ages. Subjects include: "social studies, religious education, documentaries on all subjects, but primarily about people who live ordinary lives in extraordinary ways." Submission method: query with synopsis. Submissions returned with proper SASE. Reports in 1 month. Guidelines/catalog for SAE. Pays writers in accordance with Writer's Guild standards.

Tips: Illustrators/animators: "Be informed about movements and needs in education, multi-cultural sensitivity." Looks for "social values, originality, competency in subject, global awareness."

*BILL WADSWORTH PRODUCTIONS, 2520 Longview, #308, Austin TX 78705. (512)478-2971. Director: Bill Wadsworth. Estab. 1978. Type of company: Production house. Audience: K-12. Uses films, videotapes. Recent children's productions: *Tailypo*, written by Bill Wadsworth, 16mm Folk Tale aimed at elementary age; *Another Half*, written by Bill Wadsworth, 16mm gender role pressures aimed at ages 11-17. *First Things First*, written by Bill Wadsworth, 16mm on sexuality education aimed at ages 11-17.

Children's Writing: No needs at this time. "In future grades 3-8." Subject matter varies. Submission method: query. Submissions are not returned. Reports back only if interested. Pay is negotiated.

Illustration: Hires illustrators periodically on freelance basis for: animation, storyboarding. Submission method: cover letter, résumé, business card. Art samples are filed or not returned.

Audiotapes

There are more two-career families today and working parents are not always free to read to their children. Because of this, the demand for book/cassette packages is steadily increasing. Also increasing is interest in music tapes. In order to meet these needs, most bookstores today, both chain and independent, now stock children's story and music tapes in their inventories.

Writers and songwriters can look toward the children's audiotape market as a valid marketing outlet. Represented in this section are publishers and record companies looking for good story material or unique children's music to record. Many specify an interest in reviewing both. Be sure to study each listing to determine what subject matter they prefer to review and to what age level such submissions should be geared. Pay rates to a large degree will be based on royalties for writers and songwriters or, for recording musicians, on record contracts.

This is definitely an expanding industry, but remember that you are competing against established artists who already have a track record. Presenting yourself as a professional by submitting only the material requested, and in the correct format noted, is a good first step toward getting stories or songs recorded.

BARRON'S EDUCATIONAL SERIES, 250 Wireless Blvd., Hauppauge NY 11788. (516)434-3311. FAX: (516)434-3723. Executive Vice President: Ms. Ellen Sibley. Book publisher.
Stories: Publishes 7 book/cassette packages/year. 100% of stories are fiction. Tapes aimed at preschool audience. Authors are paid in royalties of 6-10% based on wholesale price. Buys ms outright for $1,500-5,000. Average advance: $2,000. Making contact: query, submit outline/synopsis and sample chapters, submit complete ms. Reports on queries/mss in 4-12 weeks. Book catalog for 9½" × 11" SAE.

*BRENTWOOD MUSIC, INC., 316 Southgate Court, Brentwood TN 37027. (615)373-3950. FAX: (615)373-0386. Contact: Product Development—Children's Division. Music publisher, book publisher, record company, children's video. Estab. 1980.
Music: Releases 40 LPs/year; 24-30 CDs/year. Member of ASCAP, BMI and SESAC. Publishes 60-120 children's songs/year. Works with composers. For music published pays standard royalty of 50% of net receipts. Making contact: Submit demo cassette tape by mail; unsolicited submissions OK; 2 songs and lyric sheet or lead sheet. "No music can be returned unless you include a self addressed, stamped envelope. Do not sent stamps or postage only. If you want it back, send an *envelope* big enough to hold all material and the *proper* postage. No exceptions." Reports in 3-6 months. Recently recorded songs: "Mother Goose Gospel" Vol. 1 & 2, by various writers, recorded by "The Kid Connection" on Brentwood Kids Co. label (nursery rhyme tunes with Chris-

 The asterisk before a listing indicates the listing is new in this edition.

tian lyrics); "Wake Up You Sleepyhead," written and recorded by Rhett Parrish on Brentwood Kids Co. label ("Whimsical, Disney-esque").

Stories: Will consider fictional animal, fantasy or adventure aimed at preschool through 3rd or 4th grades. Authors pay is negotiable, depending on project. Making contact: query. Reports in 1 week. Recently recorded story tapes: "Something's Up Down in Bethlehem," written by Janet McMahan-Wilson (ages 4-8, Christmas story), and "Out of This World," written By Janet McMahan and Rhett Parrish, narrated by Ragan Courtney (ages 4-8, fictional space adventure with Christian message).

THE CHILDREN'S GROUP, 17 Cadman Plaza West, Brooklyn NY 11201. (718)838-2544. FAX: (718)858-8976. President: Bob Hinkle. Personal management and record company firm. Estab. 1988.
Music: Works with composers, lyricists, team collaborators. Making contact: Submit cassette, VHS or ¾" videocassette and lyric sheet. Requirements: "Call to talk with us about who's recording and how the caller's material may fit those recording." Does not return unsolicited material. Reports in a matter of weeks.
Tips: Songwriters: "As an artist manager, a submission should be appropriate to the artist(s) in mind." Trends in children's music: "Becoming more sophisticated. Selling more. Careers developing just as in rock, pop, jazz, etc."

*CHILDREN'S LEARNING CENTER, 117 W. Rockland Rd, P.O. Box 615, Libertyville IL 60048. (708)362-4060. FAX: (708)362-4653. President: Perry Johnson. Music publisher and record company (Dharma, Future). Estab. 1968.
Music: Releases 3 singles/year; 5 12-inch singles/year; 3 LPs/year; 1 CD/year. Member of BMI. Publishes 5 children's songs/year. Works with team collaborators. For music published pays standard royalty of 50%; for songs recorded pays songwriters on royalty contract (percentage royalty paid). Making contact: Submit up to 5 cassette demo tapes and lyric sheets by mail; unsolicited submissions OK. SASE or IRC's for return of unsolicited submissions. Reports in 6 months. Recently recorded songs: "Who Are You," recorded by Bill Hooper (sing along); "Alligator," recorded by Bill Hooper (body movements); and "Race Around Your Body," recorded by Bill Hooper (sing along).
Stories: Publishes 1 book/cassette package/year; ages 3-8. Any genre nonfiction. Authors are paid in royalties 50% minimum. Making contact: Submit cassette tape of story. Reports on queries/mss 6 months. Recently recorded story tape: "Active Music for Children," by Bill Hooper (ages 3-8, learning).

*THE CHRISTIAN SCIENCE PUBLISHING SOCIETY, One Norway Street, Boston MA 02115. (617)450-2033. FAX: (617)450-2017. General Publications Product Manager: Rhoda M. Ford. Book publisher "but we do issue some recordings." Estab. 1898.
Music: Releases 2 audio cassettes/year; 1 CD/year. Hires staff writers for children's music. Works with team collaborators. Making contact: Submit demo cassettte tape by mail; unsolicited submissions OK. Send cover letter with proposal, references, résumé. Does not return unsolicited submissions. Reports in 3-4 weeks.
Tips: "Since we are part of The First Church of Christ, Scientist, all our publications are in harmony with the teachings of Christian Science."
Stories: Publishes 1-2 book/cassette packages/year; 1 audio tape/year. 100% of stories are nonfiction. Will consider nonfiction for beginning readers, juveniles, teens based on the Bible (King James Version). Authors are paid royalty or outright purchase of

Always include a self-addressed stamped envelope (SASE) or International Reply Coupon (IRC) with submissions.

manuscript, "negotiated with contract." Making contact: Submit outline/synopsis and sample chapters. Include Social Security number with submission. Reports on queries/mss in 3-4 weeks. Book catalog not available but in development. Recently published and recorded story tapes: "Everyday," Executive Producer, Rhoda M. Ford, narrated by various children (children's everyday activities in which they turn to God; for grade school); "Daniel in the Lions' Den," written by Jean Horton Berg, narrated by Ralph Camargo (Bible story, beginning readers); "The Story of Peter," written by Jean Horton Bert, narrated by Larry Weber (Bible story, beginning readers); and "The Story of Jesus," written by Jean Horton Berg, narrated by Derek and Judy Holmes (Bible story, beginning readers).
Tips: Trends: "Return to classics."

FRONTLINE MUSIC GROUP/FRONTLINE BOOKS, Box 28450, Santa Ana CA 92799. (714)660-3888. FAX: (714)755-6236. Executive Vice President: Brian Tong. Music publisher, record company, book publisher. Record labels include Broken Songs, Carlotta Music, Frontline Kids. Estab. 1985.
Music: Releases 80-100 singles/year; 40-50 LPs/year; 40-50 CDs/year. Member of ASCAP and BMI. Publishes and records 50-60 children's songs/year. Hires staff writers for children's music. Works with composers, lyricists, team collaborators. For music published pays standard royalty of 50%; for songs recorded pays musicians/artists on record contract, musicians on salary for inhouse studio work, and songwriters on royalty contract. Making contact: Submit cassette demo tape and lyric sheet by mail—unsolicited submissions OK. Requirements: only Christian material, no fantasy stuff. SASE for return of submissions. Reports in 3-4 weeks. Recently recorded songs: "Fruits of the Spirit," by Terry Taylor, recorded by Sunny Lovetree on the Frontline Kids label (children's music); and "Megamouth 1 & 2," by Terry Taylor, recorded by Megamouth on the Frontline Kids label (children's music).
Tips: Songwriters: "Submit fresh material that is relevant to today's issues. Trends in children's music: "Age groupings are becoming more specialized. There is a distinct difference in likes and dislikes between 6-10 and 10-13 year olds and 14-16 year olds."
Stories: Publishes 2-4 book/cassette packages/year. 100% of stories are fiction. Will consider fictional animal, fantasy, history, sports and spy/mystery/adventure stories aimed at all juvenile audiences "if Christian." Will consider nonfictional Bible stories aimed at all juvenile audiences. Authors are paid in royalties based on retail price. Making contact: Submit complete ms. SASE for return of ms. Reports on queries in 4-6 weeks; mss in 6-8 weeks. Book catalog, ms guidelines not available. Recently recorded story tapes: "Mouse Family Christmas," by Terry Taylor (ages 3-7), and "Harry Whodunit," by Terry Taylor (ages 5-11, mystery).
Tips: Writers: "Be unusual." Trends in children's reading material: "More sophistication."

*GORDON MUSIC CO. INC./PARIS RECORDS, P.O. Box 2250, Canoga Park CA 91306. (818)883-8224. Owner: Jeff Gordon. Music publisher, record company. Estab. 1950.
Music: Releases 3-4 CDs/year. Member of ASCAP and BMI. Publishes 6-8 children's songs/year; records 10-15 children's songs/year. Works with composers, lyricists, team collaborators. For music published pays standard royalty of 50%; for songs recorded, arrangement made between artist and company. Making contact: Call first and obtain permission to submit 3-4 videocassette tapes, lyric and lead sheets. Does not return unsolicited submissions. Recently recorded children's songs: "Toy Parde," written by Kahn/Lenard, recorded by Cabo Trio on MCA label; and "My Pal Sal," written by Champ, recorded by Kids 'R' Us on Paris label.

*HARCOURT BRACE JOVANOVICH, PUBLISHERS, 1250 Sixth Avenue, San Diego CA 92101. (619)699-6810. FAX: (619)699-6777. Senior Editor: Elizabeth Van Doren. Book publisher.
Music: Works with composers, lyrists, team collaborators. "We only publish book-and-cassette packages of our most successful back-list titles, and so accept no submissions. All our artists are solicited." Reports in 4-8 weeks. Recently recorded songs: "Into the Napping House" (6 songs), written and recorded by Carl and Jennifer Shaylen on HBJ Children's Books label (popular); "The Jolly Man" (Music and read-along), written by Michael Utley, recorded by Michael Utley and Robert Greenidge on HBJ Children's Books label (popular); and "Jump!" (Music and read-along; 1 song), written and recorded by Van Dyke Parks on HBJ Children's Books label (popular).
Tips: "Our children's book-and-cassette program is very limited at this time, and we're not apt to work with unknowns. We select musicians we feel are qualified, and approach them with our project. We are not yet looking for unsolicited submissions."
Stories: Publishes 3 book/cassette packages/year. 100% of stories are fiction aimed at ages 3-10. Method of payment "determined from our history with artist and individual project." Making contact: Submit complete manuscript, outline/synopsis and sample chapters; submit through agent only. Reports on queries in 2-4 weeks; reports on mss in 4-8 weeks. Book catalog for 9 × 12 SAE and 3 first class stamps. Recently published "Into the Napping House," written by Don and Audrey Wood, narrated by Carl and Jennifer Shaylen (ages 4-10); "The Jolly Man," written and narrated by Jimmy and Savannah Jane Buffett (ages 4-10); and "Jump!," written by Van Dyke Parks and Malcolm Jones, narrated by Whoopi Goldberg (ages 4-10).

*KIDZ & COMPANY, 333 SW Park Ave., Portland OR 97205. (503)227-3591. Contact: Sandra Louise. Estab. 1983.
Music: Releases 6 singles/year; 6 12-inch singles/year. Records 6 children's songs/year. Hires staff writers for children's music. Works with composers, lyricists, team collaborators. For music published pays standard royalty of 50%. Making contact: Submit demo cassette tape by mail; unsolicited submissions OK; write or call first and obtain permission to submit a tape; write or call to arrange a personal interview. Recently recorded songs: "Girls" and "Funky," all written by T.J. Galash, recorded by Aaron Walker on Kidz & Co. label (rap).

LARRCO IND. OF TX, INC., K-Larrco Satellite Radio and T.V. Div., Box 3842, Houston TX 77253-3842. President: Dr. L. Herbst. Music publisher, book publisher. Record labels include Beverly Hills Music Publishing, Total Sound Records, Lawrence Herbst Records, Beverly Hills Records, Larrco Records, Bestway Records, D.T.I Records.
Music: Member of BMI. Hires staff writers for children's music. Works with composers, lyricists, team collaborators. For music publishers pays standard royalty of 50%; for songs recorded pays musicians/artists on record contract, musicians on salary for in-house studio work, songwriters on 50% royalty contract. Making contact: Submit a 7½ IPS reel-to-reel tape or VHS videocassette with 3 minutes worth of song and a lyric or lead sheet by mail—unsolicited submissions are OK. SASE for return of submissions. Reports in 6 weeks.
Tips: "Submit professionally recorded works." Looks for "easy to understand lyrics on all labels."
Stories: Publishes 12 book/cassette packages/year. 3% of stories are fiction; 97% nonfiction. Will consider fictional animal, fantasy, history, adventure stories aimed at all ages. Will consider all genres of nonfiction aimed at "open" audience. Authors are paid in royalties of 50%. Making contact: submit complete ms or submit cassette tape of story. SASE for return of ms; include Social Security number with submission. Reports on queries in 2 weeks; mss in 4-12 weeks.

Tips: "Keep trying." Trends in children's reading material: "More of God's stories coming out."

OAK STREET MUSIC INC., 301-140 Bannatyne Ave., Winnipeg Manitoba R3B 3C5 Canada. (204)957-0085. FAX: (204)943-3588. Director of Marketing: Stephen Berofe. Music publisher, record company, book publisher. Record labels include Oak Street. Estab. 1987.
Music: Releases 10-15 LPs/year; 1-5 CDs/year. Member of CAPAC, PROCAN, CM-RRA, Harry Fox Agency. Publishes and records 100 children's songs/year. Hires staff writers for children's music. Works with composers, lyricists. Pays standard royalty of 50% for musicians/artists on record contract, musicians on salary for inhouse studio work, songwriters on royalty contract. Making contact: Submit a cassette demo tape or VHS videocassette with 3-5 songs and a lyric sheet by mail—unsolicited submissions are OK. Requirements: "A press kit is always helpful." Reports in 2 weeks. Recorded songs: "Sandwiches," "Sandwich Polka," The People on My Street," all written and recorded by Bob King on the Oak Street label (children's music).
Tips: Songwriters: "Insure the material is accessible by children and entertaining to *all* family members." Trends: "Recordings for children are becoming more sophisticated in terms of production and attitude towards children."
Stories: Publishes 1-2 book/cassette packages/year; 1-2 audio tapes/year. 100% of stories are fiction. Will consider fictional fantasy and adventure stories aimed at 2-10 year olds. Will consider nonfictional history, animal, biography stories aimed at 2-10 year olds. Authors are paid in negotiable royalties based on wholesale price. Making contact: Submit complete ms, cassette tape of story. SASE (IRC) for return of ms. Reports on queries in 2 weeks; mss in 2-3 weeks.
Tips: "Research various award-winning stories. Try to analyze the common factors, or the most interesting features of these titles." "A plethora of low material (re-workings of traditional stories) is now available. Try to select stories that are unique, unusual yet entertaining."

PETER PAN INDUSTRIES, 88 St. Francis St., Newark NJ 07105. (201)344-4214. FAX: (201)344-0465. Vice President of Sales: Shelly Rudin. Music publisher, record company. Record labels include Parade Music, Compose Music, Peter Pan. Estab. 1927.
Music: Releases 20 singles/year; 10 12-inch singles; 45 LPs/year; 45 CDs/year. Member of ASCAP and BMI. Publishes 50 children's songs/year; records 80-90 songs/year. Works with composers, lyricists, team collaborators. For music published pays standard royalty of 50%; for songs recorded pays musicians/artists on record contract, songwriters on royalty contract. Making contact: Submit a 15 IPS reel-to-reel demo tape or VHS videocassette by mail—unsolicited submissions OK. SASE (or SAE and IRCs) for return of submissions. Reports in 4-6 weeks.
Stories: Publishes 12 book/cassette packages/year. 90% of stories are fiction; 10% nonfiction. Will consider all genres of fiction and nonfiction aimed at 6 month olds to 9 year olds. Authors are paid in royalties based on wholesale price. Making contact: Query. Reports on queries in 4-6 weeks. Book catalog, manuscript guidelines free on request.
Tips: "Tough business but rewarding. Lullabies are very popular."

PRODUCTIONS DIADEM INC., C.P. 33 Pointe-Gatineau, Québec J8T 4Y8 Canada. (819)561-4114. President: Denyse Marleau. Record company. Record label Jouvence. Estab. 1982.
Music: Releases 1-2 LPs/year; 1-2 CDs/year. Member of CAPAC. Records 16-20 songs/year. Works with composers, lyricists. For songs recorded pays musicians/artists on record contract, musicians on salary for inhouse studio work, songwriters on 10% royalty contract. Making contact: Write first and obtain permission to submit a cassette tape

with 3 songs and a lyric sheet. SASE (or SAE and IRC's). Reports in 1 month. Recorded songs: "Vive l'hiver," by Marie Marleau, (children's contemporary music); "Chers grands-parents," by Denyse Marleau, (children's contemporary music); "Mon ami l'ordinateur," (children's popular music), all recorded by DIADEM on the Jouvence label.

RHYTHMS PRODUCTIONS/TOM THUMB MUSIC, Box 34485, Los Angeles CA 90034. (213)836-4678. President: R.S. White. Record company, cassette and book packagers. Record label, Tom Thumb – Rhythms Productions. Estab. 1955.
Music: Releases 4-6 LPs/year. Member of ASCAP. Records 4 albums/year. Works with composers and lyricists. For songs recorded pays musicians/artists on record contract, songwriters on royalty contract. Making contact: Submit a cassette demo tape or VHS videotape by mail – unsolicited submissions are OK. Requirements: "We accept musical stories. Must be produced in demo form, and must have educational content or be educationally oriented." Reports in 2 months. Recorded: *Prof. Whatzit & Carmine Cat Series*, written and produced by Dan Brown and Bruce Crook on the Tom Thumb label (musical stories). Other titles include: "The Deep Sea Adventure," "The Dinosaur Adventure," "The Space Adventure," and "The Rainmakers," all on Tom Thumb label (4 cassette and book packages.)

SILVER BURDETT & GINN, 250 James St., Morristown NJ 07960-1918. (201)285-8003. Music Editor: Donald Scafuri. Music textbook publisher, grades K-8 (each grade package contains a set of recordings). Estab. 1867.
Music: Member of ASCAP. Publishes and records 200 songs/year. Hires staff writers for children's music. Works with composers, lyricists, team collaborators. For music published pays standard mechanical royalty rate; $400 set fee per song (melody and lyrics). Write first and obtain permission to submit a cassette tape and lead sheet. SASE. Reports in 3 months. Recently recorded songs: "Whistle While You Work," by Morey/Churchill, recorded by the Houston Vocal Edition on the Silver Burdette & Ginn label (juvenile pop); "The Rainbow Connection," by Williams/Ascher, recorded by Brad Diamond on the Silver Burdett & Ginn label (pop, grade 5); "Those Magic Changes," by Casey/Jacobs, recorded by the Darrell Bledsoe Singers on the Silver Burdett & Ginn label (Broadway, grade 7).
Tips: "Songs should reflect the appropriate vocal range, rhythmic sophistication and style for a particular age level. Lyrics should also be age appropriate. The songwriter should become familiar with those types of songs that are most successful in a classroom setting. (Styles could include pop, folk, 2-or 3-part choral.)"

SIMON & SCHUSTER CHILDREN'S BOOKS, 1230 Ave. of the Americas, New York NY 10020. (212)698-7257. FAX: (212)698-7677. Marketing Director: Ken Geist. Book publisher. Estab. 1927.
Stories: Publishes 4 book/cassette packages/year. 100% of stories are fiction. "Storytapes are developed using Simon & Schuster best selling and award winning children's books." Books aimed at 3-8 year olds. Pays authors in royalties of 2%. Making Contact: Submit through agent only. Book catalog free on request. Recently recorded story tapes: *Strega Nona*, by Tomie DePaola and narrated by Dom DeLuise ("Grandmother Witch" is the source of all kinds of magic in her little town; a Caldecott Honor Book aimed at 4-9 year olds); *The Velveteen Rabbit*, by Margery Williams and narrated by Kim Hunter (a children's classic aimed at 6-10 year olds); *Pumpkinville Mystery*, by Bruce Cole and narrated by Fred Gwynne (a thrilling Halloween tale of mystery, magic and suspense aimed at 6-9 year olds).

*TEXAS STAR INTERNATIONAL/LONNY TUNES MUSIC, B.M.I., P.O. Box 460086, Garland TX 75046. President: Lonny Schonfeld. Music publisher, record company. Record labels include Lollipop Farm. Estab. 1987.

Music: Releases 2 singles and 2 LPs/year. Member of BMI. Publishes and records 3-6 children's songs/year. Works with composers, team collaborators. For music published pays standard royalty of 50%. For songs recorded pays musicians on salary for inhouse studio work. Making contact: Submit demo cassette tape with no more than 3 songs and lyric sheet by mail. Looking for "stories and songs with 'positive' endings." Reports in 6-8 weeks. Recently recorded songs: "The Little Bitty Chicken," written by Charles Goodman (animal story).
Stories: Publishes 2 audiotapes/year. 100% of stories are fiction. Will consider fictional animal, fantasy, everyday life occurrences (kids, ages 2-12). Authors are paid in royalties. BMI method of payment: 50% of publishing rights. Making contact: Submit cassette tape of story. Reports on queries/mss in 6-8 weeks. Manuscript guidelines for legal size SAE and 1 first class stamp.

WATCHESGRO MUSIC PUBLISHING CO., BMI. Watch Us Climb, ASCAP. Box 1794, Big Bear City CA 92314. (714)585-4645. President: Eddie Lee Carr. Music publisher, record company. Record labels include Interstate 20 Records, Tracker Records. Estab. 1970.
Music: Releases 10 singles/year; 5 12-inch singles/year; 1 LP/year; 1 CD/year. Publishes 15 children's songs/year; records 4 children's songs/year. Works with composers, lyricists. For music published pays standard royalty of 50%; for songs recorded pays musicians/artists on record contract, musicians on salary for inhouse studio work. Making contact: Write or call first and obtain permission to submit a cassette tape. Does not return unsolicited material. Reports in 1 week. Published songs: "Little Girls," by D.C. McKinnon, recorded by Donna Cox on the Interstate 20 Records label (children's music); "Little Boys," by Donna Cox, recorded by Donna Cox on the Tracker Records label (children's music); "My House," by Donna Cox/D.C. McKinnon, recorded by Donna Cox on the Tracker label (children's music).

*WILSON RECORDS, 200 S. Glenn Dr., 555# D, Camarillo CA 93010. (805)987-3058; (805)389-1585. President/Owner: Morris Lee Wilson. Music publisher, record company. Estab. 1972.
Music: Releases 20 singles/year; 2 12-inch singles/year; 10 LPs/year; 10 CDs/year. Member of BMI. Publishes and records 5 children's songs/year. Hires staff writers for children's music. Works with composers, lyricists, team collaborators. For music published pays standard royalty of 50%; for songs recorded pays musicians/artists on record contract, musicians on salary for inhouse studio work and songwriters on royalty contract (percentage royalty paid: 50%). Making contact: Submit demo cassette or videocassette with lyric and lead sheet; write or call first and obtain permission to submit a tape. "Songs should be for children, not about children. Be innovative. Try new approaches. And work to keep a fresh song." Reports in 12 days. Recently recorded songs: "Just Say No," written by Morris Wilson/Malusine Moore, recorded by Morris Lee Wilson on Fan Fair Records label (country); and "Happy Birthday," written and recorded by Morris Wilson on Emma Banks Records label.
Tips: "Use quality cassettes. Have all songs submitted set to words and music on lead sheet and a copyright. Songs I like should be upbeat and unique in subject matter. Make sure your lyrics sound good without music. Have a strong story line and send only your best efforts.
Stories: Publishes 2 book/cassette packages/year; 10 audio tapes/year. 70% of stories are fiction; 30% are nonfiction. Will consider fictional animal, fantasy, sports aimed at ages 7-12; nonfictional education, history, sports aimed at ages 9-16. Authors are paid in royalties: 25% minimum, 50% maximum. Making contact: Query; submit outline/synopsis and sample chapters; submit cassette tape of story. Include Social Security number with submission. Reports on queries/mss in 3 weeks. Book catalog and manuscript guidelines free on request. Recently recorded story tapes: "U-B-U," written and

narrated by Morris Lee Wilson (ages 7-12, being yourself); "Me, Me, Me," narrated by Malusine Moore (ages 5-10, helping others); "Let's Talk," written and narrated by Morris Lee Wilson (ages 8-16, talking).

*WORLD LIBRARY PUBLICATIONS INC., 3815 N. Willow Rd., Schiller Park IL 60176. (708)678-0621. Editorial Director: Nicholas T. Freund. Music publisher. Estab. 1945. **Music:** Publishes 10-12 children's songs/year. Works with composers. For music published pays 10% of sales. Making contact: Submit demo cassette tape by mail; unsolicited submissions OK. "Should be religious. We are primarily a Roman Catholic publisher." Reports in 90 days. Recently published children's songs: "Let the Children Come to Me," written and recorded by James V. Marchconda on WLP cassette 7845 label (religious/catechetical); "Gather You Children," written by Peter Finn and James Chepponis (religious/catechetical); and "Mass of the Children of God," written by James V. Marchionda on WLP Cassette 7664 label (liturgical).

Many children, craving attention, seek the spotlight of the stage. In addition, children as viewers enjoy watching their peers perform live. Schools and churches are always providing theatrical outlets for their youth and appreciate good scripts.

When writing plays for children, keep in mind who the thespians will be. Are you writing a play for children to perform, or are you writing a children's play where adults will play the lead characters? This section contains markets soliciting material to be performed by both children and adults. Note that the listings contain percentages to help you determine whether adult or child actors are in demand for these roles.

Also study the listings to pick up on variations on format required by various markets. Deedra Bébout says in a close-up interview in this section many writers who submit to her misunderstand that she publishes plays, when actually she publishes prose stories written in script form. Determining publishers' and theaters' needs is pertinent.

More than ever before, the U.S. population is comprised of a wider multitude of ethnic subcultures. Scriptwriters should keep this in mind and recognize there might be a better chance at selling a script which reflects this racial diversity.

Since many theater groups produce plays on limited budgets, scripts containing elaborate staging and costumes might not be as appealing to them. Some publishers will have catalogs available so you can become more familiar with the type of work typically used.

Payment for playwrights will usually come in the form of royalties, outright sums or a combination of both. The pay scale isn't going to be quite as high as screen play rates, but writers within this profession have the added enjoyment of seeing their work performed live by a variety of groups employing a multitude of interpretations.

BAKER'S PLAYS, 100 Chauncy St., Boston MA 02111. (617)482-1280. FAX: (617)482-7613. Editor: John B. Welch. Estab. 1845. Publishes 5-8 children's plays/year; 2-4 children's musicals/year. 80% of plays/musicals written for adult roles; 20% for juvenile roles. Subject matter: "Touring shows for 5-8 year olds, full lengths for family audience and full lengths for teens." Recently published plays: _Wizard's Crystal_, by Paul Otteson (ages 8-adult), _Michel_, by Charles Webb (ages 6-12). Submission method: Submit complete ms, score and tape of songs. Reports in 4 months. Rights obtained on mss: worldwide rights. Pays writers in royalties (amount varies) or $10-100/performance.

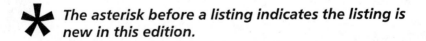 **The asterisk before a listing indicates the listing is new in this edition.**

Tips: "Looking for writers for the theater, not frustrated poets or novelists." Wants "honest, committed material dealing with today's issues."

*CHILDREN'S STORY SCRIPTS, Baymax Productions, 2219 W. Olive Ave., Suite 130, Burbank CA 91506. (818)563-6105. FAX: (818)563-2968. Editor: Deedra Bébout. Estab. 1990. Produces 30 children's scripts/year. "Except for small movements and occasionally standing up, children remain seated in Readers Theatre fashion." Publishes scripts sold to schools, camps, churches, scouts, hotels, cruise lines, etc. Wherever there's a program to teach to or entertain children. "All roles read by children except K-2 scripts. Then kids have easy lines, leader reads the narration." Subject matter: Scripts on all subjects. Targeted age range—K-8th grade, 5-13 years old. Recently published: *The Determined Maiden*, by Helen Ksypka—trying to accomplish one's goals, no matter how low the odds, for grades 5-8; *The Rain Turtle*, by Marsha Moore—Indian customs of the Lakota tribe, for grades 4-7; *Yuck-Yuck, The Different Duck*, by Ruth Kelley—discrimination, for grades K-2. No "sweet, syrupy, predictable stories." Accepts simultaneous submissions. Submissions method: submit complete manuscript. Reports in 2 weeks. Rights obtained on mss: All rights in story script form; authors retain copyrights. Pays writers in royalties; 10-15% on sliding scale, based on retail price. SASE for return of submission.
Tips: "Children's Story Scripts are essentially *prose* stories broken into parts. Descriptive narration is mixed with character dialogue. The scripts are meant to be read aloud. All the children enter at the beginning and remain in place throughout the performance. We do not hit the kids over the head with the moral or purpose of the story in the scripts. We provide discussion questions which can be used after the performance to address the purpose of the story. Writer's guidelines packet available for business-sized SASE with two first-class stampes. Guidelines explain what Children's Story Scripts are, give four-page examples from two different scripts, give list of suggested topics for scripts."

CIRCA '21 DINNER THEATRE, P.O. Box 3784, Rock Island IL 61204-3784. (309)786-2667. Producer: Dennis Hitchcock. Estab. 1977. Produces 2-3 children's plays/year; 1-2 children's musicals/year. "Prefer a cast no larger than 12." Produces children's plays for professional productions. 95% of plays/musicals written for adult roles; 5% written for juvenile roles. Recently produced plays: *Cinderella, Emperor's New Clothes* and *Jack and the Beanstalk*, all by Prince St. Players. Submission method: query with synopsis, character breakdown, tape and set description. Reports in 3 months. Payment negotiable.

CONTEMPORARY DRAMA SERVICE, Division of Meriwether Publishing Ltd., 885 Elkton Dr., Colorado Springs CO 80907. (719)594-4422. Editor: Arthur Zapel. Estab. 1969. Publishes 35-40 children's plays/year; 3 children's musicals/year. 15% of plays/musicals written for adult roles; 85% for juvenile roles. Recently published plays: *Hollywood Hotel*, by Tim Kelly—comedy three-act spoof for teens; *The Way It Is*, by Lucile McIntyre—a play about the realities of being a high school student; *Would You Believe . . . A Stable?*—a musical play for Christmas. "We do not publish plays for elementary level except for church plays for Christmas and Easter. All of our secular plays are for teens or college level." Submission method: query with synopsis, character breakdown and set description; "query first if a musical." Rights obtained on mss: all first rights. Payment varies according to type: royalty or purchase.

Refer to the Business of Children's Writing & Illustrating for up-to-date marketing, tax and legal information.

Close-up

Deedra Bébout
Editor
Children's Story Scripts
Burbank, California

"We're out to nurture the minds and souls of kids without their even noticing," says Deedra Bébout about the purpose of her company, Children's Story Scripts. Children's Story Scripts are Readers Theatre-style scripts. In other words, the story parts are divided among a number of children who read aloud from the script. Bébout says her scripts work in any setting. Besides schools, she markets them to churches, parks, recreation centers and summer camps.

Bébout's inspiration for Children's Story Scripts came from a friend in Canada who started writing scripts from fairy tales. "She asked me if I wanted to do some. I wrote eight scripts which were published in Canada. I had a lot of ideas about what scripts should be, so I formed my own company."

First and foremost, says Bébout, these stories are written to encourage kids to read. Varying parts in each script allow for those who are slower readers to participate with others, which in turn inspires confidence, encourages self expression, and promotes group interaction. Also, each script has a purpose, whether it be teaching a moral or ethic, or explaining a different lifestyle or culture. Topics can be frivolous or serious, but not preachy.

"We never 'hit the kids over the head' with the purpose of the story. The facts are disguised in the story so it's not just a dull boring list of facts," she says. "We like to let the leader talk about (the purpose of the story) afterward with a group discussion." A list of discussion questions comes in each package.

Bébout says writers who submit to her tend to misunderstand the format she's looking for. "They think they're plays and they're not. They are prose stories disguised as something else." The scripts differ from traditional theater in that they blend narration and character dialogue. "They read past tense as stories do but then the dialogue brings it into the present." The stories are not meant to be memorized, and they should be written with no elaborate staging.

Bébout says she gets 30-50 submissions a week. Publishing history of submittors is irrelevant. She notes she has accepted material from award-winning writers, but she has also accepted manuscripts from writers who have never been published. "There's always a need for material for the little tiny kids, kindergarten through second grade." Material for this age category has to have a plot, but can't be "syrupy-sweet," she says. "I think they're the most difficult category. Text has to be simple, but not simple-minded. Even kids that age are very sophisticated today."

In addition to being editor of Children's Story Scripts, Bébout also writes. Her former careers landed her in the radio and television businesses. She ended up doing sound effects for CBS at a time when gender quotas were all she needed to get started and she spent three years doing sound effects for the NBC daytime drama Santa Barbara. Although this is a far cry from her current profession, Bebout says she picked up writing skills through doing newsletters, one-liners, greeting cards and poems for friends and family.

So what makes her qualified to attempt such a venture as writing for children? "A combination of reasons; actually three—my love of the written word in stories, my theatrical background, and my deep respect for children. I just feel this is my contribution in life."

—Lisa Carpenter

THE COTERIE, 2450 Grand, Kansas City MO 64108. (816)474-6785. Artistic Director: Jeff Church. Estab. 1978. Produces 7 children's plays/year; 2 children's musicals/year. "Prefer casts of between 5-7, no larger than 15. Props and staging should be relatively simple." Produces children's plays for professional productions. 80% of plays/musicals written for adult roles; 20% for juvenile roles. "We do *not* produce puppet shows, although we may use puppets in our plays. We produce original plays, musicals and literary adaptations for ages 5 through adult." Recently produced plays: *Great Expectations*, by Barbara Field (from Charles Dickens)—a classic novel for 10 year old through adult; *Takunda*, by Charles Smith—deals with race relations and apartheid and aimed at 12 year old through adult; *Dirty Beasts*, by Judy Yeckel/Cheryl Benge (from Roald Dahl)—about friendship and intended for a 5 year old through adult audience. "We do *not* want to see 'camp' adaptations of fairytales." Submission method: query with synopsis, character breakdown and set description. Reports in 3 weeks. Rights obtained on mss: "negotiable." Pays writers in royalties; buys material outright for $500-1,500; pays $20-35/performance. SASE for return of submission.
Tips: There are "smaller casts, simpler staging requirements, strong thematic, character and plot development, 'risky' issues; (i.e. teen pregnancy, substance abuse, race relations, etc.). There is a need for non-condescending material for younger age groups (5-8) and for middle school (ages 9-13). Fairytales are fine, but they should be straightforward and non-condescending."

DRAMATIC PUBLISHING, INC., 311 Washington St., Woodstock IL 60098. (815)338-7170. Publishes plays and musicals for children and young adults. Submission method: send script, (with a cassette if a musical) and include an SASE if wish to have manuscript returned. Reports in 3-4 months. Pays writers in royalties.
Tips: Scripts should be from ½ to 1½ hours long, and not didactic or condescending. Original plays dealing with hopes, joys and fears of today's children are preferred to adaptations of old classics.

ELDRIDGE PUBLISHING CO. INC., P.O. Box 216, Franklin OH 45005. (513)746-6531. Editor: Nancy Vorhis. Estab. 1906. Publishes approximately 20 children's plays/year (5-8 for elementary; 10-12 for junior and senior high); 2-3 children's musicals/year. Prefers simple staging; flexible cast size. We "publish for elementary, middle, junior and high school, all genres." Published plays: *Frumpled Fairy Tales*, by Bill Springer, humorous retelling of 3 fairy tales, for elementary audience; *Louder Than Words*, by Linda Dumas, a collection of mimes for junior high students; *It's A Howl*, by Tim Kelley, a humorous

3-act play for high audiences. Does not want to see "anything suggestive; anything with a subject matter that is too mature." Submission method: submit complete ms, score and tape of songs (if a musical). Reports in 2 months. Rights obtained on mss: all dramatic rights. Pays writers 10% of copy sales or 35% of royalties; buys material outright for $150-300.

Tips: "We always need material which offers flexible casting; parts which can be played by boys or girls or 'group' parts which may include one or several students. We like upbeat themes with humor and physical action."

SAMUEL FRENCH, INC., 45 W. 25th St., New York NY 10010. (212)206-8990. FAX: (212)206-1429. Editor: Lawrence Harbison. Estab. 1830. Publishes 2 or 3 children's plays/year; "variable number of musicals." Subject matter: "All genres, all ages. No puppet plays." Recently published plays/musicals: *No More Secrets*, by Paul Lenzi and Geraldine Snyder—musical about child abuse; *The Gemshield Sleeper*, by Richard Slocum—sci-fi; *The Love Song of A. Nellie Goodrock*, by Richard Slocum—"mellerdrammer." "No adaptations of any of those old 'fairy tales.' No 'Once Upon a time, long ago and far away.' No kings, princesses, fairies, trolls, etc." Submission method: submit complete ms and demo tape (if a musical). Reports in 2-8 months. Rights obtained on mss: "Publication rights, amateur and professional production rights, option to publish next 3 plays." Pay for writers: "book royalty 10%; professional production royalty: 90%; amateur production royalty: 80%." SASE for return of submissions.

Tips: "Children's theater is a very tiny market, as most groups perform plays they have created themselves or have commissioned."

*GREAT AMERICAN CHILDREN'S THEATRE COMPANY, P.O. Box 92123, Milwaukee WI 53202. (414)276-4230. Artistic Director: Teri Solomon Mitze. Estab. 1975. Produces 1 children's play/year. Produces children's plays for professional productions; 100% written for adult roles.

HONOLULU THEATRE FOR YOUTH, 2846 Ualena St., Honolulu HI 96819. (808)839-9885. FAX: (808)839-7018. Acting Artistic Director: Pamela Sterling. Estab. 1955. Produces 6 children's plays/year. Subject matter: Looks for plays "celebrating cultures of the Pacific Rim, especially. Also, plays that deal with issues of concern to today's young audiences (varying in age from 6-18)." Submission method: query first with cast requirements and synopsis. SASE required for each script requested.

Tips: "Adaptations of published fiction for children to play form are the most frequently accepted types; queries could produce commissions to proceed with an adaptation, or possibly even an original work if it meets our needs and agrees with our philosophy."

*THE NEW CONSERVATORY CHILDREN'S THEATRE COMPANY & SCHOOL, 25 Van Negs Ave., San Francisco CA 94102. (415)861-4914. Executive Director: Ed Decker. Estab. 1981. Produces 6-10 children's plays/year; 3-5 children's musicals/year. Youth ages 4-19, a limited budget. Produces children's plays for "A professional theater arts training program for youths ages 4-19 during the school year and a summer session. The New Conservatory also produces educational plays for its touring company." 100% written for juvenile roles. Produced: *Earthmatters*, by Sunny Disney-Fitzchett—environmental and global concerns for 9-adults; *Get Real*, by Doug Holsclaw—AIDS education for ages 9-12; produced and published *The Inner Circle*, by Patricia Loughrey—AIDS education for ages 13-19. "We do not want to see socially relevant work." Submission method: query first; submit complete manuscript and score. Reports in 3 months. Rights obtained on mss: "negotiable." Pays writers in royalties. SASE for return of submission.

Tips: Trends: "Addressing socially relevant issues for young people and their families."

NEW YORK STATE THEATRE INSTITUTE, (formerly Patricia B. Snyder) P.A.C. 266 1400 Washington Ave., Albany NY 12223. (518)443-5222. FAX: (518)442-5318. Acting Artistic Director: Ed Lange. Estab. 1976. Produces 1-2 children's plays and 1-2 children's musicals/year. Produces family plays for professional theater. 90% of plays/musicals are written for adult roles; 10% for juvenile roles. Recently produced children's plays: *The Snow Queen*, by Adrian Mitchell and Richard Peaslee—deals with rite of passage, for a family audience; *Knockabout Boy*, by William A. Frankonis—deals with rite of passage, for a family audience; *Pied Piper*, by Adrian Mitchell and Dominick Muldowney—social commentary, for a family audience. Does not want to see plays for children only. Submission method: submit complete ms and tape of songs (if a musical). Reports in 2-3 months. Rights obtained on mss: "varies." Pay for writers: "fees vary in nature and in degree." SASE for return of submission.
Tips: Writers should be mindful of "audience *sophistication!*"

PIONEER DRAMA SERVICE, P.O. Box 22555, Denver CO 80222. (303)759-4297. FAX: (303)759-0475. Editor: Steven Fendrich. Estab. 1960. Publishes 7 children's plays/year; 2 children's musicals/year. Subject matter: Publishes plays for ages 9-high school. Recently published plays/musicals: *Nutcracker*, by Patrick R. Dorn & Bill Francoeur—unique Christmas musical for ages 10 and up; *The Empty Chair*, by Tim Kelly—one-act anti-drug drama for teens and up; *A Little Bit of Magic*, by Gail and Grant Golden—small cast musical ideal for touring for audiences 5 and up; casts 10 and up. Does not want to see "script, scores, tapes, pics and reviews." Submission method: query with synopsis, character breakdown and set description. Reports in 2 months. Rights obtained on mss: all rights. Pays writers in royalties (10% on sales, 50% royalties on productions); or buys material outright for $200-1,000.

*PITTSBURGH PLAYHOUSE JR., 222 Craft Ave., Pittsburgh PA 15213. (412)621-4445. Director: Wayne Brinda. Estab. 1949. Produces 5 children's plays/year; 1 children's musical/year. Produces children's plays for semi-professional with a college theater department: 95% of plays/musicals written for adult roles; 5% written for juvenile roles. Produced *Treasure Island*, by Fred Gaines—adapted form of novel for ages 3-14; *Snow White*, by Nick and Acaddin Dimartino—classic fairy tale for ages 3-14; *Ballad of Robin Hood*, by Michael McGovern—classic tale for ages 3-14; *Red Riding Hood* (musical) by Colette Silvestri, for ages 3-9. Does not want to see "strong social problem plays." Submissions method: query with synopsis, character breakdown and set description; first drafts. Reports in 3 weeks. Rights obtained on mss: "performance rights—negotiable." Pays writers commission/royalty.

PLAYERS PRESS, INC., P.O. Box 1132, Studio City CA 91614-0132. (818)789-4980. Vice President: R. W. Gordon. Estab. 1965. Publishes 5-25 children's plays/year; 2-15 children's musicals/year. Subject matter: "We publish for all age groups." Recently published plays/musicals: *Redclouds Revenge*, by William Hellep—play for grades 5-10; *Seven With One Blow*, by Robin Lee Sweeney—play for grades 3-7; *Raponzel N' the Witch*, by William-Alan Landes—musical for grades for 4-12. Submission method: query with synopsis, character breakdown and set description; include #10 envelope SASE with query. Reports in 3 months. Rights obtained on mss: stage, screen, TV rights. Payment varies; outright purchases are available upon written request.
Tips: "Entertainment quality is on the upswing and needs to be directed at the world, no longer just the USA."

PLAYS, THE DRAMA MAGAZINE FOR YOUNG PEOPLE, 120 Boylston St., Boston MA 02116. (617)423-3157. Managing Editor: Elizabeth Preston. Estab. 1941. Publishes 70-75 children's plays/year. "Props and staging should not be overly elaborate or costly. Our plays are performed by children in school." 100% of plays written for juvenile roles.

Subject matter: Audience is lower grades through junior/senior high. Recently published plays: *Mother for Mayor*, about a woman who has to balance politics and family, aimed at junior and senior high audiences; *Penelope, Pride of the Pickle Factory*, a melodrama set at the turn of the century, by Betty Tracey Huff, for junior/senior high; *Moby Dick*, by Adele Thane—dramatization of the Herman Melville classic, for junior and senior high audiences. Send "nothing downbeat—no plays about drugs, sex or other 'heavy' topics." Submission methods: query first on adaptations of folk tales and classics; otherwise submit complete ms. Reports in 2-3 weeks. Rights obtained on mss: all rights. Pay rates vary, on acceptance. Guidelines available; send SASE. Sample copy $3.

Tips: "Above all, plays must be entertaining for young people with plenty of action and a satisfying conclusion."

PLAYS FOR YOUNG AUDIENCES, P.O. Box 22555, Denver CO 80222. (303)759-4297. FAX: (303)759-0475. Editor: Steven Fendrich. Estab. 1989. Publishes 3 children's plays/year; 1 children's musical/year. Subject matter: Publishes plays for preschool-8th grade audience. Recently produced plays: *A Little Bit of Magic*, by Gail and Grant Golden—audiences pre-school and up—small cast musical, ideal for touring; *The Dancing Snowman*, by R. Eugene Jackson and Carl Alette, audiences pre-school and up, cast-10 and up—musical; *Nutcracker*, by Patrick R. Dorn and Bill Francoeur, ages 10 and up—unique Christmas musical. Does not want to see script, score, tape, pictures and reviews. Submission method: query first; query with synopsis, character breakdown and set description. Reports in 2 months. Rights obtained on mss: all rights. Pays writers in royalties of 10% in sales, 50% on productions; or buys material outright for $200-1,000.

STAGE ONE: THE LOUISVILLE CHILDREN'S THEATRE, 425 W. Market, Louisville KY 40202. (502)589-5946. FAX: (502)589-5779. Producing Director: Moses Goldberg. Estab. 1946. Produces 10 children's plays/year 1-3 children's musicals/year. Stage One is an equity company producing children's plays for professional productions. 100% of plays/musicals written for adult roles. "Sometimes do use students in selected productions." Recently produced plays: *Vasilsa*, by Moses Goldberg—fairy tale for 4-8 year old audiences; *Glass Menagerie*, by Tennessee Williams—deals with family tension, for a 12 year old through adult audience; *Odyssey*, by Greg Falls and Kent Beattie—a classic poem for 8-12 year old audiences. Submission method: submit complete ms, score and tape of songs (if a musical); include the author's résumé if desired. Reports in 3-4 months. Pays writers in royalties or per performance.

Tips: Looking for "stageworthy and respectful dramatizations of the classic tales of childhood, both ancient and modern; plays relevant to the lives of young people and their families; and plays directly related to the school curriculum."

TADA!, 120 West 28th St., New York NY 10001. (212)627-1732. Co-Artistic Directors: Janine Trevens and James Learned. Estab. 1984. Produces 3-4 children's plays/year; 3-4 children's musicals/year. "All actors are children, ages 6-17." Produces children's plays for professional, year-round theater. 100% of plays/musicals written for juvenile roles. Recently produced plays: *Sleepover*, by James Beloff and Philip Freedman, is an hour-long musical of the adventures during a sleepover party, for ages 2 through adult; *Wide Awake Jake*, by Alice Elliott, Robby Merkin and Faye Greenberg—boy learning to fall asleep, for ages 2 through adult; *Apt. 3*, by Davidson Lloyd—boys seek source of music in their apartment building, for ages 2 through adult. Submission method: query with synopsis, character breakdown and set description; submit complete ms, score and tape of songs (if a musical). Reports in 3 months. Rights obtained on mss: "Depends on the piece." Pays writers in royalties.

Tips: "Too many authors are writing productions, not plays. Our company is multiracial and city-oriented. We are not interested in fairy tales."

THEATRE FOR YOUNG AMERICA, 7204 W. 80th St., Overland Park KS 66204. (913)648-4600. Artistic Director: Gene Mackey. Estab. 1974. Produces 10 children's plays/year; 3-5 children's musicals/year. We use a "small cast (4-7), open thrust stage." Theatre for Young America is a professional equity company. 80% of plays/musicals written for adult roles; 20% for juvenile roles. Recently produced plays: *The Wizard of Oz*, by Jim Eiler and Jeanne Bargy—for ages 6 and up; *A Partridge in a Pear Tree*, by Lowell Swortzell—deals with the 12 days of Christmas, for ages 6 and up; *Three Billy Goats Gruff*, by Gene Mackey and Molly Jessup—Norwegian folk tales, for ages 6 and up. Submission method: query with synopsis, character breakdown and set description. Reports in 2 months. Rights obtained on mss: "production, tour rights in local area." Pays writers in royalties or $10-50/per performance.
Tips: Looking for "cross-cultural material that respects the intelligence, sensitivity and taste of the child audience."

*THEATRE-IN-THE-SCHOOLS, INC., The New England Touring Theatre, 220 East 4th St. Suite 3-2, New York NY 10009. (212)533-0416. Artistic Director: Timothy Jeffryes. Estab. 1983. Produces 1 children's play/year. 2-4 person shows, tourable, 15-30 minute set-up and breakdown. Produces for professional touring theater. 100% of plays/musicals written for adult roles. Recently produced children's plays: *Sweetwater*, by Wm. S. Leavengood—substance abuse for grades 4-10; *Folktales of Africa*, by Wm. S. Leavengood—folktales of Africa for grades 1-6; *The Road to the Constitution*, by Wm. S. Leavengood—constitution for grades 3-8. "We do not want to see musicals, large cast shows, heavy technical shows. Accepts simultaneous submissions; electronic submissions via disk or modem. Submission method: query with synopsis, character breakdown and set description. Reports in 6 months. Rights obtained on mss: "varies." Pays writers 4% royalty; outright purchase of $500-2,000.

THE YOUNG COMPANY, P.O. Box 225, Milford NH 03055. (603)673-4005. Associate Director/Literary Manager: Austin Tichenor. Estab. 1984. Produces 10-12 children's plays/year; 1-2 children's musicals/year. "Scripts should not be longer than an hour, small cast preferred; very small production budgets, so use imagination." The Young Company is a professional training program associated with American Stage Festival, a professional theater. Produced plays/musicals: *Dancing on the Ceiling*, by Austin Tichenor—adaptation of Kafka's *Metamorphosis*, for ages 7 and up; *High Pressure Zone*, music by Andrew Howard, book and lyrics by Austin Tichenor—musical about addictive behavior, for middle school and older audience; *The First Olympics*, by Eve Muson and Austin Tichenor—deals with mythology/Olympic origins, for 6 year old through adult audience. Does not want to see condescending material. Submission method: Query with synopsis, character breakdown and sample score. Rights obtained on mss: first production credit on all future materials. Pays small fee and housing for rehearsals.
Tips: Looks for "concise and legible presentation, songs that further dramatic action. Develop material with strong marketing possibilities. See your work in front of an audience and be prepared to change it if your audience doesn't 'get it.' Don't condescend to your audience. Tell them a *story*."

Special Markets

Children's coloring books, comics and greeting cards are some of the needs of the markets in this section. Because of this potpourri of demands, this section is appropriately named "special markets."

Though this section still remains small, the fact the number of listings has more than tripled from last year indicates this may be a profitable market over the long term. In addition to carrying books, children's bookstores also stock greeting cards, paper products, coloring books and educational games.

As with any section of this book, read through the listings carefully to determine subject needs and methods of submission. Since there is a variety of product needs represented by each company the materials requested for review will vary greatly.

*AMCAL, 1050 Shary Court, Concord CA 94518. (415)689-9930. FAX: (415)689-0108. Editor/Art Director: Jennifer DeCristoforo. Estab. 1975. 80% of material written and 100% illustrated by freelancers. Buys 10 freelance projects/year; receives 150 submissions/year. Greeting card lines: calendars, desk diaries, boxed Christmas cards, gift bags, ornaments, rubber stamps. AMCAL publishes high quality full color, narrative and decorative art for a wide market from traditional to contemporary. We are currently seeking delightful illustrations and verses for greeting cards. Juvenile illustration should have some adult appeal. We don't publish cartoon, humorous or gag art, or bold graphics. We sell to small, exclusive gift retailers." Greeting cards: "unrhymed, with a simple, direct sentiment."
Making Contact & Terms: "Submissions are always accepted for future lines." Reports in 1 month. Pays on acceptance. Pay negotiable/usually advance on royalty. Guideline sheets for #10 SASE and 1 first class stamp.

*A/V CONCEPTS CORP., 30 Montauk Blvd., Oakdale NY 11769. (516)567-7227. FAX: (516)567-5908. Art Director: Philip Solimene. Estab. 1969. 100% of material written and illustrated by freelancers. Buys 25 freelance projects/year; receives 100 submissions/year. Children's educational publications.
Making Contact & Terms: Reports in 10 days. Pays on publication. Writer's/illustrator's guidelines free.
Tips: Target age group: K-12.

*bePUZZLED/LOMBARD MARKETING, INC., 45 Wintonbury Avenue, Bloomfield CT 06002. (203)286-4226. FAX: (203)286-4229. Editor/Art Director: Luci Seccareccia. Estab. 1987. 100% written and illustrated by freelancers. Buys 10 freelance projects/year. Puzzles and/or games: mystery jigsaw puzzle games. Needs "to be announced via mail to list of interested freelancers."

 The asterisk before a listing indicates the listing is new in this edition.

Making Contact & Terms: Submit special puzzles in March-April for Christmas. Reports in 2-6 weeks. Material copyrighted. Purchases all rights. Pays on acceptance. Pay for puzzles $200-1,000. Writer's guideline sheet for #10 SAE and 45¢ in stamps.
Tips: Target age group: 4-6 years; 7-10 years; ages 12-adult.

*BLACKBIRD COMICS, P.O. 3211, Austin TX 78764. (512)445-5087. Editor/Art Director: John Nordland II. Estab. 1985. 100% of material written and illustrated by freelancers. Buys 3 freelance projects/year; receives 20-50 submissions/year. Comic books: creative, original, intelligently written work. Needs back up series, lettering and inking.
Making Contact & Terms: Submit seasonal comic books 6 mos-1 year in advance. Reports in 3-4 weeks. Material copyrighted. Purchases 1st & 2nd printing rights. Pays on publication. Pay for comic books is $10-50 per page (or 50% of net profit). Guideline sheet for #10 SAE and 1 first-class stamp.
Tips: Looking for superhero/action adventure/science fiction comic books. Target age group: 13 and up. Also looking for good humor books.

*BRILLIANT ENTERPRISES, 117 W. Valerio St., Santa Barbara CA 93101. Art Director: Ashleigh Brilliant. Estab. 1967. Greeting cards: wide range of humorous concepts. Greeting cards: unrhymed.
Making Contact & Terms: Reports in 3 weeks. Material copyrighted. Purchases all rights. Pays on acceptance. Pay for greeting cards $40 minimum. Writer's/illustrator's guidelines sheet for $2 and SAE.

*C.J. PUBLICATIONS, 13 Hunter, Irvine CA 92720. (714)857-9520. Art Director: C.J. Bentz-Connor. Estab. 1990. 85% of material freelance written; 95% of material freelance illustrated. Produces greeting cards (cartoon, realistic animals, fairytales, etc.), coloring books (innovative, non-traditional art) and educational puzzles and games.
Making Contact & Terms: Submit seasonal/holiday material 7 months in advance for greeting cards, 10 months in advance for coloring books, and 1 year in advance for special games and puzzles. SASE for return of submissions. Reports in 2 weeks. Pays on publication. Pays $25-150 for greeting cards; $250-400 for coloring books. Writer's/illustrator's guidelines available for 9 × 12 SASE.

*CAPUTO PUBLISHING/NOW COMICS, 332 South Michigan Ave., Suite 1750, Chicago IL 60604. (312)786-9013. FAX: (312)786-2261. Editor: Katherine Llewellyn. Art Director: Michele Mach. Estab. 1985. 50% of material written and 100% illustrated by freelancers. Receives 1,200 submissions/year. Comic books: childrens comics, mostly licensed properties, some original. Planning on coming out with children's magazine similar to Sesame Street. Needs comic art, plus spot illustrations.
Making Contact & Terms: "Unusable submissions will be returned. Others will be kept on file, but not purchased for possible future use." Reports in 2 months. Guideline sheets free.

COLORMORE, INC., P.O. Box 111249, Carrollton TX 75011-1249. (316)636-9326. President: Susan C. Koch. Estab. 1987. 50% of material written and illustrated by freelancers. Buys 2 freelance projects/year; receives 30 submissions/year. Greeting card line(s): "color-your own postcards and seasonal cards." Coloring books: "travel-related/geography/social studies." Illustrators: looks for "color-your own postcards with Texas themes."
Making Contact & Terms: Submit greeting cards 12 months in advance, special coloring books 12 months in advance. SASE. Reports in 2-4 weeks. Material copyrighted. Buys all rights, Pays on publication. Pay for greeting cards "varies"; pay for coloring books is within a 5-8% royalty range. Writer's/illustrator's guideline sheets for legal-size SAE and 1 first class stamp. Market list is regularly revised.
Tips: Target age: 5-10 years old.

*CREATE-A-CRAFT, Box 330008, Fort Worth TX 76163-0008. (817)292-1855. Editor: Mitchell Lee. Estab. 1967. Produces greeting cards, giftwrap, games, calendars, posters, stationery and paper tableware products for all ages. Works with 3 freelance artists/ year. Buys 3-5 designs/illustrations/year. Prefers artists with experience in cartooning. Works on assignment only. Buys freelance designs/illustrations mainly for greetings cards and t-shirts. Also uses freelance artist for calligraphy, P-O-P displays, paste-up and mechanicals. Considers pen & ink, watercolor, acrylics and colored pencil. Prefers humorous and "cartoons that will appeal to families. Must be cute, appealing, etc. No religious, sexual implications or off-beat humor." Produces material for all holidays and season; submit 6 months before holiday.
Making Contact and Terms: For guidelines and sample cards, send $2.50 and #10 SASE. Contact only through artist's agent. Samples are filed. Samples not filed are not returned. Report back only if interested. Write to schedule an appointment to show a portfolio, which should include original/final art, final reproduction/product, slides, tearsheets, color and b&w. Original artwork is not returned to the artist after job's completion. "Payment depends upon the assignment, amount of work involved, production costs, etc. involved in the project. Buys all rights.
Tips: "Demonstrate an ability to follow directions exactly. Too many submit artwork that has no relationship to what we produce."

ECLIPSE COMICS, P.O. Box 1099, Forestville CA 95436. (707)887-1521. FAX: (707)887-7128. Editor-in-Chief: Catherine Yronwode. Art Director: Stan Woch. Estab. 1978. 100% of material written and illustrated by freelancers. Buys "approximately 100" freelance projects/year; receives 500 submissions/year. Comic books: looks for "realistic art and stories that appeal to a broad spectrum and a variety of ages. Doesn't want to see pornography, sexist exploitation, racist stories." Writers: "All material submitted should be in (brief) outline form with 5-6 sample pages of script." Illustrators: "We will only look at samples of continuity art and cover illustrations; display pieces are not needed."
Making Contact & Terms: SASE. Pays on acceptance. Pay for comic books "varies; writer and artist split 8% royalty." Guideline sheets for #10 SAE and 1 first class stamp; guidelines and a sample comic for $1.75 and 9 × 12 SAE.

*EPHEMERA INC., 275 Capp St., San Francisco CA 94110. (415)552-4199. Editor: Ed Polish. Estab. 1980. 90% of material written and 10% illustrated by freelancers. Buys over 200 freelance projects/year; receives over 2,000 submissions/year. Novelty pin back buttons with slogans and art. Need simple and bold line art that would work on a button.
Making Contact & Terms: SASE for return of submission. Reports in 3 weeks. Material copyrighted. Pays on publication. Pays $25 per slogan or design. Guideline sheets for #10 SAE and 1 first class stamp.
Tips: Looks for "very silly and outrageously funny slogans. We also are looking for provocative, irreverent and outrageously funny *adult* humor."

*FANTAGRAPHICS BOOKS, INC., 7563 Lake City Way NE, Seattle WA 98115. (206)524-1967. FAX: (206)524-2104. Submissions Editor: Robert Boyd. Art Director: Dale Yarger. 100% of material written and illustrated by freelancers. Estab. 1975. Buys 10-15 freelance projects/year; receives 300 + submissions/year. Comic books: "We print comics of quality mostly aimed at adults, but a few for younger readers. We like projects that come wholly from the creator (writer and artist); any subject or style they use is fine. The only thing an illustrator should be aware of is that we rarely print comics in color; we prefer black-and-white art."
Making Contact & Terms: Submit seasonal comic books 9 months in advance. Reports in 6 weeks. Purchases one-time rights. Pays on publication. Pays 8% minimum for comic books. Guideline sheets for #10 SAE and 1 first-class stamp.

*FIRST PUBLISHING INC. Classics Illustrated, 435 N. LaSalle, Chicago IL 60610. (312)670-6770. FAX: (312)670-6793. Editoral Director: Wade Roberts. Art Director: Mike McCormick. Estab. 1980. 100% of material written and illustrated by freelancers. Buys 24+ freelance projects/year. Receives 200 submissions/year. Comic books.
Making Contact & Terms: Submit seasonal comic books 1 year in advance. Reports in 6 weeks. Pays 30 days after acceptance. Pay is negotiable for each project. Guideline sheets free.

*INTERCONTINENTAL GREETINGS LTD., 176 Madison Ave., New York NY 10016. (212)683-5830. Contact: Robin Lipner. Estab. 1964. 100% of material freelance written and illustrated. Bought over 200 freelance projects last year. Received "thousands" of submissions last year. Produces greeting cards and scholastic products (notebooks, pencil cases). Needs "humorous writing for greeting cards only. Greeting card (style) artwork in series of three or more. We use very little writing except for humor."
Making Contact & Terms: Accepts seasonal/holiday material year-round. SASE for return of submissions. Reports in 4 weeks. Purchases world rights under contract (for 2 years). Pays on publication. Pays $30-100 for greeting cards (per usage) and $80-200 for puzzles (per usage). "We hope to use each piece 2-20 times." Writer's/illustrator's guidelines available for SASE.
Tips: Target age group for juvenile cards: ages 1-10. Illustrators: "Use clean colors, not muddy or dark."

*MARVEL COMICS, 387 Park Avenue South, New York NY 10016. (212)696-8080. FAX: (212)576-9289. Editor-in-Chief: Tom DeFalco. Art Director: John Romita. 100% of material written and illustrated by freelancers. Comic books: mainly juvenile superhero monthlies.
Making Contact & Terms: Reports in 2-4 weeks. Material copyrighted. Purchases *all* rights, including character ownership. Pays on acceptance. Writer's/illustrator's guidelines sheet for business size SAE and 1 first class stamp.
Tips: Target age group: 12-18 year old males. *No longer considers unsolicited manuscripts.*

*MV PRESS, 5014-D Roosevelt Way NE, Seattle WA 98105. (206) 525-0632. Editor: Dennis Weber. Art Director: Cindy Murata. Estab. 1980. 96% of material freelance written and illustrated. Bought 5 freelance projects last year. Receives more than 100 submissions annually. Produces alternative b&w comics and graphic albums.
Making Contact & Terms: Submit seasonal/holiday comic book material in mid-late summer. Reports in 1-2 months. Purchases first world serial rights. Pays $400-1,500/ issue for comic books. Writer's/illustrator's guidelines for #10 SAE and 1 first class stamp.

*NEW ENGLAND COMICS, Box 1424, Brockton MS 02403. Editor: George Suarez. Art Director: Bob Polio. Estab. 1983. 100% of material written and illustrated by freelancers. Buys 3 freelance projects/year; receives hundreds of submissions/year. Comic books.
Making Contact & Terms: Submit seasonal comic books 3 months in advance. Material copyrighted. Pays on publication. Guideline sheets for #10 SAE and 1 first class stamp.

PRICE STERN SLOAN, 360 N. La Cienega Blvd., Los Angeles CA 90048. Editor: Wendy Baker Vinitsky. Estab. 1964. 90% of material written and illustrated by freelancers. Buys 50 freelance projects/year; receives hundreds of submissions/year. Publishes "activity books and board books."
Making Contact & Terms: SASE. Reports in 4-6 weeks. Rights purchased: "depends on project." Payment depends on project. Writer's/illustrator's guidelines for business-size SAE and 1 first-class stamp. "Seasonal (fall or spring issue) catalog available with SASE and $2.50 postage."

Tips: Target age group: preschool-YA. Trend toward "children's nonfiction."

*ROLLER PUBLICATIONS, P.O. Box 221295, Sacramento, CA 95822. (916)429-8522. Editor/Art Director: Andrew Roller. Estab. 1986. 20% of material written and illustrated by freelancers. Buys 30+ freelance projects/year. Receives 50+ submissions/year. Coloring books: elementary school adventures. Comic books: elementary school adventures. Puzzles and/or games: "occasionally, using our trademarked characters." Needs short, wildly humorous, zany material, one page (8½×11) camera-ready humorous pieces.
Making Contact & Terms: Submit seasonal special coloring books 3 months in advance; special games, special puzzles and comic books 3 months advance. Reports in 2 weeks. Material copyrighted. Creator keeps all rights after publication. Pays on publication Pays 1-2 contributor copies. Guideline sheets for #10 SAE and 1 first class stamp.
Tips: Looking for elementary school adventures. Target age group: 7-11.

STANDARD PUBLISHING, 8121 Hamilton Ave., Cincinnati OH 45231. (513)931-4050. FAX: (513)931-0904. Editor: Henrietta Gambill. Art Director: Frank Sutton. Estab. 1866. 100% of material illustrated by freelancers. Buys 75 freelance projects/year; receives 1,200 submissions/year. Publishes religious/value-oriented material.
Making Contact & Terms: Submit seasonal coloring books, games and puzzles 12-18 months in advance. SASE. Reports in 3 months. Material copyrighted. Buys all rights. Pays on acceptance. Writer's guidelines for SAE and 1 first class stamp.
Tips: Looks for "Bible-oriented" material, for a preschool-6th grade audience.

*SUNRISE PUBLICATION, INC., P.O. Box 2699, Bloomington IN 47402. (812)336-9900. FAX: (812)336-8712. Editors: Lori Teesch/Kim Turner. Product Design Coordinator: Nancy Jacobus. Estab. 1974. 40% of material written and 95% illustrated by freelancers. Buys 600+ freelance projects/year. Receives 1,000+/year. Greeting card lines: general greetings, holidays, note cards. Greeting cards: unrhymed verse.
Making Contact & Terms: Submit seasonal greeting cards 6-8 months in advance. Reports in 10 weeks. Material copyrighted. Pays on acceptance. Pay for greeting cards $25-125 (versing); $350 per design. Guideline sheets for #10 SAE and 1 first class stamp. Market list available to writer/illustrator.
Tips: "Bright, festive, not-to-wordy, occasion specific illustration."

WARNER PRESS, P.O. Box 2499, Anderson IN 46018. Editor: Cindy Maddox. Art Director: Dianne Deckert. Estab. 1880. 60% of material written by freelancers; 75% illustrated by freelancers. Publishes children's birthday cards, coloring and activity books, all religious-oriented. "Need fun, up-to-date stories for coloring books, with religious emphasis. Also considering activity books for Sunday school classroom use."
Making Contact & Terms: Submit seasonal greeting cards and coloring books 18 months in advance. Reports in 6 weeks. Material copyrighted. Buys all rights. Pays on acceptance. Guidelines sheet for SASE.

Young Writer's/Illustrator's Markets

There's nothing that can justify a young writer's or artist's talent more than having his work published. Children and teens—the listings in this section are for you. Included in this section are several "interactive" magazines, or rather, magazines that provide a creative outlet for their readers. Some of the magazines in this section are exclusively for children; others are adult magazines that have set aside special sections to feature the work of younger writers and illustrators.

Since most juvenile magazines are distributed through schools, churches and home subscriptions, some of the smaller, literary magazines here may not be easily found in the bookstore or library. In such a case, you may need to contact the magazine to see if a sample copy is available, and what the cost might be. It is important for writers and artists to be familiar with the editorial needs of magazines they are interested in submitting to.

Be advised that it is important to send a self-addressed stamped envelope (SASE) with proper postage affixed with each submission. This way, if the market is not interested in your work, they will send it back to you. If you do not send the SASE with your submission, you probably won't get your work back. If your work is rejected the first time you send it out, be assured you are not the first one this has happened to. Many of our best known writers and artists were turned down more times than they can count at the beginning of their careers, yet went on to be successful at their craft. The key to becoming published lies in persistence as well as talent. Keep sending out stories and artwork as you continue to improve your craft. Someday, an editor may decide your work is just what he needs.

As the adult writers and artists have been advised in other parts of this book, refer to the Business of Children's Writing & Illustrating at the beginning of this book if you're not sure how a proper query letter or manuscript looks. We have included a step by step explanation of what to include in each. Best of luck in your writing or art career!

THE ACORN, 1530 7th St., Rock Island IL 61201. (309)788-3980. Newsletter. Estab. 1989. Audience consists of "kindergarten-12th grade, teachers and other adult writers." Purpose in publishing works by children: to expose children's manuscripts to others and provide a format for those who might not have one. Children must be K-12 (put grade on manuscripts).
Magazines: 99% of magazine written by children. Word length: 500 fiction, 500 nonfiction, 32 lines poetry. Pays 1 copy of the issue the work is in. Sample copy $1. Subscription $5 for 6 issues. Submit mss to Betty Mowery, editor. Send complete ms. Will accept typewritten, legibly handwritten and/or computer printout. Reports in 1 week.
Artwork: Publishes artwork by children. Looks for "all types, size—3 × 4½ (the size of a business card). Use black ink in artwork." Pays in 1 copy of issue the work is in. Submit artwork either with manuscript or separately to Betty Mowery, editor.
Tips: "I will use occasional articles by adults, but it must relate to something that will help children with their writing—submitting or publishing. Manuscripts without SASE will not be returned."

*AGORA: THE MAGAZINE FOR GIFTED STUDENTS, AG Publications, Inc., Box 10975, Raleigh NC 27605. (919)787-6832. Magazine. 8½×11; 32 pp; offset paper and cover stock. Estab. 1986. Published "quarterly during academic year." Audience consists of "academically advanced high school and middle school students." Purpose in publishing works by children: to publicize student accomplishments; give students a chance to network. Requirements to be met before work is published: subscribe to *Agora*; a teacher's signature. Instructions for annual *Agora* Writing Competitions available— deadline April 25.

Magazines: Uses short stories (fiction-2,000 words); travel, public issues and scientific articles, literary essays, book reviews (1,500-2,000 words); short lyric poetry (25-100 lines), one-act plays, art and photos. Pays $10-25 prizes for contest winners. "We hope to increase amount as subscription base increases." Submit mss to Sally Humble, *Agora* editor.

Tips: "Very interested in illustrations that accompany a written work, depending on quality of both. The best way for submissions to get published is to participate in annual *Agora* competitions. We accept writing by middle, high school and college students *and* by adults. Major themes for 1989-90: Democracy in Eastern Europe, Economics, Oceanography and Animals/Zoos."

*BEAR ESSENTIAL NEWS FOR KIDS, P.O. Box 26908. Tempe AZ 85285. (602)345-READ. Newspaper published monthly. Audience consists of children, grades K-8 and their families. Purpose of publishing work by children: is to promote "creative and intellectual growth; contributions to self-esteem." Local programs in Arizona and California looking for major market stringers across U.S. especially school-age "Cub Reporters." Writer's guidelines available on request.

Books: Nonfiction news and features. Poetry and artwork accepted from California and Arizona students (hope to expand). Pays free copy. Children submit mss to Janet Cooper, Cub Reporter/Program Director. Send query or submit complete manuscript; teacher can submit. Will accept typewritten, legibly handwritten and/or floppy disk (Mac). Reports in 2 months.

Artwork: Publishes artwork by children. Free copy. Submit artwork to Copy Editor. Reports in 2 months.

BOYS' LIFE, 1325 Walnut Hill Ln., Box 152079, Irving TX 75015-2079. (214)580-2000. Magazine published monthly. Audience consists of boys 8-18. Requirements to be met before work is published: must be 18 or under.

Magazines: One page, which does not run every month, is written by children. Uses 3-10 fiction stories (500 words or less); nonfiction pieces (500 words or less); poetry. "We do not pay for mss." Submit mss to Jeff Csatari, special features editor. Will accept typewritten, legibly handwritten, computer printout mss. "We do not acknowledge receipt or use of ms."

*CHALK TALK MAGAZINE, Chalk Talk Publishing, 1550 Mills Rd., RR2, Sidney, BC V8L351 Canada. (604) 656-1858. Monthly magazine. 8×11; 24 pages; recycled newsprint. Estab. 1988. "*Chalk Talk* gives children the opportunity to become published

 The asterisk before a listing indicates the listing is new in this edition.

authors and inspires an enthusiasm for the written word. It is written by children for children."

Magazines: Submissions welcome from all children ages 5 to 14. The magazine contains "fun and imaginative stories and poems, true life experiences, book reviews, ecology news and concerns, and contains something different every month. Send in as many contributions as you like at one time and as often as you wish." SASE for return of ms. Contributors are not paid for their submissions.

Artwork: "Artwork reproduces best from plain paper drawn in dark crayon, felt, pen or pencil."

*CHILDREN'S ALBUM EGW PUBLISHING, Box 6086, Concord CA 94524. (415)671-9852. Magazine published bi-monthly. Audience consists of children ages 8-14. "*Children's Album* is a collection of creative thoughts and expressions dedicated to nurturing a child's positive self-image, to enlightening—without preference to age—with individuality, wisdom, and infinite imagination, to learning through fun, and to reminding—lest an adult forgets what it is like to think as a child." Writer's guidelines available on request.

Magazines: 80% of magazine written by children. Uses fiction (20 word length). Pays in 1 year subscription. Submit mss to Margo Lemas, Editor. Send query; submit complete ms. Will accept typewritten, legibly handwritten mss.

Artwork: Publishes artwork by children; submit 8½×11. Pays in 1 year subscription. Reports in 2-6 months.

CHILDREN'S DIGEST, Box 567, Indianapolis IN 46206. (317)636-8881. Magazine. Published 8 times/year. Audience consists of preteens. Purpose in publishing works by children: to encourage children to express themselves through writing. Requirements to be met before work is published: require proof of originality before publishing stories. Writer's guidelines available on request.

Magazines: 10% of magazine written by children. Uses 1 fiction story (about 200 words), 6-7 poems, 15-20 riddles, 7-10 letters/issue. "There is no payment for manuscripts submitted by readers." Submit mss to *Children's Digest* (Elizabeth A. Rinck, editor). Submit complete ms. Will accept typewritten, legibly handwritten, computer printout mss. "Readers whose material is accepted will be notified by letter. Sorry, no materials can be returned."

CHILDREN'S PLAYMATE, Box 567, Indianapolis IN 46206. (317)636-8881. Magazine. 6½×9; 48 pp; 40 lb. #5 coated, and 35 lb. uncoated paper, 40 lb. self-cover. Estab. 1928. Audience consists of children between 6 and 8 years of age. Purpose in publishing works by children: to encourage children to write. Writer's guidelines available on request.

Magazines: 10% of magazine written by children. Uses 6-7 poems, 8-10 jokes, 8-10 riddles/issue. "There is no payment for manuscripts submitted by children." Submit mss to *Children's Playmate* (Elizabeth A. Rinck, editor). Submit complete ms. Will accept typewritten, legibly handwritten, computer printout mss. "If a child's work is published, he/she will be notified by a letter. No material may be returned."

Artwork: Publishes artwork by children. "Prefers dark-colored line drawings on white paper. No payment for children's artwork published." Submit artwork to *Children's Playmate.*

Always include a self-addressed stamped envelope (SASE) or International Reply Coupon (IRC) with submissions.

CLUBHOUSE, Box 15, Berrien Springs MI 49103. (616)471-9009. Magazine. 6×9; 32 pp; 50 lb. offset paper, self cover. Estab. 1949. Publishes 1 section by kids in each issue, bimonthly. "Audience consists of kids 9-14; philosophy is God loves kids, kids are neat people." Purpose in publishing works by children: encouragement; demonstration of talent. Requirements to be met before work is published: age 9-14; parent's note verifying originality.

Magazines: 1/16th of magazine written by children. Uses adventure, historical, everyday life experience (fiction/nonfiction-1,200 words); health-related short articles; poetry (4-24 lines of "mostly mood pieces and humor"). Payment for ms: prizes for children, money for adult authors. Query. Will accept typewritten, legibly handwritten, computer printout mss. "Will not be returned without SASE." Reports in 6 weeks.

Artwork: Publishes artwork by children. Looks for all types of artwork-white paper, black pen. Pays in prizes for kids. Send black pen on white paper to Elaine Trumbo, editor. SASE—"won't be returned without SASE."

Tips: "All items submitted by kids are held in a file and used when possible. We normally suggest they do not ask for return of the item."

CREATIVE KIDS, Box 6448, Mobile AL 36660. (205)478-4700. Magazine. 8½×11; 32 pp. Estab. 1979. Published 8 times/year (Oct.-May). "All of our material is by children, for children." Purpose in publishing works by children: to create a product that is good enough for publication and to offer an opportunity for children to see their work in print. Requirements to be met before work is published: ages 5-18—must have statement by teacher or parent verifying originality. Writer's guidelines available on request.

Magazines: Uses "about 6" fiction stories (200-750 words); "about 6" nonfiction stories (200-750 words); poetry, plays, ideas to share 200-750 words/issue. Pays in free magazine/ms. Submit mss to Fay L. Gold, editor. Will accept typewritten, legibly handwritten mss. Reports in 4 weeks.

Artwork: Publishes artwork by children. Looks for "any kind of drawing, cartoon, or painting." Pays in "free magazine." Send original or a photo of the work to Fay L. Gold, editor. No photocopies. Reports in 4 weeks.

Tips: "*Creative Kids* is a magazine by kids, for kids. The work represents children's ideas, questions, fears, concerns and pleasures. The material never contains racist, sexist or violent expression. The purpose is to encourage youngsters to create a product that is good enough for publication. A person may submit one or more pieces of work. Each piece must be labeled with the student's name, birth date, grade, school, home address, and school address. Include a photograph, if possible. Recent school pictures are best. Material submitted to *Creative Kids* must not be under consideration by any other publisher. Items should be carefully prepared, proofread and double checked. All activities requiring solutions must be accompanied by the correct answers. We're looking for current topics of interest: nutrition, ecology, cleaner environment, etc."

*CREATIVE WITH WORDS, *We Are Writers, Too!*, Creative With Words Publications, P.O. Box 223226, Carmel CA 93922. Editor: Brigitta Geltrich. Semiannual anthology. Estab. 1975. "We publish the creative writing of children." Audience consists of children, schools, libraries, adults, reading programs. Purpose in publishing works by children: to offer them an opportunity to get started in publishing. "Work must be of quality, original, unedited, and not published before; age must be given (up to 19 years old)." Writer's guidelines available on request.

Books: Considers all categories except those dealing with death and murder. Uses fairy tales, folklore items (1,000 words); poetry (not to exceed 20 lines, 46 characters across). Published *We Are Writers, Too!* (anthology, children of all ages); *A Scary Halloween!* (children and adults of all ages); *A CWW Easter!* (anthology, children and adults of all ages). Pay: 20% off each copy of publication in which fiction or poetry by children appears. Submit mss to Brigitta Geltrich, editor. Query; teacher must submit; teacher and/or parents must verify originality of writing. Will accept typewritten and/or legibly handwritten mss. SASE. Reports in 2 months.

Artwork: Publishes artwork by children (language art work). Pay: 20% off every copy of publication in which work by children appears. Submit artwork to Brigitta Geltrich, editor.

*DRAGONFLY: EAST/WEST HAIKU QUARTERLY, Box 11236, Salt Lake City UT 84147. Magazine. Published quarterly. "We publish for an audience interested in haiku (a Japanese form of poetry written in many different languages). Children can write this form of poetry as well as adults can, often with a refreshing perspective. We like to encourage children to try this kind of writing." Requirements to be met before work is published: submissions with name, address, age and/or grade. Writer's guidelines available on request. "They are, however, the same as for adults."

Magazines: 1-3% of magazine written by children. Uses 1-6 haiku by younger writers. Publish more if we receive more good haiku from them. Young writers receive a free copy of the issue in which their poem appears. Submit mss to Editor: Richard Tice. Submit complete ms. Will accept typewritten, legibly handwritten, computer printout mss. SASE.

Tips: The teacher or parent should study our guidelines and a sample copy, then help the child or teen understand the form.

THE FLYING PENCIL PRESS, Box 7667, Elgin IL 60121. Books. Estab. 1988. Publishes 1 book by children/year. "Audience is general (family, schools, libraries). Philosophy is freedom of expression and creativity." Purpose in publishing works by children: to encourage and support young writers. Requirements to be met before work is published: age 8-14, following current guidelines. Writer's guidelines available on request.

Books: Uses fiction stories (up to 2,000 words); nonfiction (up to 2,000 words); poems (4-32 lines). Pays in author's copy, awards/ms. Submit ms to Charlotte Towner Graeber, editor. "We prefer fiction, nonfiction and poems to be typewritten, but will accept handwritten material if it is clear and readable. Material must be the original work of the submitting author. Enclose a self addressed stamped envelope (SASE) if you wish material we do not accept for publication to be returned. Remember to keep a copy of your writing in case the original is lost in handling or mailing. You will be notified by mail if your work is accepted for Flying Pencil publication."

Artwork: Publishes artwork by children. Artwork—black and white line art, size limit 8×10; cartoons—1 to 8 frames, black and white, size limit 8×10. Pays in copies. Artwork, illustrations and cartoons should be on unlined white paper and mailed flat, if possible. "Keep a copy of artwork in case original is lost in the mail." Submit to Charlotte Towner Graeber, editor. Reports A.S.A.P.

Tips: "Our 1991 theme is Magic, Mystery and Fantasy."

*FREE SPIRIT PUBLISHING INC., Suite 616, 400 First Ave. North, Minneapolis MN 55401. (612)338-2068. Publishes 3-8 books/year since starting in 1983 and a newsletter for 10-14 year-olds, 5 times/year. "We specialize in self-help for kids. Our main interests include the development of self-esteem, self-awareness, creative thinking and problem solving abilities, assertiveness, and making a difference in the world. Children have a lot to share with each other. They also can reach and teach each other in ways adults cannot. Additionally, we publish the works of many young people. We send writer's guidelines on request. Children only need an adult's signature assuring authenticity for the cartoon and writing contests we sponsor." Writer's guidelines available on request.

Books: Publishes psychology, self-help, how-to, education. Pays advance and royalties. Submit mss to Judy Galbraith, Publisher. Send query. Will accept typewritten mss. Reports in 1-3 months.

Magazines: 20% of magazine written by children. Uses 2-5 nonfiction articles and survey responses. Word length: 100-800. Payment for articles published by children: "A T-shirt and 3 copies of the newsletter in which they're published. Contest winners receive money and books." Submit complete ms. to Elizabeth Salzmann, Assistant Editor. Will accept typewritten, legibly handwritten mss. Reports in 2-8 weeks.
Artwork: Publishes artwork by children. "We run a cartoon contest annually. Write for details." Contest winners receive a cash prize. Write for artwork guidelines. Submit artwork to Elizabeth Salzmann.

GHOST TOWN QUARTERLY, Box 714, Philipsburg MT 59858. (406)859-3365. Magazine published quarterly. 8½ × 11; 48-52 pp; 70 lb. enamel bond paper and cover stock. Estab. 1988. "We work to preserve the history surrounding ghost towns and abandoned sites throughout the U.S., Canada and Mexico and to present this history in a manner both interesting and informative. We also feature museums and historical sites." Purpose in publishing works by children: "to add to the scope of our magazine and to give children a chance to gain recognition for their abilities." Requirements to be met before work is published: K through 12th grade; include contributor's name and address, age and name and address of school attended. Writer's guidelines available upon request.
Magazines: 4% of magazine written by children. Uses very little fiction. Uses 1-4 nonfiction articles about ghost towns and abandoned sites, museums, historical sites, interviews with people who have lived in an area now abandoned (1,000 words maximum length). Uses 1-4 poems (500 word maximum length). Pays 5¢/word on publication. Submit mss to Donna B. McLean, editor. Submit complete ms. Will accept typewritten, legibly handwritten, computer printout mss. Reports in 2-4 months.
Artwork: Publishes artwork by children "up to 8 × 10 vertical or 5 × 7 horizontal; cartoons and sketches related to our themes, depicting something based on facts." Pays $10 per cartoon; $15 per sketch, on publication. Submit "on plain paper kept free of smudges" to Donna B. McLean, editor. Reports in 2-4 months.
Tips: "We also accept photographs and pay $5 if they are published as b&w, $10 if we publish in color. Eligible for cover consideration (covers pay $50 — need to include information about photo). Best to include at least a short article with photo submission."

HIGHLIGHTS FOR CHILDREN, 803 Church St., Honesdale PA 18431. (717)253-1080. Magazine. Published monthly (July-August issue combined). "We strive to provide wholesome, stimulating, entertaining material that will encourage children to read. Our audience is children 2-12." Purpose in publishing works by children: to encourage children's creative expression. Requirements to be met before work is published: age limit 15.
Magazines: 15-20% of magazine written by children. Features which occur occasionally: "What Are Your Favorite Books?" (8-10 per year), Recipes (8-10 per year), "Science Letters" (15-20 per year). Special features which invite children's submissions on a specific topic: "Tell the Story" (15-20 per year), "You're the Reporter" (8-10 per year), "Your Ideas, Please" (8-10 per year), "Endings to Unfinished Stories" (8-10 per year). Submit complete mss to the Editor. Will accept typewritten, legibly handwritten, computer printout mss. Responds in 3-6 weeks.
Artwork: Publishes artwork by children. No cartoon or comic book characters. No commercial products. Submit black-and-white artwork for "Our Own Pages." Color for others. Features include "Creatures Nobody Has Ever Seen" (5-8 per year) and "Illustration Job" (18-20 per year). Responds in 3-6 weeks.

*KIDS' BOOKS BY KIDS, Beyond Words Publishing, Inc., Route 3, Box 492B, Hillsboro OR 97123. (503)647-5109. Book publisher. Publishes 1-2 books by children per year. Looks for "books that encourage creativity and an appreciation of nature in children." Wants to "encourage children to write, create, dream and believe that it is possible to

be published. The books must be unique, be of national interest and the child must be personable and promotable."
Books: Publishes stories and joke books. Pays in royalties. Submit manuscript to Cynthia Black, editor. Query or have teacher submit. Will accept typewritten or computer printed mss. Responds in 3 months.

*LIFEPRINTS, Blindskills, Box 5181, Salem OR 97304. (503)581-4224. Magazine. 8½ × 11; 52 pp; 60 lb. paper and 110 lb. cover stock. Estab. 1983. Published 4 times/ year. Magazine includes blind and visually impaired successes, teenagers.
Magazines: Uses nonfiction anecdotal material. We do not pay; nonprofit. Editor: Carol M. McCarl. Will accept manuscripts in typed, brailled, or in cassette formats. A small honorarium is awarded to students whose articles are published in *Lifeprints*. Articles published in *Lifeprints* are written for visually-impaired or blind people.

*THE LOUISVILLE REVIEW, University of Louisville, 315 Bingham Humanities, Louisville KY 40292. Magazine published annually (spring). Purpose in publishing works by children: "To give children a place to be published in an adult literary magazine." Requirements to be met before work is published: Grades K-12.
Magazines: 25% of magazine written by children. Uses 4-5 fiction stories, 30-40 poems/ issue. Pays 1 copy. Submit mss to Sena Naslund, Faculty Editor. Submit complete ms with signed permission from parents or guardian to publish if accepted. Will accept typewritten mss. Reports in 3 months.

MERLYN'S PEN: The National Magazine of Student Writing, Box 1058, East Greenwich RI 02818. (401)885-5175. Magazine. Published every 2 months during the school year, September to May. "We publish 150 manuscripts annually by students in grades 7-10. The entire magazine is dedicated to young adults' writing. Our audience is classrooms, libraries and students from grades 7-10." Requirements to be met before work is published: writers must be in grades 7-10 and must follow submission guidelines for preparing their manuscripts. When a student is accepted, he/she, a parent and a teacher must sign a statement of originality.
Magazines: 100% of magazine written by adolescents. Uses 6-8 short stories, plays (fiction); 2-3 nonfiction essays; poetry; letters to the editor; editorials; reviews of previously published works; reviews of books, music, movies. No word limit on any material. Pays for ms in three copies of the issue and a paperback copy of *The Elements of Style* (a writer's handbook). Also, a discount is offered for additional copies of the issue. Submit mss to R. Jim Stahl, editor. Submit complete ms. Will only accept typewritten mss. "All rejected manuscripts have an editor's constructive critical comment in the margin." Reports in 11 weeks.
Artwork: Publishes artwork by young adults, grades 7-10. Looks for black and white line drawings, cartoons, color art for cover. Pays in 3 copies of the issue to the artist, and a discount is offered for additional copies. Send unmatted original artwork. Submit artwork to R. Jim Stahl, editor. Reports in 11 weeks.
Tips: "All manuscripts and artwork must be submitted with a cover sheet listing: name, age and grade, home address, home phone number, school name, school phone number, school address, teacher's name and principal's name. SASE must be large enough and carry enough postage for return."

MY FRIEND, 50 St. Paul's Ave., Jamaica Plain, Boston MA 02130. (617)522-8911. Magazine. Published 10 times/year. Audience consists of children ages 6-12, primarily Roman Catholics. Purpose in publishing works by children: to stimulate reader participation and to encourage young Catholic writers. Requirements to be met before work is published: we accept work from children ages 6-16. Requirements regarding originality included in guidelines. Writer's guidelines available for SASE.

Close-up

Mike Joyer
Portland, Oregon

Zach Robert
Littleton, Colorado

Once upon a time two little boys got bored on a summer day and decided to write a book. Then one day a couple of years later they thought it would be really swell to get it published. One of them opened the yellow pages to the publishers section, and with closed eyes randomly chose a publisher. He called the publisher and asked to have the book published. The publisher loved the idea and published the book. The end.

The irony of this writer's fairy tale is that for Zach Robert, 12, and Mike Joyer, 11, it really happened. Their book, *100 Excuses for Kids* was published in April 1990 by Kids' Books By Kids, an imprint of Beyond Words Publishing. 20,000 copies were printed.

The two boys have been friends since preschool days when they both lived in Denver. They sat down one day, back when they were 8 and 9 years old, and started writing excuses. According to Zach, "We just started writing up excuses. After we had done about five chapters, we figured we wouldn't get it published or anything, but we'd use it for ourselves. We kept on doing them until we had 10 chapters."

Mike, who has since moved to Oregon, took the text and kept it in his closet. One day, about two years after starting the project, Mike talked to the people at Beyond Words Publishing and mailed them the manuscript. They agreed to publish the book provided the boys come up with 14 more chapters. "We did those individually, with each one of us having assigned chapters, as well as together over the phone," explains Zach.

According to Mike, they maintained creative control even for the illustrations. Each added his own illustrations, which were later redone by an artist for the published version. He stresses even though the final art was drawn by someone else, the concepts for all the drawings were theirs.

Presently both the boys and Beyond Words Publishing are hoping the book will attract enough interest for a second excuses book, this one to be called *America's Best Excuses for Kids*. For this book, other kids around the country will be invited to send their best excuses for consideration. Kids who have their excuses published in the book will get their name listed as well as a free copy of the book.

"I've learned if you believe you can do something, you really can," says Zach, reflecting on his experience. Regarding the press he received over the book, he says, "I had to know every single thing about the book, so I was reading it over and over in order to prepare for the interviews. I had to know everything down pat." The veteran excuse-maker's advice to getting something published is simple: "Write something you know a lot about."

Mike says persistence is the key. "Call around to publishers and see what they say. If it sounds reasonable, send in your manuscript. If it gets rejected the first time, keep trying until someone publishes it."

Both boys admit they were very lucky in getting published and recognize it's rarely that easy. Zach says being kids probably gave them an edge as far as the publicity they received. After all, says Mike, "it's not every day that a kid gets a book published." The occurrence is so rare, in fact, that both boys had trouble convincing their classmates they were published authors. Mike says his friends didn't believe him until he brought the actual book into school one day.

The success of the excuses in the book depends on each kid's parents, says Mike, who grudgingly admits to having not-so-gullible parents. Perhaps that's why his post-*Excuses* life has remained unchanged. When asked if he gets any star treatment, he says, "Well, not really. I still have to do all the chores."

—Lisa Carpenter

Mike Joyer and Zach Robert are international authorities in the art of making excuses. Because of extensive research (testing excuses on family and friends), their book includes the right things to say in order to stay up late, get candy and get out of doing homework.

Tips: "Our 'Junior Reporter' feature gives young writers the chance to do active research on a variety of topics. Children may ask for an 'assignment' or suggest topics they'd be willing to research and write on. This would be mainly where our interest in children's writing would lie."

THE MYTHIC CIRCLE, Mythopoeic Society, Box 6707, Altadena CA 91001. Editor: Tina Cooper and Christine Lowentrout. Art Director: Lynn Maudlin. Quarterly magazine. Circ. 150. Fantasy writer's workshop in print featuring reader comments in each issue. 5% of publication aimed at juvenile market.
Nonfiction: How-to, interview/profile. "We are just starting with nonfiction—dedicated to how to write and publish." Buys maximum of 4 mss/year. Average word length: 250-2,000. Byline given.
How to Contact/Writers: Fiction: send complete ms. Nonfiction: query. SASE (IRC) for answer to query and return of ms. Reports on queries/mss in 1 month. Will consider photocopied, computer printout (dark dot matrix) and electronic submissions via disk (query for details).
Illustration: Buys 10 illustrations/issue; buys 40 illustrations/year. Preferred theme or style: fantasy, soft science fiction. Will review ms/illustration packages submitted by authors/artists; ms/illustration packages submitted by authors with illustrations done by separate artists; illustrator's work for possible use with fiction/nonfiction articles and columns by other authors.
How to Contact/Illustrators: Ms/illustration packages: complete with art. Illustrations only: Send tear sheets. Reports on art samples in 3-6 weeks. Original artwork returned at job's completion (only if postage paid).
Terms/Writers & Illustrators: Pays on publication. Buys one-time rights. Pays in contributor copies. Sample copy $5. Writer's guidelines free with SAE and 1 first-class stamp.
Tips: "We are a good outlet for a story that hasn't sold but 'should' have—good feedback and tips on improvement. We do have a 'Mythopoeic Youth' section with stories and art by those under 18 years."

*THE PIKESTAFF FORUM, P.O. Box 127, Normal IL 61761. (309)452-4831. Magazine published annually; "we hope to eventually get out two issues per year." "The basic audience of *The Pikestaff Forum* is adult; in each issue we have a Young Writers feature publishing writing and artwork by young people aged 7 through 17. Purpose in publishing works by children: Our purpose is twofold: (1) to put excellent writing by young people before the general public, and (2) to encourage young people in developing their self-confidence and powers of literary expression. Requirements to be met before work is published: Work must be by young people aged 7 through 17; it must be original, previously unpublished, and submitted by the authors themselves (we do *not* wish parents or teachers to submit the work); the person's age at the time the piece was written must be stated." Writer's guidelines available on request.
Magazines: 10% of magazine written by children. Uses 1-3 fiction stories, 7-10 poems/issue. Poetry always welcome. Author or artist receives three free copies of the issue in which the work appears, and has the option of purchasing additional copies at a 50% discount. Submit mss to Robert D. Sutherland, Editor/Publisher. Submit complete ms. Will accept typewritten, legibly handwritten, computer printout mss.
Artwork: Publishes artwork by children. No restrictions on subject matter; "should be free-standing and interesting (thought-provoking). *Black and white only* (dark image); we cannot handle color work with our format." Artist receives three free copies of the issue in which the work appears, and has the option of purchasing additional copies at a 50% discount off cover price. In black and white, clearly marked with artist's name, address and age at the time the work was created. Submit artwork to Robert D. Sutherland, Editor/Publisher. Reports in 3 months. "We do not wish teachers to submit for

their students, and we do not wish to see batches of works which are simply the product of school assignments."

*PURPLE COW, The Newspaper for Teens and Young Adults, 3500 Piedmont Road NE Suite 415, Atlanta GA 30305. (404)239-0642. Newspaper published monthly. "All of our articles are written *by* teens. Our target market is teenagers and youth adults (ages 12-19). Our philosophy is to give teens quality reading material, positive messages, and a healthy means of communications within the community. Our articles are predominately written by an area teen board, which are a representative group of writers from all local high schools. Freelance work *is* accepted on college and career issues." Writer's guidelines available on request.
Magazines: Uses 15 nonfiction stories/issue (200-700 word length). Payments range from $10-25. Pays on publication; writer retains all rights. Submit mss to Melissa Goldman, Editor. Submit complete ms. Will accept typewritten mss.
Artwork: Publishes artwork by children. Looks for music, comics, issue-related. Submit artwork to Melissa Goldman, Editor.
Tips: "Please note that there are additional Purple Cows in Birmingham, Dallas and Charlotte. You may feel free to approach these publications separately. These publications have acceptance policies similar to those of the Atlanta Purple Cow."

REFLECTIONS, Box 368, Duncan Falls OH 43734. (614)674-5209. Magazine. Published January and June. Purpose in publishing works by children: to encourage writing. Requirements to be met before work is published: statement of originality and signed by teacher or parent. Writer's guidelines available on request (with SASE).
Magazines: 100% of magazine written by children. Uses 1-3 fiction stories (1,000-2,000 words); 1-3 nonfiction articles (1,000-2,000 words); poetry. Pays in contributor's copy. Editor: Dean Harper. Submit complete ms. Will accept typewritten, legibly handwritten, computer printout mss. "Please include your name, age, school, address, and your teacher's name. Be certain to include a self-addressed stamped envelope with your manuscripts. Make the statement that this is your own original work, then date it and sign your name. Your teacher or parent should also sign it." Reports in 2 weeks.
Artwork: Publishes artwork by children. Pays in contributor's copy. Editor: Dean Harper. SASE. Reports in 2 weeks.

SCHOLASTIC SCOPE, 730 Broadway, New York NY 10003. (212)505-3000. Magazine published weekly. "*Scope* is a language arts magazine for junior high and high school students reading below level (approximately 5th grade level)." Purpose in publishing works by children: to encourage readers to write, to entertain readers. Requirements to be met before work is published: proof of original work, signed by parent or teacher. Writer's guidelines available on request.
Magazines: 20% of magazine written by children. Uses fiction, nonfiction and poetry. Submit ms to Adrienne Su, associate editor. Submit complete ms. Will accept typewritten, legibly handwritten, computer printout mss. SASE.

SHOE TREE, National Association for Young Writers, 215 Valle del Sol Dr., Santa Fe NM 87501. (505)982-8596. Magazine. 6 × 9; 64 pp; 70# Lakewood 390 PPI paper, 10 pt. C15 cover stock. Estab. 1984. Published 3 times/year. "We urge young writers to use writing as a serious form of communication. The goal of NAYW is to encourage children's writing. We accept only the finest work by young writers, ages 6-14." Writer's guidelines available on request.
Magazines: 95% of magazine written by children; one adult author-to-author column. Uses 5-10 fictional stories; 2-6 nonfiction articles; and personal narratives, humor, book reviews, 6-10 poems. Pays with 2 complimentary copies. Sheila Cowing, editor-in-chief.

Mary Thomas, 12, of Sante Fe, New Mexico did this illustration for Shoe Tree. *"She writes as well as draws and has a strong sense of whimsey; hence she had a good time creating 'Aussie' animals to go with Sara Rosenbaum's story ('The Aussie Murder Mystery')," says Sheila Cowing, editor-in-chief. The magazine solicits from young artists ages 6-14.*

Submit complete ms. Will accept typewritten, legibly handwritten, computer printout mss. Reports in 2 months.

Artwork: Publishes artwork by children. "We use art mostly for illustration. Send, or have teacher send, samples of artwork and then we solicit. Also use pictures for full-color or b&w cover." Pays with 2 complimentary copies. Submit artwork by student or teacher, either photocopy or original. Sheila Cowing, editor-in-chief. Reports in 1 months.

*SKIPPING STONES, Multicultural Children's Quarterly, 80574 Hazelton, Cottage Grove OR 97424. (503)942-9434. Articles Editor: Arun N. Toke. Fiction Editor: Amy Klauke. Quarterly magazine. 8½ × 11; 32 pages; recycled 50 lb. paper quality; recycled 80 lb. cover stock. Estab. 1988. Circulation 3,000-4,000. "*Skipping Stones* is a multicultural, nonprofit, children's magazine to encourage cooperation, creativity and celebration of cultural and environmental richness. It offers itself as a creative forum for communication among children from different lands and backgrounds."

Magazines: Fiction accepted only by young writers (under 19 years of age). Word length for fiction: 2 pages. Byline given.
Poetry: Publishes poetry by young, unpublished writers.
How to Contact/Writers: Send complete manuscript. Reports on queries in 1 month; on ms in 2 months. Accepts simultaneous submissions.
Artwork: Will review all varieties of manuscript/illustration packages. Reports back to artists in 2 months.
Terms/Writers and Illustrators: "We are not able to pay cash. We are glad to give a few copies of the magazine in which your contribution is published. Sample copy for $4 and 8½ × 11 SAE with 4 first class stamps.
Tips: "Think, live and write as if you were a child. Let the 'inner child' within you speak out—naturally, uninhibited." Wants "material that gives insight on cultural celebrations, lifestyle, custom and tradition, glimpse of daily life in other countries and cultures. Photos, songs, artwork are most welcome if they illustrate/highlight the points."

SKYLARK, 2233 171st St., Hammond IN 46323. (219)989-2262. Editor: Marcia Jaron. Art Director: Cathy Kadow. Children's Editor: Cheryl Dipple. Annual magazine. Circ. 500-750. 15% of material aimed at juvenile audience. Presently accepting material by children, not adults. "We are presently focusing on writing and drawings by children and do not want to see material submitted by adults at this time. Our goal for the special children's section of our magazine is to encourage young talent."
Magazines: Uses animal, contemporary, fantasy, history, humorous, problem solving, religious, romance, science fiction, sports, spy/mystery/adventure (fiction and nonfiction). Does not want to see material about Satan worship, graphic sex. Byline given.
How to Contact/Writers: Fiction/nonfiction: Send complete ms. Reports on queries/mss in 6 months. Will consider simultaneous submissions.
Artwork: Wants to see artwork by children.
How to Contact/Illustrators: Illustrations only: Artwork. Reports on art samples in 6 months. Original artwork returned at job's completion "if SASE is included with artwork."
Terms/Writers & Illustrators: Pays in contributor's copies. Sample copy $3 with SAE. Writer's/illustrator's guidelines free with SASE.
Tips: Writers: "Do not send handwritten material, typed double-spaced only." Illustrators: "Use ink; pencil does not reproduce well. Also, send black and white only."

*THE SOW'S EAR POETRY JOURNAL, 245 McDowell St., Bristol TN 37620. (615)764-1625. Magazine published quarterly. "Our audience includes serious poets throughout the USA. We publish school-aged poets in each issue to encourage young writers and to show our older audience that able young poets are writing. We request young poets to furnish age, grade, school and list of any previous publication." Writer's guidelines available on request.
Magazines: 3% of magazine written by children. Uses 1-5 poems (1 page). Pays 1 copy. Submit complete ms. Will accept typewritten, legibly handwritten mss. Reports in 3 months.
Artwork: Publishes artwork by children. "Prefer line drawings. Any subject or size that may be easily reduced or enlarged. Must be black & white." Pays 1 copy. Submit artwork to Mary Calhoun, Graphics Editor. Reports in 3 months.

STONE SOUP, The Magazine by Children, Children's Art Foundation, Box 83, Santa Cruz CA 95063. (408)426-5557. Articles/Fiction Editor, Art Director: Ms. Gerry Mandel. Bimonthly magazine. Circ. 12,000. "We publish fiction, poetry and artwork by children through age 13. Our preference is for work based on personal experiences and close observation of the world."

Magazines: 100% of magazine written by children. Uses animal, contemporary, fantasy, history, problem solving, science fiction, sports, spy/mystery/adventure fiction stories. Does not want to see classroom assignments and formula writing. Buys 50 mss/year. Byline given. Pays on acceptance. Buys all rights. Pays $10 each for stories and poems, $15 for book reviews. Contributors also receive 2 copies. Sample copy $2. Free writer's guidelines. Uses animal, interviews/profile, problem solving, travel nonfiction articles. "We don't publish straight nonfiction, but we do publish stories based on real events and experiences." Buys 10 mss/year. Byline given. Send complete ms. Reports in 6 weeks.

Artwork: Buys 6 illustrations/issue; 30/year. Send samples of artwork. Pays $8 for b&w illustrations. Contributors receive 2 copies. Sample copy $2. Free illustrator's guidelines. Reports in 6 weeks. Original artwork returned at job's completion. All artwork must be by children through age 13.

STRAIGHT MAGAZINE, Standard Publishing, 8121 Hamilton Ave., Cincinnati OH 45231. (513)931-4050. Magazine. 6×7; 12 pp; newsprint paper and cover stock. Estab. 1951. Weekly magazine includes fiction pieces and articles for Christian teens 13-19 years old to inform, encourage and uplift them. Purpose in publishing works by children: give them an opportunity to express themselves. Requirements to be met before work is published: must submit their birth date and Social Security number (if they have one). Writer's guidelines available on request, "included in regular guidelines."

Magazines: 15% of magazine written by children. Uses fiction (500-1,000 words); personal experience pieces (500-700 words); poetry (approx. 1 poem per issue). Pays flat fee for poetry; per word for stories/articles. Submit mss to Carla J. Crane, editor. Submit complete ms. Will accept typewritten and computer printout mss. Reports in 4-6 weeks.

Artwork: Publishes artwork by children. Looks for "anything that will fit our format." Pays flat rate. Submit artwork to Carla Crane, editor. Reports in 4-6 weeks.

SUNSHINE MAGAZINE, Henrichs Publications, Inc., Box 40, Sunshine Park, Litchfield IL 62056. (217)324-3425. Magazine published monthly. "General audience."

Magazines: "Two pages/issue written by children." Uses fiction, nonfiction and poetry (up to 200 words). Pays in copies. Submit mss to Editor. Submit complete ms. Will accept typewritten, legibly handwritten, computer printout mss. Reports in 3 months.

THUMBPRINTS, 928 Gibbs St., Caro MI 48723. (517)673-6653. Newsletter. Monthly. "Our newsletter is designed to be of interest to writers and allow writers a place to obtain a byline." Purpose in publishing works by children: to encourage them to seek publication of their work. Writer's guidelines available on request, "same guidelines as for adults."

Newsletter: Percentage of newsletter written by children "varies from month to month." Pays in copies. Submit ms to Janet Ihle, editor. Submit complete ms or have teacher submit. Will accept typewritten and computer printout mss. Reports in 6-8 weeks.

Artwork: Publishes artwork by children. Looks for art that expresses our monthly theme. Pays in copies. Send pencil or ink drawing no larger than 3×4. Submit artwork to Janet Ihle, editor.

Tips: "We look forward to well written articles and poems by children. It's encouraging to all writers when children write and are published."

TURTLE, Ben Franklin Literary & Medical Society, Children's Better Health Institute, 1100 Waterway Blvd., Box 567, Indianapolis IN 46206. (317)636-8881. Magazine. *"Turtle* is generally a health-related magazine geared toward children from ages 2-5. Purpose in publishing works by children: we enjoy giving children the opportunity to exercise

their creativity." Requirements to be met before work is published: for ages 2-5, publishes artwork or pictures that you have drawn or colored all by yourself. Writer's guidelines available on request.
Artwork: Publishes artwork by children. There is no payment for children's artwork. All artwork must have the child's name, age and complete address on it. Submit artwork to *Turtle* Magazine Executive Editorial Director: Beth Wood Thomas. "No artwork can be returned."

*VIRGINIA WRITING, Longwood College, Farmville VA 23901. (804)395-2160. Magazine published twice yearly. *"Virginia Writing* publishes prose, poetry, fiction, nonfiction, art, photography, music, and drama from Virginia high school students and teachers. The purpose of the journal is to publish 'promise.' The children must be attending a Virginia high school, preferably in no less than 9th grade (though some work has been accepted from 8th graders). Originality is strongly encouraged. The guidelines are also in the front of our magazine." No profanity or racism accepted.
Magazines: 75% of magazine written by children. Uses 17 nonfiction short stories, 56 poems and prose/issue. Submit mss to Billy C. Clark, Founder and Editor. All works: submit complete ms. Will accept typewritten mss. Reports as soon as possible.
Artwork: Publishes artwork by children. All types of artwork, including that done on computer. All work is returned upon publication in a non-bendable, well protected package with a cover letter. Submit artwork to Billy C. Clark. Reports as soon as possible.
Tips: "All works should be submitted with a cover letter describing student's age, grade and high school currently attending."

*WHOLE NOTES, P.O. Box 1374, Las Cruces NM 88004. (505)382-7446. Magazine published every even numbered year. "We look for original, fresh perceptions in writing. General audience. We try to recognize excellence in creative writing by children as a way to encourage and promote imaginative thinking." Writer's guidelines available on request.
Magazines: 25% of magazine written by children. Uses 1-3 fiction short, short stories—any kind (length open), 30 poems/issue (length open). Pays 2 complimentary copies. Submit mss to Nancy Peters Hastings, Editor. Submit complete ms. Will accept typewritten, legibly handwritten mss. Reports in 1 week.
Artwork: Publishes artwork by children. Looks for black and white line drawings which can easily be reproduced. Pays complimentary copy of issue. Send clear photocopy. Submit artwork to Nancy Peters Hastings, Editor. Reports in 1 week.

WOMBAT: A JOURNAL OF YOUNG PEOPLE'S WRITING AND ART, 365 Ashton Dr., Athens GA 30606. (404)549-4875. Newspaper, (slick cover/ newsprint interior). Published 4 times a year. "Illiteracy in a free society is an unnecessary danger which can and must be remedied. *Wombat*, by being available to young people and their parents and teachers, is one small incentive for young people to put forth the effort to learn to read and write (and draw) better, to communicate better, to comprehend better and—hopefully—consequently, to someday possess greater discernment, judgment and wisdom as a result." Purpose in publishing works by children: to serve as an incentive, to encourage them to work hard at their reading, writing and—yes—drawing/art skills, to reward their efforts. Requirements to be met before work is published: ages 6-16; all geographic regions; statement that work is original is sufficient.
Magazines: 95% of magazine written by children. Have one 2-4 page "Guest Adult Article" in most issues/when available (submitted). Uses any kind of fiction (3,000 words maximum) but avoid extreme violence, religion or sex (approaching pornography); uses any kind of nonfiction of interest to 6-16 year olds (3,000-4,000 words); cartoons, puzzles and solutions, jokes and games and solutions. Pays in copies and frameable certificates.

Submit mss to Publisher: Jacquelin Howe. Submit complete ms. Teacher can submit; parents, librarians, students can submit. Will accept typewritten, legibly handwritten, computer printout mss. Responds in 1-2 weeks with SASE; up to 12 months with seasonal or holiday works (past season or holiday). Written work is not returned. SASE permits *Wombat* to notify sender of receipt of work.

Artwork: Publishes artwork by children. Looks for: works on paper, not canvas. Photocopies OK if clear and/or reworked for clarity and strong line definition by the artist. Pays in copies and frameable certificates. Submit artwork to Publisher: Jacquelin Howe. "Artwork, only, will be returned if requested and accompanied by appropriate sized envelope, stamped with sufficient postage."

Tips: *"Wombat* is, unfortunately, on 'hold' probably throughtout this entire school year; therefore, we are asking people to please query as to when/if we will résumé publication, before subscribing or submitting works to *Wombat* right now."

WRITER'S GAZETTE NEWSLETTER, Trouvere Co., Rt. 2 Box 290, Eclectic AL 36024. Newsletter published monthly. 8½ × 11; 8 pp; 20# bond paper and cover stock. Estab. 1981. Readers are other writers. Purpose in publishing work by children: to give them the early experience and encouragement to continue to write.

Magazines: 1% of magazine written by children. Uses 1-3 fictional stories (800 words average); and 1-4 nonfiction articles (800 words average). Pays $1-50 or copy of publication. Submit ms to Brenda Williamson, editor. Will accept typewritten, legibly handwritten, computer printout form. Reports in 1-6 weeks.

Artwork: Publishes artwork by children. Looks for "simple drawings." Pays in copy of publication.

*WRITING, 60 Revere Drive, Northbrook IL 60062. (708)205-3000. Magazine published monthly. "To teach students to write and write well; grades 7-12. No formal guidelines; but letter is sent if request received."

Magazines: Small percentage of magazine written by children. Uses 1-10 mss/issue. Submit mss to Alan Lenhoff, Editor. Submit complete ms; either child or teacher may submit. Prefer typewritten mss.

*YOUNG HARTLAND/HARTLAND QUARTERLY, 7747 Ravensridge, Shrewsbury MO 63119-5505. (313)750-9134. Semiannual magazine. Purpose in publishing works by children: "Encourage the writing and publication of children's poetry." Contributors must be in grades 2-10. Writer's guidelines available on request. SASE must accompany all requests and mss.

Magazines: 90% of magazine written by children. Uses 50 poems/issue. Pays 2 copies to child. Submit mss to Dianna Drinkard, Editor. Submit complete ms. Will accept typewritten, legibly handwritten mss. Reports in 1 month.

*YOUNG VOICES MAGAZINE, P.O. Box 2321, Olympia WA 98507. (206)357-4683. Magazine published bi-monthly. "Young Voices is by elementary and middle school/ junior high students for people interested in their work." Writer's guidelines available on request.

Magazines: Uses 20 fiction stories, 5 nonfiction stories, 5 book reviews/poetry/issue. Pays $3-5 on acceptance. Submit mss to Steve Charak, Editor/Publisher. Submit complete ms. Will accept typewritten, legibly handwritten mss. Reports in 3 months.

Artwork: Publishes artwork by children. "Prefer work that will show up in black and white." Pays $3-5 on acceptance. Submit artwork to Steve Charak. Reports in 3 months.

Contests & Awards

Publication is not the only way to get your work recognized. Placing in a contest or winning an award truly validates the time spent on a craft, including writing and illustrating. Even for those who don't place, many competitions offer the chance to obtain valuable feedback from judges and other established writers or artists.

The popularity of contests among writers and illustrators is evident this year in our 27 new listings. Not all of these contests are geared strictly for professionals. Many are designed for "amateurs" who haven't yet been published. Still others are open only to students. Contests for students in this section are marked with a double dagger (‡). Contests really can be viable vehicles to gain recognition in the industry.

Be sure to study the guidelines and requirements for each contest. Note whether manuscripts and artwork should be unpublished or previously published. Also, be aware that awards vary with each contest. Where one contest may award a significant monetary amount, another may award a certificate or medal.

You will notice that some contests require nominations. If you are interested in being recommended for such an award, be sure to bring it to your editor's or art director's attention. Such a nomination is a good publicity tool for the publisher as well as yourself.

Read through the listings that interest you, then send away for more information to gain specifics about the types of written or illustrated material reviewed, word length and any qualifications you should know about, such as rights to prize-winning material.

AIM Magazine Short Story Contest, P.O. Box 20554, Chicago IL 60620. (312)874-6184. Contest Directors: Ruth Apilado, Mark Boone. Annual contest. Estab. 1983. Purpose of the contest: "We solicit stories with social significance. Youngsters can be made aware of social problems through the written word and hopefully they will try solving them." Unpublished submissions only. Deadline for entries: August 15, 1991. SASE for contest rules and entry forms. SASE for return of work. No entry fee. Awards $100. Judging by members of staff. Contest open to everyone.

*ALBERTA WRITING FOR YOUTH COMPETITION, Alberta Culture & Multiculturalism, 12th Fl., CN Tower, 10004-104 Ave., Edmonton Alberta T5J 0K5 Canada. (403)427-2554. Contact: Judy Hayman, consultant. Contest/award held every two years. Estab. 1980. Purpose of the contest/award: to encourage and develop writers in the juvenile market in Alberta. Unpublished submissions only. Deadline for entries: December 31 (even years). SASE for contest/award rules and entry forms. No entry fee. Awards for best book manuscript, $2,000 cash award from Alberta Culture and Multiculturalism, $1,000 cash advance against royalties from publisher, $1,500 12-month option for film/television from Allarcom Limited, book publishing from Doubleday Canada Ltd. Judging by independent panel of qualified judges. "Should publishing co-sponsor choose to publish winning manuscript, rights are purchased." Requirements for entrants: only those Canadian citizens or landed immigrants resident in Alberta at the time of submission and for a period of 12 out of the preceding 18 months. "Book likely to be published by Doubleday Canada Ltd., usually within 18 months of winning the competition."

‡AMERICA & ME ESSAY CONTEST, Farm Bureau Insurance, 7373 W. Saginaw, Box 30400, Lansing MI 48909. (517)323-7000. Communications/Advertising Technician: Blythe Redman. Annual contest/award. Estab. 1968. Purpose of the contest/award: to give Michigan 8th graders the opportunity to express their thoughts/feelings on America and their roles in America. Unpublished submissions only. Deadline for entries: mid-November. SASE for contest/award rules and entry forms. "We have a school mailing list. Any school located in Michigan is eligible to participate." Entries not returned. No entry fee. Awards savings bonds and plaques for state top ten ($500-1,000), certificates and plaques for top 3 winners from each school. Judging by home office employee volunteers. Requirements for entrants: "participants must work through their schools or our agents' sponsoring schools. No individual submissions will be accepted. Top ten essays and excerpts from other essays are published in booklet form following the contest. State capital/schools receive copies."

*‡AMHA MORGAN ART CONTEST, American Morgan Horse Assoc., Box 960, Shelburne VT 05482. (802)985-4944. Communications Director: Tracey Holloway. Annual contest/award. The art contest consists of three categories: Morgan art (pencil sketches, oils, water colors, paintbrush), Morgan cartoons, Morgan speciality pieces (sculptures, carvings). Unpublished submissions only. Deadline for entries: December 1. SASE for contest/award rules and entry forms. Entries not returned. Entry fee is $2. Awards $50 first prize and AMHA ribbons to top 5 places. "All work submitted becomes property of The American Morgan Horse Association. Selected works may be used for promotional purposes by the AMHA." Requirements for entrants: "We consider all work submitted." Works displayed at the annual convention.
Tips: This year the Morgan Horse Association, Inc. will be sponsoring two judgings. The first will be divided into three age groups: 13 years and under, 14-21 years and adult. The second judging will be divided into three categories and open to all ages. The top 5 places will receive official Art Contest Ribbons. Each art piece must be matted, have its own application form and its own entry fee.

‡AVON FLARE YOUNG ADULT NOVEL COMPETITION, Avon Books, 105 Madison Ave., New York NY 10016. (212)481-5609. Contest held every two years. Estab. 1983. Purpose of the contest/award: to find and encourage teenage writers. Unpublished submissions only. Deadline for entries: August 31 of odd numbered years. SASE for contest/award rules and entry forms. SASE for return of entries. No entry fee. Awards a $2,500 advance. Judging by the editors of Avon Books. Rights to winning material purchased. Requirements for entrants: "you are eligible to submit a manuscript if you will be no younger than 13 and not older than 18 years of age as of December 31. The book will be published one year after selection."
Tips: "Each manuscript should be approximately 125 to 200 pages, or about 30,000 to 50,000 words. All manuscripts must be typed, double-spaced, on a single side of the page only. Be sure to keep a copy of your manuscript; we cannot be responsible for the manuscripts. With your manuscript, please enclose a letter that includes your name, address, telephone number, age, and a short description of your novel." For information contact Lisa Norment, associate editor.

MARGARET BARTLE ANNUAL PLAYWRITING AWARD, Community Children's Theatre of Kansas City, 8021 E. 129th Terrace, Grandview MO 64030. (816)761-5775. Chairman: E. Blanche Sellens. Annual contest/award. Estab. 1950. Unpublished submissions

 The double dagger before a listing indicates the contest is for students.

WOULD YOU USE THE SAME CALENDAR YEAR AFTER YEAR?

Of course not! If you scheduled your appointments using last year's calendar, you'd risk missing important meetings and deadlines, so you keep up-to-date with a new calendar each year. Just like your calendar, *Children's Writer's & Illustrator's Market* changes every year, too. Many of the editors move or get promoted, rates of pay increase, and even editorial needs change from the previous year. You can't afford to use an out-of-date book to plan your marketing efforts!

So save yourself the frustration of getting manuscripts returned in the mail, stamped MOVED: ADDRESS UNKNOWN. And of NOT submitting your work to new listings because you don't know they exist. Make sure you have the most current writing and marketing information by ordering *1992 Children's Writer's & Illustrator's Market* today. All you have to do is complete the attached post card and return it with your payment or charge card information. Order now, and there's one thing that won't change from your *1991 Children's Writer's & Illustrator's Market* - the price! That's right, we'll send you the 1992 edition for just $16.95. *1992 Children's Writer's & Illustrator's Market* will be published and ready for shipment in February 1992.

Let an old acquaintance be forgot, and toast the new edition of *Children's Writer's & Illustrator's Market*. Order today!

(See other side for more helpful children's writing books)

More Books to Help You Get Published!

Writing for Children & Teenagers
by Lee Wyndham/revised by Arnold Madison
Filled with practical know-how and step-by-step instruction, including how to hold a young reader's attention, where to find ideas, and vocabulary lists based on age level, this third edition provides all the tips you need to flourish in today's children's literature market.
265 pages/$12.95, paperback

The Children's Picture Book: How to Write It, How to Sell It
by Ellen E. M. Roberts
If you'd like to try your hand at writing children's picture books, this guide is for you. It answers virtually every question about the writing and selling process: how to choose a subject, plot a story, work with artists and editors, and market your book. Includes advice from professional picture book writers and editors, plus a list of agents who handle picture books.
189 pages/$18.95, paperback

How to Write & Illustrate Children's Books
Edited by Treld Pelkey Bicknell & Felicity Trotman
A truly comprehensive guide that demonstrates how to bring freshness and vitality to children's text and pictures. Numerous illustrators, writers, and editors contribute their expert advice.
143 pages/$22.50

Use coupon on other side to order today!

only. Deadline for entries: January. SASE for contest/award rules and entry forms. SASE for return of entries. No entry fee. Awards $500. Judging by a committee of five.

*THE IRMA SIMONTON BLACK BOOK AWARD, Bank Street College of Education, 610 West 112th Street, New York NY 10025. (212)222-6700. Contact: Linda Greengrass. Annual award. Estab. 1972. Purpose of the award: "The award is given each spring for a book for young children, published in the previous year, for excellence of both text and illustrations." Entries must have been published during the previous calendar year. Deadline for entries: January after book is published. "Publishers submit books to us by sending them here to me at the Bank Street library. Authors may ask their publishers to submit their books. Out of these, three to five books are chosen by a committee of older children and adults. These books are then presented to children in selected second, third and fourth grade classes here and at a few other cooperating schools on the east coast. These children are the final judges who pick the actual award. The award is a scroll (one each for the author and illustrator, if they're different) with the recipient's name and a gold seal designed by Maurice Sendak."

BOOK OF THE YEAR FOR CHILDREN, Canadian Library Association, Ste. 602, 200 Elgin St., Ottawa ON K2P 1L5 Canada. (613)232-9625. Chairperson, Canadian Association of Children's Librarians. Annual contest/award. Estab. 1947. "The main purpose of the award is to encourage writing and publishing in Canada of good books for children up to and including age 14. If, in any year, no book is deemed to be of award calibre, the award shall not be made that year. To merit consideration, the book must have been published in Canada and its author must be a Canadian citizen or a permanent resident of Canada." Previously published submissions only; must be published between January 1 and December 1. Deadline for entries: January 1. SASE for contest/award rules and entry forms. Entries not returned. No entry fee. Awards a medal. Judging by committee of members of the Canadian Association of Children's Librarians. Requirements for entrants: Contest open only to Canadian authors or residents of Canada. "Winning books are on display at CLA headquarters."

*BOOK PUBLISHERS OF TEXAS CHILDREN'S/YOUNG PEOPLE'S AWARD, P.O. Box 9032, Wichita Falls TX 76308-9032. (817)692-6611 ext. 4123. Contact: James Hoggard. Send to above address for list of judges to whom entries should be submitted. Annual award. Purpose of the award: "To recognize notable achievement by a Texas writer of books for children or young people or by a writer whose work deals with a Texas subject. The award goes to the author of the winning book, a work published during the calendar year before the award is given. Judges list available each October. Deadline is first postally operative day of January." Previously published submissions only. SASE for award rules and entry forms. No entry fee. Awards $250. Judging by a panel of three judges selected by the TIL Council. Requirements for entrants: The writer must have lived in Texas for two consecutive years at some time, or the work must have a Texas theme.

 The asterisk before a listing indicates the listing is new in this edition.

*THE BOSTON GLOBE-HORN BOOK AWARDS, The Boston Globe & The Horn Book, Inc., The Horn Book, 14 Beacon St., Boston MA 02108. (617)227-1555. Contest/Award Directors: Stephanie Loer and Anita Silvey. Writing Contact: Stephanie Loer, children's book editor for *The Boston Globe*, 298 North St., Medfield MA 02052. Annual contest/award. Estab. 1967. "Awards are for picture books, nonfiction and fiction. Two honor books are also chosen for each category." Books must be published between July 1, 1990 through June 30, 1991. Deadline for entries: May 1, 1991. "Publishers usually nominate books." Award winners receive $500 and silver engraved bowl, honor book winners receive a silver plate." Judging by three judges involved in children's book field who are chosen by Anita Silvey, editor-in-chief for *The Horn Book* and Stephanie Loer, children's book editor for *The Boston Globe*. "*The Horn Book* publishes speeches given at awards ceremonies. The book must be available/distributed in the U.S. The awards are given at the fall conference of the New England Library Association."

*BUCKEYE CHILDREN'S BOOK AWARD, State Library of Ohio, 65 S. Front St., Columbus OH 43266-0334. (614)644-7061. Treva Pickenpauch, Chairperson. Correspondence should be sent to Floyd C. Dickman at the above address. Award every two years. Estab. 1981. Purpose of the award: "The Buckeye Children's Book Award Program, was designed to encourage children to read literature critically, to promote teacher and librarian involvement in children's literature programs, and to commend authors of such literature, as well as to promote the use of libraries. Awards are presented in the following three categories: Grades K-2, Grades 3-5 and Grades 6-8." Previously published submissions only. The book must have been originally copyrighted in the United States within the last three years preceding the nomination year. Deadline for entries: February 1st. "The nominees are submitted by this date during the even year and the votes are submitted by this date during the odd year. This award is nominated and voted upon by children in Ohio. It is based upon criteria established in our bylaws. The winning authors are awarded a special plaque honoring them at a special banquet given by one of the sponsoring organizations. The BCBA Board oversees the tallying of the votes and announces the winners. The book must have been written by an author, a citizen of the United States and originally copyrighted in the U.S. within the last three years preceding the nomination year. The award-winning books are displayed in a historical display housed at the Columbus Metropolitan Library in Columbus, OH."

CALDECOTT AWARD, Association for Library Service to Children, division of the American Library Association, 50 E. Huron, Chicago IL 60611. (312)944-6780. Executive Director ALSC: Susan Roman. Annual contest/award. Estab. 1938. Purpose of the contest/award: to honor the artist of the most distinguished picture book for children published in the U.S. Must be published year preceding award. Deadline for entries: December. SASE for contest/award rules and entry forms. Entries not returned. No entry fee. "Medal given at ALA Annual Conference during the Newbery/Caldecott Banquet."

CALIFORNIA WRITERS' CONFERENCE AWARDS, California Writers' Club, 2214 Derby St., Berkeley CA 94705. (415)841-1217. "Ask for contest rules before submitting entries." Contest/award offered every two years. Next conference, July 12-14, 1991. Purpose of the contest/award: "the encouragement of writers." Categories: adult fiction, adult nonfiction, juvenile fiction or nonfiction, poetry and scripts. Unpublished submissions only. SASE for contest/award rules and entry forms. SASE for return of entries. Entry fee is $5. Awards: "First prize in each category is free tuition to the Conference; second prize is cash and third a certificate." Judging by "published writer-members of California Writers' Club." Requirements for entrants: "Open to any writer who is not a member of California Writers' Club. Winners in previous contests of California Writers' Club not eligible."

CANADA COUNCIL GOVERNOR GENERAL'S LITERARY AWARDS, 99 Metcalfe St., P.O. Box 1047, Ottawa, Ontario K1P 5V8 Canada. (613)598-4376. Officer, Writing and Publishing Section: Josiane Polidori. Annual contest/award. Estab. 1976. Purpose of contest/award: to encourage Canadian authors and illustrators of books for young people as well as to recognize the importance of their contribution to literary activity. Must be published between December 1, 1990 and October 31. Eligible books are submitted by publishers (5 copies must be sent to Canada Council). All books must be received by September 30. The Council will also accept by that date finished copies of titles having an official publication date of up to October 31. Submission forms available on request. Entries not returned. No entry fee. Awards $10,000 Canadian. Judging by practicing writers, illustrators plus librarian or critic.

CHILD STUDY CHILDREN'S BOOK AWARD, Child Study Children's Book Committee at Bank St. College, 610 West 112 St., New York NY 10025. (212)222-6700. Chairperson: Anita Dare. Annual contest/award. Estab. 1943. Purpose of the contest/award: "To honor a book for children or young people which deals realistically and in a positive way with problems in their world." Must be previously published "within the current year." Submissions: "From publisher's review copies that are submitted for our annual recommended booklist, we select a winner." Entries not returned. No entry fee. Awards $500 and plaque. Judging by committee members. Works will be displayed "in our annual booklist and on display for one year in Bank St. College Library."

CHILDREN'S BOOK AWARD, Sponsored by Federation of Children's Book Groups. 30 Senneleys Park Rd., Northfield Birmingham B31 1AL England. (021)427-4860. Coordinator: Jenny Blanch. Annual contest/award. Estab. 1980. Purpose of the contest/award: "The C.B.A. is an annual prize for the best children's book of the year judged by the children themselves." Previously unpublished submissions only. Deadline for entries: December 31. Entries not returned. Awards "a magnificent silver and oak trophy worth over $6,000 and a portfolio of children's work." Judging by children. Requirements for entrants: Work must be fiction and published during the current year (poetry is ineligible). Work will be published in our current "Pick of the Year" publication.

CHILDREN'S CHOICE AWARD, Harris County Public Library, Suite 200, 49 San Jacinto, Houston TX 77002. (713)221-5350. Director: Elizabeth J. Ozbun, Children's Specialist. Annual contest/award. Estab. 1978. Purpose of the contest/award: "The objective of the program is for children to select their favorite author, to read and to use the public library. Children are free to select any published author." Deadline for entries: "Election is held in March. Children are given a blank ballot and are invited to fill in the name of their favorite author. The winning author receives a framed certificate." Judging by "children. The author with the most votes wins. Dr. Seuss 1978, Judy Blume 1979-1990." **Tips:** "Each child receives a pin with the theme, 'I VOTED.' Starting in 1988 the design used on the pin was from a child's design which was selected from entries in the Design the Button contest. The winning child receives a book of his/her choice."

*CHILDREN'S READING ROUND TABLE AWARD, Children's Reading Roundtable of Chicago, 3930 North Pine Grove, #1507, Chicago IL 60613. (312)477-2271. "Entries are made by nomination by CRRT Members only." Annual award. Estab. 1953. Purpose of the award: longtime commitment to children's books. Award recipients have been authors, editors, educators, and illustrators.

Refer to the Business of Children's Writing & Illustrating
for up-to-date marketing, tax and legal information.

THE CHRISTOPHER AWARD, The Christophers, 12 E. 48 St., New York NY 10017. (212)759-4050. Christopher Awards Coordinator: Peggy Flanagan. Annual contest/ award. Estab. 1969 (for young people; books for adults honored since 1949). Previously published submissions only; must be published between January 1 and December 31. Deadline for entries: "books should be submitted all year." Entries not returned. No entry fee. Awards a bronze medallion. Books are judged by both reading specialists and young people. Requirements for entrants: "only published works are eligible and must be submitted during the calendar year in which they are first published."
Tips: "The award is given to works, published in the calendar year for which the award is given, that 'have achieved artistic excellence, affirming the highest values of the human spirit.' They must also enjoy a reasonable degree of popular acceptance."

*‡CRICKET LEAGUE, *Cricket*, the Magazine for Children, 315 5th Street, Peru IL 61354. (815)224-6643. Address entries to: Cricket League. Monthly. Estab. 1973. "The purpose of Cricket League contests is to encourage creativity and give children an opportunity to express themselves in writing, drawing, painting, or photography. There are two contests each month. Possible categories include story, poetry, art, or photography. Each contest relates to a *specific theme* described on each *Cricket* issue's Cricket League page. Entries which do not relate to the current month's theme cannot be considered." Unpublished submissions only. Deadline for entries: the 25th of each month. Cricket League rules, contest themes and submission deadline information can be found in the current issue of *Cricket*. "We prefer that children who enter the contests subscribe to the magazine, or that they read *Cricket* in their school or library." No entry fee. Awards children's books or art/writing supplies. Judging by *Cricket* Editors. Obtains right to print prizewinning entries in magazine. Requirements for entrants: Any child age 14 or younger can enter. Restrictions of mediums for illustrators: Usually artwork must be black and white only. Refer to contest rules in current *Cricket* issue. Winning entries are published on the Cricket League pages in the *Cricket* magazine 3 months subsequent to the issue in which the contest was announced.

*DELACORTE PRESS PRIZE FOR A FIRST YOUNG ADULT NOVEL, Delacorte Press, Books for Young Readers Department, 666 Fifth Ave., Dept BFYR, New York NY 10103. (212)765-6500. Contest/Award Director: Lisa Oldenburg. Annually. Estab. 1982. Purpose of the contest/award: To encourage the writing of contemporary young adult fiction. Previously unpublished submissions only. "Entries must be submitted between Labor Day and New Year's Day of the following year. The real deadline is a December 31 postmark. Early entries are appreciated." SASE for contest/award rules. Awards a $1,500 cash prize and a $6,000 advance against royalties on a hardcover and paperback book contract. Judged by the editors of the Books for Young Readers Dept. of Delacorte Press. Rights acquired "only if the entry wins or is awarded an Honorable Mention." Requirements for entrants: The writer must be American or Canadian and must *not* have previously published a YA novel. He may have published anything else.
Tips: "Books (manuscripts) should have a contemporary setting, be suitable for ages 12-18, and be between 100 and 224 pages long. *Summaries are urgently requested.*

THE MARIE-LOUISE D'ESTERNAUX POETRY SCHOLARSHIP CONTEST, The Brooklyn Poetry Circle, Apt. 51, 61 Pierrepont St., Brooklyn NY 11201. (718)875-8736. Chairperson: Gabrielle Lederer. Annual contest/award. Estab. 1965. Purpose of the contest/ award: "to encourage students between the age of 16 and 21 to write poetry." Previously unpublished submissions only. Deadline for entries: April 15. SASE for contest rules. Entries not returned. No entry fee. Awards first place: $50; 2nd place: $25. Judging by three members (critics) of the Brooklyn Poetry Circle. Requirements for entrants: Open to *students* between 16 and 21 years of age.

*DREXEL CITATION, Drexel University, College of Information Studies, Philadelphia PA 19104. (215)895-2474. Director: Shelley G. McNamara. Annual award. Purpose of the award: "The Drexel citation is an award that was established in 1963 and given at irregular intervals since that time to honor Philadelphia or Philadelphia area authors, illustrators, publishers or others who have made outstanding contributions to literature for children in Philadelphia. The award is co-sponsored by The Free Library of Philadelphia. The recipient is selected by a committee representing both the College of Information Studies and The Free Library of Philadelphia. There is only one recipient at any given time and that recipient is recognized at an annual conference on children's literature presented each year in the spring on the Drexel campus. The recipient receives an individually designed and hand-lettered citation at a special award luncheon during the conference."

*SHUBERT FENDRICH MEMORIAL PLAYWRIGHTING CONTEST, Pioneer Drama Service, Inc., P.O. Box 22555, Denver CO 80222. (303)759-4297. Director: Steven Fendrich. Annual contest/award. Estab. 1990. Purpose of the contest/award: "To encourage the development of quality theatrical material for educational and community theater." Previously unpublished submissions only. Deadline for entries: March 1st. SASE for contest/award rules and entry forms. No entry fee. Awards $1,000 royalty advance and publication. Judging by Editors. All rights acquired when work is published. Requirements for entrants: Any writers currently published by Pioneer Drama Service are not eligible.

CAROLYN W. FIELD AWARD, Pennsylvania Library Association, 3107 N. Front St., Harrisburg PA 17110. (717)233-3113. Executive Director: Margaret S. Bauer, CAE. Annual contest/award. Estab. 1983. Purpose of the contest/award: "To honor outstanding Pennsylvania children's authors/illustrators." Previously published submissions only; must be published January-December of year of award." Deadline for entries: March 1. SASE for contest/award rules and entry forms. SASE for return of entries. No entry fee. Awards a medal, citation and luncheon honoring award winner. Judging by "children's librarians." Requirements for entrants: "Writer/illustrator must be a Pennsylvania resident." Works displayed at "PLA annual conference each fall."

DOROTHY CANFIELD FISHER CHILDREN'S BOOK AWARD, Vermont Department of Libraries, Vermont State PTA and Vermont Congress of Parents and Teachers, % Southwest Regional Library, Pierpoint Ave., Rutland VT 05701. Chairman (currently): Betty Lallier. Annual contest/award. Estab. 1957. Purpose of the contest/award: to encourage Vermont children to become enthusiastic and discriminating readers by providing them with books of good quality by living American authors published in the current year. Previously published entries are not eligible. Deadline for entries: "January of the following year." SASE for contest/award rules and entry forms. No entry fee. Awards a scroll presented to the winning author at an award ceremony. Judging is by the children grades 4-8. They vote for their favorite book. Requirements for entrants: "the book must be copyrighted in the current year. It must be written by an American author living in the U.S."

‡FLORIDA STATE WRITING COMPETITION, Florida Freelance Writers Assoc., P.O. Box 9844, Fort Lauderdale FL 33310. (305)485-0795. Juvenile Chairman: Ginger Kuh. Annual contest/award. Estab. 1984. Short Fiction: all age groups judged together/ages 6-8 — 400-900 words; Teen (ages 9-12 yrs.) — 500-1,000 words; Teen/Young Adult — 1,500-2,000 words. Nonfiction: All age groups judged together/ages 9-12: 1,000 words maximum, ages 6-8 — 500 words maximum, ages Teen/Young Adult — 2,000 words maximum. Special Categories: Edwin V. Pugh Award — best historical article; Florida Federation of Wildlife Award — best conservation article. Book Chapter (fiction or nonfiction: ages

6-8−800 words maximum; ages 9-12−1,000 words maximum; teen/YA−3,000 words maximum. Judging criteria: Interest and readability within age group, writing style and mechanics, originality, salability. Deadline: March 15. For copy of official entry form, send #10 SASE.

*FOSTER CITY ANNUAL WRITERS CONTEST, Foster City Committee for the Arts, 650 Shell Blvd., Foster City CA 94404. Contest Chairman: Ted Lance. Annual contest/ award. Estab. 1974. Categories: fiction, humor, children's story, rhymed verse, blank verse. Unpublished submissions only. Contest is kicked off in April each year and ends August 31. SASE for contest/award rules. SASE for return of entries. Entry fee is $5 for each entry. Awards $300 first prize for the best fiction work of not more than 3,000 words; $300 first prize for the best entry in the category of prose humor; $300 first prize for the best children's story of not more than 2,000 words; $300 each first prize for the best works in rhymed verse, blank verse. Poetry work not to exceed two double-spaced pages in length. Only one poetic work judged per entry fee. Rosettes will be awarded also in all five categories for first prize and honorable mention. Judging by members of the Peninsula Press Club. Requirements for entrants: entries must be original, previously unpublished and in English.

DON FREEMAN MEMORIAL GRANT-IN-AID and WORK-IN-PROGRESS GRANT, (Grant for a Contemporary Novel for young people, nonfiction research grant, grant for a work whose author has never had a book published), SCBW, P.O. Box 66296, Mar Vista Stn., Los Angeles CA 90066. Estab. 1974. Purpose of contest/award: to assist illustrator members of The SCBW. SASE for contest/award rules and entry forms. SASE for return of entries. No entry fee. Awards $1,000 plus a $500 runner-up grant. Judging by panel of people in the field. Requirements for entrants: must be SCBW member.

GOLD MEDALLION BOOK AWARDS, Evangelical Christian Publishers Association, Suite 106B, 950 W. Southern Ave., Tempe AZ 85282. (602)966-3998. Director: Doug Ross. Annual contest/award. Estab. 1975. Deadlines for entries: December 1. SASE for contest/award rules and entry form. "The work must be submitted by the publisher." Entry fee is $175 for non-members. Awards a Gold Medallion plaque.

GOLDEN KITE AWARDS, Society of Children's Bookwriters, Box 66296, Mar Vista Station, Los Angeles CA 90066. (818)347-2849. Coordinator: Sue Alexander. Annual contest/award. Estab. 1973. "The works chosen will be those that the judges feel exhibit excellence in writing, and in the case of the picture-illustrated books−in illustration, and genuinely appeal to the interests and concerns of children. For the fiction and nonfiction awards, original works and single-author collections of stories or poems of which at least half are new and never before published in book form are eligible− anthologies and translations are not. For the picture-illustration awards, the art or photographs must be original works (the texts−which may be fiction or nonfiction− may be original, public domain or previously published). Deadline for entries: December 15. SASE for contest/award rules. Self-addressed mailing label for return of entries. No entry fee. Awards statuettes and plaques. The panel of judges will consist of two children's book authors, a children's book artist or photographer (who may or may not be an author), a children's book editor and a librarian." Requirements for entrants: "Must be a member of SCBW." Works will be displayed "at national conference in August."
Tips: Books to be entered, as well as further inquiries, should be submitted to: The Society of Children's Book Writers, % Sue Alexander, 6846 McLaren, Canoga Park, CA 91307.

HIGHLIGHTS FOR CHILDREN **FICTION CONTEST**, 803 Church St., Honesdale PA 18431. (717)253-1080. "Mss should be addressed to Fiction Contest. Editor: Kent L. Brown Jr." Annual contest/award. Estab. 1980. Purpose of the contest/award: to stimulate interest in writing for children and reward and recognize excellence. Unpublished submissions only. Deadline for entries: February 28; entries accepted after January 1 only. SASE for contest/award rules and entry forms. SASE for return of entries. No entry fee. Awards 3 prizes of $1,000 each in cash (or, at the winner's election, attendance at the Highlights Foundation Writers Workshop at Chautauqua). Judging by *Highlights* editors. Winning pieces are purchased for the cash prize of $1,000. Requirements for entrants: contest open to any writer. Winners announced in June.
Tips: "This year's contest is for mystery stories up to 900 words. Stories should be consistent with *Highlights* editorial requirements. No violence, crime or derogatory humor."

AMELIA FRANCES HOWARD-GIBBON MEDAL, Canadian Library Association, Ste. 602, 200 Elgin St., Ottawa ON K2P 1L5 Canada. (613)232-9625. Chairperson, Canadian Association of Children's Librarians. Annual contest/award. Estab. 1971. Purpose of the contest/award: "the main purpose of the award is to honor excellence in the illustration of children's book(s) in Canada. To merit consideration the book must have been published in Canada and its illustrator must be a Canadian citizen or a permanent resident of Canada." Previously published submissions only; must be published between January 1 and December 31. Deadline for entries: February 1. SASE for contest/award rules and entry forms. Entries not returned. No entry fee. Awards a medal. Judging by selection committee of members of Canadian Association of Children's Librarians. Requirements for entrants: illustrator must be Canadian or Canadian resident. Winning books on display at CLA Headquarters.

*L. RON HUBBARDS'S ILLUSTRATORS OF THE FUTURE CONTEST, L. Ron Hubbard Library, P.O. Box 3190, Los Angeles CA 90078, (213)466-3310. Director: Frank Kelly-Freas. Annual contest. Estab. 1988. Purpose of the contest: "To find, reward and publicize new speculative fiction illustrators, so that they may more easily attain to professional illustrating careers." Unpublished submissions only. Deadlines: December 31, March 31, June 30, September 30. SASE for contest rules and entry forms. No entry fee. Awards quarterly: $500 to each of three winners; awards annual grand prize: $4,000. Requirements for entrants: "The Contest is open to those who have not previously published more than three black-and-white story illustrations, or more than one process-color painting, in media distributed to the public. Open to works of science fiction and fantasy." Black and white mediums only. "Winners receive offers of publication of their story illustration in the 'L. Ron Hubbard Presents Writers of The Future' series of annual anthologies from Bridge Publications. Quarterly co-winners enter a second competition for the annual Grand Prize of $4,000 illustrating assigned stories. All quarterly winners are brought to the annual Hubbard Awards event, where the Grand Prize winner is announced."

*L. RON HUBBARD'S WRITERS OF THE FUTURE CONTEST, L. Ron Hubbard Library, P.O. Box 1630, Los Angeles CA 90078. (213)466-3310. Director: Algis Budrys. Annual contest. Estab. 1984. Purpose of the contest: "To find, reward and publicize new speculative fiction writers, so that they may more easily attain to professional writing careers." Unpublished submissions only. Quarterly Deadlines: December 31, March 31, June 30, September 30. SASE for contest rules and entry forms. No entry fee. Awards Quarterly: 1st Place $1,000; 2nd Place $750; 3rd Place $500. Annual Grand Prize: $4,000. Requirements for entrants: "Contest is open to any new or amateur writer—must not have professionally published a novel or novella, or more than three short stories. Contest is for short stories or novellas of science fiction or fantasy. Winners and some finalists receive offers of publication in the 'L. Ron Hubbard Presents Writers of the Future' series of annual anthologies from Bridge Publications, Inc. WOTF Anthology authors are invited to a special writing-career management workshop, with travel, tuition and lodging paid by the contest."

INDIAN PAINTBRUSH BOOK AWARD, Wyoming Library Assoc., Box 1387, Cheyenne WY 82003. (307)632-7622. Contest/Award Director: Laura Grott. Annual contest/award. Estab. 1986. Purpose of contest/award: to encourage the children of Wyoming to read good books. Previously published submissions only, published between 1986 and 1989 (for 1991 nominations list). Deadline for entries: April 1. Books can only be submitted for the nominations list by the children of Wyoming. No entry fee. Awards a plaque. Judging by the children of Wyoming (grades 4-6) voting from a nominations list of 20. Requirements for entrants: only Wyoming children may nominate: books must be published in last 5 years, be fiction, have good reviews: final list chosen by a committee of librarians.

INTERNATIONAL READING ASSOCIATION CHILDREN'S BOOK AWARD, Sponsored by the Institute for Reading Research-International Reading Association, 800 Barksdale Rd., P.O. Box 8139, Newark DE 19714-8139. (302)731-1600. FAX: (302)731-1057. Public Information Associate: Wendy L. Russ. Annual contest/award. To submit a book for consideration, send 10 copies to: Eileen M. Burke, 48 Bayberry Rd., Trenton NJ 08618. Categories: young readers—4-10, older readers—10-16. Must be published between January 1990 and December 1990. Deadline for entries: December 1 of each year. SASE for contest/award rules and entry forms. Awards a $1,000 stipend and medal. Requirements for entrants: Must be a writer's first or second book. Award is presented each year at annual convention.

IOWA TEEN AWARD, Iowa Educational Media Association, 2211 Northwestern, Ames IA 50010. (515)232-0307. Co-Chairmen: Norma Sisson and Twyla Kerr. Annual contest/award. Estab. 1983. Purpose of contest/award: to allow students to read high quality literature and to have opportunity to select their favorite from this list. Must have been published "in last 3-4 years." Deadline for entries: August 1. "Media specialists, teachers and students nominate possible entries." Awards a brass apple and opportunity to speak at IEMA annual convention. Judging by students in 6-9th grade. Requirements: To be of recent publication, so copies can be ordered for media center collections and to be nominated by media specialists on a scale of 1-5. Works displayed "at participating schools in Iowa."

*IUPUI YOUTH THEATRE PLAYWRITING COMPETITION AND SYMPOSIUM, Indiana University-Purdue University at Indianapolis, 525 North Blackford Street, Indianapolis IN 46202. (317)274-2095. Director: Dorothy Webb. Entries should be submitted to W. Mark McCreary, Literary Manager. Contest/award every two years. Purpose of the contest/award: "To improve both the artistic quality and quantity of dramatic literature for young audiences and to explore literary and artistic standards of dramatic literature intended for young people." Unpublished submissions only. Deadline for entries: October 1. SASE for contest/award rules and entry forms. No entry fee. "Awards will be presented to the top ten finalists. Four cash awards of $1,000 each will be received by the top four playwrights of whose scripts will be given developmental work culminating in polished readings showcased at the Symposium held on the IUPUI campus. Major publishers of scripts for young audiences, directors, producers, critics and teachers attend this Symposium and provide useful reactions to the plays. If a winner is unable to be involved in preparation of the reading and to attend the showcase of his/her work, the prize will not be awarded. Remaining finalists will receive certificates." Judging by professional directors, dramaturgs, publishers, university professors.

Tips: "Write for guidelines and entry form."

THE EZRA JACK KEATS NEW WRITER AWARD, Writing Contact: Hannah Nuba, Director, %The New York Public Library Early Childhood Resource and Information Center, 66 Leroy St., New York NY 10014. (212)929-0815. Biennial contest/award. Estab. 1986. Purpose of the contest/award: "Award to writers of books done in the tradition of Ezra Jack Keats that appeal to very young children, capture universal qualities of childhood in a multicultural world and portray strong family relationships." Previously published submissions only: Must be published the year of contest or the year before. Deadline for entries: December. SASE for contest/award rules and entry form. Entries not returned. No entry fee. Awards silver Ezra Jack Keats Medal and $500. "Books that reflect the tradition of Ezra Jack Keats: represent the multicultural nature of the world and extend the child's awareness and understanding of other cultural/ethnic groups; capture the universal qualities of childhood; portray strong family relationships; appeal to children ages 9 and under. The author should have published no more than six books. Picture books are judged on the outstanding features of the the text. Candidates need not be both author and illustrator."

KERLAN AWARD, Kerlan Collection, 109 Walter Library, 117 Pleasant St. SE, University of Minnesota, Minneapolis MN 55455. (612)624-4576. Curator: Karen Nelson Hoyle. Annual award. Estab. 1975. "Given in recognition of singular attainments in the creation of children's literature and in appreciation for generous donation of unique resources to the Kerlan Collection." Previously published submissions only. Deadline for entries: November 1. Anyone can send nominations for the award, directed to the Kerlan Collection. No materials are submitted other than the person's name. No entry fee. Award is a laminated plaque. Judging by the Kerlan Award Committee—three representatives from the University of Minnesota faculty (from the College of Education, the College of Home Economics, and the College of Liberal Arts); one representative from the Kerlan Collection; one representative from the Kerlan Friends; one representative from the Minnesota Library Association. Requirements for entrants: open to all who are nominated. Anyone can submit names. "For serious consideration, entrant must be a published author and/or illustrator of children's books (including young adult fiction) and have donated original materials to the Kerlan Collection."

*JANUSZ KORCZAK AWARDS, Joseph H. and Belle R. Braun Center for Holocaust Studies, Anti-Defamation League, 823 United Nations Plaza, New York NY 10017. (212)490-2525. FAX: (212)867-0779. Contest/Award Director: Dr. Dennis B. Klein. Estab. 1980. Purpose of contest/award: The award honors books for and about children which best exemplify Janusz Korczak's principles of selflessness and human dignity. SASE for contest/award rules and entry forms. No entry fee. Judging by an interdisciplinary committee of leading scholars, editors, literary critics and educators. Press release will announce winners.

‡ELIAS LIEBERMAN STUDENT POETRY AWARD, Poetry Society of America, 15 Gramercy Park, New York NY 10003. (212)254-9628. Contest/Award Director: Elise Paschen. Annual contest/award. Purpose of the contest/award: Award is for the best unpublished poem by a high or preparatory school student (grades 9-12) from the U.S. and its territories. Unpublished submissions only. Deadline for entries: December 31. SASE for contest/award rules and entry forms. Entries not returned. No entry fee. Award: $100. Judging by a professional poet. Requirements for entrants: Contest open to all high school and preparatory students from the U.S. and its territories. School attended, as well as name and address, should be noted. Line limit: none. "The award-winning poem will be included in a sheaf of poems that will be part of the program at the award ceremony, and sent to all PSA members."

VICKY METCALF BODY OF WORK AWARDS, Canadian Authors Association, 121 Avenue Rd. #104, Toronto ON M5R 2G3 Canada. (416)926-8084. Attn: Awards Chairman. Annual contest/award. Estab. 1963. Purpose of the contest/award: to honor a body of work inspirational to Canadian youth. Deadline for entries: December 31. SASE for contest/award rules and entry forms. Entries not returned. No entry fee. Awards $2,000. Judging by panel of CAA-appointed judges including past winner.
Tips: "The prizes are given solely to stimulate writing for children by Canadian writers," said Mrs. Metcalf when she established the award. "We must encourage the writing of material for Canadian children without setting any restricting formulas."

VICKY METCALF SHORT STORY AWARD, Canadian Authors Association, 121 Avenue Rd. #104, Toronto ON M5R 2G3 Canada. (416)926-8084. Attn: Awards Chairman. Annual contest/award. Estab. 1982. Purpose of the award: to honor writing by a Canadian inspirational to Canadian youth. Previously published submissions only; must be published between January 1 and December 31. Deadline for entries: December 31. SASE for contest/award rules and entry forms. Entries not returned. No entry fee. Awards $1,000 to Canadian author and $1,000 to Canadian editor of winning story. Judging by CAA-selected panel including past winners.

THE MILNER AWARD, Atlanta-Fulton Public Library/Friends of the Atlanta Fulton Public Library, One Margaret Mitchell Square, Atlanta GA 30303. (404)730-1710. Exec. Director: Rennie Jones Davant. Annual contest/award. Estab. 1983. Purpose of the contest/award: "The Milner Award is an annual award to a living American author of children's books. Selection is made by the children of Atlanta voting for their favorite author during Children's Book Week." Previous winners not eligible. "The winning author is awarded a specially commissioned work of the internationally famous glass sculptor, Hans Frabel, and a $1,000 honorarium." Requirements for entrants: "Winner must be an American author, able to appear personally in Atlanta to receive the award at a formal program."

*‡MISSISSIPPI VALLEY POETRY CONTEST, North American Literary Escadrille, P.O. Box 3188, Rock Island IL 61204. Director: Sue Katz. Annual contest. Estab. 1971. Categories for adults, high school, junior high and elementary students. Unpublished submissions only. Deadline for entries: September 15. SASE for contest rules and entry forms. Entry fee of $3 will cover up to 5 poems submitted. Cash awards from $30-125. Requirements for entrants: Open to any student or adult poet, writer or teacher.

NATIONAL JEWISH BOOK AWARD FOR CHILDREN'S LITERATURE, (Shapolsky Award), JCCA Jewish Book Council, 15 E. 26th St., New York NY 10010. (212)532-4949. Awards Coordinator: Dr. Marcia W. Posner. Annual contest/award. Estab. 1950. Previously published submissions only; must be published in 1990 for 1991 award. Deadline for entries: November 19. SASE for contest/award rules and entry forms. Entries not returned. No entry fee. Awards $750. Judging by 3 authorities in the field. Requirements for entrants: contest for best Jewish children's books, published only for ages 8-14. Books will be displayed at the awards ceremony in NYC in June.

‡THE 1991 NATIONAL WRITTEN & ILLUSTRATED BY . . . AWARDS CONTEST FOR STUDENTS, Landmark Editions, Inc., Box 4469, Kansas City MO 64127. (816)241-4919. Contest/Award Director: Teresa Melton. Annual awards contest with 3 published winners. Purpose of the contest/award: to encourage and celebrate the creative efforts of students. There are three age categories (6-9 years of age; 10-13; and 14-19). Unpublished submissions only. Deadline for entries: May 1. Contest rules available for self-addressed, business-sized envelope, stamped with 45¢ postage."Need to send a self-addressed, sufficiently stamped book mailer with book entry" for its return. No entry fee. Prize: "Book is published." Judging by national panel of educators, editors, illustrators and authors. "Each student winner receives a publishing contract allowing Landmark to publish the book. Copyright is in student's name and student receives royalties on sale of book. Books must be in proper contest format and submitted with entry form signed by a teacher or librarian. Students may develop their illustrations in any medium of their choice, as long as the illustrations remain two-dimensional and flat to the surface of the paper." Works will be published in 1992, Kansas City, MO for distribution nationally and internationally. Winner and runners-up in each age category will receive college scholarships from the R.D. and Joan Dale Hubbard Foundation: winner, $5,000; second place, $2,000; third, fourth, and fifth places, $1,000 each.

NEW JERSEY AUTHOR AWARD, Alumni Association, NJ Institute of Technology, Newark NJ 07076. (201)596-3449. Director: Dr. Herman A. Estrin. Annual contest/award. Estab. 1960. Purpose of the contest/award: "To honor New Jersey authors of published books." Previously published submissions only; must be published September, 1989 to December, 1991. Deadline for entries: January 30, 1991. SASE for contest/award rules and entry forms. Entries not returned. No entry fee. Awards "an author's citation and a guest invitation to NJ Authors Banquet." Judging by "publishers of books written by NJ authors. March 19, 1991, NJ Authors' works will be displayed in the lounge of student center at NJIT."

‡NEW JERSEY POETRY CONTEST, NJIT Alumni Association, 323 Martin Luther King Blvd., Newark NJ 07102. (201)596-3441. Contest Director: Dr. Herman A. Estrin. Annual contest/award. Estab. 1977. Purpose of the contest/award: to encourage young poets to write poetry and to have it eventually published. Unpublished submissions only. Deadline for entries: February 10. SASE for contest rules and entry forms. Entries not returned. No entry fee. Awards a citation with the poet's name and the name of the poem. Also, the poem will be published in an anthology. Judging by teachers of English. *Requirements for entrants: poet must be a NJ resident.* "The published anthology can be obtained through NJIT Alumni office."

NEWBERY MEDAL AWARD, Association for Library Service to Children—division of the American Library Association, 50 E Huron, Chicago IL 60611. (312)944-6780. Executive Director, ALSC: Susan Roman. Annual contest/award. Estab. 1922. Purpose of the contest/award: for the most distinguished contribution to American children's literature published in the U.S. Previously published submissions only; must be published prior to year award is given. Deadline for entries: December. SASE for contest/award rules and entry forms. Entries not returned. No entry fee. Medal awarded at banquet during annual conference. Judging by Newbery Committee.

THE NOMA AWARD FOR PUBLISHING IN AFRICA, Kodansha Ltd., % Hans Zell Associates, 11 Richmond Rd. P.O. Box 56, Oxford OX1 3EL England. (0865)511428. Telex: 940/2872ZELLG. FAX: (0865)793298. Secretary of the Managing Committee: Hans M. Zell. Annual contest/award. Estab. 1979. Purpose of contest/award: To encourage publications of works by African writers and scholars in Africa, instead of abroad, as is still too often the case at present. Categories of books eligible for the Award are scholarly or academic, books for children, literature and creative writing, including fiction, drama and poetry. Previously published submissions only. 1991 Award given for book published in 1990. Deadline for entries: end of February. Submissions must be made

 The double dagger before a listing indicates the contest is for students.

through publishers. Conditions of entry and submission forms are available from the secretariat. Entries not returned. No entry fee. Award is $5,000. Judging by the Managing Committee (jury): African scholars and book experts and representatives of the international book community. Chairman: Professor Asiola Irele. Requirements for entrants: author must be African, and book published in Africa. "Winning titles are displayed at appropriate international book events."

THE SCOTT O'DELL AWARD FOR HISTORICAL FICTION, 1100 E. 57th St., Chicago IL 60037. Award Director: Mrs. Zena Sutherland. Annual contest/award. Purpose of the contest/award: "To promote the writing of historical fiction of good quality." Previously published submissions only; must be published between January 1 and December 31 of each year. Deadline for entries: December 31. "Publishers send books, although occasionally a writer sends a note or a book." SASE for contest/award rules and entry forms. No entry fee. Award $5,000. Judging by the advisory committee of *The Bulletin of the Center for Children's Books* at the University of Chicago." Requirements for entrants: "Must be published by a U.S. publisher in the preceding year; must be by an American citizen; must be set in the North or South American continent; must be historical fiction."

*‡OHIO GENEALOGICAL SOCIETY ESSAY/ART CONTEST, Ohio Genealogical Society, Box 2625, Mansfield OH 44906. (419)522-9077. Director: Tacy A. Arledge. Annual contest. Estab. 1985. Purpose of the contest: "The purpose is to foster an interest in the child's ancestry and heritage. The essay division requires knowledge of proper research techniques, documentation, proper grammar and footnoting. The art division includes paintings, songs, poetry, needlework, photography, etc. and is designed to encourage creativity involving a family's heritage." Unpublished submissions only. Deadline for entries: March 1. SASE for contest rules and entry forms. No entry fee. Monetary awards. All essays submitted become property of OGS. All winning entries become property of OGS. Requirements for entrants: "Out-of-state children submitting entries must be a member of OGS, or child/grandchild/great grandchild of an OGS member. All children living in Ohio are eligible to enter, regardless of OGS membership."
Tips: There are 2 divisions—junior division includes students in third grade thru the age of 13; senior division are students over 13 through seniors in high school.

OHIOANA BOOK AWARDS, Ohioana Library Association, 1105 State Departments Bldg., 65 S. Front St., Columbus OH 43215. (614)466-3831. Director: Linda R. Hengst. Annual contest/award. "The Ohioana Book Awards are given to books of outstanding literary quality. Up to 6 Book Awards are given each year. Awards may be given in the categories of: fiction, nonfiction, children's literature, poetry and books about Ohio or an Ohioan. Books must be received by the Ohioana Library during the calendar year prior to the year the Award is given and must have a copyright date within the last two calendar years." Deadline for entries: December 31. SASE for contest/award rules and entry forms. No entry fee. "Any book that has been written or edited by a person born in Ohio or who has lived in Ohio for at least five years" is eligible.

HELEN KEATING OTT AWARD FOR OUTSTANDING CONTRIBUTION TO CHILDREN'S LITERATURE, Church and Synagogue Library Association, Box 19357, Portland OR 97219. (503)244-6919. Chair of Committee: Tacy Woods. Annual contest/award. "This award is given to a person or organization that has made a significant contribution to promoting high moral and ethical values through children's literature." Deadline for entries: February 1. "Recipient is honored in July during the conference." Awards certificate of recognition and a conference package consisting of registration, meals and housing. "A nomination for an award may be made by anyone. It should include the name, address and telephone number of the nominee plus the church or synagogue relationship where appropriate. Nominations of an organization should include the name of a contact person. A detailed description of the reasons for the nomination should be given, accompanied by documentary evidence of accomplishment. The person(s) making the nomination should give his/her name, address and telephone number and a brief explanation of his/her knowledge of the nominee's accomplishments. Elements of creativity and innovation will be given high priority by the judges.

*PLEASE TOUCH MUSEUM BOOK AWARD, Please Touch Museum, 210 N. 21st St., Philadelphia PA 19103. (215)963-0667. Curator of Education: Mary Ann Baron. Annual award. Estab. 1985. Purpose of the award: "Award is given to an outstanding concept book for children three and younger." Previously published submissions only. Deadline for entries: December 15. SASE for award rules and entry forms. No entry fee. Includes Book Award Celebration Day, hologram to winner and citation from Mayor. Judging by selected jury of children's literature experts, librarians, literacy officials and child development specialists. Education store purchases books for selling at Book Award Celebration Day and throughout the year.

‡PUBLISH-A-BOOK CONTEST, Raintree Publishers, 310 W. Wisconsin Ave., Milwaukee WI 53203. (414)273-0873. FAX: (414)273-0877. Vice President for Marketing and Sales: Julia G. Mayo. Send written entries: PAB Contest. Annual contest/award. Estab. 1984. Purpose of the contest/award: to stimulate 4th, 5th and 6th graders to write outstanding stories for children. Unpublished submissions only. Deadline for entries: January 31. SASE for contest/award rules and entry forms. "Entries must be sponsored by a teacher or librarian." Entries not returned. No entry fee. Grand prizes: Raintree will publish four winning entries in the fall of 1990. Each winner will receive a $500 advance against an author royalty contract and ten free copies of the published book. The sponsor named on each of these entries will receive 20 free books from the Raintree catalog. Honorable mentions: each of the twenty honorable mention writers will receive $25. The sponsor named on each of these entries will receive ten free books from the Raintree catalog. Judging by an editorial team. Contract issued for Grand Prize winners. Payment and royalties paid. Requirements for entrants: contest is open only to 4th, 5th and 6th graders enrolled in a school program in the United States or other countries. Books will be displayed and sold in the United States and foreign markets. Displays at educational association meetings, book fairs. "We also have a separate contest for children in grades 2 and 3, established in 1989. All of the above is the same with the exception of the grades, deadline of March 1 and number of winners will be one."

‡ANNA DAVIDSON ROSENBERG AWARD FOR POEMS ON THE JEWISH EXPERIENCE, Judah L. Magnes Museum, 2911 Russell St., Berkeley CA 94705. (415)849-2710. Poetry Award Coordinator: P. Friedman. Annual award. Estab. 1986-87. Purpose of the contest/award: to encourage poetry in English on the Jewish experience. Previously unpublished submissions only. Deadline for entries: August 31. SASE for contest/award rules and entry forms. SASE for list of winners. Awards $100-1st Prize, $50-2nd Prize, $25-3rd Prize; honorable mention certificates; *$25 Youth Commendation (poets under 19)*. Judging by committee of 3. There will be a reading of winners in December at Museum. Prospective anthology of winning entries.
Tips: Write for entry form and guidelines *first*; entries must follow guidelines and be accompanied by entry form.

*CARL SANDBURG LITERARY ARTS AWARDS, Friends of the Chicago Public Library, 78 E. Washington St., Chicago IL 60602. (312)269-2922. Annual contest/award. Categories: fiction, nonfiction, poetry, children's literature. Published submissions only; must be published between June 1 and May 31 (the following year). Deadline for entries: September 1. SASE for contest/award rules and entry forms. Entries not returned.

No entry fee. Awards trophy and $1,000. Judging by authors, reviewers, book buyers, librarians. Requirements for entrants: native born Chicagoan or presently residing in the six-county metropolitan area. Two copies submitted by September 1. All entries become the property of the Friends.

‡SEVENTEEN FICTION CONTEST, Smith Corona, 9th Fl., 850 Third Ave., New York NY 10022. (212)759-8100. Fiction Editor: Adrian Nicole LeBlanc. Annual contest/award. Unpublished submissions only. Deadline for entries: January 31. SASE for contest/award rules and entry forms. Entries not returned. No entry fee. Awards cash prize. Judging by "external readers, in-house panel of editors." If first prize, acquires first North American rights for piece to be published. Requirements for entrants: "Our annual fiction contest is open to anyone between the ages of 13 and 21 on January 31. Submit only original fiction that has never been published in any form other than in school publications. Stories should be between 1,500 and 3,000 words in length (six to twelve pages). All manuscripts must be typed double-spaced on a single side of paper. Submit as many original stories as you like, but each story must include your full name, address, birth date and signature in the top right-hand corner of the first page. Your signature on submission will constitute your acceptance of the contest rules."

SFWA NEBULA AWARDS, Science Fiction Writers of America, Inc., Box 4335, Spartanburg SC 29305. (803)578-8012. Executive Secretary: Peter Dennis Pautz. Annual contest/award. Estab. 1966. Purpose of the contest/award: to recognize meritorious achievement of short stories, novelettes, novellas and novels published the previous calendar year in the science fiction/fantasy genre. Previously published submissions only; must be published between January 1 and December 31 of the previous calendar year. "Works are nominated and selected by our active membership." Entries not returned. Awards a trophy. Judging by the active membership of the SFWA, Inc.

‡SHOE TREE CONTESTS, National Association for Young Writers, Inc., 215 Valle del Sol Dr., Santa Fe NM 87501. (505)982-8596. Editor: Sheila Cowing. Contest/award offered 3 times a year/one each fiction, nonfiction, poetry. Estab. 1984. "The purpose of the awards is to stimulate young writers to do their best work. Fiction, poetry, nonfiction." Unpublished submissions only. Deadline for entries: December 1, fiction; April 1, poetry; June 1, nonfiction. SASE for contest/award rules and entry forms. No entry fee. Awards first prize $25, second prize $10, honorable mention; all receive publication in *Shoe Tree*: "All writers may have work reprinted elsewhere after they write requesting permission, providing credit is given to *Shoe Tree*." Works will be published in the issue of *Shoe Tree* following due date.
Tips: "Contests are open to all children between the ages of 6-14, first grade through eighth, at the time of entry. A statement of authenticity signed by the student and by a parent, teacher, or guardian must accompany the entry. Student's name, address, age and the names of his or her school and teacher must accompany the entry."

CHARLIE MAY SIMON BOOK AWARD, Arkansas Elementary School Council, Arkansas Dept of Education, #4 Capitol-305-B, Little Rock AR 72201. (501)682-4371. Award Director: James A. Hester. Annual contest/award. Estab. 1970. Purpose of contest/

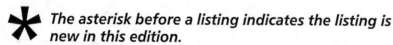

The asterisk before a listing indicates the listing is new in this edition.

award: to promote reading—to encourage reading of quality literature and book discussion. Previously published submissions only; must be published between January 1 and December 31 of calendar year; all books must have recommendations from 3 published sources. No entry fee. Awards a medallion. Contest open to entry by any writer, provided book is printed in year being considered.

GEORGE G. STONE CENTER FOR CHILDREN'S BOOKS RECOGNITION OF MERIT AWARD, George G. Stone Center for Children's Books, The Claremont Graduate School, 131 E. 10th St., Claremont CA 91711-6188. (714)621-8000 ext. 3670. Contest/ Award Director: Doty Hale. Annual contest/award. Estab. 1965. Purpose of the contest/ award: given to an author or illustrator of a children's book or for a body of work for the "power to please and expand the awareness of children and teachers as they have shared the book in their classrooms." Previously published submissions only. SASE for contest/award rules and entry forms. Entries not returned. No entry fee. Awards a scroll by artist Richard Beasley. Judging by a committee of teachers, professors of children's literature and librarians. Requirements for entrants: "nominations are made by students, teachers, professors and librarians. Award made at annual Claremont Reading Conference in spring (March)."

*SYDNEY TAYLOR MANUSCRIPT COMPETITION, Association of Jewish Libraries, 15 Goldsmith St., Providence RI 02906. (401)274-1117. Director: Lillian Schwartz. Annual contest. Estab. 1985. Purpose of the contest: "This competition is for unpublished writers of fiction. Material should be for readers aged 8 to 12 years, with universal appeal that will serve to deepen the understanding of Judaism for all children, revealing positive aspects of Jewish life." Unpublished submissions only. Deadline for entries: January 15. SASE for contest rules and entry forms. No entry fee. Awards $1,000. Judging by qualified judges from within the Association of Jewish Libraries. Requirements for entrants: Must be an unpublished author.

‡VERY SPECIAL ARTS YOUNG PLAYWRIGHTS PROGRAM, Very Special Arts Education Office, John F. Kennedy Center for the Performing Arts, Washington D.C. 20566. (202)628-2800. Janet Rice, Program Director. Annual contest/award. Estab. 1984. "All scripts must address or incorporate some aspect of disability." Unpublished submissions only. Deadline for entries: February 19, 1991. Deadline changes each year according to production date. Write to Young Playwrights Coordinator for contest/award rules and entry forms. No entries returned. No entry fee. Judging by Artists Selection Committee. "Very Special Arts retains the rights for videotaping and broadcasting on television and/or radio." Requirements for entrants: Scripts must be written by students between the ages of 12 and 18. "Script will be selected for production at the John F. Kennedy Center for the Performing Arts, Washington D.C."

‡VFW VOICE OF DEMOCRACY, Veterans of Foreign Wars of the U.S., 34th & Broadway, Kansas City MO 64111. (816)756-3390. Director: Gordon Thorson. Annual contest/ award. Estab. 1960. Purpose of the contest/award: to give high school students the opportunity to voice their opinions about their responsibility to our country and to convey them via the broadcast media to all of America. Deadline for entries: November 15. SASE for contest/award rules and entry forms. SASE for return of entries. No entry fee. Awards prizes with monetary awards ranging from $1,000-18,000. Requirements for entrants: "10th, 11th and 12th grade students in public, parochial and private schools in the United States and overseas are eligible to compete. Former national and/or 1st place state winners are not eligible to compete again. U.S. citizenship is required."

*THE STELLA WADE CHILDREN'S STORY AWARD, AMELIA Magazine, 329 E St., Bakersfield CA 93304. (805)323-4064. Editor: Frederick A. Raborg, Jr. Annual contest/ award. Estab. 1988. Purpose of the contest/award: with decrease in the number of religious and secular magazines for young people, the juvenile story and poetry must be preserved and enhanced. Unpublished submissions only. Deadline for entries: August 15. SASE for contest/award rules and for return of entries. Entry fee is $5 per adult entry; there is no fee for entries submitted by young people under the age of 17, but such entry must be signed by parent, guardian or teacher to verify originality. Awards $125 plus publication. Judging by editorial staff. Previous winners include Maxine Kumin and Sharon E. Martin. "We use First North American serial rights only for the winning manuscript." Contest is open to all interested. If illustrator wishes to enter only an illustration without a story, the entry fee remains the same. Illustrations will also be considered for cover publication. Restrictions of mediums for illustrators: no restrictions, though submitted photos should be no smaller than 5×7. Illustrations (drawn) may be in any medium. "Winning entry will be published in the most appropriate issue of either AMELIA, CICADA or SPSM&H—subject matter would determine such. Submit clean, accurate copy."

‡**WE ARE WRITERS, TOO!**, Creative With Words Publications, Box 223226, Carmel CA 93922. (408)649-1862. Contest/Award Director: Brigitta Geltrich. Annual contest/award. Estab. 1975. Unpublished submissions only. Deadline for entries: May 31. SASE for contest/award rules and entry forms. SASE for return of entries "if not winning poem." No entry fee. Awards publication is an anthology. Judging by selected guest editors and educators. Contest open to children only (up to and including 18 years old). **Tips:** Writer must request contest rules.

*****WESTERN HERITAGE AWARDS**, National Cowboy Hall of Fame, 1700 NE 63rd St., Oklahoma City OK 73111. (405)478-2250. Director of Public Relations: David Sullivant. Annual contest/award. Estab. 1961. Purpose of the contest/award: The WHA is presented annually to encourage the accurate and artistic telling of great stories of the West. Categories include fiction, nonfiction, children's books, poetry. Must have been published in previous contest year. Previously published submissions only; must be published the calendar year before the awards are presented. Deadline for entries: December 31. SASE for contest/award rules and entry forms. Entries not returned. No entry fee. Awards a Wrangler award, a reproduction of a C.M. Russell bronze. Judging by a panel of judges selected each year with distinction in various fields of western art and heritage. Requirements for entrants: the material must pertain to the development or preservation of the West, either from a historical or contemporary viewpoint. Historical accuracy is vital. "There is an autograph party preceding the awards. Film clips are shown during the awards presentation."

LAURA INGALLS WILDER AWARD, Association for Library Service to Children—a division of the American Library Association, 50 E. Huron, Chicago IL 60611. (312)944-6780. Executive Director, ALSC: Susan Roman. Contest/award offered every 3 years. Purpose of the contest/award: to recognize an author or illustrator whose books, published in the U.S., have over a period of years made a substantial and lasting contribution to children's literature. Awards a medal. Judging by committee which chooses several authors—winner is chosen by vote of ALSC membership.

*****PAUL A. WITTY SHORT STORY AWARD**, International Reading Association, 800 Barksdale Road, P.O. Box 8139, Newark DE 19714-8139. (302)731-1600. Chair of Committee: Dorothy Grant Hennings. Annual contest. Estab. 1986. Purpose of award: "The entry must be an original short story appearing in a young children's periodical that regularly publishes short stories for children. (These would be periodicals generally aimed at readers to about age twelve.) The awarded short story should serve as a reading and literary standard by which readers can measure other writing and should encourage young readers to read by providing them with enjoyable and profitable reading." Previously published submissions only. Deadline for entries: "The entry must have been published for the first time in the eligibility year; the short story must be submitted during the calendar year of publication; thus a story will be considered but one time; the story may be entered into the award competition by its publisher. A story may be entered into the competition by members of the subcommittee or other members of IRA. Anyone wishing to nominate a short story should send it to the designated Paul A. Witty Short Award Subcommittee Chair as early as possible. The chair will then request that the publisher send two copies of the story in manuscript form by the stated deadline. Both fiction and nonfiction writing are eligible; each will be rated according to characteristics that are appropriate for the genre." Interested authors should send inquiry to IRA in Newark, DE. Award is $1,000 and recognition at the annual IRA Convention.

*ALICE LOUISE WOOD OHIOANA AWARD FOR CHILDREN'S LITERATURE, Ohioana Library Association, 1105 State Departments Bldg., 65 S. Front St., Columbus OH 43215. (614)466-3831. Director: Linda R. Hengst. Annual award. Estab. 1991. Purpose of the award: "Award of $1,000 to an Ohio author whose body of work has made, and continues to make, a significant contribution to literature for children or young adults." SASE for award rules and entry forms. Requirements for entrants: "Born in Ohio, or lived in Ohio for a minimum of five years; established a distinguished publishing record of books for children and young people; body of work has made, and continues to make, a significant contribution to the literature for young people; Through whose work as a writer, teacher, administrator, or through community service, interest in children's literature has been encouraged and children have become involved with reading."

YOUNG ADULT CANADIAN BOOK AWARD, % Unionville Library, 15 Library Lane, Markham, Ont. L3R 5C4. (416)477-2641. Contest/Award Director: Nancy E. Black. Annual contest/award. Estab. 1981. Purpose of contest/award: "To recognize the author of an outstanding English-language Canadian book which appeals to young adults between the ages of 13 and 18 that was published the preceding calendar year. Information is available for anyone requesting. We approach publishers, also send news releases to various journals, i.e. *Quill & Quire*." Entries are not returned. No entry fee. Awards a leather-bound book, sometimes author tour. Requirement for entrants: a work of fiction (novel or short stories), the title must be a Canadian publication in either hardcover or paperback, and the author must be a Canadian citizen or landed immigrant. Award given at the Canadian Library Association Conference.

*YOUNG PEOPLE'S AWARD, Friends of American Writers, 15237 Redwood Lane, Libertyville IL 60048. Director: Roma Rosen. Annual award. Estab. 1922. Previously published submissions only. Deadline for entries: December 31. SASE for awards rules and entry forms. No entry fee. Awards $700—first prize, $400—second prize. Author cannot have published more than 3 books.

YOUNG READER'S CHOICE AWARD, Pacific Northwest Library Association, 133 Suzzallo Library, FM-30, Graduate School of Library and Information Science, Seattle WA 98195. (206)543-1897. Secretary: Carol Doll. Award Director: Terry Hyer, 812 E. Clark, Pocatello, ID 83201. Annual contest/award. Estab. 1940. Purpose of the contest/award: to promote reading for enjoyment. Previously published submissions only; must be published 3 years before award year. Deadline for entries: February 1. SASE for contest/award rules and entry forms. No entry fee. Awards a silver medal, struck in Idaho silver. "Children vote for their favorite (books) from a list of titles nominated by librarians, teachers, students and other interested persons."

‡YOUNG WRITER'S CONTEST, Young Writer's Contest Foundation, Box 6092, McLean VA 22106. (703)893-6097. Executive Director: Kathie Janger. Annual contest/award. Estab. 1984. Purpose of the contest/award: to challenge first through eighth graders and to give them recognition; in so doing, we aim to improve basic communication skills. Unpublished submissions only. Deadline for entries: November 30. SASE for contest/ award rules and entry forms. Entries not returned. Entry fee is $15 per school (or, if school does not participate, the individual may pay the fee). "All participating students and schools receive certificates; winners' entries are published in our anthology: *Rainbow Collection: Stories and Poetry by Young People.*" Judging by writers, editors, journalists, teachers, reading specialists. "All rights surrounding winners' entries are given to YWCF, via consent and release form. Participants must be currently enrolled in grades 1-8; no more than 12 entries per school may be submitted; we accept poems, stories and essays. *Rainbow Collection: Stories and Poetry by Young People* is published in May of each year, and is distributed (25,000 cc. in 1989) to libraries, school systems and charitable organizations. The YWCF complements classroom writing programs and creates a cycle of encouragement and performance; writing is critical to all fields of endeavor; we reward the students' efforts — not just the winners.' "

Resources

Agents

Many children's writers and illustrators, especially those who are just beginning, are confused about whether to utilize the services of an agent. The decision about obtaining an agent's services is strictly one that each writer or illustrator must decide for himself. There are some who are confident enough with their own negotiation skills and feel acquiring an agent is not in their best interest. Still, others scare easily at the slightest mention of business and are not willing to sacrifice valuable writing or illustrating time for the time it takes to market their work. Before you put any thought into whether to contact an agent, read on to become familiar with what an agent can — and cannot — do.

Children's writers and illustrators really don't need agents to sell projects. In fact, many agents elude children's books because they are not as profitable as adult books. This section contains the names and addresses of agencies that will take a look at children's books. With an agent, however, it is possible to expedite the process of getting your work looked at, especially with publishers that will not accept unagented submisssions.

When agreeing to have a reputable agent represent you, keep in mind he should be familiar with the needs of the current market and evaluate your manuscript accordingly. He should also be able to determine the quality of your piece and whether it is salable. Upon selling your manuscript, your agent should be able to negotiate a favorable contract. Also, sometimes royalty statements can be confusing; your agent should be able to clear up any questions you have about monetary payments. One advantage to having an agent be the "go-between" is his acting as the bad guy during the negotiations. This allows you, as an individual, to preserve your good faith with the publisher.

Keep in mind, though, that however reputable the agent is, he has limitations. An agent's representation does not guarantee sale of your work. It just means he sees potential in your writing or art. Though an agent may offer criticism or advice on how to improve your book, he cannot make you a better writer or give you fame.

Agents typically charge a 15 percent commission from the sale of your writing or art material. Such fees will be taken from your advance and royalty earnings. If your agent sells foreign rights to your work, he will deduct 20 percent because he will most likely be dealing with an overseas agent with whom he must split the fee.

Some agents offer reading services. If you are a new writer, you will probably be charged a fee of less than $75. Many times, if an agent agrees to represent you, the fee will be reimbursed (though not always). If you take advantage of an agency's critique service, you will probably pay a range of $25-200 depending on the length of the manuscript. The purpose of a critique service is not to polish the manuscript, but to offer advice based on the agent's knowledge of what sells in juvenile publishing. Prior to engaging in a reading or critique service, you should find out up front what results to expect. The listings in this section specify whether such services are available, the fee, and whether the fee is refundable upon an agreement to represent you. Also note in the listings the percentage of agency income derived from these services. You may want to be wary of agencies with high percentages in this area. Unfortunately, there are "quacks" in this business who are more interested in earning their money from services than from selling books. Other standard fees incurred from an agent include miscellaneous expenses such as photocopying, phone bills, postage or messenger services.

Be advised that not every agent is open to representing a writer or artist who doesn't have some sort of track record. Your manuscript or artwork, and query or cover letters, must be attractive and professional looking. Your first impression must be that of an organized, articulate person.

Feel free to investigate an agent before contacting him. Determine how familiar — and successful — he is with selling to children's publishers. Hopefully, the following listings will provide an essential first step. Included in them is information regarding reporting time on queries/manuscripts/art samples, possible reading or critique fees, and the miscellaneous expenses mentioned earlier. Also, when possible, information about rights marketed, contract requirements (i.e., how long the agreement runs and what expenses you are responsible for) and other special services is included.

ARTISTS INTERNATIONAL, 7 Dublin Hill Road, Greenwich CT 06830. (203)869-8010. FAX: (203)869-8274. Contact person: Michael Brodie. Estab. 1971. Represents 25 artists. 15 artists in picture books, 12 in young readers, 20 in middle readers, 6 in young adults/teens, 20 illustrators who specialize in juvenile art. Prefers to review new material via slide, tearsheets and SAE. Commission: 30% on domestic and foreign sales. 100% of business derived from commission on ms sales.

CAROL BANCROFT & FRIENDS, 7 Ivy Hill Rd., Box 959, Ridgefield CT 06877. (203)438-8386. Owner: Carol Bancroft. Estab. 1972. Member of SCBW. Represents 40 illustrators. Prefers to review new material via a portfolio. Reports in 2 months on illustrations. Handles 30% picture books, 10% young readers, 10% middle readers, 10% young adults. Commission: 25% on domestic sales. Offers a criticism service.

BOOKSTOP LITERARY AGENCY, 67 Meadow View Rd., Orinda CA 94563. (415)254-2664. Agent: Kendra Marcus. Estab. 1985. Member of SCBW. Clients specialize in picture books, young readers, middle readers, young adult books, illustration of own books, juvenile art. 50% of clients are new/unpublished writers; 30% new/unpublished illustrators. Qualifications for representation: must have high-quality work that will sell to the trade market. Prefers to review new material via the entire ms. Reports in 6 weeks on a ms or ms/illustration package. Has sold *Mustache*, by Soto (picture book — Putnam); *Stargone John*, by McKenzie (early chapter — Holt); *Winter Fox*, by Brutschy (picture book — Knopf); *Horns Antlers, Teeth, Tusks*, by Raumon (picture book — Lothrop. Commission: 15% on domestic sales, 20% on foreign sales. Criticism service fee:

$25 an hour. 75% of business derived from commission on ms sales; 25% from criticism services.

ANDREA BROWN, LITERARY AGENCY, 1081 Alameda, Suite 71, Belmont CA 94002. (415)508-8410. FAX: (415)508-8416. President: Andrea Brown. Estab. 1981. Member of ILAA; WNBA. 15-18 clients specialize in picture books, 10 in young readers, 20-25 in middle readers, 10-12 in young adult books, many writers illustrate own books, 10 clients specialize in juvenile art. 25% of clients are new/unpublished writers; 5% new/ unpublished illustrators. Reviews new material via query with outline/proposal. Published writers should send samples of work published. Taking on very few brand new writers." Reports in approximately 1-3 weeks on a query, 1-4 months on a ms, 8 weeks on a ms/illustration package, 1-3 weeks on illustrations. Handles (approximately) 30% nonfiction, 40% fiction, 10% ms/illustration package, 20% illustrations only. Has sold *Seven Little Hippos*, by Mike Thaler/Jerry Smath (picture book—Simon & Schuster); *Wild Goat*, by Caroline Arnold (Young Reader—Morrow); *Ethics*, by Susan Terkel (Middle—Lodestar/Dutton). Commission: 15% on domestic sales, 20% on foreign sales. All business derived from commission on ms sales.
Tips: Trends: "YA is finally coming back; more nonfiction on unusual subjects; lots of topics for picture books."

MARIA CARVAINIS AGENCY, INC., 235 W. End Ave., New York NY 10023. (212)580-1559. President: Maria Carvainis. Estab. 1977. Member of Independent Literary Agents Association, Writers Guild of America, Authors Guild of America, and Romance Writers of America. Represents 60 clients. 15% of clients specialize in young adult books. 15% of clients are new/unpublished writers. Accepting new clients. Qualifications for representation: "I look for three criteria to be met: 1) a strong writing talent 2) a special story or book concept and 3) a strong execution of the story or book concept." Prefers to learn of new authors and their projects via a letter query with SASE. Reports in 2-3 weeks, if not earlier, on a query, 4-12 weeks on a ms. Handles 100% fiction (10% middle readers, 90% young adults). "I would like to see more children's and middle-grade books and nonfiction. Has sold *The Tub People*, by Pam Conrad (children's, Harper & Row); *Stonewords*, by Pam Conrad (young adult, Harper & Row); *The Most Embarrassing Mother in the World*, by Peter Filichia (young adult, Avon). Commission: 15% on domestic sales, 20% on foreign sales. Criticism service only offered to agency's clients. "I offer evaluation of the strength of the book's development and execution of its potential given my experience for more than a decade as an editor at Macmillan Publishing, Basic Books, Avon Books and Crown Publishers." 100% of business derived from commission on ms sales.

MARTHA CASSELMAN, LITERARY AGENT, Box 342, Calistoga CA 94515-0342. (707)942-4341. "Regret we cannot return long-distance phone queries; please query by mail with SASE." Estab. 1978. Member of ILAA. Represents 6 clients in juvenile and young adults. 2 clients specialize in picture books. 2 illustrators specialize in juvenile art. 60% of clients are new/unpublished writers. Qualifications for representation: "Authors should be familiar with the field." Commission: 15% domestic sales, plus 10% foreign sales. 90% of business derived from commission/ms sales. "I do some consultation on contracts on an hourly rate." Charges for copying, overnight mailing services. "I have

"Picture books" are geared toward the preschool—8 year old group; "Young readers" to 5-8 year olds; "Middle readers" to 9-11 year olds; and "Young adults" to those 12 and up.

made a cautious entry into the juvenile and young adult market. Sales have been to reputable publishers."

SJ CLARK LITERARY AGENCY, 410 W. Richmond Ave., Pt. Richmond CA 94801. Owner: Sue Clark. Estab. 1982. Represents 12 clients. 1 client specializes in picture books, 2 in young adults/teens, 1 writer also illustrates own manuscript. 95% of clients are new/unpublished writers. Prefers to review new material via query then entire ms. Ms/illustration packages: send "copy of final art." Reports in 1-2 months on a query, 2-3 months on a ms, 2-3 months on a ms/illustration package. Handles 95% fiction, 10% young readers, 30% middle readers, 55% young adults. Commission: 20% on domestic sales. 100% of business derived from commission on ms sales.

RUTH COHEN, INC., Box 7626, Menlo Park CA 94025. (415)854-2054. President: Ruth Cohen. Estab. 1982. Member of ILAA. Represents 60-70 clients. 7 clients specialize in picture books, 20 in young readers, 10 in young adult books, 5 writers illustrate own books, 5 clients specialize in juvenile art. 50% of clients are new/unpublished writers. Qualifications for representation: "Submission of quality material in the form of a partial ms and illustrations (if illustrator has been published before) or a partial ms for older children if author has not been published before; plus list of credits and SASE. Prefers to review new material via an outline plus 3 opening chapters; ms/illustration packages (must include SASE). Reports in 14 days on a query, 21 days on a ms or ms/illustration package, 14 days on illustrations. Has sold *I Really Am a Princess*, by Shields (ages 4-8, picture book—Dutton); *Cousin Marlene is Driving Me Crazy*, by Kleitsch (ages 4-8—Dutton); *Secrets of a Rain Forest*, by Dorros (ages 4-8—Scholastic); *Christopher Columbus*, by Lernson (ages 8-12—Lodester). Commission: 15% domestic sales; 20% foreign sales. Charges for foreign/telex or phone calls and overseas mailing.

CRAVEN DESIGN STUDIOS, INC., 234 Fifth Ave., 4th Floor, New York NY 10001. (212)696-4680. President: Tema Siegel. Estab. 1981. Represents 20 illustrators. Qualifications for representation: "Illustrators should have a few years experience and have some published pieces. How many pieces published does not matter as much as how good they are and how well they represent a specific style." Ms/illustrations packages: submit samples—photocopies that do not have to be returned—or a self addressed mailer. Will call for portfolio if interested. Reports in 2 weeks on illustrations. Handles 100% illustrations (10% picture books, 10% young readers, 3% middle readers, 2% young adults); also 85% textbooks. Commission: 25% domestic sales; 25% foreign sales. 100% of business derived from commission on illustrations.

*RICHARD CURTIS ASSOCIATES, 171 E. 74th St., New York NY 10021. (212)772-7363. Estab. 1974. Represents 150 clients. Head of Children's Books: Ms. Rob Cohen. Member of ILAA. Handle 25% nonfiction, 75% fiction (25% picture books, 25% young readers, 25% young adults). So far, only one illustrator. Qualifications for representation: "We will consider only children's book authors who have already sold books." Query format: outline plus sample chapters or, for short juvenile books, will take illustrations. For longer young adult books, 1 or 2 sample chapters would be preferable. Query only for illustrators. Response in 2 weeks on a query, 4 weeks on ms and ms/illustration packages. Some better known clients: young adult author John Bellairs and

Always include a self-addressed stamped envelope (SASE) or International Reply Coupon (IRC) with submissions.

illustrator Barry Moser. Commission: 15% domestic sales; 20% foreign sales. 100% of business derived from commission on ms sales.

Tips: "This is a difficult market and we are just getting started, so we have very strict standards for acceptance. But we love to see good books."

EDUCATIONAL DESIGN SERVICES, INC., P.O. Box 253, Wantagh NY 11793. (718)539-4107 or (516)221-0995. President: B. Linder. Vice President: E. Selzer. Estab. 1979. Represents 14 clients; young adult/teen, writers of textual material for education market only. 75% of clients are new/unpublished writers. Prefers to review new material via query, entire ms, outline/proposal, outline plus sample chapters and/or portfolio. Reports in 4-6 weeks on query or ms. Has sold *United States Government* (7-9 year olds, Minerva Books); *New York State History* (8-9 year olds, Amsco Book Co.); *Nueva Histeria de los Estados Unidos* (Minerva). Commission: 15% on domestic sales, 25% on foreign sales. All business derived from commission/ms sales. Other fees: "long-distance phone calls, office expenses and mailing costs." No response without SASE.

PETER ELEK ASSOCIATES, Box 223, Canal St. Station, New York NY 10013. (212)431-9368. FAX: (212)966-5768. Executive Assistant: Anne C.J. Roche. Estab. 1979. Represents 30 clients. 8 clients specialize in picture books, 8 in young readers, 2 in middle readers, 1 in young adult books, 5 clients specialize in juvenile art. 20% of clients are new/unpublished writers; 50% new/unpublished illustrators. Accepting new clients "very selectively." Qualifications for representation: "intent on making a career as a professional writer; experience writing for children (not simply a teacher, librarian or parent)." Prefers to review new material via a query; with outline proposal. Reports in 14 days on a query, 21 days on a ms or ms/illustration package. Handles 30% nonfiction (60% picture books, 40% middle readers); 50% fiction (60% picture books, 20% young readers, 20% middle readers); 20% ms/illustration package (80% picture books, 10% young readers, 10% middle readers). Has sold *My First Computer Book*, by Tedd Arnold (beginner, Workman); *Secrets of Reserving*, by Sara Bisel (middle reader, Scholastic); *The Simple People*, by Tedd Arnold (picture book, Dial Book for Young Readers). Commission: 15% domestic sales; 20% foreign sales. If required, charges for ms copying, courier charges. 100% of business derived from commission on ms sales.

Tips: "Sadly too many individuals are encouraged by 'schools' and writing courses to believe that they are innovative and have the ability to write for children. Few have studied publishers' catalogs and bookstore/library shelves to see what is already there."

ETHAN ELLENBERG/LITERARY AGENT, #5-C, 548 Broadway, New York NY 10012. (212)431-4554. President: Ethan Ellenberg. Estab. 1984. Represents 60 clients. 3 clients specialize in picture books, 1 in young readers, 1 writer illustrates own books. 50% of clients (in children's books) are new/unpublished writers; 50% new/unpublished illustrators. (In adult books 80% of clientele published before.) Qualifications for representation: a professionally prepared manuscript and/or illustrations ready for submission to publishers. "Query, sample chapters or entire ms are all acceptable to submit as long as they include SASE. No preference." Reports in 2-3 weeks for all submissions, no matter what. Handles 50% fiction, 50% ms/illustration package. Has sold *Antics*, by Cathy Hepworth (ages 2-adult, picture book, Putnam's); *While You're Asleep*, by Cathy Hepworth (ages 2-10, picture book, Walker). Commission: 15% domestic sales; 20% foreign sales. "The only expense I charge is a photocopying fee for duplication of ms for submission."

Tips: "I am actively seeking new clients and I look forward to hearing from anyone serious about children's books. Before opening my own agency I was in charge of the contracts for juvenile publishing at Bantam, so I know the field well. I enjoy children's books and I'm excited about the opportunities the field has."

*ANN ELMO AGENCY INC., 60 E. 42 St., New York NY 10165. (212)661-2880, 2881, 2883. President: Ann Elmo; or Lettie Lee. Estab. 1945. Member of SAR, Authors League, Dramatist Guild. Represents 50 regular clients. 5 clients specialize in young readers, 3 in young adult books, 5 writers illustrate own books. Qualifications for representation: "Writers need not have credits in juvenile writing to be accepted as long as they have valid ideas in marketable form." Prefers to review new material via a query or entire ms; ms/illustration packages (typed double-spaced). Reports in 1 week on ms, 4-8 weeks on ms/illustration package. Commission: 15% domestic sales; 25% foreign sales.

*CHARLOTTE GUSAY, LITERARY AGENT, 10532 Blythe, Los Angeles CA 90064. (213)559-0831. Estab. 1988. Member of Pen International. Represents 9 clients. 5 clients specialize in picture books, 5 in young readers, 5 in middle readers, 1 in young adult books, 3 writers illustrate own books, 3 clients specialize in juvenile art. 90% of clients are new/unpublished writers; 66% new/unpublished illustrators. Qualifications for representation: "Exceptional quality; prefer nonsexist; enjoy ethnic!" Prefers to review "final art and text or published samples." Reports in 3-6 weeks. Handles (approximately) 35% nonfiction (35% picture books, 60% young readers, 30% middle readers, 10% young adult); 30% fiction (40% picture books, 60% young readers, 30% middle readers, 10% young adult); 30% ms/illustration packages (60% picture books, 50% Young Readers, 40% Middle Readers, 10% Young Adult); illustrations (50% picture books, 40% young readers, 10% young adult). Has sold *A Visit to the Art Galaxy*, Annie Reiner (6 and up, Green Tiger Press). Commission: 15% domestic sales, 25% foreign sales, 25% illustration only. Children's book proposals are $1/page, $50 minimum. Write for fee schedules, critiquing information and agency terms. "A one-time nonrefundable marketing fee is required of authors upon signing with the agency. The author is responsible for reproduction of and supplying manuscripts (or books) to the agency for submission to publishers or producers, as well as reimbursement for long distance phone, Fed Ex, and FAX expenses." 95% of business derived from commission on ms sales.; 5% from reading fees or criticism services. Payment of a criticism fee *does not* ensure that agency will represent writer.
Tips: Trends: "Innovation and exceptional art illustration. Emerging ethnic consciousness."

HEACOCK LITERARY AGENCY, INC., Suite #14, 1523 6th St., Santa Monica CA 90401. (213)393-6227. President: Jim Heacock. Vice President: Rosalie Heacock. Estab. 1978. "We'll send free brochure on our services if writers will request and enclose SASE." Member of ILAA (Independent Literary Agents Association); Association of Talent Agents. Represents 50 clients. 5 clients specialize in picture books, 5 in young readers. Qualifications for representation: "Each must have been published by a *major* house at least four times in the recent past." Prefers to review new material via query, outline/proposal and/or outline plus sample chapters. Reports in 2 weeks on query, 4 weeks on ms/illustration package. Handles 15% nonfiction, 15% young adults; 25% fiction, 25% young readers; 60% ms/illustration package, 30% picture books, 30% young readers. Recently sold titles: *The High Rise Glorious Skittle Skattle Skat Rorious Sky Pie Angel Food Cake*, by Richard Jesse Watson (illustrations) & Nancy Willard (ages 4-8 picture book, Harcourt Brace); *Weird Parents*, by Audrey Wood (ages 4-8 picture book, Dial Books Young Readers); *Never Cry Moose*, by Mark and Brenda Weatherby (ages 4-8 picture book, Harcourt Brace). Commission: 15% on domestic sales (on first $50,000 earnings each year, then 10% for balance of year); 25% on foreign sales (if sold direct 15% – if agent used 25%). Other fees: "Our out-of-pocket actual costs for postage, telephone, packing, photocopies, etc." 95% of business derived from commission on ms sales; 5% from consultant contracts in advising authors or negotiating contracts for them. "This charge is $125 per hour plus expenses. We do not have time for criticisms."

Tips: "We prefer to restrict our efforts to a small and select group of highly talented writers and offer a maximum personal service. Equally so for illustrators with national award-winning potential."

J. KELLOCK & ASSOCIATES LTD., 11017-80 Ave., Edmonton Alberta T6G 0R2 Canada. (403)433-0274. President: Joanne Kellock. Estab. 1981. Represents approximately 35 clients. 5 clients in picture book (artists only), 13 in young adult books, 17 junior/juvenile. 30% of clients are new/unpublished writers; 1% new/unpublished illustrators. Qualifications for representation: "It is always preferable to acquire a writer who has one or two books on the market, but new talent must be looked at providing any project is well thought out, professionally written, competition studied, and required age group carefully considered. Helpful if illustrators have a reputation as an artist, and are VERY serious about becoming an illustrator for children's material. They must love such children's books." Prefers to review new material via a query; outline/proposal; outline plus 3 complete sample chapters; or one finished piece of art work, 3 b&w sketches. Reports in 1 week on a query, 3-4 weeks on a ms, 2 weeks on a ms/illustration package, 1 week on illustrations. Handles 2% nonfiction picture books, and 5% middle readers; 3% fiction picture books, 15% young readers and 12% young adults; 4% ms/illustration package picture books, 2% young readers, 15% middle readers, 9% young adults; 3% illustration only picture books, 15% middle readers, 9% young adult books. Has sold *A Promise to the Sun*, by Tololwa Marti Mollet (pre-school, Little, Brown & Company); *I Spent My Summer Vacation Kidnapped Into Space*, by Martyn Godfrey (juvenile, Scholastic Inc); *The Orphan Boy*, by Tololwa Marti Mollel (ages 3-5, Oxford University Press and Clarion Books); *Is It O.K If This Monster Stays For Lunch*, by Martyn Godfrey (ages 3-5, Oxford University Press). Commission: 15% English language sales; 20% foreign sales. SASE required for return of material. "Cannot mail to U.S. with U.S. Postage, send International Postage or cash. In both cases double the amount of mailing cost to me. I basically concern myself with style working with subject/whether or not work fits into the right age group; character development, action, point of view/voice. My reader sometimes deals with ms from new writers." Charges for postage and long distance calls. 70% of business derived from commission on ms sales and 30% from reading fees/criticism service.
Tips: "I do very well with sales of children's work, and consequently more and more writers of this material seek me out. I fight hard for my children's writers, particularly if sale is to Canadian publisher, as here children's writers are still somehow considered second class. I also sell TV/film, but only if option originates from a book for which I kept such rights for author."

BARBARA S. KOUTS, LITERARY AGENT, 788 Ninth Ave., New York NY 10019. (212)265-6003. Literary Agent: Barbara Kouts. Estab. 1980. Member of ILAA. Represents 25 clients. 8 clients specialize in picture books, 10 in young readers, 5 in young adult books, 2 writers illustrate own books. 60% of clients are new/unpublished writers. Qualifications for representation: "I am looking for writers with some background in writing (i.e., published stories or articles). But I will look at new material, too." Prefers to review new material via a query. Reports in 1-2 weeks on query, 3-4 weeks on ms. Handles 30% nonfiction (10% picture books, 45% middle readers, 45% young adult books); 70% fiction (30% picture books, 30% young readers, 30% middle readers, 10% young adult books). Has sold *The Talking Eggs*, by Robert San Souci (picture book); *Beethoven's Cat*, Elisabeth McHugh (middle grade novel); *Beyond Safe Boundaries*, by Margaret Sacks (young adult novel). Commission: 10% domestic sales; 20% foreign sales. Charges photocopying fee. 100% of business derived from commission on ms sales.

LIGHTHOUSE LITERARY AGENCY, P.O. Box 1000, Edgewater FL 32132-1000. Director: Sandra Kangas. Estab. 1988. Member of Authors Guild. Represents 68 clients. 8 clients specialize in picture books, 6 in young readers, 6 in young adult books. 35% of clients are new/unpublished writers. Qualifications for representation: "Some prior success is a plus, but not a requirement. More important is a professional work attitude. We enjoy working with authors who are receptive to criticism, those who realize that good writing is the art of rewriting." Prefers to review entire ms. "Do not send your only copy." Ms/illustration packages: send quality copies of artwork. Do not send original artwork until requested to do so. Reports in 1 month on a query, ms, ms/illustration package or illustrations. Handles 30% nonfiction (50% picture books, 25% young readers, 25% middle readers); 70% fiction (50% picture books, 25% young readers, 25% middle readers). Recent sales: *The Goose Got Loose*, by Happel (Little, Brown), *Power PR*, by Hill (Fells). Commission: 15% domestic sales; 20% foreign sales. 85% of business derived from commission on ms sales; Reading fee $45.
Tips: "Due to the volume of submissions received, we are more apt to accept for marketing work by writers with a track record. We will still read material from new writers."

RAY LINCOLN LITERARY AGENCY, Elkins Park House, #107-B, 7900 Old York Road, Elkins Park PA 19117. (215)635-0827. CEO: Mrs. Ray Lincoln. Estab. 1974. Represents 25 adult and 20 children's book authors. 2 clients specialize in picture books, 5 in young readers, 5 in middle readers, 8 in young adults/teens. 20% of clients are new/unpublished writers. Qualifications for representation: "must have a fresh, appealing style. I handle nonfiction as well as fiction in both juvenile and adult categories." Prefers to review new material via query (first); sample chapters later, if sample is of interest. "I then request the full manuscript." Reports in 1-2 weeks on a query, 3-4 weeks on a ms. Handles 25% nonfiction (10% middle readers, 15% young adults); 75% fiction (10% picture books, 25% young readers, 15% middle readers, 25% young adults). Recently sold titles: *Fourth-Grade Rats*, by Jerry Spinelli (Scholastic), *Will The Nurse Make Me Take My Underwear Off?*, by Joel Schwartz (Dell), *A Capital Capitol City*, by Suzanne Hilton (Atheneum). Offers criticism service. 100% of business derived from commission on ms sales.
Tips: "I particularly like the 5 and up categories, including young adult, and plan to expand."

SCOTT MEREDITH LITERARY AGENCY, INC., 845 Third Ave., New York NY 10022. (212)245-5500. FAX: (212)755-2972. Vice-President and Editorial Director: Jack Scovil. Estab. 1946. Represents 2,000 clients. 25 clients specialize in picture books, 35 in young readers, 35 in middle readers, 50 in young adults/teens, 5 writers also illustrate their own manuscripts. "The 2,000 (represented) are established authors, though we also work with new writers." Qualifications for representation: "If an author has sold a book to a major publisher, or three to lesser publishers, we'll read a new script without charge, and take on the author for commission representation if we find the script salable and consider the author generally promising." Prefers to review new material via entire ms or "at least one" sample chapter; ms/illustration packages: send "final text but rough sketches, since different publishers have different size requirements, etc., for finished art." Reports in a day or two on a query, 2 weeks on a ms, 2 weeks on a ms/illustration package; "We guarantee decision on all submissions within 2 weeks." Handles 35% nonfiction (20% picture books, 20% young readers, 30% middle readers, 30% young adults); 45% fiction (20% picture books, 20% young readers, 30% middle readers, 30 % adults); 20% ms/illustration package, 70% picture books, 20% young readers, 25%

Refer to the Business of Children's Writing & Illustrating for up-to-date marketing, tax and legal information.

middle readers, 5% young adults. "We don't represent illustrators: only writers who also illustrate. However, we'll sometimes accept a straight illustration assignment for a client." Recently sold *Barney's Horse*, by Syd Hoff (Harper and Row, picture book); *Harvey's Wacky Parrot Adventure*, by Eth Clifford (Houghton-Mifflin, middle readers); *The Young Astronauts*, by Jack Anderson and Shariann Lewitt (Zebra Books, YA). Commission: 10% on domestic sales, 20% on foreign sales. Reading/criticism service: "We don't call it a 'reading' fee since the single fee covers a detailed response on why we've determined that the material is salable or unsalable, and assistance in revisions (without further charge) where we consider revisions necessary to make a script salable." Critiques range "anywhere from 2 single-spaced pages to as many as a dozen or more. Reports are based on multi-readings by staff and written by Scott Meredith personally with staff assistance." Other fees: "No charge for local calls and ordinary mail; we charge long distance calls (such as a rare call to foreign publishers) or shipments by FedEx at our cost only." 90% of business derived from commission on ms sales, 10% from reading/criticism services. "If we find a script salable, or it becomes salable following our suggested revisions, we will represent the author; but we won't take on a script and represent its author if the submission is irreparably unsalable."
Tips: The juvenile publishing market is "very strong now. It was weak for a while when government subsidies slowed down and school systems decreased buying, but that's rectified itself. And juvenile publishers in most cases are starting to pay higher advances. We used to tell potential juvenile writers, rather apologetically, that advances were absurdly low buy royalties often went on forever and added up nicely; but now even advances are pretty respectable. They're not the lottery-winner advances paid for some adult books, but at least they're well into the thousands rather than the hundreds."

MEWS BOOKS LTD., 20 Bluewater Hill, Westport CT 06880. (203)227-1836. President: Sidney B. Kramer. Estab. 1975. Represents 50 "active at one time" clients. 10 picture books; 20 young readers; 30 writers illustrating own mss; 1 client specializes in juvenile art. 20% of clients are new/unpublished writers. Qualifications for representation: "We look for professional handling of material presented. If material calls for illustration, send very rough sketches so that the ultimate work can be visualized. Recommendation by published author or expert is useful. Work should have clear purpose and age delineation. Previously published authors (in any category) have greater credibility with publishers." Prefers to review new material via query; character and plot outline/proposal. No original illustrations are accepted by us. "We try to process material within 30 days." SASE. Have sold to Simon & Schuster, Western Publishing, Crown, *Parents*. Commission: 15% domestic sales; 20% foreign sales. 100% of business derived from commission on ms sales. For accepted proposals, minimum fee is $350 (covers circulation to 4-5 publishers).
Tips: "President offers individual, domestic and international legal service to authors in need of negotiating assistance (as an attorney and former publisher). The agency offers extensive foreign representation."

MULTIMEDIA PRODUCT DEVELOPMENT, INC., 410 S. Michigan Ave., Chicago IL 60605. (312)922-3063. FAX: (312)922-1905. President: Jane Jordan Browne. Estab. 1971. Represents 100 clients of whom 12 write juveniles. 4 clients specialize in picture books, 4 in young readers, 2 in middle readers, 2 in young adults/teens. 5% of clients are new/unpublished writers. Qualifications for representation: "They must be published authors." Prefers to review new material via a query with SASE required for reply. Handles 25% nonfiction (30% picture books, 15% young readers, 15% middle readers, 15% young adults—100% of 25%); 75% fiction (30% picture books, 15% young readers, 15% middle readers, 15% young adults—100% of 75%). Recently sold *Upside Down*, by Mary Jane Miller (ages 10-14, Viking); *Dinosaur James*, by Scott Taylor (ages 4-8, Morrow); *May Makes a Million*, by Charlotte Herman (ages 6-9, Henry Holt). Commission: 15% on domestic sales, 20% on foreign sales. Additional fees charged for "photo-copies, foreign postage and phone/fax." 100% of commission derived from commission on ms sales.

PAMELA NEAIL ASSOCIATES, 27 Bleecker St., New York NY 10012. (212)673-1600. FAX: (212)673-7687. Contact: Lisa Allyn Worth. Estab. 1982. Member of SPAR, Soci-ety of Illustrators. Represents 15 clients. 5 clients specialize in picture books, 5 in young readers, 5 in young adult books, 5 clients specialize in juvenile art. Qualifications for representation: "We represent illustrators and are willing to review work. Artists should send promos and slides—NO ORIGINALS, and if they wish the materials returned, must include a SASE." Prefers to review printed promos, no originals.

THE NORMA-LEWIS AGENCY, 521 Fifth Ave., New York NY 10175. (212)751-4955. Partner: Norma Liebert. Estab. 1980. 50% of clients are new/unpublished writers. Pre-fers to review new material via a query; ms/illustration packages: do not send any original artwork, send reproductions only. Reports in 2 weeks on a query, 4 weeks on a ms; 4 weeks on ms/illustration packages. Handles 50% nonfiction, 50% fiction. Commission: 15% domestic sales; 20% foreign sales. 100% of business derived from commission on ms sales.

SIDNEY E. PORCELAIN AGENCY, Box 1229, Milford PA 18337-1229. (717)296-6420. Manager: Sidney Porcelain. Estab. 1951-2. Represents 20 clients. 3 clients specialize in picture books, 1 in young adults/teens, 1 writer also illustrates own manuscripts. 80% of clients are new/unpublished writers. Prefers to review new material via query and portfolio. Reports in 1 week on a query, 2 weeks on a ms, 2 weeks on a ms/illustration package. Handles 50% fiction (40% middle readers, 10% young adults). Commission: 10% on domestic sales, 20% on foreign sales. 100% of business derived from commission on ms sales. Critique ms for a fee depending on length.

*PUBLISHERS' GRAPHICS, 251 Greenwood Ave., Bethel CT 06801. (203)797-8188. President: Paige C. Gillies. Estab. 1970. Member of GAG (Graphic Artists Guild). 80% of clients specialize in picture books, 80% in young readers, 60% in middle readers, 40% in young adult readers, 5% writers who also illustrate their own manuscripts, 90% illustrators who specialize in juvenile art. 1% of clients are new/unpublished writers; 20 new/unpublished illustrators. Prefers black & white photocopies of art with a note and SASE. Reports in up to 4 weeks.

*PESHA RUBINSTEIN, LITERARY AGENT, 37 Overlook Terrace #LD, New York NY 10033. (212)781-7845. Estab. 1990. Represents 20 clients. 3 clients specialize in picture books, 2 in young readers, 1 in young adult books. Other clients are adult fiction and nonfiction. Represents 2 writers who also illustrate their own manuscripts. 90% of clients are new/unpublished writers; 10% new/unpublished illustrators. Qualifications for representation: "No previous publication required. Author must have a feel for original, interesting and entertaining children's books." Prefers to review new material via a query (for YA material), entire manuscript (for children's books for under age

 The asterisk before a listing indicates the listing is new in this edition.

10); ms/illustration packages: "text, rough sketches with at least two drawings more fully developed." Reports in 2 weeks on a query, 3 months on a ms or ms/illustration package, 2 months on illustrations. Commission: 15% on domestic and foreign sales. Other fees: only "postage fees if such fees are a result of author's late delivery. Express mail if a deadline must be met." 100% of business derived from commission on ms sales.

Tips: "I think the most original and exciting art in the U.S. today is finding its biggest forum in children's books. This affects picture books positively in that the illustrations are more and more fascinating. As for texts, I find that editors pick up when I mention the word "series," for either fiction or nonfiction works."

S.I. INTERNATIONAL, 43 E. 19th St., New York NY 10003. (212)254-4996. FAX: (212)995-0911. Children's Director: Mr. Don Bruckstein. Estab. 1958. Member of Graphic Artists Guild. Represents 25 clients. 5 clients specialize in picture books, 5 in young readers, 6 in young adult books, 2 writers illustrate own books, 17 clients specialize in juvenile art. Qualifications for representation: "previous illustration work published." Prefers to review new material via a portfolio. Reports in 2 weeks on ms/illustration package, 1 week on illustrations. Commission: 25% domestic sales; 35% foreign sales.

RICHARD W. SALZMAN ARTIST REPRESENTATIVE, 1352 Hornblend St., San Diego CA 92109. (619)272-8147. San Francisco number: (415)751-7935. FAX: (619)272-0180. Associate: Kathy Joiner. Estab. 1982. Member of Society of Photo & Artist Representatives, GAG, AIGA. Represents 28 clients. 18 clients specialize in picture books, 18 in young readers, 18 in middle readers 18 in young adults/teens, 12 illustrators specialize in juvenile art. Qualifications for representation: "design based solely on portfolio." Prefers to review new material via "mailed samples—try to include some for us to keep on file. Slides are acceptable." Handles 20% nonfiction; 20% fiction; 20% ms/illustration package; 30% illustrations only. Commission: 25% on domestic sales, 30% on foreign sales. Criticism service fee: "$75 per hour—illustration & photo only"; verbal criticism service. Additional fees: "cost of portfolio and 75% of any advance cost." 75% of business derived from commission on ms sales; 5% from criticism services.

SCHLESSINGER-VAN DYCK AGENCY, 12 S. 12th St., 2814 P.S.F.S. Building, Philadelphia PA 19107. (215)627-4665. Partner/Agent: Barrie Van Dyck. Estab. 1987. Represents 55 clients. 4 clients specialize in picture books, 8 in middle readers, 4 in young adults/teens. 40% of clients are new/unpublished writers. Qualifications for representation: "We prefer authors with publishing credentials but it is not mandatory. We are selecting authors carefully according to quality of writing, in both fiction and nonfiction." Prefers to review new material via query (for fiction); outline/proposal for nonfiction. Reports in 2 weeks on a query, 4 weeks on a ms. Handles 50% nonfiction, 50% fiction. Sold *The Bread Sister of Sinking Creek,* by Robin Moore (Harper & Row, ages 9-14); *Maggie Among the Seneca,* by Robin Moore (Harper & Row, age 9-14); *Amazing Lizards,* by Jayne Pettit (Scholastic, age 8-12). Commission: 15% on domestic sales, 20% on foreign sales. Other fees: office expense fee, long distance phone, UPS mailing, duplicating of manuscripts. 100% of business derived from commission on ms sales.

SINGER MEDIA, CORP., 3164 Tyler Ave., Anaheim CA 92801. Associate Editor: Dorothy Rosati. Estab. 1940. Represents 100+ clients. 20 clients specialize in picture books, 10 in young readers, 40 in young adults/teens. 20% of clients are new/unpublished writers, 20% cartoonists. Qualifications for representation: "We syndicate to foreign markets and like to obtain reprint rights." Prefers to review new material via query and entire ms; ms/illustration: send final text. Reports in 3 weeks. Recently sold titles: *Juvenile Activity Books* (PSI, Ottenheimer University). Commission: 20% on domestic sales, 25% on foreign sales, 50% on syndication. Reading fee: "We charge $250 which is

minimal when compared with the fees of other professionals. If we succeed in placing the manuscript with a publisher, this fee will be refunded in full. This is only a one-time payment." Critiques are comprised of "professional evaluation by published authors." 98% of business derived from commission on ms sales; 2% from reading/criticism services."
Tips: "We like books and scripts of interest to the international market."

*GUNTHER STUHLMANN, AUTHOR'S REPRESENTATIVE, P.O. Box 276, Becket MA 01223. (413)623-5170. Associate: Barbara Ward. Estab. 1954. Qualifications for representation: Established publication record. "We are taking on few new clients right now, and we have worked mostly in the YA markets in the past, but are not very active in that area now." Prefers to review new material via a query. Commission: 10% on domestic sales, 20% on foreign sales. 100% of business derived from commission on ms sales.

WRITERS HOUSE, 21 W. 26 St., New York NY 10010. (212)685-2400. Executive Vice President: Amy Berkower; Director: Susan Cohen. Contact: Megan Howard. Estab. 1973. Member of ILAA. Represents 300 clients. Clients specialize in picture books, young readers, young adult books, illustrators writing own book. Small percent of clients are new/unpublished writers. Accepting new clients "on a limited basis." Qualifications for representation: "material we think we can sell and a person we'd like to work with." Prefers to review new material via a query or outline plus 2 sample chapters. Reports on a query in 2-3 weeks, 6-8 weeks on a ms, 2-3 weeks on ms/illustration package. Handles mostly fiction; smaller % of nonfiction and ms/illustration packages. Susan Cohen has sold *Root-A-Toot-Toot*, by Anne Rockwell (picture book, Macmillan), *Frances In The Fourth Grade*, (middle grades series, Knopf), and *The Raincatchers*, by Jean Thesman (YA, Houghton-Mifflin). Amy Berkower has sold *Babysitters Club*, by Ann Martin (middle grade series, Scholastic), *Paper Doll*, by Elizabeth Feuer (YA, FSG), and *I Found An Elf By Myself*, by Bernie Most (picture book, Harcourt Brace Jovanovich). Commission: 10% domestic sales; 20% foreign sales. Charges for extraordinary expenses (big photocopying jobs, telexes, messengers) deducted from disbursements to writers. Most of business % derived from commission on ms sales; some from foreign and performance rights sales, and agency also represents submission rights for some small publishers.

Though the term "networking" sounds so "business-like," creative people such as writers and artists can benefit by the contacts that can be made through the organizations listed in this section. Professional organizations provide a writer or artist with a multitude of educational, business and legal services. Much of these services come in the form of newsletters, workshops or seminars that provide tips about how to be a better writer or artist, types of business records to keep, health and life insurance coverage you should carry or organizational competitions to be aware of.

As you read through the listings included here you will notice that some are open to professionals only, some are geared for amateurs and still others have different membership levels. Feel free to write for more information regarding any group that sounds interesting to ascertain its membership qualifications as well as services offered to members.

In addition to the educational benefits of belonging to a professional organization is the added "social" aspect of learning from peers and having a support system to help you through "dry" creative or financial periods. Also, you never know when "knowing someone" may expedite the goal-achieving process. Membership in a writer's or artist's group also presents to a publisher an image of being serious about your craft. Of course, this provides no guarantee that your work will be published, but it offers an added dimension of credibility.

ACTION FOR CHILDREN'S TELEVISION (ACT), 20 University Rd., Cambridge MA 02138. (617)876-6620. President: Peggy Charren. Purpose of organization: "ACT is a national nonprofit children's television advocacy organization working to encourage diversity in children's television and to eliminate commercial abuses targeted to young children." Qualifications for membership: "payment of $20 yearly membership dues." Membership cost: "Begins at $20, members may contribute more if they wish." Sponsors workshops/conferences; open to nonmembers. "ACT sponsors annual Achievement in Children's Television Awards for children's television series, home videos and public service campaigns." Awards a certificate. Contest open to nonmembers.

AMERICAN SOCIETY OF JOURNALISTS AND AUTHORS, 1501 Broadway, New York NY 10036. (212)997-0947. Executive Director: Alexandra Cantor. Qualifications for membership: "Need to be a professional nonfiction writer published 8-10 times in general circulation publications." Cost of membership: "Initiation fee—$50; annual dues—$120. Group sponsors annual conference May 4th, 1991; monthly workshops in NYC. Workshops/conferences open to nonmembers. Publishes a newsletter for members that provides confidential information for nonfiction writers. Sponsors contests that are open to nonmembers.

THE AUTHORS GUILD, 234 W. 44th St., New York NY 10036. (212)398-0838. Assistant Director: Peggy Randall. Purpose of organization: membership organization of 6,700 members that offers services and information materials intended to help authors with the business and legal aspects of their work, including contract problems, copyright matters, freedom of expression and taxation. Qualifications for membership: book author published by an established American publisher within 7 years or any author who has had three works, fiction or nonfiction, published by a magazine or magazines of general circulation in the last 18 months. Associate membership also available. Annual dues-$90. Different levels of membership include: associate membership with all rights except voting available to an author who has work in progress but who has not yet met the qualifications for active membership. This normally involves a firm contract offer from a publisher. Workshops/conferences: "The Guild and Authors League of America conduct several symposia each year at which experts provide information, offer advice, and answer questions on subjects of interest and concern to authors. Typical subjects have been the rights of privacy and publicity, libel, wills and estates, taxation, copyright, editors and editing, the art of interviewing, standards of criticism and book reviewing. Transcripts of these symposia are published and circulated to members." Symposia open to members only. "The *Author's Guild Bulletin*, a quarterly journal, contains articles on matters of interest to writers, reports of Guild activities, contract surveys, advice on problem clauses in contracts, transcripts of Guild and League symposia, and information on a variety of professional topics. Subscription included in the cost of the annual dues."

THE AUTHORS RESOURCE CENTER, Box 64785, Tucson AZ 85740-1785. (602)325-4733. Executive Director: Martha R. Gore. Purpose of organization: to help writers, graphic artists and illustrators understand the business and professional realities of the publishing world—also have literary agency (opened March 1, 1987) and artists agency (opened January 1990) that markets members' books and illustrations to publishers. Qualifications for membership: serious interest in writing or illustrating. Membership cost: $50 per year for aspiring and published members. "Professional development workshops are open to members at a discount and to the general public. TARC instructors are actively publishing and often have academic credentials. The *Tarc Report* is published bimonthly and includes information about markets, resources, legal matters, writers workshops, reference sources, announcement of members' new books, reviews and other news important to members. Sample copy is $3. Subscription included in membership fee. *TARC* was established in 1984."

CALIFORNIA WRITERS' CLUB, 2214 Derby St., Berkeley CA 94705. (415)841-1217. Secretary: Dorothy V. Benson. Purpose of organization: "We are a nonprofit professional organization open to writers to provide writing and market information and to promote fellowship among writers." Qualifications for membership: "publication for active members; expected publication in five years for associate members." Membership cost: entry fee, $20; annual dues $25. (Entry fee is paid once.) Workshops/conferences: "Biennial summer conference, July 12-14, 1991, at Asilomar, Pacific Grove, CA; other conferences are held by local branches as they see fit." Conferences open to nonmembers. "Newsletter, which goes out to all CWC members, to newspapers and libraries, publishes the monthly meetings upcoming in the eight branches, plus the achievements of members, and market and contest opportunities." Sponsors contest. CWC's "major contest is for nonmembers, every two years, and first prize in each of 5 categories is free tuition to the biennial conference; second prize is cash; and third prize a certificate."

CANADIAN AUTHORS ASSOCIATION, 121 Avenue Rd. #104, Toronto ON M5R 2G3 Canada. (416)926-8084. Contact: Executive Director. Purpose of organization: to help "emerging" writers and provide assistance to professional writers. Membership is di-

 The asterisk before a listing indicates the listing is new in this edition.

Your Guide to Getting Published

Learn to write publishable material and discover the best-paying markets for your work. Subscribe to *Writer's Digest*, the magazine that has instructed, informed and inspired writers since 1920. Every month you'll get:

- Fresh markets for your writing, including the names and addresses of editors, what type of writing they're currently buying, how much they pay, and how to get in touch with them.
- Insights, advice, and how-to information from professional writers and editors.
- In-depth profiles of today's foremost authors and the secrets of their success.
- Monthly expert columns about the writing and selling of fiction, nonfiction, poetry and scripts.

Plus, a $12.00 discount. Subscribe today through this special introductory offer, and receive a full year (12 issues) of *Writer's Digest* for only $18.00—that's a $12.00 savings off the $30 newsstand rate. Enclose payment with your order, and we will add an extra issue to your subscription, absolutely **free**.

Detach postage-free coupon and mail today!

Subscription Savings Certificate

Save $12.00

Yes, I want professional advice on how to write publishable material and sell it to the best-paying markets. Send me 12 issues of *Writer's Digest* for just $18...a $12 discount off the newsstand price. (Outside U.S. add $4 and remit in U.S. funds.)

- ☐ Payment enclosed (Send me an extra issue free—13 in all)
- ☐ Please bill me

Writer's DIGEST

Guarantee: If you are not satisfied with your subscription at any time, you may cancel it and receive a full refund for all unmailed issues due you.

Name (please print)

Address   Apt.

City

State   Zip

Basic rate, $24.

VMCW1

Writer's ®
DIGEST

How would you like to get:

- up-to-the-minute reports on new markets for your writing
- professional advice from editors and writers about what to write and how to write it to maximize your opportunities for getting published
- in-depth interviews with leading authors who reveal their secrets of success
- expert opinion about writing and selling fiction, nonfiction, poetry and scripts
- ...all at a $12.00 discount?

vided into two categories for individuals: Active (voting): Persons engaged in writing in any genre who have produced a sufficient body of work; Associate (non-voting): Persons interested in writing who have not yet produced sufficient material to qualify for Active membership, or those who, though not writers, have a sincere interest in Canadian literature. Persons interested in learning to write may join the Association for one year at a reduced rate. Membership cost: $90-active members, $90-associates, $60-introductory rate. Workshops/conferences: 70th Annual Conference, June 20-26, 1991 in Ottawa, ON. "The conference draws writers, editors and publishers together in a congenial atmosphere providing seminars, workshops, panel discussions, readings by award-winning authors, and many social events." Open to nonmembers. Publishes a newsletter for members only. Also publishes a quarterly journal and a bienniel writer's guide available to nonmembers. "The Association created a major literary award program in 1975 to honor writing that achieves literary excellence without sacrificing popular appeal. The awards are in four categories—fiction, (for a full-length novel); nonfiction (excluding works of an instructional nature); poetry (for a volume of the works of one poet); and drama (for a single play published or staged). The awards consist of a handsome silver medal and $5,000 in cash; they are funded by Harlequin Enterprises, the Toronto-based international publisher." Contest open to nonmembers. Also contests for writing by students and for young readers (see Vicky Metcalf and Canadian Author & Bookman Awards).

*THE CHILDREN'S BOOK COUNCIL, INC., 568 Broadway, New York NY 10012. (212)966-1990. Purpose of organization: "A nonprofit trade association of children's and young adult publishers, CBC promotes the enjoyment of books for children and young adults, and works with national and international organizations to that end. The CBC has sponsored National Children's Book Week since 1945." Qualifications for membership: Trade publishers of children's and young adult books are eligible for membership. Membership cost: "Individuals wishing to receive mailings from the CBC (our semi-annual newsletter, CBC FEATURES and our materials brochures) may be placed on our mailing list for a one-time-only fee of $15. Publishers wishing to join should contact the CDC for dues information." Sponsors workshops and conferences. Publishes a newsletter with articles about children's books and publishing. Listings of free or inexpensive materials from publishers.

CHILDREN'S READING ROUND TABLE OF CHICAGO, #1507, 3930 N. Pine Grove, Chicago IL 60613. (312)477-2271. Information Chairperson: Marilyn Singer. Purpose of organization: "to support activities which foster and enlarge children and young adults' interest in reading and to promote good fellowship among persons actively interested in the field of children's books." Qualifications for membership: "Membership is open to anyone interested in children's books. There are no professional qualifications; however, the majority of our members are authors, freelance writers, illustrators, librarians, educators, editors, publishers and booksellers." Membership cost: $12 for year (June 1 through May 31), applicable to members within our Chicago meeting area; Associate Membership, $8, limited to persons outside the Metropolican Chicago Area or who are retired. "All members have same privileges, which include attendance at meetings; newsletter, *CRTT Bulletin*; yearbook published biennially; and access to information about CRRT special activities." Workshops/conferences: Children's Reading Round Table Summer Seminar for Writers & Illustrators, given in odd-numbered years. The 3-day seminar, at a Chicago college campus, usually in August, features guest speakers and a variety of profession-level workshops, manuscript critiquing and portfolio appraisal. Enrollment is open members and nonmembers; one fee applicable to all. Meals included, housing extra. Also, Children's Reading Round Table Children's Literature Conference, given in even-numbered years. One-day program, at a Chicago college campus, usually in early September. Program includes guest authors and educators, variety of workshops, exhibits, bookstore, lunch. Enrollment open to members and nonmembers; one fee applicable to all. *CRRT Bulletin, Children's Reading Round Table of Chicago* is published seven times a year, in advance of dinner meetings, and contains articles; book reviews; special sections of news about authors and artists; librarians and educators; publishers and booksellers. An Opportunity Column provides information about professional meetings, workshops, conferences, generally in the Midwest area. The *Bulletin* is available to members on payment of dues. Sample copies may be requested. Awards: "We do give an honorary award, the Children's Reading Round Table Annual Award, *not* for a single book or accomplishment but for long-term commitment to children's literature. Award includes check, lifetime membership, plaque. Nominations can be made *only* by CRRT members; nominees are not limited to membership."

*GRAPHIC ARTISTS GUILD, 11 West 20th St., New York NY 10011. (212)463-7730. Executive Director: Paul Basista. Purpose of organization: "To unite within its membership all professionals working in the graphic arts industry; to improve the economic and social conditions of professional artists and designers; to improve industry standard." Qualification for full membership: 51% of income derived from artwork. Associate members include those in allied fields, students and retirees. Initiation fee: $25. Full memberships $100-175/year. Associate membership $55-95/year. Sponsors "Eye to Eye," a national conference exploring the relationships between artists/artists and artists/clients. Publishes newsletter. "Advocates the advancement and protection of artists' rights and interests."

INTERNATIONAL BLACK WRITERS, Box 1030, Chicago IL 60690. (312)995-5195. Executive Director: Mable Terrell. Purpose of organization: to encourage, develop and display writing talent. Qualifications for membership: the desire to write and willingness to work to excel in the craft. Membership cost: $15/year. Different levels of membership include: senior citizens and youth. Workshops/conferences: 1991 conference, June 15-17, Chicago IL. Open to nonmembers. Publishes a newsletter detailing issues of importance to writers, competitions. Nonmembers subscription: $15/year. Sponsors an annual writing competition in poetry, fiction and nonfiction. Deadline: May 30th. Awards include plaque and certificates. Contest open to nonmembers.

*LEAGUE OF CANADIAN POETS, 24 Ryerson Ave., Toronto, Ontario M5T 2P3 Canada. (416)363-5047. FAX: (416)860-0826. Executive Director: Angela Rebeiro. President: Maria Jacobs. The L.C.P. is a national organization of published poets. Our constitutional objectives are to advance poetry in Canada and to promote the professional interests of the members. Qualifications for membership: full—publication of at least one book of poetry by a Canadian publisher; associate membership—an active interest in poetry, demonstrated by several magazine/periodical publication credits. Membership fees: full—$160/year, associate—$30/year. Hold an Annual General Meeting every spring; some events open to nonmembers. "We also organize reading programs in schools and public venues. We publish a newsletter which includes information on poetry/poetics in Canada and beyond. Also publish the books *Poetry Markets for Canadians*; *Who's Who in the League of Canadian Poets*; *When is a Poem* (teaching guide) and its accompanying anthology of Canadian Poetry *Here is a Poem*; plus a series of cassettes. We sponsor a National Poetry Contest, open to Canadians living here and abroad." Rules: Unpublished poems of any style/subject, under 75-lines, typed, with name/address on separate sheet. $5 entry fee per poem. $1,000-1st prize, $750-2nd, $500-3rd; plus best 50 published in an anthology, Inquire with SASE. Contest open to nonmembers. Organize three annual awards: The Gerald Lampert Memorial Award for a first book of poetry published in Canada in the preceding year; The Pat Lowther Memorial Award for a book of poetry written by a woman in the preceding year; The F.R. Scott

Translation Award for a translation of poetry by a Canadian in the previous year. Please write for more details.

*NATIONAL WRITERS CLUB, Ste. 620, 1450 S. Havana, Aurora CO 80012. (303)751-7844. Executive Director: James Lee Young. Purpose of organization: association for freelance writers. Qualifications for membership: associate membership — must be serious about writing; professional membership — published and paid (cite credentials). Membership cost: $50-associate; $60-professional; $15 setup fee for first year only. Workshops/conferences: TV/Screenwriting Workshops, NWC Annual Summer Conference (usually July) Literary Agency, Editing and Critiquing services. National Writer's School. Open to nonmembers. Publishes industry news of interest to freelance writers; how-to articles; market information; member news and networking opportunities. Nonmember subscription $18. Sponsors poetry contest; short story/article contest; book manuscript contest. Awards cash awards for top three winners; books and/or certificates for other winners; honorable mention certificate places 11-20. Contests open to nonmembers.

*NATIONAL WRITERS UNION, 13 Astor Place, 7th Floor, New York NY 10003. (212)254-0279. Associate Director: Anne Wyville. Purpose of organization: Advocacy for freelance writers. Qualifications for membership: "Membership in the NWU is open to all qualified writers, and no one shall be barred or in any manner prejudiced within the Union on account of race, age, sex, sexual preference, disability, national origin, religion or ideology. You are eligible for membership if you have published a book, play, three articles, five poems, one short story or an equivalent amount of newsletter, publicity, technical commercial, government or insitutional copy. You are also eligible for membership if you have written an equal amount of unpublished material and you are actively writing and attempting to publish your work." Membership Dues: Annual writing income under $5,000, $55/year; annual writing income $5,000-25,000, $95/year; annual writing income over $25,000, $135/year. "National union newsletter quarterly, issues related to freelance writing and to union organization. Nonmember subscription $15.

*PEN AMERICAN CENTER, 568 Broadway, New York NY 10012. (212)334-1660. Purpose of organization: "To foster understanding among men and women of letters in all countries. International PEN is the only worldwide organization of writers and the chief voice of the literary community. Members of PEN work for freedom of expression wherever it has been endangered." Qualifications for membership: "The standard qualification for a writer to join PEN is that he or she must have published, in the United States, two or more books of a literary character, or one book generally acclaimed to be of exceptional distinction. Editors who have demonstrated commitment to excellence in their profession (generally construed as five years' service in book editing), translators who have published at least two book-length literary translations, and playwrights whose works have been professionally produced, are eligible for membership. An application form is available upon request from PEN Headquarters in New York. Candidates for membership should be nominated by two current members of PEN. Inquiries about membership should be directed to the PEN Membership Committee. Friends of PEN is also open to writers who may not yet meet the general PEN membership requirements. PEN sponsors more than fifty public events at PEN Headquarters in New York, and at the branch offices in Boston, Chicago, Houston, San Francisco and Portland, Oregon. They include tributes by contemporary writers to classic American writers, dialogues with visiting foreign writers, symposia that bring public attention to problems of censorship and that address current issues of writing in the United States, and readings that introduce beginning writers to the public. PEN's wide variety of literary programming reflects current literary interests and provides informal occasions for writers to meet each other and to welcome those with an interest in literature. Events are all open to the public and are usually free of charge. The Children's Book Authors' Committee sponsors regular public events focusing on the art of writing for children and young adults and on the diversity of literature for juvenile readers. National union newsletter covers PEN activities, features interviews with international literary figures, transcripts of PEN literary symposia, reports on issues vital to the literary community. All PEN publications are available by mail order directly from PEN American Center. Individuals must enclose check or money order with their order. Subscription: $8 for 4 issues; sample issue $2. Pamphlets and brochures all free upon request. Sponsors several competitions per year. Monetary awards range from $700-12,750.

SCIENCE FICTION WRITERS OF AMERICA, INC., P.O. Box 4335, Spartanburg SC 29305. (803)578-8012. Executive Secretary: Peter Dennis Pautz. Purpose of organization: to encourage public interest in science fiction literature and provide organization format for writers/editors/artists within the genre. Qualifications for membership: at least one professional sale or other professional involvement within the field. Membership cost: annual active dues—$56; affiliate—$39; one-time installation fee of $10; dues year begins July 1. Different levels of membership include: affiliate requires one professional sale or professional involvement; active requires three professional short stories or one novel published. Workshops/conferences: annual awards banquet, usually in April or May. Open to nonmembers. Publishes newsletter. Nonmember subscription: $12.50 in U.S. Sponsors SFWA Nebula® Awards for best published SF in the categories of novel, novella, novelette, and short story. Awards trophy. Contest open to nonmembers.

SOCIETY OF CHILDREN'S BOOK WRITERS, Box 66296, Mar Vista Station, Los Angeles CA 90066. (818)347-2849. Chairperson, Board of Directors: Sue Alexander. Purpose of organization: to assist writers and illustrators working or interested in the field. Qualifications for membership: an interest in children's literature and illustration. Membership cost: $35/year. Different levels of membership include: full membership—published authors/illustrators; associate membership—unpublished writers/illustrators. Workshops/conferences: 30-40 events around the country each year. Open to nonmembers. Publishes a newsletter focusing on writing and illustrating children's books. Sponsors Don Freeman Award for illustrators, 4 grants in aid.

*SOCIETY OF ILLUSTRATORS, 128 E. 63rd St., New York NY 10021. (212)838-2860. Director: Terrence Brown. Purpose of organization: To promote interest in the art of illustration for working professional illustrators and those in associated fields. "Cost of membership: Initiation fee—$200. Annual dues for Non-Resident members (those living more than 125 air miles from SI's headquarters) are $207. Dues for Resident Artist Members are $352 per year, Resident Associate Members $411." Different levels of membership include: *Artist Members* "shall include those who make illustration their profession" and through which they earn at least 60% of their income. *Associate Members* are "Those who earn their living in the arts or who have made a substantial contribution to the art of illustration." This includes art directors, art buyers, creative supervisors, instructors, publishers and like categories. "All candidates for membership are admitted by the proposal of one active member and sponsorship of four additional members. The candidate must complete and sign the application form which requires a brief biography, a listing of schools attended, other training and a résumé of his or her professional career." Candidates for *Artist* membership, in addition to the above

Refer to the Business of Children's Writing & Illustrating for up-to-date marketing, tax and legal information.

Close-up

Sue Alexander
Chairperson of the Board of Directors
The Society of Children's Book Writers
Los Angeles, California

"We are probably the best source of information about the children's book field," says Sue Alexander, chairperson of the board of directors for the Society of Children's Book Writers (SCBW).

The Society of Children's Book Writers was started by approximately 30 Los Angeles writers in 1968. Today the SCBW boasts a nationwide membership in excess of 6,500.

Two memberships are available: Full members are writers and illustrators who have had work for children or young adults published. Associate memberships are open to anyone with an interest in the field. In addition to publishing a bimonthly newsletter, the SCBW also publishes informational pieces on contracts, copyrights and grants for works in progress, to name a few. The only cost to members for these publications is the cost of the postage.

Alexander, herself a fulltime writer of picture books and easy readers, has had 22 books published since 1973. Two of her current books include *Who Goes Out On Halloween?* and *World Famous Muriel and the Magic Mystery.* She says she's been writing all her life, or at least since she was eight years old. Though no longer a novice, her involvement in the SCBW has made her aware of the basic questions most beginners have.

Alexander says the current boom in children's books is due to the increased enthusiasm about education. "You have a group of parents who married later, has more money and recognizes the value of reading for children."

Young adult novels are slumping for reasons of economics, she says. "Young people of 13-14 don't have $14.95 in their pockets to buy (hardcover) books and they wouldn't be caught dead walking into a children's bookstore. So they are going to bookstores in malls and buying the cheaper paperbacks. Therefore, the hardcover book sales in YA books have had to fall back on the traditional market for children's books—libraries and schools. Unfortunately, libraries and schools don't have as much money as they used to."

Alexander says she's pleased to see nonfiction becoming more popular and feels it started in part when *Lincoln, A Photobiography* (by Russell Freedman) received the 1988 Newbery Medal. Also, publishers have become more aware of how nonfiction should look and have done wonders with presenting it, she says. In addition, nonfiction paperbacks are becoming more widespread, and in turn, more accessible.

Initial problems experienced by beginning illustrators involve the way they present artwork to publishers. "What they need to show are kinds of things seen in children's books," says Alexander. "Very often the portfolios I see, the art is wonderful, but very esoteric. We (the SCBW) try to give guidance in that area." The most common misconception of beginning writers is they don't understand a writer is not responsible for the illustrations, she says. Also, "they (writers) don't read children's books and so haven't a clue what's going on. They are depending on their memories of the books they read as children. The memory of a book is not as valid as the book itself."

— Lisa Carpenter

---

requirements, must submit examples of their work. Sponsors The Annual of American Illustration. Awards include gold and silver medals. Open to nonmembers. Deadline: October 1.

*WOMEN WRITERS WEST, Box 1637, Santa Monica CA 90406. (213)657-0108. President: Rita White. "Women Writer's West (WWW) is a nonprofit, non-political support group for women and men who write. Through this network, we exchange information on the many readings, workshops, classes and literary events that take place in Southern California. Membership is open to all who support and encourage creativity. Our members are published and to-be-published, fiction writers, poets, nonfiction writers, freelancers, TV and screenwriters, and diary keepers, as well as practitioners of the teaching and healing arts." Cost of membership: $20/year. Workshops/conferences: monthly meeting includes speaker or workshop; annual 1-day conference—1991 date unknown, usually spring. Publishes newsletter about writing. Nonmember subscription: $10.

*WOMEN'S NATIONAL BOOK ASSOCIATION, 160 Fifth Ave., New York NY 10010. (212)675-7804. President: Patti Breitman. Purpose of organization is "to provide service to the book community; to support women in the book community. Anyone who loves books may join. Membership costs vary from chapter to chapter." Each chapter publishes a monthly newsletter and national newsletter published three times a year.

*THE WRITERS ALLIANCE, Box 2014, Setauket NY 11733. Executive Director: Kiel Stuart. Purpose of organization: "A support/information group for all types of writers." Membership cost: $15/year, payable to Kiel Stuart. A group membership costs $25. Different levels of membership include: corporate/group—$25, individual—$15. Publishes newsletter for all writers who use (or want to learn about) computers. Nonmember subscription $15—payable to Kiel Stuart.

Workshops

No professional can ever know all he needs to know about his craft or the business aspects involved in maintaining a profit. Keeping up with trends in publishing, as well as changes in tax and copyright law, are only some of the topics covered by writing and illustration workshops.

Be aware that not every workshop included here relates specifically to juvenile writing or illustrating. Special courses for mystery, science fiction, western and romance writing are genres which transfer nicely to middle- and young adult readers plus general workshops in watercolors and oils for illustrators to enhance technique.

These listings will provide you with information describing what courses are offered, where and when, and the costs. Some of the national writing and art organizations also offer regional workshops throughout the year. Write for information.

*CAPE LITERARY WORKSHOPS, Cape Cod Writers Conference, % Cape Cod Conservatory, Route 132, West Barnstable MA 02668. (508)775-4811. Executive Director: Marion Vuilleumier. Writer and illustrator workshops geared toward intermediate, advanced levels. Summer workshops offered in children's book writing and children's book illustration. Workshops held in July and early August. Conference held third week in August. Intensive workshops meet Monday-Friday from 9-1. Afternoons and evenings are used to do assignments and enjoy Cape Cod attractions. Class sizes limited. Cost of workshop: $385; includes registration and tuition. Materials, room and board extra. "It is not necessary to have works-in-progress but those who do will find these workshops especially helpful. Participants are encouraged to send current work in advance."
Tips: Send for brochure for more information on workshops and accommodations.

*CLARION SCIENCE FICTION & FANTASY WRITING WORKSHOP, Lyman Briggs School, E-28 Holmes Hall, MSU, East Lansing MI 48824-1107. (517)353-6486. Administrative Assistant: Mary Sheridan. Writer and illustrator workshop geared toward intermediate levels. Emphasizes science fiction and fantasy. "An intensive workshop designed to stimulate and develop the talent and techniques of potential writers of speculative fiction. Previous experience in writing fiction is assumed. Approximately 25 participants will work very closely together over a six week period, guided by a series of professional writers of national reputation." Workshop held summer—June 23-August 3, 1990. Length of session: six weeks. Class size: 17-25. Cost of tuition (7 credits of upper level course work): $500-600 for Michigan resident, $1,300-1,400 for non-Michigan resident (depending on educational status and whether credit is desired). Lodging (single room) and meal costs are being negotiated. Requirements prior to registration: submission of two manuscripts (up to 2,500 words each) for review, and a completed application form with a $25 application fee. Write for more information.

*DILLMAN'S CREATIVE WORKSHOPS, 3305 Sand Lake Lodge Lane, Lac du Flambeau WI 54538. (715)588-3143. Coordinators: Amber Weldon or Dennis Robertson. "All levels of art workshops (watercolor, acrylics, pastels and oils) geared to all different levels." 1991 schedule includes a wide variety. Write for tentative 1991 schedule. Workshops held mid May through mid October. Length of each session: usually 5 days/6 nights—sometimes weekends. Maximum class size: 25. Writing and/or art facilities available: 3-4 separate studios—fully equipped. Cost varies from $600-800. This includes

room, board and tuition. $100-350 tuition only for people staying off-grounds.
Tips: Write for brochure.

DRURY COLLEGE/SCBW WRITING FOR CHILDREN WORKSHOP, Drury College, Springfield MO 65802. (417)865-8731. Assistant Director, Continuing Education: Lynn Doke. Writer and illustrator workshop geared toward beginner, intermediate, advanced, professional levels. Emphasizes all aspects of writing for children and teenagers. Classes/courses offered include: "An Inside View of Illustration at a Children's Book Publishing House," "Everything Is True, and Nothing Is True: How to Write from Your Own Life," "Teen Girls Who Date Football Players Too Much and Other Ways to Gag Editors: Avoiding All-Too-Common Mistakes," "How to Write for Teenagers When You Aren't One Anymore." One-day workshop held in November. Length of each session: 1 hour. Manuscript and portfolio consultations (by appointment only). Maximum class size: 25-30. $45 registration fee; individual consultations $25. Send SASE for more information.

HIGHLIGHTS FOUNDATION WRITERS WORKSHOP AT CHAUTAUQUA, 711 Court St., Honesdale PA 18431. (717)253-1192. Conference Director: Jan Keen. Writer workshops geared toward beginner, intermediate, advanced levels. Classes/courses offered include: "Children's Interests," "Writing Dialogue," "Beginnings and Endings," "Science Writing," "My Stories for Young Readers." Workshops held July 20-27, 1991, Chautauqua Institution, Chautauqua, NY. Length of each session: 1½ hrs. Maximum class size: 100. Cost of workshop: $1,500 (if registered before April 25, early bird rate is $985); includes registration fee, gate ticket fee, workshop supplies and all meals. Write for more information.

*MAINE WRITERS WORKSHOP, 2 Central St., Rockport ME 04856. (207)236-8581. Assistant to Director: Joan Rosenberg. Founder and Director, David H. Lyman. "These workshops are for professional writers who have a history of published work. Newspaper writers may wish to develop their craft in writing novels, or to improve their travel writing. Professional travel writers may wish to begin work on their first novel, or need help overcoming a block. Writers without a history of published work are discouraged from attending, but are accepted if samples of their work show talent and dedication. A résumé *must* accompany your application indicating your publishing career." "The Children's Story Workshop" was featured in 1990. Workshops held in summer and fall. Length of each session: 1 week. Maximum class size: varies. Cost of workshop: $450 tuition; room and board $375-575.
Tips: Send for brochure on workshops and accommodations.

*MARITIME WRITERS' WORKSHOP, Dept. Extension & Summer School, P.O. Box 4400, University of New Brunswick, Fredericton, New Brunswick E3B 5A3 Canada. (506)453-4646. Week-long workshop geared to all levels and held in July. Length of each session: 3 hours per day. Group workshop plus individual conferences, public readings, etc. Maximum class size: 10-12. Cost of workshop: $220 tuition. Meals and

 The asterisk before a listing indicates the listing is new in this edition.

accommodations extra. 10-20 ms pages due before conference (deadline announced). Scholarships available.

*PERSPECTIVES IN CHILDREN'S LITERATURE CONFERENCE, 226 Furcolo Hall, University of Massachusetts, Amherst MA 01003. (413)545-4325. Director of Conference: Masha K. Rudman. Writer and illustrator workshops geared to all levels. Emphasis varies from year to year. Workshops held first or second week in April. Length of each session: classes are 1-hour sessions. Maximum class size: 100. Cost of workshop: about $45.

ROBERT QUACKENBUSH'S CHILDREN'S BOOK WRITING AND ILLUSTRATING WORKSHOP, 460 East 79th St., New York NY 10021. (212)744-3822. Contact: Robert Quackenbush. Writer and illustrator workshops geared toward beginner, intermediate, advanced, professional levels. Emphasizes picture books from start to finish. Classes/courses offered include: fall and winter courses, extend 10 weeks each — 1½ hour/week; July workshop is a full five day (9 a.m.-4 p.m.) extensive course. Workshops held fall, winter and summer. Maximum class size: 8. Writing and/or art facilities available: work on the premises; art supply store nearby. Cost of workshop: $450 for instruction. Write for more information.

SEMINARS FOR WRITERS, % Writers Connection, Ste. 180, 1601 Saratoga-Sunnyvale Rd., Cupertino CA 95014. (408)973-0227. FAX: (408)973-1219. Program Director: Meera Lester. Writer's workshops geared toward beginner, intermediate levels. Length of each session: six-hour session usually offered on a Saturday. Maximum class size: 35-40. Occasional seminars on writing for children (approximately 2-3 per year). Bookstore of 200 titles of writing, reference and how-to books. Monthly newsletter by subscription. Write for more information.

SEVENTH ANNUAL CHILDREN'S LITERATURE CONFERENCE, Hofstra University, U.C.C.E., 232 Memorial Hall, Hempstead NY 11550. (516)560-5997. Writers/Illustrators Contact: Lewis Shena, director, Liberal Arts Studies. Writer and illustrator workshops geared toward beginner, intermediate, advanced, professional levels. Emphasizes: fiction, nonfiction, poetry, submission procedures, picture books. Workshops held April 27, Saturday, 9:30 a.m.-4:30 p.m. Length of each session: 2 hours. Maximum class size: 20. Cost of workshop includes: 2 workshops, reception, lunch, panel discussions with guest speakers, e.g. "What An Editor Looks For." Write for more information. Co-sponsored by Society of Children's Book Writers.

SOUTHERN CALIFORNIA SOCIETY OF CHILDREN'S BOOK WRITERS ILLUSTRATORS DAY, 11943 Montana Ave. #105, Los Angeles CA 90049. (213)820-5601, 457-3501. Regional Advisor: Judith Enderle. Illustrator workshops geared toward beginner, intermediate, advanced, professional levels. Emphasizes illustration and illustration markets. Conference includes: presentations by art director, children's book editor, and panel of artists/author-illustrators. Workshops held annually in November. Length of session: full day. Maximum class size: 100. "Editors and art directors will view portfolios. We want to know if each conferee is bringing a portfolio or not." Cost of workshop: $60 members, $65 students, $70 nonmembers; bring your lunch, handouts included.
Tips: "This is a chance for illustrators to meet editors/art directors and each other. Writers Day held in February."

*SPLIT ROCK ARTS PROGRAM, University of Minnesota, 306 Wesbrook Hall, 77 Pleasant St. SE, Minneapolis MN 55455. (612)624-6800. Registrar: Vivien Oja. Writer and illustrator workshops geared toward intermediate, advanced, professional levels. Workshops offered in writing and illustrating books for children and young people. 1991 workshops begin July 7. Length of each session: One week intensive, Sunday night to Saturday noon. 2 college credits available. Maximum class size: 16. Workshops held on the University of Minnesota-Duluth campus. Cost of workshop: $250-280; includes tuition and fees. Amounts vary depending on course fee, determined by supply needs, etc. **Tips:** Complete catalogs available April 1. Call or write anytime to be put on mailing list. Some courses fill very early.

SUMMER WRITERS CONFERENCE, Hofstra U - U.C.C.E. - Memorial 232, Hempstead NY 11550. (516)560-5997. Writers/Illustrators Contact: Lewis Shena, director, Liberal Arts Studies. Writer workshops geared toward beginner, intermediate, advanced, professional levels. Emphasizes fiction, nonfiction, poetry, children's literature, stage/screen. Classes/courses offered: "Besides workshops, we arrange a series of readings and discussions." Workshops held Monday-Friday—2 weeks—July 8-19, 1991. Length of each session: daily, approximately 2½ hours of workshop and 1-2 hours of informal meetings. Maximum class size: 20. Writing/art facilities available: lecture room, tables, any media required will be gotten. Cost of workshop: noncredit, approximately $525; includes 2 workshops per day—special readings—special speakers. Dorm rooms available at additional cost. Write for more information.

VASSAR INSTITUTE OF PUBLISHING AND WRITING: CHILDREN'S BOOKS IN THE MARKETPLACE, Box 300, Vassar College, Poughkeepsie NY 12601. (914)437-5900. Program Coordinator: Maryann Bruno. Director: Barbara Lucas. Writer and illustrator workshops geared toward beginner, intermediate, advanced, professional levels. Emphasizes "the editorial, production, marketing and reviewing processes, on writing fiction and nonfiction for all ages, creating the picture book, understanding the markets and selling your work." Classes/courses offered include: "Writing Fiction," "The Editorial Process," "How to Write a Children's Book and Get It Published." Workshop in 1991, June 16-23. Length of each session: 3½-hour morning critique sessions, afternoon and evening lectures. Maximum class size: 55 (with three instructors). Cost of workshop: approximately $600, includes room, board and tuition for all critique sessions, lectures, and social activities. "Proposals are pre-prepared and discussed at morning critique sessions. Art portfolio review given on pre-prepared works." Write for more information.
Tips: "This conference gives a comprehensive look at the publishing industry as well as offering critiques of creative writing and portfolio review."

*WILLAMETTE WRITERS 21ST ANNUAL WRITERS CONFERENCE, 9045 SW Barbur Blvd, Suite 5A, Portland OR 97219. (503)452-1542. Conference Chair: Linda Stirling Wanner. Writer workshops geared toward beginner, intermediate, advanced, professional levels. Emphasizes all areas of writing. Classes/courses offered include: romance writing; A-B-C's of writing; A-B-C's of writing, basic techniques; desk top publishing; How to Research—Step by Step Process; science fiction panel, dialogue, etc. Opportunities to meet one-on-one with leading literary agents and editors. Workshops held third week of August 1991. Length of each session: 1½ hours. Write for more information.

*WORKING WRITERS RETREAT—SCBW NW, 12180 Southwest Ann Place, Tigard OR 97223. (503)639-5754. Retreat Chair: Margaret Bechard. Writer workshop geared toward intermediate, advanced levels; illustrator workshop geared toward beginner, intermediate levels. "We have craft lectures with published authors who usually discuss how they got started, how they work and how they market. We also have an editor who usually discusses market trends. In the mornings, we have craft lectures. The afternoons are devoted to small groups where participants can critique manuscripts, exchange ideas or meet with the faculty." Retreat held in June 21-26, 1991 at Silver Falls Conference Center. "We basically go all day. Although participants may choose to not attend everything." Maximum class size: There are 40 participants. Small groups are usually 5-10 people. Cost of workshop: 1990 prices: $255 (members of SCBW-NW, $10/year for membership), $280 (nonmembers); double occupancy room (single $45 more), 5 nights, all meals, all events.

*WRITING FOR YOUNG PEOPLE, 1908 S. Goliad, Amarillo TX 79106. (806)353-4925 or 358-3717. Writer and illustrator workshops geared toward beginner, intermediate levels. Emphasizes "varying aspects of writing for the children's market, especially technique and marketing; basic information the artist needs to get started as an illustrator." Classes/courses offered include: 1990 presentations—"Everything Is True and Nothing Is True": "Writing from Your Own Life"; "Recipe for a Middle Grade Novel"; "Nonfat, Non-taxable, Non-seasonal Non-secrets to Nonfiction"; "Are Happy Days Here Again?: Children's Publishing in the 90's"; "Nuts and Bolts for the Freelance Illustrator." Workshops held in October. Length of each session: one-day conference (8:30-4:00). Cost of workshop: $45; includes all sessions and lunch.
Tips: Location—Region XVI Education Service Center, Amarillo, TX. "Our event is a one-day conference with 3-4 speakers experienced in some facet of the children's market (authors, editors, librarians, booksellers, illustrators), Ms evaluations offered for additional fee." Sponsored by Society of Children's Book Writers, West Texas Chapter.

Market conditions are constantly changing! If you're still using this book and it is 1992 or later, buy the newest edition of Children's Writer's & Illustrator's Market *at your favorite bookstore or order directly from* Writer's Digest Books.

Advance. A sum of money that a publisher pays a writer prior to the publication of a book. It is usually paid in installments, such as one-half on signing the contract; one half on delivery of a complete and satisfactory manuscript. The advance is paid against the royalty money that will be earned by the book.

All rights. The rights contracted to a publisher permitting a manuscript's use anywhere and in any form, including movie and book-club sales, without additional payment to the writer.

Anthropomorphization. To attribute human form and personality to things not human (such as animals).

ASAP. Abbreviation for as soon as possible.

B&W. Abbreviation for black and white artwork or photographs.

Backlist. A publisher's list of books not published during the current season but still in print.

Biennially. Once every two years.

Bimonthly. Once every two months.

Biweekly. Once every two weeks.

Bleed. Area of a plate or print that extends beyond the actual trimmed sheet to be printed.

Book packager. Draws all elements of a book together, from the initial concept to writing and marketing strategies, then sells the book package to a book publisher and/or movie producer. Also known as book producer or book developer.

Business-size envelope. Also known as a #10 envelope, it is the standard size used in sending business correspondence.

Camera-ready. Art that is completely prepared for copy camera platemaking.

Caption. A description of the subject matter of an illustration or photograph; photo captions include names of people where appropriate. Also called cutline.

Clean-copy. A manuscript free of errors and needing no editing; it is ready for typesetting.

Contract. A written agreement stating the rights to be purchased by an editor or art director and the amount of payment the writer or illustrator will receive for that sale.

Contributor's copies. Copies of the issues of magazines sent to the author or illustrator in which his/her work appears.

Copy. Refers to the actual written material of a manuscript.

Copyediting. Editing a manuscript for grammar usage, spelling, punctuation, and general style.

Copyright. A means to legally protect an author's/illustrator's work. This can be shown by writing ©, your name, and year of work's creation.

Cover letter. A brief letter, accompanying a complete manuscript, especially useful if responding to an editor's request for a manuscript. A cover letter may also accompany a book proposal. A cover letter is not a query letter.

Cutline. See caption.

Disk. A round, flat magnetic plate on which computer data is stored.

Division. An unincorporated branch of a company.

Dot-matrix. Printed type in which individual characters are composed of a matrix or pattern of tiny dots.

Dummy. Hand-made mock-up of a book.

Final draft. The last version of a "polished" manuscript ready for submission to the editor.

First North American serial rights. The right to publish material in a periodical before it appears in book form, for the first time, in the United States or Canada.

Flat fee. A one-time payment.

GAG. Graphic Artists Guild.

Galleys. The first typeset version of a manuscript that has not yet been divided into pages.

Gatefold. A page larger than the trim size of a book which is folded so as not to extend beyond the edges.

Genre. A formulaic type of fiction, such as adventure, mystery, romance, science fiction or western.

Glossy. A black and white photograph with a shiny surface as opposed to one with a non-shiny matte finish.

Gouache. Opaque watercolor with an appreciable film thickness and an actual paint layer.

Halftone. Reproduction of a continuous tone illustration with the image formed by dots produced by a camera lens screen.

Hard copy. The printed copy of a computer's output.

ILAA. Independent Literary Agents Association, Inc.

Illustrations. May be artwork, photographs, old engravings. Usually paid for separately from the manuscript.

Imprint. Name applied to a publisher's specific line or lines of books.

IRC. International Reply Coupon; purchased at the post office to enclose with text or artwork sent to a foreign buyer to cover his postage cost when replying or returning work.

Keyline. Identification, through signs and symbols, of the positions of illustrations and copy for the printer.

Kill fee. Portion of the agreed-upon price the author or artist receives for a job that was assigned, worked on, but then canceled.

Layout. Arrangement of illustrations, photographs, text and headlines for printed material.

Letter-quality submission. Computer printout that looks like a typewritten manuscript.

Line drawing. Illustration done with pencil or ink using no wash or other shading.

Mechanicals. Paste-up or preparation of work for printing.

Middle reader. The general classification of books written for readers 9-11 years of age.

Modem. A small electrical box that plugs into the serial card of a computer, used to transmit data from one computer to another, usually via telephone lines.

Ms, mss. Abbreviation for manuscript(s).

One-time rights. Permission to publish a story in periodical or book form one time only.

Outline. A summary of a book's contents in 5-15 double spaced pages; often in the form of chapter headings with a descriptive sentence or two under each one to show the scope of the book.

Package sale. The editor buys manuscript and illustrations/photos as a "package" and pays for them with one check.

Payment on acceptance. The writer or artist is paid for his work at the time the editor or art director decides to buy it.

Payment on publication. The writer or artist is paid for his work when it is published.

Photocopied submissions. Submitting photocopies of an original manuscript instead of sending the original. Do not assume that an editor who accepts photocopies will also accept multiple or simultaneous submissions.

Photostat. Black-and-white copies produced by an inexpensive photographic process using paper negatives; only line values are held with accuracy. Also called stat.

Picture book. A type of book aimed at the preschool to 8-year-old that tells the story primarily or entirely with artwork.

PMT. Photostat produced without a negative, somewhat like the Polaroid process.

Print. An impression pulled from an original plate, stone, block, screen or negative; also a positive made from a photographic negative.

Proofreading. Reading a manuscript to correct typographical errors.

Query. A letter to an editor designed to capture his/her interest in an article you purpose to write.

Reading fee. An arbitrary amount of money charged by some agents and publishers to read a submitted manuscript.

Reporting time. The time it takes for an editor to report to the author on his/her query or manuscript.

Reprint rights. Permission to print an already published work whose rights have been sold to another magazine or book publisher.

Response time. The average length of time it takes an editor or art director to accept or reject a manuscript or artwork and inform you of the decision.

Rights. What you offer to an editor or art director in exchange for printing your manuscripts or artwork.

Rough draft. A manuscript which has been written but not checked for errors in grammar, punctuation, spelling or content. It usually needs revision and rewriting.

Roughs. Preliminary sketches or drawings.

Royalty. An agreed percentage paid by the publisher to the writer or illustrator for each copy of his work sold.

SAR. Society of Author's Representatives.

SASE. Abbreviation for self-addressed, stamped envelope.

SCBW. Society of Children's Book Writers.

Second serial rights. Permission for the reprinting of a work in another periodical after its first publication in book or magazine form.

Semiannual. Once every six months.

Semimonthly. Twice a month.

Semiweekly. Twice a week.

Serial rights. The rights given by an author to a publisher to print a piece in one or more periodicals.

Simultaneous submissions. Sending the same article, story, poem or illustration to several publishers at the same time. Some publishers refuse to consider such submissions. No simultaneous submissions should be made without stating the fact in your letter.

Slant. The approach to a story or piece of artwork that will appeal to readers of a particular publication.

Slush pile. What editors call the collection of submitted manuscripts which have not been specifically asked for.

Software. Programs and related documentation for use with a particular computer system.

Solicited manuscript. Material which an editor has asked for or agreed to consider before being sent by the writer.

SPAR. Society of Photographers and Artists Representatives, Inc.

Speculation (Spec). Writing or drawing a piece with no assurance from the editor or art director that it will be purchased or any reimbursements for material or labor paid.

Subsidiary rights. All rights other than book publishing rights included in a book contract, such as paperback, book club and movie rights.

Subsidy publisher. A book publisher who charges the author for the cost of typesetting, printing and promoting a book. Also vanity publisher.

Synopsis. A brief summary of a story or novel. If part of a book proposal, it should be a page to a page and a half, single-spaced.

Tabloid. Publication printed on an ordinary newspaper page turned sideways.

Tear sheet. Page from a magazine or newspaper containing your printed story, article, poem or ad.

Thumbnail. A rough layout in miniature.

Transparencies. Positive color slides; not color prints.

Unsolicited manuscript. A story, article, poem, book or artwork sent without the editor's or art director's knowledge or consent.

Vanity publisher. See subsidy publisher.

Word length. The maximum number of words a manuscript should contain as determined by the editor or guidelines sheet.

Word processor. A computer that produces typewritten copy via automated typing, text-editing, and storage and transmission capabilities.

Young adult. The general classification of books written for readers ages 12-18.

Young reader. The general classification of books written for readers 5-8 years old. Here artwork supports the text as opposed to picture books.

Key to Symbols

* *Symbol indicating listing is new in this edition*
■ *Symbol indicating a market subsidy publishes manuscripts*
‡ *Symbol indicating a contest is for students*

The age-level index is set up to help you more quickly locate book markets geared to the age group(s) for which you write or illustrate. Read each listing carefully and follow the publisher's specific information about the type(s) of manuscript(s) each prefers to read and the style(s) of artwork each wishes to review.

Picture books (preschool-8-year-olds)

Advocacy Press
Aegina Press/University Editions
Aladdin Books/Collier Books for Young Readers
Alyson Publications, Inc.
American Bible Society
Arcade Publishing
Atheneum Publishers
Barrons Educational Series
Beacon Press
Beyond Words Publishing
Bradbury Press
Branden Publishing Co.
Bright Ring Publishing
Carolina Wren Press/Lollipop Power Books
Carolrhoda Books, Inc.
Charlesbridge
Chronicle Books
Clarion Books
Cloverdale Press
Cobblehill Books
Concordia Publishing House
Council for Indian Education
Crocodile Books, USA
Crown Publishers (Crown Books for Children)
Davenport, Publishers, May
Delacorte Press
Dial Books for Young Readers
Double M Press
Doubleday
Dutton Children's Books
Eakin Publications
Eerdmans Publishing Company, Wm. B.

Esoterica Press
Farrar, Straus & Giroux
Four Winds Press
Godine, Publisher, David R.
Golden Books
Green Tiger Press
Harbinger House, Inc.
Harcourt Brace Jovanovich
HarperCollins Children's Books
Harvest House Publishers
Hendrick-Long Publishing Company
Holiday House Inc.
Holt & Co., Inc., Henry
Homestead Publishing
Houghton Mifflin Co.
Humanics Children's House
Ideals Publishing Corporation
Jalmar Press
Jewish Publication Society
Jones University Press/Light Line Books, Bob
Jordan Enterprises Pub. Co., Inc.
Joy Street Books
Just Us Books, Inc.
Kar-Ben Copies, Inc.
Kendall Green Publications
Kingsway Publications
Knopf Books for Young Readers
Kruza Kaleidoscopix, Inc.
Lion Books, Publisher
Lion Publishing Corporation
Little, Brown and Company
Lodestar Books
Lothrop, Lee & Shepard Books
McElderry Books, Margaret K.
Magination Press
March Media, Inc.

Metamorphous Press
Morehouse Publishing Co.
Muir Publications, Inc, John
Multnomah Press
NAR Publications
Oddo Publishing, Inc.
Orchard Books
Our Child Press
Parenting Press, Inc.
Paulist Press
Pelican Publishing Co. Inc.
Perspectives Press
Philomel Books
Pippin Press
Pocahontas Press, Inc.
Potter Inc., Clarkson N.
Price Stern Sloan
Prometheus Books
Random House Books for
Young Readers
Read'n Run Books
Rosebrier Publishing Co.
St. Paul Books and Media
Scholastic Hardcover
Scholastic, Inc.
Scribner's Sons, Charles
Speech Bin, Inc., The
Standard Publishing
Stemmer House Publishers,
Inc.
TAB Books
Trillium Press
Tyndale House Publishers
Volcano Press
Walker and Co.
Warner Juvenile Books
Waterfront Books
Winston-Derek Publishers,
Inc.
Women's Press

Young readers (5-8-year-olds)

Accent Books
Advocacy Press
Aegina Press/University Editions
Aladdin Books/Collier Books
for Young Readers
American Bible Society
Arcade Publishing
Atheneum Publishers
Barrons Educational Series
Beacon Press
Behrman House Inc.
Beyond Words Publishing

Bradbury Press
Bright Ring Publishing
Carolina Wren Press/Lollipop Power Books
Carolrhoda Books, Inc.
China Books
Chronicle Books
Clarion Books
Cloverdale Press
Cobblehill Books
Colormore, Inc.
Concordia Publishing House
Council for Indian Education
Crossway Books
Crown Publishers (Crown
Books for Children)
Delacorte Press
Dial Books for Young Readers
Dillon Press, Inc.
Double M Press
Doubleday
Dutton Children's Books
Eakin Publications
Eerdmans Publishing Company, Wm. B.
Esoterica Press
Farrar, Straus & Giroux
Free Spirit Publishing
Godine, Publisher, David R.
Golden Books
Harbinger House, Inc.
Harcourt Brace Jovanovich
HarperCollins Children's
Books
Harvest House Publishers
Hendrick-Long Publishing
Company
Herald Press
Holiday House Inc.
Holt & Co., Inc., Henry
Homestead Publishing
Houghton Mifflin Co.
Humanics Children's House
Ideals Publishing Corporation
Incentive Publications, Inc.
Jalmar Press
Jewish Publication Society
Jones University Press/Light
Line Books, Bob
Jordan Enterprises Pub. Co.,
Inc.
Joy Street Books
Just Us Books, Inc.
Kar-Ben Copies, Inc.

Kendall Green Publications
Kingsway Publications
Kruza Kaleidoscopix, Inc.
Lerner Publications Co.
Liguori Publications
Lion Publishing Corporation
Little, Brown and Company
Lothrop, Lee & Shepard
 Books
Lucas/Evans Books
McElderry Books, Margaret
 K.
Magination Press
March Media, Inc.
Maryland Historical Press
Meadowbrook Press
Metamorphous Press
Morehouse Publishing Co.
Multnomah Press
NAR Publications
Oddo Publishing, Inc.
Orchard Books
Our Child Press
Parenting Press, Inc.
Paulist Press
Perspectives Press
Philomel Books
Pippin Press
Players Press, Inc.
Pocahontas Press, Inc.
Potter Inc., Clarkson N.
Price Stern Sloan
Prometheus Books
Random House Books for
 Young Readers
Read'n Run Books
Rockrimmon Press, Inc., The
St. Anthony Messenger Press
St. Paul Books and Media
Scholastic Hardcover
Scholastic, Inc.
Scribner's Sons, Charles
Shoe Tree Press
Speech Bin, Inc., The
Sri Rama Publishing
Standard Publishing
Stemmer House Publishers,
 Inc.
TAB Books
Trillium Press
Tyndale House Publishers
Volcano Press
Walker and Co.
Waterfront Books
Watts, Inc., Franklin
Weigl Educational Publishers

Winston-Derek Publishers,
 Inc.
Women's Press

Middle readers (9-11-year-olds)

Addison-Wesley Publishing
 Co.
Aegina Press/University Editions
Aladdin Books/Collier Books
 for Young Readers
American Bible Society
Arcade Publishing
Archway/Minstrel Books
Atheneum Publishers
Avon Books
Barrons Educational Series
Beacon Press
Behrman House Inc.
Beyond Words Publishing
Bradbury Press
Bright Ring Publishing
Carolrhoda Books, Inc.
China Books
Chronicle Books
Clarion Books
Cloverdale Press
Cobblehill Books
Concordia Publishing House
Council for Indian Education
Crossway Books
Crown Publishers (Crown
 Books for Children)
Delacorte Press
Dial Books for Young Readers
Dillon Press, Inc.
Double M Press
Doubleday
Dutton Children's Books
Eakin Publications
Eerdmans Publishing Company, Wm. B.
Enslow Publishers Inc.
Faber and Faber, Inc.
Farrar, Straus & Giroux
Four Winds Press
Free Spirit Publishing
Godine, Publisher, David R.
Golden Books
Greenhaven Press
Harbinger House, Inc.
Harcourt Brace Jovanovich
HarperCollins Children's
 Books

Harvest House Publishers
Haypenny Press
Hendrick-Long Publishing
  Company
Herald Press
Holiday House Inc.
Holt & Co., Inc., Henry
Homestead Publishing
Houghton Mifflin Co.
Incentive Publications, Inc.
Jewish Publication Society
Jones University Press/Light
  Line Books, Bob
Jordan Enterprises Pub. Co.,
  Inc.
Joy Street Books
Just Us Books, Inc.
Kendall Green Publications
Kingsway Publications
Knopf Books for Young
  Readers
Kruza Kaleidoscopix, Inc.
Lerner Publications Co.
Liguori Publications
Lion Books, Publisher
Lion Publishing Corporation
Little, Brown and Company
Lodestar Books
Lothrop, Lee & Shepard
  Books
Lucas/Evans Books
Lucent Books
McElderry Books, Margaret
  K.
March Media, Inc.
Maryland Historical Press
Meadowbrook Press
Metamorphous Press
Misty Hill Press
Morehouse Publishing Co.
Mosaic Press
Muir Publications, Inc, John
Multnomah Press
New Day Press
Oddo Publishing, Inc.
Orchard Books
Our Child Press
Pando Publications
Parenting Press, Inc.
Paulist Press
Pelican Publishing Co. Inc.
Perspectives Press
Philomel Books
Pippin Press
Players Press, Inc.
Pocahontas Press, Inc.

Potter Inc., Clarkson N.
Press of MacDonald & Rein-
  ecke, The
Price Stern Sloan
Prometheus Books
Random House Books for
  Young Readers
Read'n Run Books
Rockrimmon Press, Inc., The
Rosen Publishing Group, The
St. Anthony Messenger Press
St. Paul Books and Media
Sandlapper Publishing Co.,
  Inc.
Scholastic Hardcover
Scholastic, Inc.
Scribner's Sons, Charles
Shoe Tree Press
Skylark/Books for Young
  Readers
Speech Bin, Inc., The
Standard Publishing
Star Books, Inc.
Stemmer House Publishers,
  Inc.
Sterling Publishing Co., Inc.
TAB Books
Thistledown Press Ltd.
Trillium Press
Tyndale House Publishers
Volcano Press
Voyageur Publishing Co., Inc.
Walker and Co.
Waterfront Books
Watts, Inc., Franklin
Weigl Educational Publishers
Winston-Derek Publishers,
  Inc.
Women's Press

Young adults (12 and up)

Aegina Press/University Edi-
  tions
Aladdin Books/Collier Books
  for Young Readers
Alyson Publications, Inc.
American Bible Society
Archway/Minstrel Books
Atheneum Publishers
Avon Books
Barrons Educational Series
Behrman House Inc.
Bradbury Press
Branden Publishing Co.
Clarion Books

Cloverdale Press
Cobblehill Books
Concordia Publishing House
Consumer Report Books
Council for Indian Education
Crossway Books
Crown Publishers (Crown Books for Children)
Davenport, Publishers, May
Delacorte Press
Dial Books for Young Readers
Double M Press
Dutton Children's Books
Eakin Publications
Eerdmans Publishing Company, Wm. B.
Enslow Publishers Inc.
Faber and Faber, Inc.
Facts on File
Farrar, Straus & Giroux
Free Spirit Publishing
Golden Books
Greenhaven Press
Harcourt Brace Jovanovich
HarperCollins Children's Books
Harvest House Publishers
Haypenny Press
Hendrick-Long Publishing Company
Herald Press
Holiday House Inc.
Holt & Co., Inc., Henry
Homestead Publishing
Houghton Mifflin Co.
Incentive Publications, Inc.
Jewish Publication Society
Jones University Press/Light Line Books, Bob
Jordan Enterprises Pub. Co., Inc.
Joy Street Books
Kendall Green Publications
Kingsway Publications
Knopf Books for Young Readers
Lerner Publications Co.
Liguori Publications
Lion Books, Publisher
Lion Publishing Corporation
Little, Brown and Company
Lodestar Books
Lothrop, Lee & Shepard Books
Lucas/Evans Books

McElderry Books, Margaret K.
Maryland Historical Press
Meadowbrook Press
Meriwether Publishing Ltd.
Metamorphous Press
Misty Hill Press
Morehouse Publishing Co.
Naturegraph Publisher, Inc.
New Day Press
Orchard Books
Our Child Press
Pando Publications
Paulist Press
Pelican Publishing Co. Inc.
Perspectives Press
Philomel Books
Players Press, Inc.
Pocahontas Press, Inc.
Prometheus Books
Read'n Run Books
Rosen Publishing Group, The
St. Anthony Messenger Press
St. Paul Books and Media
Sandlapper Publishing Co., Inc.
Scholastic Hardcover
Scholastic, Inc.
Scribner's Sons, Charles
Shaw Publishers, Harold
Shoe Tree Press
Speech Bin, Inc., The
Standard Publishing
Stemmer House Publishers, Inc.
TAB Books
Texas Christian University Press
Thistledown Press Ltd.
Trillium Press
Voyageur Publishing Co., Inc.
Walker and Co.
Waterfront Books
Watts, Inc., Franklin
Weigl Educational Publishers
Winston-Derek Publishers, Inc.
Women's Press
W.W. Publications

Age-Level Index Magazine Publishers

The age-level index is set up to help you more quickly locate magazine markets geared to the age group(s) for which you write or illustrate. Read each listing carefully and follow the publisher's specific information about the type(s) of manuscript(s) each prefers to read and the style(s) of artwork each wishes to review.

Picture books (preschool-8-year-olds)
Chickadee
Cochran's Corner
Cricket Magazine
Day Care and Early Education
DynaMath
Highlights for Children
Humpty Dumpty's Magazine
Ladybug, the Magazine for Young Children
My Friend
National Geographic World
Nature Friend Magazine
Pennywhistle Press
Scienceland
Sing Out!
Together Time
Turtle Magazine
Tyro Magazine
Wee Wisdom Magazine
Young Salvationist

Young readers (5-8-year-olds)
Atalantik
Chickadee
Child Life
Children's Playmate
Cochran's Corner
Cricket Magazine
Day Care and Early Education
DynaMath
Friend
Friend Magazine, The
Highlights for Children
Home Altar, The
Hopscotch

Humpty Dumpty's Magazine
Jack and Jill
Kid City
Ladybug, the Magazine for Young Children
Lighthouse
My Friend
Nature Friend Magazine
Noah's Ark
Pockets
Scienceland
Sing Out!
Single Parent, The
Six Lakes Arts
Tyro Magazine
USKids®
Wee Wisdom Magazine
Wonder Time
YABA Framework
Young American
Young Judaean

Middle readers (9-11-year-olds)
Atalantik
Boys' Life
Bradley's Fantasy Magazine, Marion Zimmer
Cat Fancy
Child Life
Children's Digest
Clubhouse
Cobblestone
Cochran's Corner
Cricket Magazine
Crusader
Current Health I
Discoveries
Dolphin Log
DynaMath
Faces
Friend Magazine, The

Highlights for Children
Home Altar, The
Hopscotch
International Gymnast
Jack and Jill
Junior Trails
Kid City
Lighthouse
Mad Magazine
My Friend
National Geographic World
Nature Friend Magazine
Noah's Ark
Odyssey
On The Line
Owl Magazine
Pennywhistle Press
R-A-D-A-R
Ranger Rick
Scope
Shofar
Sing Out!
Single Parent, The
Six Lakes Arts
Superscience
Take 5
Teen Dream
3-2-1 Contact
Touch
Tyro Magazine
USKids®
Venture
Wee Wisdom Magazine
World of Busines$ Kids, The
YABA Framework
Young American
Young Crusader, The
Young Judaean
Zillions

Group
Guide Magazine
Hicall
Highlights for Children
InSights
International Gymnast
Keynoter
Lighthouse
Listen
Mad Magazine
My Friend
Nature Friend Magazine
New Era Magazine
Odyssey
Owl Magazine
Pennywhistle Press
Pioneer
Scholastic Math Magazine
Scope
Seventeen Magazine
Sing Out!
Single Parent, The
Six Lakes Arts
Starwind
Story Friends
Straight
Take 5
Teen Dream
'Teen Magazine
Teen Power
3-2-1 Contact
TQ
Tyro Magazine
Venture
Voice
With
World of Busines$ Kids, The
YABA Framework
Young American
Young Salvationist
Youth Update
Zillions

Young adults (12 and up)

Aim Magazine
Animal Tales
Atalantik
Bradley's Fantasy Magazine,
    Marion Zimmer
Careers
Clubhouse
Cobblestone
Cochran's Corner
Current Health II
Delirium
DynaMath
Exploring
Faces

General Index

A

Accent Books 39
Acorn, The 203
Action for Children's Television (ACT) 251
Addison-Wesley Publishing Co. 40
Advocacy Press 40
Aegina Press/University Editions 41
Aerial Image Video Services 177
Agora: The Magazine for Gifted Students 204
Aim Magazine 125
Aim Magazine Short Story Contest 219
Aladdin Books/Collier Books for Young Readers 42
Alberta Writing for Youth Competition 219
Alyson Publications, Inc. 42
AMCAL 198
America & Me Essay Contest 220
American Bible Society 43
American Society of Journalists and Authors 251
AMHA Morgan Art Contest 220
Anderson Films, Ken 178
Animal Tales 126
Arcade Publishing 43
Archway/Minstrel Books 44
Artists International 240
Atalantik 126
Atheneum Publishers 44
Authors Guild, The 251
Authors Resource Center, The 252
A/V Concepts Corp. 198
Avon Books 45
Avon Flare Young Adult Novel Competition 220

B

Bakers Plays 190
Bancroft & Friends, Carol 240
Bantam Doubleday Dell (see Doubleday 63)
Barron's Educational Series 46, 182
Bartle Annual Playwriting Award, Margaret 220
Beacon Press 46
Bear Essential News for Kids 204
Behrman House Inc. 47
bePUZZLED/Lombard Marketing, Inc. 198
Beyond Words Publishing 48
Black Book Award, The Irma Simonton 221
Blackbird Comics 199
Book of the Year for Children 221
Book Publishers of Texas Children's/Young People's Award 221
Bookstop Literary Agency 240
Boston Globe-Horn Book Awards, The 222
Boys' Life 127, 204
Bradbury Press 48
Bradley's Fantasy Magazine, Marion Zimmer 128
Branden Publishing Co. 49
Brentwood Music, Inc. 182
Bright Ring Publishing 49
Brilliant Enterprises 199
Brown Literary Agency, Andrea 241
Buckeye Children's Book Award 222

C

C.J. Publications 199
Caldecott Award 222
California Writers' Club 252
California Writers' Conference Awards 222
Canada Council Governor General's Literary Awards 223
Canadian Authors Association 252
Cape Literary Workshops 259

Caputo Publishing/Now Comics 199
Careers 128
Carolina Wren Press/Lollipop Power Books 50
Carolrhoda Books, Inc. 51
Carvainis Agency, Inc., Maria 241
Casselman, Martha, Literary Agent 241
Cat Fancy 129
Chalk Talk Magazine 204
Charlesbridge 52
Chickadee 129
Child Life 130
Child Study Children's Book Award 223
Children's Album 205
Childrens Book Award 223
Children's Book Council, Inc, The 253
Children's Choice Award 223
Children's Digest 130, 205
Children's Group, The 183
Children's Learning Center 183
Children's Playmate 131, 205
Children's Reading Round Table Award 223
Children's Reading Round Table of Chicago 253
Children's Story Scripts 191
Children's Writer's & Illustrator's Market 52
China Books 52
Choices 131
Christian Science Publishing Society, The 183
Christopher Award, The 224
Chronicle Books 53
Circa '21 Dinner Theatre 191
Clarion Books 53
Clarion Science Fiction & Fantasy Writing Workshop 259
Clark Literary Agency, SJ 242
Clearvue 178
Cloverdale Press 56
Clubhouse 132, 206
Cobblehill Books 56
Cobblestone 133
Cochran's Corner 133
Cohen, Inc., Ruth 242
Colormore, Inc. 57, 199
Concordia Publishing House 57

Consumer Report Books 58
Contemporary Drama Service 191
Coterie, The 193
Council for Indian Education 58
Craven Design Studios, Inc. 242
Create-A-Craft 200
Creative Kids 206
Creative with Words 206
Cricket League 224
Cricket Magazine 134
Crocodile Books, USA 59
Crossway Books 59
Crown Publishers (Crown Books for Children) 60
Crusader 134
Current Health I 135
Current Health II 135
Curtis Associates, Richard 242

D

Davenport, Publishers, May 60
Day Care and Early Education 135
Delacorte Press 61
Delacorte Press Prize for a First Young Adult Novel 224
Delirium 135
Dell Publishing (see Delacorte Press 61)
D'Esternaux Poetry Scholarship Contest, The Marie-Louise 224
Dial Books for Young Readers 61
Dillman's Creative Workshops 259
Dillon Press, Inc. 62
Dimension Films 178
Discoveries 136
Dolphin Log 136
Double M Press 63
Doubleday 63
Dragonfly: East/West Haiku Quarterly 207
Dramatic Publishing, Inc. 193
Drexel Citation 225
Drury College/SCBW for Children Workshop 260
Dutton Children's Books 63 (also see Cobblehill Books

56, Lodestar Books 85)
DynaMath 137

E

Eakin Publications 64
Eclipse Comics 200
Educational Design Services,
  Inc. 243
Educational Video Network
  179
Eerdmans Publishing Com-
  pany, Wm. B. 65
Eldridge Publishing Co. Inc.
  193
Elek Associates, Peter 243
Ellenberg/Literary Agent,
  Ethan 243
Elmo Agency Inc., Ann 244
Enslow Publishers Inc. 65
Ephemera Inc. 200
Esoterica Press 65
Exploring 137

F

Faber and Faber, Inc. 66
Faces 138
Facts on File 66
Fantagraphics Books, Inc.
  200
Farrar, Straus & Giroux 66
Fendrich Memorial Play-
  wrighting Contest, Shub-
  ert 225
Field Award, Carolyn W. 225
First Publishing Inc. 201
Fisher Children's Book
  Award, Dorothy Canfield
  225
Florida State Writing Compe-
  tition 225
Flying Pencil Press, The 207
Foster City Annual Writers
  Contest 226
Four Winds Press 67
Free Spirit Publishing 68, 207
Freeman Memorial Grant-In-
  Aid, Don 226
French, Inc., Samuel 194
Friend 138
Friend Magazine, The 139

Frontline Music Group/
  Frontline Books 184

G

Gallaudet University Press
  (see Kendall Green Publi-
  cations 81)
Ghost Town Quarterly 208
Godine, Publisher, David R.
  68
Gold Medallion Book
  Awards 226
Golden Books 69
Golden Kite Awards 226
Gordon Music Co. Inc./Paris
  Records 184
Graphic Artists Guild 254
Great American Children's
  Theatre Company 194
Green Tiger Press 69
Greenhaven Press 69
Group 139
Guide Magazine 140
Gulliver Books (see Harcourt
  Brace Jovanovich 70)
Gusay, Literary Agent, Char-
  lotte 244

H

Harbinger House, Inc. 70
Harcourt Brace Jovanovich
  70, 185
Harper & Row Junior Books
  (see HarperCollins Chil-
  dren's Books 71)
HarperCollins Children's
  Books 71
Harvest House Publishers 72
Haypenny Press 72
HBJ Children's Books (see
  Harcourt Brace Jovanov-
  ich 70)
Heacock Literary Agency,
  Inc. 244
Hearst Corp., The (see Avon
  Books 45)
Hendrick-Long Publishing
  Company 73
Herald Press 73
Hicall 140

*Can't find a listing? Check Other Book Publishers, page
123, and Other Magazine Publishers, page 176, for
additional names.*

High Adventure 141
Highlights Foundation Writers Workshop at Chautauqua 260
Highlights for Children 141, 208
Highlights for Children Fiction Contest 227
Holiday House Inc. 74
Holt & Co., Inc., Henry 74
Home Altar, The 142
Homestead Publishing 75
Honolulu Theatre for Youth 194
Hopscotch 142
Houghton Mifflin Co. 75 (also see Clarion Books 53)
Howard-Gibbon Medal, Amelia Frances 227
Hubbard's Illustrators of the Future Contest, L. Ron 227
Hubbard's Writers of the Future Contest, L. Ron 227
Humanics Children's House 76
Humpty Dumpty's Magazine 144

I
Ideals Publishing Corporation 76
Incentive Publications, Inc. 77
Indian Paintbrush Book Award 228
InSights 145
Intercontinental Greetings Ltd. 201
International Black Writers 254
International Gymnast 146
International Reading Association Children's Book Award 228
Iowa Teen Award 228
Iupui Youth Theatre Playwriting Competition and Symposium 228

J
Jack and Jill 146
Jalmar Press 77
Jewish Publication Society 78
Jones University Press/Light Line Books, Bob 78

Jordan Enterprises Pub. Co., Inc. 79
Joy Street Books 79
Junior Trails 146
Just Us Books, Inc. 79

K
Kar-Ben Copies, Inc. 80
KDOC-TV 179
Keats New Writer Award, The Ezra Jack 229
Kellock and Associates Ltd., J. 245
Kendall Green Publications 81
Kerlan Award 229
Keynoter 147
Kid City 148
Kids' Books by Kids 208
Kidz & Company 185
Kingsway Publications 81
Knopf Books for Young Readers 82
Korcazk Awards, Janusz 229
Kouts, Literary Agent, Barbara S. 245
Kruza Kaleidoscopix, Inc. 82

L
Ladybug, the Magazine for Young Children 148
Larrco Ind. of TX, Inc. 185
League of Canadian Poets 254
Lerner Publications Co. 83
Lieberman Student Poetry Award, Elias 229
Lifeprints 209
Lighthouse 149
Lighthouse Literary Agency 246
Liguori Publications 83
Lincoln Literary Agency, Ray 246
Lion Books, Publisher 84
Lion Publishing Corporation 84
Listen 149
Little, Brown and Company 85 (also see Joy Street Books 79)
Lodestar Books 85
Lothrop, Lee & Shepard Books 86
Louisville Review, The 209
Lucas/Evans Books 86

Lucent Books 88

M

McElderry Books, Margaret K. 89
McGraw-Hill, Inc. (see TAB Books 116)
Macmillan Publishing Co. (see Aladdin Books/Collier Books for Young Readers 42, Atheneum Publishers 44, Bradbury Press 48, Four Winds Press 67, Margaret K. McElderry Books 89, Charles Scribner's Sons 112)
MAD Magazine 150
Magination Press 89
Maine Writers Workshops 260
March Media, Inc. 90
Maritime Writers' Workshop 260
Marshmedia 179
Marvel Comics 201
Maryland Historical Press 90
Meadowbrook Press 91
Meredith Literary Agency, Inc., Scott 246
Meriwether Publishing Ltd. 91
Merlyns Pen, The National Magazine of Student Writing 209
Metamorphous Press 92
Metcalf Body of Work Awards, Vicky 230
Metcalf Short Story Award, Vicky 230
Mews Books Ltd. 247
Milner Award, The 230
Mississippi Valley Poetry Contest 230
Misty Hill Press 92
Morehouse Publishing Co. 92
Morrow Co., William (see Lothrop, Lee & Shepherd Books 86)
Mosaic Press 93

Muir Publications, Inc, John 93
Multimedia Product Development, Inc. 247
Multnomah Press 94
MV Press 201
My Friend 151, 209
Mythic Circle, The 212

N

NAR Publications 95
National Geographic World 151
National Jewish Book Award for Children's Literature 230
National Writers Club 255
National Writers Union 255
National Written & Illustrated by .. Awards Contest for Students, The 1991 230
Nature Friend Magazine 152
Naturegraph Publisher, Inc. 95
Neail Associates, Pamela 248
New Conservatory Children's Theatre Company & School, The 194
New Day Press 95
New England Comics 201
New Era Magazine 152
New Jersey Author Award 231
New Jersey Poetry Contest 231
New York State Theatre Institute 195
Newbery Medal Award 231
Noah's Ark 153
Noma Award for Publishing in Africa, The 231
Norma-Lewis, The 248
NTC Publishing Group 179

O

Oak Street Music Inc. 186
Oddo Publishing, Inc. 95
O'Dell Award for Historical Fiction, The Scott 232

Can't find a listing? Check Other Book Publishers, page 123, and Other Magazine Publishers, page 176, for additional names.

Odyssey 153
Odyssey Paperbacks (see
    Harcourt Brace Jovanov-
    ich 70)
Ohio Genealogical Society
    Essay/Art Contest 232
Ohioana Book Awards 232
Olive Jar Animation 180
On The Line 153
Orchard Books 96
Ott Award for Outstanding
    Contribution to Children's
    Literature, Helen Keating
    232
Our Child Press 96
Owl Magazine 154

P
Pando Publications 97
Parenting Press, Inc. 97
Paulist Press 98
Pelican Publishing Co. Inc. 99
Pen American Center 255
Pennywhistle Press 154
Perspectives in Children's
    Literature Conference
    261
Perspectives Press 100
Peter Pan Industries 186
Philomel Books 100
Pikestaff Forum, The 212
Pioneer 155
Pioneer Drama Service 195
Pippin Press 101
Pittsburgh Playhouse Jr. 195
Players Press, Inc. 102, 195
Plays for Young Audiences
    196
Plays, The Drama Magazine
    for Young People 195
Please Touch Museum Book
    Award 233
Pocahontas Press, Inc. 102
Pockets 155
Porcelain Agency, Sidney E.
    248
Potter Inc., Clarkson N. 103
Press of MacDonald & Rein-
    ecke, The 103
Price Stern Sloan 103, 201
Productions Diadem Inc. 186
Prometheus Books 104
Publish-A-Book Contest 233
Publishers' Graphics 248
Purple Cow 213
Putnam & Grosset Group,

The (see Philomel Books
    100)

Q
Quackenbush's Children's
    Book Writing and Illus-
    trating Workshop, Robert
    261

R
R-A-D-A-R 156
Random House (see Clark-
    son N. Potter Inc. 103)
Random House Books for
    Young Readers 105
Ranger Rick 156
Read'n Run Books 105
Reflections 213
Rhythms Productions/Tom
    Thumb Music 187
Rockrimmon Press, Inc., The
    106
Roller Publications 202
Rosebrier Publishing Co. 106
Rosen Publishing Group, The
    106
Rosenberg Award for Poems
    on the Jewish Experience,
    Anna Davidson 233
Rubinstein, Literary Agent,
    Pesha 248

S
S.I. International 249
St. Anthony Messenger Press
    107
St. Paul Books and Media 107
Salzman Artist Representa-
    tive, Richard W. 249
Sandburg Literary Arts
    Award, Carl 233
Sandlapper Publishing Co.,
    Inc. 108
Schlessinger-Van Dyck
    Agency 249
Scholastic Hardcover 108
Scholastic, Inc. 111
Scholastic Math Magazine
    157
Scholastic Scope 213
Science Fiction Writers of
    America, Inc. 256
Scienceland 157
Scojtia Publishing Co. (see
    Jordan Enterprises Pub-
    lishing Co. 79)

Scope 158
Scribner's Sons, Charles 112
Seminars for Writers 261
Seventeen Fiction Contest 234
Seventeen Magazine 158
Seventh Annual Childrens Literature Conference 261
SFWA Nebula Awards 234
Shaw Publishers, Harold 112
Shoe Tree 213
Shoe Tree Contests 234
Shoe Tree Press 113
Shofar 158
Silver Burdett & Ginn 187
Simon & Schuster Children's Books 187
Simon Book Award, Charlie May 234
Sing Out! 159
Singer Media, Corp. 249
Single Parent, The 159
Sinnot and Associates, Inc. 180
Six Lakes Arts 160
Skipping Stones 161, 214
Skylark 215
Skylark/Books for Young Readers 113
Society of Children's Book Writers 256
Society of Illustrators 256
Southern California Society of Children's Book Writers Illustrators Day 261
Sow's Ear Poetry Journal, The 215
Speech Bin, Inc., The 113
Split Rock Arts Program 261
Sri Rama Publishing 114
Stage One: The Louisville Children's Theatre 196
Standard Publishing 114, 202
Star Books, Inc. 115
Starwind 161
Stemmer House Publishers, Inc. 115
Sterling Publishing Co., Inc. 116

Stone Center for Children's Books Recognition of Merit Award, George G. 235
Stone Soup 215
Story Friends 162
Straight 163
Straight Magazine 216
Stuhlmann, Author's Representative, Gunther 250
Summer Writers Conference 262
Sunrise Publication, Inc. 202
Sunshine Magazine 216
Superscience 163

T
TAB Books 116
Tada! 196
Take 5 164
Taylor Manuscript Competition, Sydney 235
Teen Dream 164
'Teen Magazine 164
Teen Power 165
Texas Christian University Press 117
Texas Star International/ Lonny Tunes Music, B.M.I. 187
Theatre for Young America, Inc. 197
Theatre-In-The-Schools, Inc. 197
Thistledown Press Ltd. 117
3-2-1 Contact 165
Thumbprints 216
Together Time 166
Touch 166
TQ 168
Treehaus Communications, Inc. 180
Trillium Press 117
Turtle 216
Turtle Magazine 168
Tyndale House Publishers 118
Tyro Magazine 169

Can't find a listing? Check Other Book Publishers, page 123, and Other Magazine Publishers, page 176, for additional names.

U

USKids® 170

V

Vassar Institute of Publishing and Writing: Children's Books in the Marketplace 262
Venture 170
Very Special Arts Young Playwrights Program 235
VFW Voice of Democracy 235
Virginia Writing 217
Voice 171
Volcano Press 118
Voyager Books (see Harcourt Brace Jovanovich 70)
Voyageur Publishing Co., Inc. 118

W

W.W. Publications 119
Wade Children's Story Award, The Stella 235
Wadsworth Productions, Bill 181
Walker and Co. 119
Warner Juvenile Books 120
Warner Press 202
Watchesgro Music Publishing Co. 188
Waterfront Books 120
Watts, Inc., Franklin 121 (also see Orchard Books 96)
We Are Writers, Too! 236
Wee Wisdom Magazine 171
Weigl Educational Publishers 121
Western Heritage Awards 236
Western Publishing (see Golden Books 69)
Whole Notes 217
Wilder Award, Laura Ingalls 236
Willamette Writers 21st Annual Writers Conference 262
Wilson Records 188
Winston-Derek Publishers, Inc. 121
With 171
Witty Short Story Award, Paul A. 236

Wombat: A Journal of Young People's Writing and Art 217
Women Writers West 258
Women's National Book Association 258
Women's Press 122
Wonder Time 172
Wood Ohioana Award for Children's Literature, Alice Louise 237
Working Writers Retreat— SCBW NW 262
World Library Publications Inc. 189
World of Busines$ Kids, The 172
Writers Alliance, The 258
Writer's Gazette Newsletter 218
Writers House 250
Writing 218
Writing for Young People 263

Y

YABA Framework 173
Yolen Books, Jane (see Harcourt Brace Jovanovich 70)
Young Adult Canadian Book Award 237
Young American 173
Young Company, The 197
Young Crusader, The 174
Young Hartland/Hartland Quarterly 218
Young Judaean 174
Young People's Award 237
Young Readers's Choice Award 237
Young Salvationist 175
Young Voices Magazine 218
Young Writer's Contest 238
Youth Update 175

Z

Zillions 176

Other Books of Interest
for Children's Writers and Illustrators

Annual Market Books

Artist's Market, edited by Lauri Miller $21.95

Humor & Cartoon Markets, edited by Bob Staake (paper) $16.95

Novel & Short Story Writer's Market, edited by Robin Gee (paper) $18.95

Photographer's Market, edited by Sam Marshall $21.95

Poet's Market, by Judson Jerome $19.95

Songwriter's Market, edited by Brian Rushing $19.95

Writer's Market, edited by Mark Kissling $24.95

Writing for Children

The Children's Picture Book: How to Write It, How to Sell It, by Ellen E. M. Roberts (paper) $18.95

Families Writing, by Peter R. Stillman $15.95

How to Write & Illustrate Children's Books, by Treld Pelkey Bicknell & Felicity Trotman $22.50

Nonfiction for Children: How to Write It, How to Sell It, by Ellen E. M. Roberts $16.95

Writing for Children & Teenagers, 3rd Edition, by Lee Wyndham/Revised by Arnold Madison (paper) $12.95

Writing Young Adult Novels, by Hadley Irwin & Jeannette Eyerly $14.95

Illustration

Fantasy Art, by Bruce Robertson $24.95

Painting Watercolor Portraits that Glow, by Jan Kunz $27.95

People Painting Scrapbook, by J. Everett Draper $26.95

Putting People in Your Paintings, by J. Everett Draper $22.50

Reference Books

Beginning Writer's Answer Book, edited by Kirk Polking (paper)$13.95

The Complete Guide to Self-Publishing, by Tom & Marilyn Ross (paper) $16.95

How to Write a Book Proposal, by Michael Larsen (paper) $10.95

How to Write with a Collaborator, by Hal Bennett with Michael Larsen $11.95

Knowing Where to Look: The Ultimate Guide to Research, by Lois Horowitz (paper) $15.95

Literary Agents: How to Get & Work with the Right One for You, by Michael Larsen $9.95

Time Management for Writers, by Ted Schwarz $10.95

12 Keys to Writing Books that Sell, by Kathleen Krull (paper) $12.95

The 29 Most Common Writing Mistakes & How to Avoid Them, by Judy Delton (paper) $9.95

Word Processing Secrets for Writers, by Michael A. Banks & Ansen Dibell (paper) $14.95

The Writer's Book of Checklists, by Scott Edelstein (self-cover) $16.95

The Writer's Digest Guide to Manuscript Formats, by Dian Dincin Buchman & Seli Groves $17.95

How to Sell Your Photographs & Illustrations, by Elliott & Barbara Gordon (paper) $16.95

Business & Legal Forms for Authors & Self Publishers, by Tad Crawford (paper) $15.95

Graphics/Business of Art

Airbrushing the Human Form, by Andy Charlesworth (cloth) $19.95

Artist's Friendly Legal Guide, by Conner, Karlen, Perwin & Spatt (paper) $18.95

Basic Graphic Design & Paste-Up, by Jack Warren (paper) $13.95

Color Harmony: A Guide to Creative Color Combinations, by Hideaki Chijiiwa (paper) $15.95

Complete Airbrush & Photoretouching Manual, by Peter Owen & John Sutcliffe (cloth) $24.95

The Complete Book of Caricature, by Bob Staake (cloth) $18.95

The Complete Guide to Greeting Card Design & Illustration, by Eva Szela (cloth) $27.95

Creative Ad Design & Illustration, by Dick Ward (cloth) $32.95

Design Rendering Techniques, by Dick Powell (cloth) $29.95

Dynamic Airbrush, by David Miller & James Effler (cloth) $29.95

Getting It Printed, by Beach, Shepro & Russon (paper) $29.50

The Graphic Artist's Guide to Marketing & Self Promotion, by Sally Prince Davis (paper) $15.95

Handbook of Pricing & Ethical Guidelines—7th Edition, by Graphic Artists Guild (paper) $22.95

How to Draw & Sell Cartoons, by Ross Thomson & Bill Hewison (cloth) $18.95

How to Draw & Sell Comic Strips, by Alan McKenzie (cloth) $18.95
How to Succeed as an Artist in Your Hometown, by Stewart Biehl (paper) $24.95
How to Understand & Use Design & Layout, by Alan Swann (paper) $19.95
The Creative Artist, by Nita Leland (cloth) $27.95
Business & Legal Forms for Fine Artists, by Tad Crawford (paper) $12.95
Business & Legal Forms for Illustrators, by Tad Crawford (paper) $15.95
Marker Rendering Techniques, by Dick Powell & Patricia Monahan (cloth) $32.95
The Professional Designer's Guide to Marketing Your Work, by Mary Yeung (cloth) $29.95
Type: Design, Color, Character & Use, by Michael Beaumont (paper) $19.95
Typewise, by Kit Hinrichs with Delphine Hirasuna (cloth) $39.95

Watercolor

Getting Started in Watercolor, by John Blockley (paper) $19.95
Painting Nature's Details in Watercolor, by Cathy Johnson (paper) $21.95
Tony Couch Watercolor Techniques, by Tony Couch (paper) $14.95
Watercolor Painter's Solution Book, by Angela Gair (cloth) $24.95
Watercolor Tricks & Techniques, by Cathy Johnson (cloth) $24.95
Watercolor Workbook, by Bud Biggs & Lois Marshall (paper) $21.95
Watercolor: You Can Do It!, by Tony Couch (cloth) $26.95

Mixed Media

Colored Pencil Drawing Techniques, by Iain Hutton-Jamieson (cloth) $24.95
Exploring Color, by Nita Leland (paper) $22.95
Getting Started in Drawing, by Wendon Blake (cloth) $24.95
Keys to Drawing, by Bert Dodson (paper) $19.95
The North Light Illustrated Book of Painting Techniques, by Elizabeth Tate (cloth) $27.95
Oil Painting: A Direct Approach, by Joyce Pike (cloth) $26.95
Oil Painting: Develop Your Natural Ability, by Charles Sovek (cloth) $27.95
Painting Seascapes in Sharp Focus, by Lin Seslar (paper) $21.95
Pastel Painting Techniques, by Guy Roddon (paper) $19.95
The Pencil, by Paul Calle (paper) $17.95
Realistic Figure Drawing, by Joseph Sheppard (paper) $19.95
Decorative Painting for Children's Rooms, by Rosie Fisher (cloth) $29.95

A complete catalog of Writer's Digest Books and North Light Books is available **FREE** by writing to the address shown below. To order books directly from the publisher, include $3.00 postage and handling for 1 book, $1.00 for each additional book. Allow 30 days for delivery.

Writer's Digest Books/North Light Books
1507 Dana Avenue, Cincinnati, Ohio 45207
Credit card orders call TOLL-FREE
1-800-289-0963

Write to this same address for information on *Writer's Digest* magazine, Writer's Digest Book Club, Writer's Digest School, Writer's Digest Criticism Service, North Light Book Club, Graphic Artist's Book Club, *The Artist's Magazine*, *HOW* Magazine and *Story* Magazine.

Prices subject to change without notice.